MALAYSIA
SINGAPORE · BRUNEI

TRAVELLER'S HANDBOOK

Stefan Loose • Renate Ramb
translated by David Crawford

**MALAYSIA - SINGAPORE - BRUNEI
TRAVELLER'S HANDBOOK**

ISBN 3-922025-16-1

Published by
Stefan Loose Publications
Koertestrasse 22
D 1000 Berlin 61
Germany

First English Edition January 1986

Printed in Germany by
Kösel GmbH & Co.

Maps and Design by
Klaus Schindler

Translated from the 1st German Edition by
David Crawford

© Stefan Loose 1984, **1986**

All rights reserved. No part of this publication may be reproduced, stored in a retrieval system or transmitted in any form by any means, electronic, mechanical, photocopying, recording or otherwise, except brief extracts for the purpose of review, without the written permission of the publisher and copyright owner.

Send 12 US$ for a copy of Malaysia, Singapore, Brunei Traveller's Handbook to Stefan Loose Publications, Koertestrasse 22, D 1000 Berlin 61, Germany, and the book is airmailed to anywhere in the world.

TABLE OF CONTENTS

INTRODUCTION 5

PEOPLE & COUNTRY 8

GEOGRAPHY 9
FLORA & FAUNA 12
ECOLOGY 16
POPULATION 19
HISTORY 23
GOVERNMENT & POLITICS 31
ECONOMY 33
RELIGION 37
LANGUAGE & LITERATURE 44
THE MEDIA 46
ART & CULTURE 51

GENERAL INFORMATION 52

ENTRY FORMALITIES 56
CLIMATE & TRAVEL SEASONS 59
PLANE TICKETS 63
HEALTH 66
OUTFIT 72
VALUABLES 75
MONEY 77
WEIGHTS & MEASURES 81
MAIL & TELEPHONE 82
GETTING AROUND 86
ACCOMMODATIONS 93
FOOD & DRINK 96
FESTIVALS & HOLIDAYS 102
PHOTOGRAPHY 106
TOURIST INFORMATION 107
WOMEN BACKPACKERS 108
ALIEN 109

CONTENTS

PENINSULAR MALAYSIA 113

KUALA LUMPUR 113
FROM KUALA LUMPUR TO PENANG 130
    Fraser's Hill (130), Cameron Highlands (131)
    Pulau Pangkor (140), Lumut (141), Ipoh (142),
    Kuala Kangsar (145), Taiping (146)
PENANG 149
FROM PENANG TO PADANG BESAR 167
    Gunung Jerai (168), Gerik (170), Alor Setar
    (171), Pulau Langkawi (174)
FROM KL TO JOHORE BHARU 180
    Seremban (180), Port Dickson (186), Malacca
    (187), Johore Bharu (197)
FROM JORHORE BHARU TO KUANTAN 200
    Desaru (200), Mersing (202), Pulau Tioman
    (204), Endau (205), Pekan (207),
    Kuantan (208)
KELANTAN 211
    Kota Bharu (212)
TRENGGANU 219
    Kuala Trengganu (220), Marang (223),
    Kuala Dungun (226)
FROM KUANTAN TO KL 230
    Tasek Chini (230), Taman Negara (234)

SARAWAK 242
    Kuching (244), Bako National Park (250), from
    Kuching to Brunei (251), Bandar Sri Aman (254),
    Sibu (256), Kapit (158), Overland from Belaga to
    Bintulu (260), Bintulu (260), Niah Caves (261),
    Miri (262), Gunung Mulu National Park (254),
    Bareo (264)

BRUNEI 267
    Bandar Seri Begawan (268)

SABAH 273
    Kota Kinabalu (274), Mount Kinabalu (279),
    from Kota Kinabalu to Brunei (282)
    from Kota Kinabalu to Kudat (286)
    from Kota Kinabalu to Tawau (287)

SINGAPORE 292
    The City (294), Chinatown (296), Little
    India (298), Arab Street (298), Central
    Park (299), Parks and Gardens (300),
    The Offshore Islands (301)

CONTENTS

SUGGESTED READING 319

SUBJECT INDEX 324

INDEX OF TOWNS 328

TABLE OF MAPS

Peninsular Malaysia	8	East Coast 3	217
Kuala Lumpur	116	Kuala Trengganu	221
KL Center	117	Marang	223
Cameron Highlands	135	East Coast 4	227
Pulau Pangkor	137	Taman Negara	237
Ipoh	143	Kuala Tembeling	241
Penang	153	Sarawak	242
Penang Island	165	Kuching	245
Alor Setar	171	Bako National Park	250
West Coast	173	Sibu	257
Pulau Langkawi	177	Miri	263
Seremban	184	Brunei	267
West Coast	185	Bandar Seri Begawan	269
Malacca	191	Sabah	273
Peninsula (south)	195	Kota Kinabalu	275
Johore Bharu	199	Mount Kinabalu	281
East Coast 1	203	Kinabalu National Park	283
Pulau Tioman	205	Sandakan	287
Pekan	207	Singapore Island	292
Kuantan	209	City 1 (Chinatown)	295
East Coast 2	210	City 2 (northeast)	299
Kota Bharu	213	City 3 (Orchard Rd.)	309

TABLE OF PHOTOGRAPHS

Country Road, Sabah	9
Iban Longhouse, Sarawak	11
Timbering, Sabah	17
Lumbered Landscape, East Coast West Malaysia	18
People in Penang	20
Dayak in Sarawak	21
Colonial Architecture, Kuala Lumpur	35
Mosque, Mersing	39
Chinese Burial, Mersing	41
Batik, Kota Bharu	55
Back Home	83
Trishaw Driver, Kota Bharu	89
Train Station, Kuala Lumpur	95
Public Transport, Northern Sabah	111
Skyline, Kuala Lumpur	121
Batu Caves near Kuala Lumpur	124
Tea Plantation in Cameron Highlands	133
Ubudiah Mosque, Kuala Kangsar	147
Street Scene, Penang	149
Pantai Merdeka near Gunung Jerai	169
Malay Musician	181
Pulau Rawa, East Coast	201
Malay Seamstress	211
Batu Rakit, East Coast	229
Orang Asli on Sungai Tembeling	235
Trophy Heads, Museum Kuching	243
River Crossing	253
Boat Dock, Kapit	259
Kampong Ayer, Bandar Seri Begawan, Brunei	271
Tamu, Sabah	277
Rungus Woman, Sabah	291
General Post Office, Singapore	293
The Merlin, Singapore	303

INTRODUCTION

This new **Malaysia-Singapore-Brunei Traveller's Handbook** is the fruit of many trips we've enjoyed with friends, parents, and our three-year-old son. Our travel companions have been particularly helpful in providing new insights.

Numerous letters have crossed our desk from readers of **South-East Asia Handbook** who'd enjoy even more background information. But what traveller wants to cart a tome of more than 600 pages? That's why we decided to publish a **Traveller's Handbook** series.
There's space for 80 additional pages covering geography, economics, fauna & flora. Malaysia's ethnic make-up religions, art and culture. And, of course, we greatly expanded upon the practical travel tips found in **South-East Asia Handbook**.
Another important reason for this book is that many readers can only spend four to six weeks on the road, and so wisely choose to travel just one country intensively.

Malaysia is an ideal vacation land, offering something for everybody. You'll find fantastic sandy beaches, coral reefs, remote islands, unspoiled jungles, and proto-Malayan tribes living in an almost lost technological era.
Singapore and Brunei on the other hand, aren't holiday attractions, yet it's hard to avoid them. The dynamism of the Singapore people has propelled the citystate within a few years from the Third World into an industrial society. Brunei boasts the highest per capita income in Asia thanks to large oil reserves. But higher prices in both countries reflect this prosperity in comparison to Malaysia.

We try to double check all our info, but the world is changing. Because a travel guide is only as useful as it is up to date, we use word processing to bring you revised editions annually. **Write to us about your experiences, new spots we've missed, or if that restaurant we recommend has deteriorated.**

"Sounds nice, but what will it cost?" - every traveller needs to pose this question when planning a trip. But nothing stands still in today's world: houses come down, roads are built, restaurants change hands, and prices rise. We want to give you concrete tips on things that change (in addition to century old monuments). But price information is quickly outdated. We mention the inflation rate for each country, so you can judge how much things have changed.

Malaysia may not be the cheapest country in the world, but you can live cheaper than in the 'West'. Many travellers are seduced to travel cheap: cheap hotels, cheap food, cheap buses, and budget flights. Occasionally you'll be invited to dinner by someone with far less money than you have; so even there you can save. Travelling cheap, for as long as possible, sometimes becomes an aim in itself.

Few backpack travellers blow their budget on luxuries they can't afford at home. In Malaysia or Singapore, your dinner bill could easily exceed the monthly income of your waiter or a rubber-plantation worker. Keep an eye on the relationship between local income and your expenses.

If you plan to see all of Malaysia in two weeks, then you won't have much use for this book. Such tours will show you the latest in tourist services, but that scrambled-egg culture is Hilton-Hyatt not Malaysian. Living in a tourist ghetto, many tourists never meet anybody who isn't employed by the tourist industry. The consolation is that the country is thereby somewhat sheltered from the tourist invasion.

Those who do take to the road on their own will find themselves immersed in the local culture. That means you learn more about the countries you're visiting, but also requires you show consideration for the traditions and habits of your hosts.

You won't be able to prevent the relentless onslaught of 'western civilization' into the deepest regions of the tropical rain forests. It's happened! The farther your travels take you from the Penang - Kuala Lumpur - Malacca - Singapore trail, the more consideration you should give to local culture and taboos. Make an effort to inform yourself by doing some of the suggested reading.

Another important source of information are newspapers and magazines. Two regional magazines, the 'Far Eastern Economic Review' and 'Asiaweek', report weekly on the political, economic and cultural situation in Asia. Keep informed on what's happening around you!

If at first you think the cities are very western oriented, you'll discover with further exposure more and more discrepancies between western and Asian mentality. Then notice the differences between Indian-Hindu plantation workers, Muslim kampong inhabitants, Chinese industrial managers, and the Punan still hunting with blowpipes.

Particularly in rural areas, you'll be exposed to the problems of the Third World. They used to be called developing nations because the western world assumed that everyone would want to industrialize into carbon copies of Detroit. For centuries the white race was noted in the Third World for its preachy, self-righteous attitude. With the end of colonial imperialism, it'd be a shame to see the rise of cultural imperialism through tourist colonies.

Much has been written about Third World tourism. The problems are apparent to everyone who travels with their eyes open. At the same time such trips help you to reconsider your values and better understand other people and cultures.

We hope that you travel with your eyes open, with a will to understand, and of course, enjoy Malaysia, Singapore, and Brunei!

PEOPLE & COUNTRY

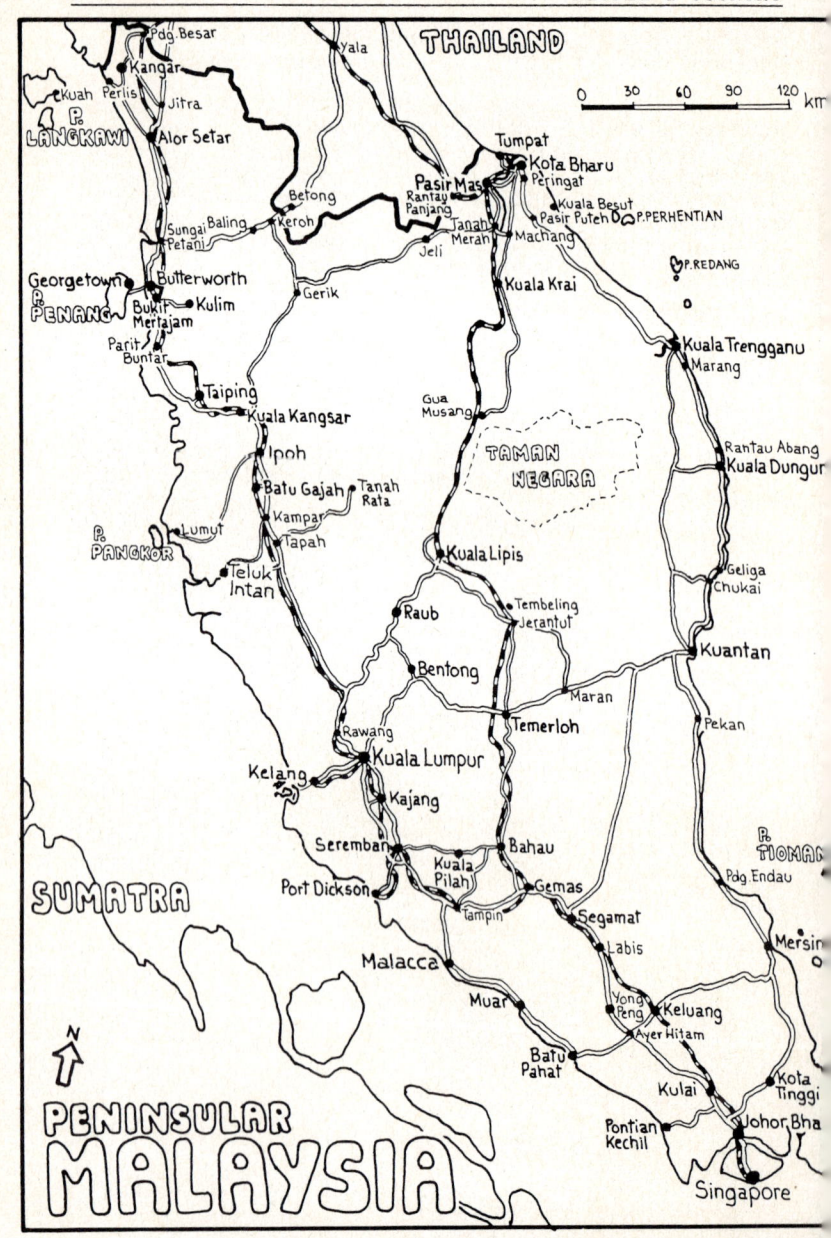

PEOPLE & COUNTRY

GEOGRAPHY

The **Federation of Malaysia** isn't a naturally defined geographical entity; rather a country in two clumps separated by 600 km of the South China Sea. Peninsular Malaysia (also called 'West Malaysia' or simply 'Malaya') runs south from 7° north latitude along a large Asian continental peninsula. Sabah and Sarawak form the eastern Malaysian territories located in the north and northeast of the island Borneo (Kalimantan). Malaysia's total area of 330,434 km^2 is home to more than 15 million people.

At the southern tip of the Malay peninsula, 2.5 million people inhabit the 618 km^2 island **Republic of Singapore**. A causeway, built in 1924, connects Singapore to the Malaysian mainland.

The **Sultanate of Brunei** (population 250,000 over 5765 km^2) claims less than one percent of the island of Borneo. Brunei is split into two parts by Sarawak's Limbang Valley.

All three states are independent countries, members of ASEAN (Association of South East Asian Nations) and due to their British colonial heritage, members of the British Commonwealth.

The **Malay Peninsula** was formed about 150 million years ago. Running north to south are several almost parallel chains of folded mountains. The main chain stretches from Thailand to Malacca. Despite their hard granite consistency, millions of years of erosion has washed them down. The tallest mountain, Gunung Tahan, boasts just 2187 m. Even so, the mountains determine local climate, particularly planting seasons on the east and west coasts. And they form a natural boundary hindering access between the coasts.

The **mountains** are covered with tropical jungle, which below 500 m gives way to highland agriculture (mostly rubber and palm oil). Large tin reserves are situated west of the main mountain chain at the edge of the granite mountains. Limestone, slate and sandstone are the main ingredients. Around Ipoh and Kuala Lumpur, you'll find bizarre countryside and deep caves carved by erosion of the limestone formations.

The **coastal plains**, created by sedimentary deposits, rise just 30 m above sea level, and are covered with rice paddies. The land here is extremely wet, but also generally more fertile than further inland. There, erosion robs the soil of fertility, requiring special conservation efforts.

The **flatlands on the West coast** are between 20 km (Kedah) and 60 km (Perak, Selangor) wide. However, the east coast (except in the Kelantan Delta) is just a long, narrow strip. The ground in the northern regions of the east coast is very porous and therefore suitable for sturdy arid crops such as coconut palms, casuarina, and tapioca. Keep in mind that the coast takes the full brunt of pounding surf during northeast monsoon season, except in the regions sheltered by mangrove, tidewater swamps. Whole strips of coast can be washed away, or conversely, entire harbours buried in sand.

PEOPLE & COUNTRY

The **southern end of the Malay Peninsula** (Southern Pahang, Johore) is hill country interspersed with several great swamp regions - Tasek Bera, Tasek Chini, and the tidewater region between Endau and Pekan. They were created by sluggish river waters, spreading out in wide bands across the flatlands. Due to the narrow width of the peninsula, the longest river, Sungei Pahang, is just 330 km long. Sand and sediment are washed down from the mountains by heavy rains. As the streams spread out and lose force, this soil is deposited from the plains to the delta creating alluvial soil.

The countryside in **Sarawak and Sabah**, unlike on the Malay Peninsula, varies greatly, even within small areas. The island's geological development has never been peaceful. New mountains were being created by volcanic eruption, sometimes building up layers several kilometres high. Under great pressure, they crumble and are eventually eroded away. In Brunei this process created tremendous oil reserves. Sabah boasts the 4101 m high Mount Kinabalu, the highest mountain in South-East Asia.

FLORA & FAUNA

Of all the tropical regions in the world, South-East Asia boasts the greatest variety of flora and fauna. One reason is the region's long history of climatic stability. It's presumed that the climate in Malay rain forests hasn't changed in 150 million years. Although the Malay Peninsula bedecks only 0.09 % of the earth's surface, about 8500 plant species grow here. That's about the same number found in all of North America. In some parts of Malaysia, such as Mount Kinabalu, the diversity is especially impressive due to changes in altitude. Botanists have discovered 800 types of orchid and 400 varieties of fern. The country's fauna is just as rich. Native to Malaysia are 200 species of mammal, 675 varieties of bird and 120 species of snake. Most creatures find their habitats in the **tropical rain forest**.

"Though it is midday it is very dark and very sombre. The sun cannot pierce the dense foliage of the branches of the giant trees, and so heavily do shadows lie upon shadows that the very green seems almost black." That's how George Maxwell described the Malay jungle in 1907 in his wonderful book 'In Malay Forests'. Gigantic **tualang** trees over 70 m tall join with other huge trees in forming the jungle roof. Frequently such giants stretch up even above the leafy roof. In the **virgin forest** it's possible to distinguish between several clearly defined levels. The thick leaves of the highest trees take the full brunt of the tropical sun and are subject to temperature shifts ranging from 32° C at noon and 22° C at night. At the same time humidity falls from 100 % to 60 % at night. Below the protective leaves, however, there's little variation either in temperature or humidity. Hence the virgin rain forest has two separate climatic zones within a few meters of each other.

At the 10-20 m level, a second layer of tree leaves competes for life-giving light by stretching for the sky. Further below in the twilight of the rain forest, you'll find plants which require little light but thrive on humidity growing between the heavy roots and hanging vines (liana). At the lower levels, the green of the forest is only seldom broken by colourful plants. Many types of orchid are epiphytic and grow on other plants at the upper levels of the rain forest. The rare **Rafflesia**, may be the largest flower in the world with a span of over 1 m in diameter, but it's still a parasite. It grows on a certain type of vine on the ground.

PEOPLE & COUNTRY

When you come to a clearing during your jungle trek, notice how suddenly the vegetation changes. No wonder, with the sun burning down to the undergrowth. Grass, shrubs and other plants flourish, creating impassable thickets.

Where the virgin rain forest has been pruned by logging, the natural ecological cycle and humus production is disrupted. The luscious vegetation gives the impression of extremely fertile soil. But the humus layer is generally very thin. Where the jungle has been logged over, no new organic material is added to the soil. And the humus layer is quickly washed away without the protection of leaves and roots. If nothing is done with the soil, a **secondary jungle** is formed in time, featuring much fewer species, generally low trees and bushes.

Animal habitats in the tropical rain forest, as in the case of plants, are determined by the varied climatic conditions at different levels of the forest. **Hornbill, Slow Loris, Gibbon**, and many species of insects, live only at the upper level.

All jungle mammals are threatened with extinction, including the **Elephant** (found today in Sabah where it was originally imported as a work animal), the **Sumatran Rhinoceros** (estimated population on the Malay Peninsula: 100), **Tapir**, and **Tiger**. Once upon a time the jungles of Malaya were home to the practically extinct **Java Rhinoceros**; today only 50 of the creatures survive in the Javanese nature preserve, Ujong Kulon. The rhino has fallen victim to poacher's greed because its horn is a coveted, traditional Chinese aphrodisiac. Holding its own is the **Seladang**, a type of wild cattle. Native to South-East Asia is the **Kancil** (mouse deer); just 20 cm tall, it's the world's smallest hoofed animal.

Besides the tiger, the following beasts of prey are threatened with extinction in Malaysia: the **Leopard, Black Panther, Clouded Leopard, Leopard Cat** and other wild cats. Prettiest of all is the 'kucing mas' or **Golden Cat**. However, it is unlikely that you would ever see one of the large cats or any large wild animal in the wild.

You're much more likely to run into some of the various species of ape, particularly the **Gibbon** and the **Macaque**. One type of macaque monkey is called 'berok' by the Malays. Red-brown and with short tails, they run around the jungle floor on all fours. Young male animals are captured and trained to work in the villages, harvesting coconuts. They're great at climbing the tall palms and twisting the ripe nuts until they fall to the ground. Well-trained monkeys can harvest 700 nuts in a working day.

PEOPLE & COUNTRY

The islands of Borneo and Sumatra are the only natural habitats of Asia's anthropoid ape, the **Orangutan.** A hundred years ago, Alfred Russel Wallace estimated the population on both islands to be about one million. Today only 1500 to 2000 of the creatures survive in the forests of Sarawak and Sabah. The 'mawas', as it is called in Malay, has no natural enemies other than man. But its natural habitat is being pushed back by civilization. Even today, despite strict conservation laws, particularly on Kalimantan, mother orangutans are killed in order to capture its young. Rehabilitation centers, like the one at Sepilok (Sabah), can do little to prevent the species' extinction. Since 1964, young orangutans have been trained here to survive in a new life in the wild. The **Proboscis Monkey** (nasalis larvatus) is only found on Borneo.

Tropical rain forests are frequented by 'gliders'. Just on Borneo, there're 14 types of **Flying Squirrels.** The largest, the giant flying squirrel, sports a wingspan of almost 1 m, with a body length of 50 cm. Then there's the **Flying Lemur**, which reaches the size of a house cat, the **Flying Lizard**, and the **Flying Frog.** All these creatures have developed the ability to glide, enabling them to get around fast in the leafy jungle roof.

Malaysia's largest reptile is the **Estuarine Crocodile** which can reach 10 m in length. The smallest amphibian is the tiny **Forest Frog.** Of the 120 odd snake species found in Malaysia, only sixteen are poisonous. But just five of these are deadly:
the **King Cobra, Black Cobra, Wagler's Pit Viper** (which populate the snake temples of Penang), the **Banded Krait**, and the **Coral Snake.** The longest snake in the world, the **Reticulated Python**, enjoys its habitat in Malaysia. Pythons reach 10 m in length and weigh up to 140 kg. They like to enwrap and strangle their prey, consisting of mostly small mammals, apes or birds. Sometimes pythons even find their way into cities. Once the police of Singapore had considerable trouble getting a full grown python down from a lamppost on Orchard Road.

PEOPLE & COUNTRY   15

Green in all its variations is about the only colour found in the rain forest. Flowers grow in most cases only in the upper levels. Just an occasional butterfly (coming in all colours and sizes) adds a few spots of moving colour. The **Atlas Moth** boasts a wingspan of 25 - 30 cm. Estimates speak of 150,000 species of insects living in Malaysia, with up to 50,000 types within each species. Among the prettiest butterflies are the **Malay Lacewing** and the **Raja Brooke.** Strangely, the male and female Raja Brooke butterflies have different habitats. Only the males are found around waterfalls and clearings, while the females live in the upper levels of the forest. Quite impressive is the **Rhinoceros Beetle,** which can reach 5 cm in length. **Red Weaving Ants** build nests out of leaves and bits of leaves, held together by a thread-like secretion. Should you bump into one of their nests by accident (only an idiot would do it intentionally), you'll find out how aggressive they can be.

The fauna we've discussed up to now inhabit the damp lowland tropical rain forest. At 1000 m in altitude, the term becomes **tropical mountain forest** or 'montane forest', where you'll find completely different vegetation. Among the trees, species of oak and tropical evergreens dominate. In the upper regions the flora is a lot like in the Himalayas. The forests are often covered with fog, and plaits of moss cover tree trunks and slopes. Even though only a small portion of Malaysia is covered with tropical mountain forest, its ecological importance is great. Extremely rare types of plants and animals live here, and great amounts of precipitation are absorbed and stored.

Particularly on the coast opposite of Sumatra, but also in Sarawak and Sabah, **mangrove forests** form one almost never-ending grove. They might be just a few trees in width, or up to 20 km wide. In Malaysia there are three basic types of mangrove, all of which use a brace-root system to support themselves above the slimy swamps. Frequently sandbanks are formed in the sea in front of the mangroves, which pushes the mangrove swamps inland. Just 1000 years ago, Palembang, the capital of Sri Vijaya was right on the sea; today it's located 100 km inland.

ECOLOGY

One of Malaysia's main ecological problems is shared with its neighbouring countries: the size of the tropical rain forests is being ever reduced, and with it, more than just trees are dying. Scientists studying satellite photos estimate that 1.2% of the world's rain forests are logged yearly. That works out to about 21 hectare (51.89 acres) per minute. Already, 38 % of South-East Asia's rain forests are gone.

Though tropical rain forests cover just 13 % of the earth's surface, their ecological importance is far disproportionate to size. They have tremendous capacity to convert the sun's energy into organic material, and to store surplus water which they release in times of drought. Along with animals and microorganisms (bacteria, fungi, etc.) which live on the ground and reconvert organic materials into minerals, it forms the most efficient natural ecosystem on our planet. Constant rates of energy from the sun and high humidity produce extremely rapid vegetation growth. The flora and fauna aren't subject to seasonal variations of climate found in more moderate latitudes. These are some of the reasons why South-East Asia's rain forests have spawned such diversity of life forms. Studies of the virgin forests in Brunei have turned up 220 different species of trees within a 20,000 m^2 area.

Over the course of thousands of years, man had little effect on the ecology of South-East Asia's tropical rain forests. Relatively small areas were logged, mostly around ancient towns, and for agriculture. Slash and burn agriculture, as practised by native inhabitants, affected increasing acreage of jungle, but then the rain forest was only sparsely populated. In the early days of European colonial rule, little large-scale logging took place because the Europeans were mostly interested in spices and metals.

Just 100 years ago, 99 % of the Malay Peninsula was covered by forest; today it's about half. At the turn of the century, ever larger sections of land tasted the plow as rubber production increased. Then after WW II, demand for wood increased enormously in Japan and in the West. Logging in the jungles achieved alarming proportions. But relatively few types of trees (in Peninsular Malaysia just 150 of 2500 species) are economically viable. Many unneeded trees are damaged by improper logging. Large forest roads are carved to get the wood out faster. Just to get one valuable tree, many others are either cut down or damaged. On the other hand, if logging is done properly, young sprouts and seedlings are able to survive in the soil along with other less useful species, permitting the jungle to regenerate.

But the major cause of the disappearing tropical rain forest in South-East Asia is the population explosion, requiring a constant increase in land under tillage. Malaysia's population increased from 6.1 million in 1950 to 14.3 million in 1980. Estimates for 1985 are about 16.4 million.

Take for example the increase in area under agriculture in Pahang Tenggara, a 11,500 km^2 region of southeast Pahang. As recently as 1972 when an international consulting firm began studying agricultural potential, almost 90 % of Pahang Tengarra was covered by jungle. Since then about 25,000 hectares (61775 acres) have been logged annually. By 1990, agriculture will have increased to 50 %. The diversity of species and productivity of vegetation in the ever-damp rain forest will be lost. Instead, the country will be covered with endless palm oil plantations.

Forecasts for the year 2002 speak of one third of South-East Asia becoming infertile bushland, covered with lalang grass, because of land mismanagement. Due to population growth, the ecologically efficient lowland rain forests will go over to agricultural usage. The structure of remaining jungle regions will change as many species of plants and animals become extinct under pressure from expanding civilization. Lumber companies will redouble efforts in the remaining unspoiled regions. Topsoil erosion, flooding and periods of drought will increase because lalang grasslands and agricultural land have only a fraction of the jungle's ability to store water and protect against soil erosion.

POPULATION

According to official estimates (1985), Malaysia has a population of more than 15 million people; 12.8 million of whom live on Peninsular Malaysia. But keep in mind that this a population of tremendous ethnic, linguistic, cultural and religious diversity.

It's confusing keeping track of terms such as **Malaya** and **Malaysia** or **Malay** and **Malaysian**. 'Malaya' is the old term used by the British to denote Peninsular Malaysia. 'Malaysia' is the name of the country founded in 1962, whose citizen (called 'Malaysians') are 45 % ethnic Malay, 36 % ethnic Chinese, 9 % ethnic Indian (Tamil), and 8 % from the various proto-Malayan tribes. These figures are for the entire country including Sarawak and Sabah. On Peninsular Malaysia (the mainland), Malays form a majority of 54 %.

Ethnic Malays exercise more or less political control; though mathematically they're just another minority. Their language is **Bahasa Malaysia**, and their culture is based on Islam. The Muslim belief is the most important differentiator between Malays and non-Malays. But among the Malays, you'll find differences in dialect, culture and appearance. Regional differences are particularly marked between the east coast (Kelantan/Trengganu) and west coast (Kedah/Perlis). The Minangkabau culture in Negri Sembilan is a prime example of immigration from the Indonesian archipelago. Many Malays have among their ancestors Bugis, Minangkabau, Javanese, or other people of Indonesia. Ethnic Malays make up less than 20 % of the population in Sarawak. Generally these are members of aboriginal tribes who have converted to Islam and acquired Malay culture.

Chinese immigration only reached major proportions in the 19th century when demand for plantation and tin-mine labor was high in the British colony. Chinese immigrants, seeking their fortune in South-East Asia, were drawn mostly from southern provinces of the Middle Kingdom. China back then was plagued by famine and turmoil. Many emigrants (generally merchants and craftsmen), paid for their own passage. Their goal was to make their fortune and eventually return home. Many succeeded.

The industrious Chinese are quite unlike the very relaxed and less materialistic Malays. However, most of the immigrants were unskilled workers (coolies) shipped by slave traders from China to the harbors of Singapore or Penang.

The Chinese population may be one ethnic minority, but it is much less homogenous in language and religion than the Malays. The people of southern China speak a number of different languages, requiring people from different regions to speak together in Mandarin (the Chinese national language), English, or Bahasa Malaysia. A small group called **Baba Chinese** speak a Malay derivative language, though their traditions (ancestor worship, marriage and burial ceremonies) are still very Chinese. They date their origins in the region to the several hundred members of the royal household brought by the Chinese princess Hang Liu when she married Sultan Mansur Shah of Malacca in the 15th century.

The Chinese make up about a third of the population in Sarawak, while in Sabah they're about 20 %. Many Chinese emigrated to the northwest coast of Borneo during the 19th century and up through the 1920s. Like in the rest of South-East Asia, they were drawn from southern China (Hokkien, Hakka, Teochew, Cantonese, and Hainanese).

Over the course of generations, the immigrants have gained strength economically and control a major part of the economy. Still, in the eyes of many Malays, the Chinese are synonymous with loansharks and cutthroats. Chinese minorities have the same problem everywhere in South-East Asia.

PEOPLE & COUNTRY

Particularly in the 19th century, contract labourers from southern **India** were brought by hundreds of thousands to work on the rubber plantations, and at railway and road building. Estimates speak of 4.2 million Indians arriving between 1786 and 1953. Like the Chinese coolies, most of them returned to their homelands when their contracts expired. A much smaller group provided the services of administrative officers, office workers, doctors, lawyers and teachers. It was the Sri Lanka Tamils and Indians from Kerala who got these better-paid positions. Northern Indians (Sikhs, Bengalis, and Pashtuns) found positions in the army, police and guards. Indians still are overrepresented in these professions.

About 50,000 **Orang Asli** ('native people' in Malay) live in the jungles and along the coast of Peninsular Malaysia. Members of these diverse tribes have little in common other than that they were all here before the ethnic Malays. They include 1800 **Negritos** (the most ancient inhabitants living in the northern jungle regions) or the **proto-Malays** which include about 1800 **Orang Laut** (the 'sea people').

The largest group is the 30,000 strong **Senoi**, which can be subdivided into the **Temiar, Semai, Mah Meri,** and **Semok Beri.** They are all said, like the Negritos, to have migrated into the region between 6-8000 years ago. Their skin, however, is lighter than the nomadic Negritos, and they practice slash-and-burn agriculture. They have been driven out of their original settlements into less accessible jungles.

The ethnic make up in the states of Sarawak and Sabah is even more complex. **Dayak** is the general term used today to denote the proto-Malay population of Kalimantan. Of the 1,294,000 people in Sarawak, about half are proto-Malayan. There are an estimated 200 different tribes on the island of Kalimantan. The most important ethnic group in Sarawak are the Iban, who make up about a third of the population. Other ethnic groups: Land-Dayak 10 %, Melanau 5 %, Malays 20 %, Chinese 30 %, and other tribes (Kayan, Kenyah, Kelabit, Murut, Punan) 5 %.
The 1,002,000 inhabitants of Sabah break down: Kadazan 30 %, Chinese 22 %, Bajau 15 %, Murut 5 %, other tribes 20 %. There are 22 different ethnic groups living in Sabah.

Of the 2.5 million people living in **Singapore**, 76 % are of Chinese origin, 15 % are Malay and 7 % Indian. The remainder consist of Europeans and Eurasians. The official languages, unlike in Malaysia, are English, Malay, Tamil and Mandarin. However, the Chinese national language, Mandarin, is spoken only by a small minority, with most Chinese sticking to their local dialects. About 42 % of the Singapore Chinese are Hokkien, 22 % Teochew, 17 % Cantonese, 7 % Hainanese, and 7 % Hakka, just to name a few.
In the school system, pupils can choose between schools set up for four different mother tongues: English, Mandarin, Thamil and Malay. The English schools are becoming evermore popular as many Chinese families choose to speak English in the home. It is hard to predict what affects this will have on the historical and cultural identities of the different ethnic groups.

Of the 250,000 inhabitants of **Brunei**, 54 % are ethnic Malay and 26 % ethnic Chinese, who (like everywhere else in South-East Asia) control trade and small industries. The 16 % of proto-Malay origins belong mainly to the tribes: Iban, Kadazan, Murut, and Kedayan. About 4 % of the population are American and Australian specialists working in the oil industry and administration.

****
THIS BOOK IS ALIVE
and changing, like the world, like Malaysia. That's why we print frequent new editions. Play a part in this change, write to us. Address in front of book.
****

HISTORY

Once upon a time the Malay Peninsula formed a land bridge over which about 5000 years ago the **proto-Malays** (Austronesians) migrated from continental Asia to the East Indies and Polynesia. They pushed the former peninsula inhabitants (whose descendants are the **Senoi** and **Semang**) back into remote jungle areas.

The proto-Malay immigrants had a late-stone age culture, marked by simple crop rotation in agriculture. They raised barley and rice, along with bananas, sugar cane, coconuts, cucumbers and bamboo; plus they tamed pigs and cattle. Their simple stone tools became improved over the course of their migration. They utilized outrigger canoes, with which they reached Madagascar and Easter Island. Around the year 100 AD, proto-Malays reached the island of Samoa - 9,500 km as the crow flies from Malaysia.

A second wave of Austronesian immigration arrived on the Malay peninsula between 400 and 300 BC. These **deutero-Malays** used iron tools and in fertile regions introduced the terracing of wet-rice.

During the first century AD, trade relations were well established between China and India utilizing various harbors on the coast of Peninsular Malaysia. Land routes, over which goods were transported, stretched from coast to coast. City-states with cultural and religious connections to India grew up around the harbors.

Langkasuka, situated in what is now northern Malaysia (probably Kedah), was a Malay-Hindu power center for almost 1000 years. Ancient Malay oral and written tradition remembers the mythical land 'Alang-kah-suka'; even the legends of the Orang Asli (Malaysia's most ancient remaining inhabitants) speak of a mythical kingdom.

In the 7th and 8th centuries, the Indies as well as large chunks of the mainland were ruled by **Sri Vijaya**. Langkasuka, Kelantan, Pahang and Trengganu were forced to pay tribute. Chinese travellers tell of a powerful trading and seafaring state. Buddhism was the official religion and ancient Malay, written in Sanskrit, the major language. The oldest writings yet discovered in the region date from that period.

In the second half of the 13th century, the Central Javanese power, **Majapahit**, became a major power in South-East Asia. For about 100 years the Malay peninsula was a permanent place of confrontation between Majapahit and the Thai Kingdom, Ayutthaya. In 1349, Temasik (today Singapore) was conquered by the Thais.

The beginnings of Islam on the Malay Peninsula are difficult to date. Persian and Arabian traders in the 13th century first brought the Buddhist and Hindu influenced population into contact with the teachings of Mohammed. The first to establish Islam as its official religion were the kingdoms of North Sumatra. Marco Polo wrote in 1292 of Islam's sturdy roots in Perlak and Pasai, two kingdoms on Sumatra. A stone fragment discovered near Kuala Berang, the **Trengganu Stone**, contains the oldest Malay inscription with arabic lettering. It testifies a Malay-Islamic kingdom in 1380 in present-day Trengganu, whose ruler was called Raja Mandulika.

About the same time, several Islamic Sultanates were established on the coast of Borneo, Brunei being the most important.

Never forget that high cultures existed in South-East Asia long before the arrival of Europeans. For hundreds of years, active contacts were maintained with the world's two greatest civilizations of the time, politically and culturally: India and China. These relations were disturbed by the arrival of Europeans on the Asian stage. It would be several hundred years before Asian self-determination returned to the region.

For more than 100 years, **Malacca** was the most important political and economic center in South-East Asia. It is assumed that the city was founded in 1398 and grew to 40,000 inhabitants by 1450. **Parameswara**, a Malay prince from Palembang (Sumatra), was forced to flee the Majapahit Kingdom after a failed coup d'etat. He fled first to Temasek (today Singapore), but was driven away by the fearsome Thais. In 1398 he landed at a small fishing village on the west coast of peninsular Malaysia. Its Minangkabau inhabitants lived from fishing, and were infamous pirates. Within 80 years, Malacca ruled the Malay peninsula up to Songkhla, the Riau and Lingga Archipelagos, as well as large parts of Sumatra. This quick expansion was only possible with the condonation of the Chinese Emperor who needed a strong vassal in the region. Malacca sent a number of delegations to the imperial court of the Middle Kingdom.

Malacca at that time was the most cosmopolitan city in the world. It was home to Arabs, Chinese, Indians, Javanese, Thais, as well as Bugis, Persians, Gujaratis, Klings and Acenese. Many factors contributed to the city's development. The first of these was her geographical location at the natural meeting place of the northeast and southwest monsoon. Trading ships from both east and west could use the trade winds to reach her and pick up cargo. A Portugese captain wrote home, "Malacca is the richest seaport in the world, with the most merchants and full of trading goods."

In 1498 **Vaso da Gama** rounded the tip of Africa and landed in India. Portugal's goal was control of the lucrative spice trade which until then had been under the control of Indian, Arab, and Persian merchants.

In 1511, Viceroy **Alfonso d'Albuquerque** conquered Malacca with a force of just 800 Portugese and 300 Malabar Indians. Internal weaknesses had become increasingly apparent under the last Sultan, Mahmud Shah. Non-Malay merchants and traders were too heavily taxed – they conspired openly with the Portuguese. Corruption and intrigue were the rule in the ruling circles.

Over the next 130 years, the Portuguese made Malacca the pillar of their Asian colonies. Trade flourished; and Portugese policy was farsighted when compared to the Dutch colonial empire which would succeed it.

In 1641, after a six month siege of the city by **Dutch** troops and troops of its ally the Sultan of Johore (who was a direct descendant of the last sultan of Malacca), the Portugese governor surrendered the city.

At the end of the 17th century, a new wave of immigration hit the sparsely populated Malay peninsula. **Minangkabau** from Sumatra settled in the south and founded their own principalities which joined together at the end of the 18th century to form a confederation (Negri Sembilan = Nine States). The **Bugis,** a seafaring and trading people from southern Sulawesi, settled along the coast, establishing their own states or seizing control of Malay sultanates. Johore and Selangor were ruled by Bugis.

Toward the end of the 17th century, the **Johore Empire** had achieved roughly the geographical dimensions of Malacca. Goods from the East Indies and Peninsular Malaysia were traded in the capital Batu Sawar on the Johore River. Even Dutch ships from Malacca laid anchor here.

After the conquest of Malacca by the Dutch, the city never regained her former beauty and influence. International trade increasingly moved via the Sultanate of **Aceh** on the north coast of Sumatra, through Dutch **Batavia** and through the capital of the ever more powerful **Johore Kingdom**.

In 1824 the Dutch traded their now unprofitable Malacca colony for the British possession, Bencoolen (Benkulu), on Sumatra. From then until the independence of Malaysia in 1957, the Union Jack flew over the city (quickly forgetting three years of Japanese occupation).

Not until 1786 did **England** make inroads on Malaya. Sir Francis Light made a treaty with the Sultan of Kedah ceding the island of Penang. The East India Company needed a base on the Straits of Malacca for their lucrative trade with China (opium to China; tea, silk, and porcelain to India and the homeland). **Stamford Raffles**, governor of the Dutch East Indies during the Napoleonic Wars, took possession of Singapore for the British Empire in 1819. In 1826 the colonies of Penang, Malacca, Dindings (Pangkor) and Singapore were consolidated into the **Straits Settlement.**

In Malaya there were several quite powerful sultanates, some of which were controlled by the Thai Kingdom (Perlis, Kedah, Kelantan, Trengganu). On the other hand, due to the Industrial Revolution, Britain had new economic interests in the region: first with 'colonial goods', then as a market for England. The colonies took on importance as suppliers of raw materials for industrial production. For example, demand for tin in Great Britain rose between 1800 to 1871 from just 11,000 tons to 136,000 tons.

Between 1874 and 1896, the Sultanates of Perak, Selangor, Pahang, and Negri Sembilan became British protectorates by way of treaty. The sultans were only permitted to make political decisions with the concurrence of the 'British Resident'. Only questions of Malay customs and religion were left to the sultans. In 1896 the **Federated Malay States** were created comprising the sultanates mentioned above. In 1909 Thailand signed over all her rights in the northern sultanates (Kedah, Perlis, Kelantan, and Trengganu) to the British. Johore joined the Federation in 1914.

Through a complicated system of treaties, Britain managed to bring the whole of Malaya under its political control. Somerset Maugham's short story descriptions of Malaya and the north coast of Borneo in the 1920s and '30s offer worthy illustrations of this period. Tin and rubber became the most important exports. Huge plantations, mostly owned by British monopolies, ranged over the land.

The history of the Malaysian states of **Sarawak** and **Sabah** is closely connected to that of **Brunei**. The language cripples in England managed to turn the Malay word 'Berunai' (= Brunei) into Borneo (pronounced 'borneeoh'). This European name was given to the third largest island in the world. Today the whole island is called Kalimantan meaning 'island of rivers'. Extensive trade relations existed already between the north coast of Kalimantan and the Chinese Empire 1500 years ago. With the arrival of the European powers, first Portugal and then Spain, the traditional social and economic structure was greatly changed. In 1521, Brunei was attacked by the fleet of world circumnavigator, Magellan. Brunei, which also controlled a large part of the southern Philippines, was conquered by superior Spanish weaponry. Century long trade links were broken. A similar policy was also practised by the Dutch. Brunei was reduced to a mini-state. Pirates made the coasts unsafe.

In 1841, **James Brooke**, one of the cliché types who 'built' the British Empire, sailed his ship The Royalist along the coast of Sarawak. The Iban and Malays at that time were in rebellion against the Sultan of Brunei because he, or rather his proxy in Kuching, was forcing people to work in antimon mines. James Brooke knew right away how to pick sides. In the Sultan's cause he used his ship's firepower to 'restore law and order' as pacification measures of this kind are still called. Out of gratitude, the Sultan of Brunei made James Brooke, Raja of Sarawak, with the right to all state income in return for a pittance of $2500 a year from Brooke. So the White Rajas of Sarawak were born. From 1853 to 1904, the area was expanded to its present size.

Until the 1930s, rebellions were common daily occurrences. The peacekeeping measures of the White Raja have gone down in history as great and heroic acts for the general good of Sarawak. If this really was the case, remains questionable. The Brookes gave the country an administration, it is true, and allowed the different nationalities some say. But they also conducted bloody campaigns against ethnic groups unwilling to submit completely to White Raja rule.

The most important rebellions against the White Raja:
1857 - A rebellion of Chinese coolies and settlers in Bau. They were able to capture Kuching. Later 3-4000 were killed by British troops.
1858-61 - Uprising of the Iban under the leadership of the legendary Rentap on the Sungei Skrang.
1863 - Retaliation action against the Kayan on the Rejang.
1896-1909 - Resistance of the Iban on Batang Ai under the leadership of Bantin.
1931-34 - Rebellion under Asun on the Sungei Kanowit.

The British empire forced the Sultan of Brunei to cede the island of Labuan in 1846. The weakened sultan had no choice when faced with the threatening canon of Her Majesty's fleet.

Until 1888, Sabah was controlled and ruled by the privately owned British **North Borneo Company**. Two English merchants bought this part of Borneo from the Sultan of Brunei, but at the same time made payments to the Sultan of Sulu (Philippines) because the title was unsettled (President Marcos later staked a claim to Sabah). In 1888, Brunei and Sabah became British protectorates.

Between 1894 and 1905, the Mat Salleh Revolt broke out in Sabah. It began with the murder of two Dayak traders. **Mat Salleh**, headman of the village, was ordered charged. First he refused to give himself up to a police unit; later he swore on the Koran to obey the laws of Sabah. In 1895 he showed up in Sandakan with a large number of armed followers to bring a complaint against the North Borneo Company. The governor of the day rejected it as unfounded. An arrest order for Mat Salleh was issued in 1896, but he disappeared into the jungle. In 1897 he appeared again on the island of Gaya with a group of armed men und burned everything to the ground with the exception of his birthplace village. The Company's security forces were mostly Dayak from Sarawak. During the following military campaigns, head-hunting of the rebels was permitted. Villages were destroyed and the inhabitants killed. But not until 1900 was a large military force able to capture Mat Salleh and some of his supporters in Tambunan. Mat Salleh was killed, but 'peace' would not return for another five years.

During WW II the whole island was occupied by Japanese troops. In 1945, the major towns of Sabah were completely destroyed by American and Australian bomber attacks. After the Japanese capitulation, the third White Raja of Sarawak, Charles Vyner Brooke, turned his private country over to the British Crown after negotiating a royal compensation for himself.

In December 1942 **Japanese** troops landed at Songkhla, Patani and Kota Bharu. Two months later Singapore fell. Until the 12th of September 1945, Malaya was ruled by the Japanese military. The Japanese secret police (Kempetai) set up a brutal system of repression under which the Chinese particularly suffered. The army plundered the country along with Japanese companies (Mitsui and Mitsubishi profited greatly). Japanese was required in all schools, and the different nationalities were played off against each other. Resistance mounted. Under the leadership of the Malayan Communist Party (MCP) a guerilla war was waged against the occupiers. Parallel resistance movements can be found in Burma, Indochina, and the Philippines.

A nationalist movement developed relatively late in Malaysia compared to other South-East Asian countries. There were several reasons: The population was divided among three large ethnic groups, each with diverging interests. The Chinese were and are China oriented. The Malays lived mostly as small farmers in traditional villages. The Indians generally worked on the plantations. There wasn't a real national feeling binding these ethnic groups.

Malay historians see the awakening of Islamic fervour around the turn of the century as the beginning of Malay nationalism. The radicals of the 20s and 30s were stronlgy influenced by Indonesian nationalism, they even called for Malaya's annexation by the burgeoning Indonesian State. Not until after WW II did the various ethnic groups begin forming political parties. The most important Malay party was **UMNO** (United Malays National Organisation). Shortly thereafter the Chinese established the **MCA** (Malayan Chinese Association). The Indians set up the **MIC** (Malayan Indian Congress).

The armed struggle of the MCP recontinued two years after the war. In 1948, a state of emergency was declared which was only lifted in 1960. Estimates speak of 20-25,000 dead on both sides.

In 1955 the three political parties (UMNO, MIC, MCA) founded the Alliance and won 51 of a total of 52 seats in the Federal Legislative Council. After top level talks between UMNO chairman **Tunku Abdul Rahman** and the British government the independence of Malaya was fixed on August 31st 1957. As expected Tunku Abdul Rahman became the first Premier of the new country.

Political parties were also created in **Singapore** after the war, but they were more left wing than in Malaysia. The first National Assembly was elected in 1959 with the **PAP** (People's Action Party) winning 43 of 51 seats. The party's chairman, **Lee Kuan Yew** became Premier.

In 1963 Singapore joined the **Federation of Malaysia**. The reasons lay in British fears that Singapore might drift even further to the left, plus almost universal conviction that the island could never survive economically on its own. The PAP under Lee Kuan Yew forced left-wing elements out of the PAP. They quickly founded their own party called **Barisan Socialis**. Just two years later, Singapore seceded from the federation. Economic, political, and racial differences were the cause.

Since then, the PAP has ruled the city state with an iron hand. Still the planned capitalistic economy seems to be a success.

In early 1982 the National Front (formerly the Alliance) won an overwhelming majority at the polls in Malaysia. **Premier Mahathir** has a mandate including 90 % of the seats in the house of representatives. The election result also shows for the first time since 1957 that parties seeking to represent just one nationality (Party Islam for the Malays or Democratic Action Party for the Chinese) don't have a chance. After heavy racial unrest in 1969, there's hope for better relations between the races.

THE STATES OF MALAYSIA: AREA AND POPULATION

KEDAH	Alor Setar	9,516 km^2	1.102,200
PERLIS	Kangar	,806 km^2	147,726
KELANTAN	Kota Baru	14,960 km^2	877,575
PERAK	Ipoh	20,748 km^2	1.762,288
PAHANG	Kuantan	35,932 km^2	770,644
PENANG	Georgetown	1,014 km^2	911,585
SELANGOR	Shah Alam	8,216 km^2	1.467,441
NEGRI SEMBILAN	Seremban	6,708 km^2	563,955
MALACCA	Malacca	1,664 km^2	453,153
TRENGGANU	Kuala Trengganu	13,130 km^2	542,280
JOHORE	Johore Baru	19,958 km^2	1.601,504
SABAH	Kota Kinabalu	76,409 km^2	1.002,608
SARAWAK	Kuching	125,450 km^2	1.294,753
FED. DISTRICT	Kuala Lumpur	,244 km^2	937,875

GOVERNMENT & POLITICS

The **Merdeka Constitution** was worked out by constitutional lawyers in London before the independence of Malaysia in 1956-57. Based on western-democratic models, human rights such as personal freedom, freedom of movement, freedom of religion, freedom of assembly, equality before the law, and the right to organize unions were all guaranteed.

Malaysia's parliament consists of a lower house (**Dewan Rakyat**) elected by the people, and an upper house (**Dewan Negara**) of whose 58 members 26 are elected by the local state parliaments and the rest appointed by the **Yang di-Pertuan Agong** (King). The king is elected for a term of five years by the nine Malaysian sultans and the governors of the other states (Penang, Malacca, Sarawak, Sabah) out of the ranks of the Sultans. So Malaysia and the United Arab Emirates are the only countries in the world with elected monarchies.

Since the election of 1981, the ruling National Front party under Premier **Datuk Seri Mahathir Mohamad** enjoys a mandate of 140 seats out of 154 representatives in the lower house. It is a coalition of the largest and most important parties representing the three main ethnic groups. Traditionally the **UMNO** (United Malays National Organisation) picks the Premier and most important ministers.

Elected at the same time as the lower house are the local parliaments of the 11 states. Here too the National Front won 280 of 312 seats. Only in Kelantan did the Party Islam make a come back. The appearance of Islamic fundamentalists, particularly in Kelantan and Trengganu, has presented a problem for Mahathir. Unlike his predecessors, who were very Great Britain oriented, he has tried to put the post-colonial era behind him. Economically that has meant closer ties to Japan and Korea, as well as to the Persian Gulf and the Pacific Nations.

Malaysia's foreign policy is based on non-alliance and regional cooperation. However, still intact is the **Five Power Defence Agreement** with New Zealand, Singapore, Great Britain and Australia (which has two squadrons of Mirage fighter aircraft stationed at Butterworth. Other defence agreements exist with Thailand and Indonesia. They permit troops of each country to pursue communist guerillas across each other's borders.

Singapore has been ruled since 1959 by the **PAP** (People's Action Party) under **Lee Kuan Yew**. Opposition parties do exist, but have little chance in Lee Kuan Yew's "Rugged Society". Only in 1981 and later on in 1984 did opposition politicians of the **Worker's Party**, to everyone's amazement, win parliamentary seats in elections. That was a traumatic experience for the PAP!

The old-guard leadership of Singapore which steered the country through independence and the break with the Federation of Malaysia, will be replaced in coming years by a new generation. Lee Kuan Yew has developed a staff of competent politicians and technocrats to succeed him in order to ensure a smooth succession.

As in Malaysia, western democracy can't necessarily be grafted with South-East Asia's very different tradition. The political leadership of Singapore, despite western education, is still highly influenced by Confucian thought. The common good is given priority over individual freedom. It is the responsibility of the political elite to guarantee a peaceful and orderly society. Lee Kuan Yew has been practising this Confucian ideal for 25 years. Under his leadership, Singapore has developed the second-highest per capita income in Asia. The material affluence of most inhabitants is quickly apparent to visitors.

PEOPLE & COUNTRY

The tiny Sultanate of Brunei received its independence on December 31, 1983. Until then it was a British Protectorate. **Sultan Hassanal Bolkiah** has added his country to the ranks of ASEAN (Association of South East Asian Nations). Political contacts with neighboring countries have been intensified, and cooperation with Malaysia will probably be very close. Trained personnel who once came mainly from Great Britain, will be trained in Malaysia before assuming administrative positions. Till now, the Sultan's rule has been quite autocratic.

ECONOMY

Almost 40 % of Malaysia's population of 15 million are employed in **agriculture** (including fishing and forestry). This produces, however, only 23 % of GDP. Typical Asian small farms are mostly found in the north (Kelantan, Trengganu, Perlis, Kedah). Wet rice, vegetables, spices, sugar cane, and coconut palms are grown. In some parts of Malaysia, **double cropping** is practised with state support, bringing two harvests per year.

Tourists, though, will take home memories of the **plantations,** especially **rubber** and **palm-oil.** Today they're no longer wholly owned by multinationals (Dunlop, Sime Darby, Guthrie, Harrisons). They have generally been taken over by Malaysian holdings. Less noticeable, but equally important to national rubber production, are small holdings: farms under 40 ha (98.8 acres). Most of these farms have just 1-6 ha. The state subsidizes farmers as best it can. It provides inexpensive seedlings, credit, and subsidies.

Malaysia produces 42 % of the world's **natural rubber.** Demand for this raw material is sinking, however, due to increasing use of synthetics and a general fall in world demand. The government, therefore, is supporting the planting of palm oil and other products. Malaysia provides about 80 % of the world's **palm oil** production. According to research by the Palm Oil Research Institute, it is possible to convert palm oil into a fuel comparable to diesel oil. Its by-products include methane gas and paper flakes.

Major rubber producers have joined together to form the ANRPC (Association of Natural Rubber Producing Countries) in order to stabilize prices by cutting production.

The most important Malaysian export products today are oil and petro chemicals (38 % of 1984 exports). Vast reserves are suspected off the coasts of Sabah, Sarawak, and Trengganu. At the end of 1983, around 400,000 barrels a day were being produced. Malaysia consumes only about 200,000 barrels per day. Petronas, the state-owned oil company has signed production contracts with some multinational oil companies, but in the future wants to produce all the oil itself.

Malaysia is also the leader in **tin** production turning out 38 % of world output. In the export balance, however, this metal is only in fifth place at 5 %. Tin is mostly used for tin cans and by the electric industry.

Western style **industry** only began developing in the 1960s as measures were taken to increase exports. Manufacturing now produces 21 % of the GDP. Economic growth in the early 1980s floated between 10 and 11.5 % becoming the major force in economic development. Today almost 1 million Malaysians are employed by industry (in 1970 just 270,000).

Foreign investment is generously encouraged, but also planned and controlled by the Federal Industrial Development Authority. Expansion is sought in those industries which will reduce imports and expand exports.

Malaysia's **balance of trade** showed red figures in 1981 for the first time in many years. Sinking demand and falling world market prices for tin, oil, rubber and wood were major reasons. But by 1983, balance of trade figures were again written in black.

Trade, industry, banks and insurance companies are still disproportionately controlled by ethnic Chinese. Through state support for the **'bumiputra'** (in Malay = sons of the earth), an attempt is being made to enlarge the percentile holdings of the ethnic Malays. This policy has made it just about impossible for a Chinese to get a license to run a hotel or taxi. Many wealthy Chinese get around this problem by using Malays as straw partners.

Oil is the dominant element in the **Brunei** economy; oil and gas make up 95 % of the sultanate's export earnings.

PEOPLE & COUNTRY

175 000 barrels a day are shipped by the Brunei Shell Petroleum Company making Brunei 30th in the ranks of oil exporting nations. In 1982 the state earned 7 billion B$ but was only able to spend 1.8 billion B$. This small sultanate is said to have nearly 26 billion B$ in currency reserves.

The fourth Five Year Development Plan calls for expanding the economy, social services and cultural life. Agriculture and forestry are to be furthered and the infrastructure improved. An express way parallel to the coast is under construction. The country's interior has no roads at all. Neither is there a direct connection between the two parts of the country. But even the most inaccessible longhouses have micro-wave connections to Brunei's telephone system.

80 % of all food is imported. Agriculture is largely restricted to farmers producing for their own needs. Few large farms are of economic importance. In the interior, slash and burn agriculture is used to create fields. The loss of woodcover is so great that scientists have been warning of the negative effects: including the feared loss of the entire coastal jungle in the near future.

The state is supporting the establishment of new industries: without much success till now. The largest natural gas liquefaction facility in the world went on line at Lumut in 1973 to serve Japan's needs. The facility is 10 % state owned with Shell and Mitsubishi splitting the rest.

Singapore too has felt the effects of the world recession. In the 1970s the gross national product grew at an amazing rate (1978-82 it was 8.8 %), but it's now levelled off at about 0.5 %. The driving force behind this prosperity has been the building industry with growth of 31 %. By the end of this decade, US$5 billion will be spent on the **MRT** (Mass Rapid Transit) rail system. That should keep the building industry in good shape for a while to come.

Since 1979, at government initiative, a program called the **Second Industrial Revolution** is under way. The intent is to increase Singapore's industrialization. An attempt is being made to switch from labor intensive to capital intensive industries. Skilled workers are available and job training programs abound.

Jurong Industrial Estate is a result of the first big state supported industrialization program in the 1960s and the early '70s. For years the appliance and electronics industry produced color TVs, calculators, car radios and cassette recorders. Now the move is into high quality computers and electronic measuring devices. The textile and wood-processing industries, begun in the early stages of industrialization, now play an ever smaller role.

Singapore is Asia's largest oil-refining center (number three in the world after Houston and Rotterdam). But in 1983 it was only operating at 70 % of capacity. Crude oil is imported from neighboring Indonesia and Malaysia and exported to Japan and the rest of South-East Asia. However, Indonesia and Malaysia are also building refineries, leading to talk of Singapore's over-capacity. Oil refining accounts for one-third of Singapore's industrial production.

The workforce is structured as in no other South-East Asian country. 36 % are employed in industry, 40 % in sales and services, 23 % by public service and only 1.4 % in fishing and agriculture. Compare this to Indonesia where you have 11 % in industry, 25 % in sales and services, 15 % in public services, and 54 % in fishing and agriculture.

All together, Singapore has (after Japan) the highest standard of living in Asia. Splendid economic development over the country's eighteen years has worked to the benefit of everyone. Not only has the industry taken off; Singapore has become the financial center of South-East Asia.

RELIGION

A number of very different religions coexist in the multi-ethnic state of Malaysia. The ethnic Chinese adhere to Taoism, Buddhism and Christianity. There is an Indian-Hindu minority. Even today, people in the isolated jungle regions of Sarawak and Peninsular Malaysia are **Animist**. Christian **missionaries** have left their mark on many of Borneo's proto--Malay tribes. Malays and small numbers of Indians are Muslim, making Islam the national religion. But the Malaysian constitution guaranties freedom of religion.

Malay Muslims may not be so orthodox as their Middle Eastern brothers in faith, but Islamic fundamentalists do make headlines here too. In 1978 Muslim extremists stormed a Hindu temple near KL. Four of the attackers were killed by Indian temple guards. In 1980 a group of fanatic Muslims attacked a police station in Batu Pahat (Johore); several people died. On the other hand, Islamic political parties weren't able to achieve a breakthrough at the polls in 1982. Only in the east coast states of Kelantan and Trengganu did they have a notable success. At the same time, Islamic extremists are up in arms against the other nationalities. Maintaining the balance between Muslim Malays, Hindu Indians, and Taoist or Buddhist Chinese is one of the major tasks of every government.

Islam is the adherence to the teaching of the 7th-century Arabian prophet **Mohammed.** Mohammed, himself, is said to be the last of a series of great prophets (Adam, Noah, Moses, Jesus, etc.). In 622 AD, Mohammed was forced to flee from Mecca to Medina. This marks year 'one' of the Islamic calendar.

The basic principle of Islam is the belief in just one God. "There is no other God besides Allah, and Mohammed is his Prophet." Allah is the creator, keeper, and renewer of all things. The will of Allah, to which all people must submit, is expressed in the holy book, the **Koran**. It is seen as the word of God as related to Mohammed by the archangel Gabriel. The first part, divided into 114 surah, depicts ethical and spiritual teachings along with the Last Judgement. The remaining surah discuss social doctrine, plus political and moral principles which guide the religious community.

From the beginning Islam has had a social component manifested in the equality and fraternity of the faithful. Therefore, in the ideal Islamic state, there are no contradictions between religious or secular power, nor between the community and religious consciousness. This dual nature - religious and temporal - set it above all established religions of the time. Christians and Jews are tolerated because they follow the Holy Book; but non-believers must be brought to the true faith by **jihad** (holy war).

The expansion of Islam in the first centuries after Mohammed's death is truly amazing. A large part of the known world, from Spain to India and central Asia were conquered in the name of Islam. Arabian, Persian, and Indian traders brought the faith to the Hindu and Buddhist empires of South-East Asia.

The **five fundamental principles** of Islam were proclaimed shortly after the prophet's death forming the foundation of the faith.
Profession of Faith (tahajjuud) - There is no other God besides Allah, and Mohammed is his Prophet. The profession, which forms the basis for admission to the community, must be spoken at least once in a lifetime - loud, error free, and be understood completely both in heart and mind.
Prayer - Although the Koran only mentions three daily prayers, the second principle of Islam stipulates five. The muezzin of the mosque calls the faithful to prayer. Before each prayer, the hands, feet, and face have to be washed. The imam stands before the faithful, facing Mecca, reciting from the Koran. Twice the congregation falls to its knees and calls out "Allahu akhbar" (God is great). According to strict teaching, the five prayers must be performed daily; however today, even very religious Moslems can't always keep pace.
Zakat - the Koran set forth a yearly tax. The Holy scriptures are very explicit on this point: grain and fruit are taxed at 10 %, if the land is irrigated by man then 5 %. Money and precious metals are taxed at 2 1/2 %. In most Islamic countries, these payments, which the Koran specifies should be used primarily to relieve the poor, are collected on a voluntary basis.
Fasting - during the ninth month of the Islamic calendar **'Ramadan'**, fasting is required from sunrise to sunset. Forbidden during the day are eating, drinking and smoking.
Haj - every muslim must make a pilgrimage to Mecca, "if they can afford it" and if the family left behind has the means to care for itself. The high point of every pilgrimage is a visit to the **Ka'bah**, a square structure in the middle of the Great Mosque of Mecca, built of stone from Mecca's

PEOPLE & COUNTRY

mountains. According to ancient tradition, the holy relic is wrapped in black brocade. In the eastern corner of the Ka'bah is the famous black stone, which is kissed and touched by pilgrims.

Malaysia, like other Islamic countries, has official institutions supporting pilgrims on their Haj, which must take place during the last month of the year as reckoned by the Islamic calendar.

The Malays discovered Islam hundreds of years ago, but **ancient traditions and taboos** from Malay Animistic and Hindu heritage still remain. Supernatural beings, spirits, fairies and ghosts play a part in many aspects of Malay village life and are not seen to be in contradiction with monotheistic Islam. Spirits are omnipresent, existing in animals, plants, trees and on mountains. But even in the human head, protecting spirits are known to gather which shouldn't be annoyed. For that reason, no Malay likes having his or her head or hair touched. That might frighten the spirits. The concept of mutual respect can be traced back to Animistic tradition too. A Malay would never be scornful of a neighbor, because this would incur the wrath of the neighboring house spirits who are pledged to serving their masters. Many illnesses are believed caused by evil spirits. In order to heal them, the **dukun**, a sort of traditional medicine man, is called. More serious illnesses are treated by a **pawang** or **bomoh**. The exorcist ceremonies can last several days.

Taboos are actions or behavioral patterns which are forbidden by society or the community. So babies aren't permitted to chew on a stick of sugar cane at night; they'd be sucking blood out of their mothers who would then die. That's just one of thousands of taboos sprung up around babies. If you're eating 'ketupat' (rice wrapped in coconut or palm leaves), never rip open the package; otherwise you're liable to get lost later. Every ethnic group in Malaysia has its own taboos for burials: Malays dress simply and inconspicuously, Indians only wear white, while ethnic Chinese wear either black or blue. A lot of taboos are still strictly kept; while others are neglected or forgotten. When you stay with Malays you'll see them trying to be indulgent with foreigners when they behave improperly or break a taboo.

The **Chinese religions** consist of a complex system of beliefs and religious cults, some handed down by ancient folklore, others originating with Buddhism, Taoism, and the teachings of the philosopher Confucius.

One factor dominates the religious life of most Chinese: **ancestor worship**. Death is thereby not considered a breaking of family ties, but rather an intrinsical part. The first responsibility of the deceased's children is to assure a proper burial, held according to strict tradition. Even after death, the departed won't be forgotten for many generations. In their honor a family tree is made, generally 25 - 30 cm long and 6 cm wide. On the front is written the name and birthday of the deceased (and today usually a photo), on the back are the names of preceding ancestors. The family tree occupies a place of respect on the family altar. The spirit of the deceased remains here and is presented daily offerings. Frequently small bowls with food and drink are placed on the altar along with joss sticks (incense). But the soul of the departed is never neglected in its grave. Contentment of its soul is of great importance to the well being of the family A soul in torment endangers the health and affluence of each member of the family. That's why the graves are visited several times each year by family members.

According to **superstition**, there are many benevolent gods (shen) and evil spirits and demons (kuei). Temples are built in honor of the gods according to the means of the congregation, ranging from palaces to simple shrines. The faithful can visit these places at any time to seek the aid and advice of the divine. In strict Buddhist temples, only statues of Buddha are found – but most Chinese temples contain statues of other deities besides the main god or goddess. Very popular is the goddess **Kuan-yin**, who according to legend was transformed from the male Buddhist Bodhisattva Avalokitesvara into the Goddess of Mercy. The Goddess of Mercy Temple in Penang is dedicated to her.

Chinese temple life is fascinating for outsiders, but also difficult to understand. There are, for example, no scheduled religious services, rather every petitioner decides for his or herself when it is time to pay a visit. The statue of the temple deity, flanked by two guards, sits behind the altar. Candles and joss sticks burn. Offerings, such as food and drink are spread on the altar. Petitioners knee or bow before the gods, burning temple money in order to send it to the ancestors in the great beyond. Often the temple deity will be asked to show approval or disapproval of a major personal decision. The answer is resolved either mechanically by the throwing of two wooden blocks, or by an oracle which works by pulling a small numbered stick out of a bamboo container.

The teachings of the philosophers **Confucius** (551-479 BC) and **Laotse** (lived in the 3rd or 4th century BC, considered the founder of Taoism) are not religious in nature per se, rather ethical and moral teachings that only much later received some religious connotations. In the 1st century AD, **Buddhism** made its appearance. Each of these three currents are seen as parts of a great whole by Chinese. In a geography book on China from 1915, I found the following statement, "In every Chinese burial procession, no matter how long or short it might be, there are Buddhist and Taoist monks busy praying for the departed, and these monks aren't hired by Buddhists or Taoist, but rather by Confucians."

Most of the Malay Indians are **Hindu**. According to the ancient classical definition, a Hindu is someone who acknowledges the caste system, who recognizes the four phases of life, who accepts the teachings of the transmigration of souls, and who sees the Veda and its succeeding literature as their guiding principles.

The **caste system** (priests, nobility, freemen, slaves) which still rules India, is of much less importance in Malaysia and Singapore because the contract labor imported from India almost invariably belonged to the lower castes. The caste system teaches that each person has an equally important function on the earth, but not an equal status in society. Each individual has their own predetermined responsibility to fulfil, according to the ultimate order of all things (dharma).

The **four stages of life** are: chaste student, householder, forester, and ascetic. In the fourth phase, the ascetic (sannyasin) is able to achieve complete separation from bodily sensation. Fire dancers and self-mutilators have achieved this phase; while a Hindu in the second phase is invited to give himself up to sensual and materialistic experiences. The famous Kamasutram or the Temple of Khajuraho with its erotic reliefs are expressions there of.

The teaching of the **transmigration of the soul**, or the belief that freedom from the circle of reincarnations, is dependent on individual (kharma), and the good and bad deeds committed in the present lifetime. The goal is to become one with **Brahman**, the essential divine reality of the universe.

PEOPLE & COUNTRY

The **Weda** (holy revelation) was written over 3000 years ago in an ancient form of Sanskrit by Indo-Aryan peoples, but few Brahmans today are able to read or interpret the texts. According to Indian beliefs, these texts have existed since the beginning of time, and were transmitted to the people of the earth by holy prophets.

In a Hindu pantheon, the most important gods are embodiments of Brahma. **Brahma**, the creator; **Vishnu**, the preserver and protector; and **Shiva**, the destroyer.

Vishnu, who appears in numerous incarnations, is often depicted with four arms and blue skin. The most important incarnations of Vishnu are **Rama**, the good prince from the epic Ramayana, and **Krishna** from the epic Mahabharata. Both Buddha and Jesus are also said to be incarnations of Vishnu. Shiva is the god of the Brahmans, who pray to his Lingga (phallus). His two sons are particularly honored: **Skanda**, the six-headed god of war whose cult is quite strong in Southern India; and **Ganesha**, the elephant-headed god of scribes and remover of obstacles. In Malaysia, **Subrimaniam**, an incarnation of Skanda is especially honored. Along with belief in a god-filled world (including several million different deities), there is the tendency in Hinduism to see many gods as the various masks of one single god.

For western visitors, it's hard to come to grips with all the religions. Religious taboos even determine eating habits. A Malay Muslim would never consider eating pork, but the Chinese love it. A Hindu will turn his nose when he sees a Malay or Chinese eating beef. For him the cow is a holy animal; while for Muslims the pig is unclean and therefore unfit for consumption.

LANGUAGE & LITERATURE

Malayan languages, the most important subfamily of the Austronesian languages (Indonesian, Melanesian, Micronesian and Polynesian languages) are spoken by 200 to 250 million people. However, there are distinct regional and dialectic variances. The most important Malay languages are Javanese, Sundanese, Balinese, Minangkabau, Acenese, Buginese, and Madurese. The dialect found on the east coast of Sumatra, in the Riau & Lingga Archipelagos, and the Malay Peninsula (particularly in the south) has gained acceptance in this century as the 'lingua Franca' facilitating written communication between the Indonesian islands and the Malay Peninsula. Even today, Riau-Malayan is the prestige dialect, forming the basis of two national language, Bahasa Indonesia and **Bahasa Malaysia.**

Even before the arrival of Europeans, **'Bazar Malayan'** (melayu pasar) was the extra-regional means of communication in the archipelago. Bazar Malayan was a necessity due to strong trade relations between city states. It is a sort of pidgin language utilizing simplified grammar and syntax. The Javanese form of Bazar Malayan was used by the Dutch as a colonial language. This inspired the young Indonesian national independence movement, of the 1920s, to make Malayan the national language of Indonesia, calling it **Bahasa Indonesia** (Indonesian language).

On the peninsula, Arabic was taught and spoken in Koran schools until into the 19th century. Malayan was simply a means of communication which nobody considered using for theology or serious study. **Munshi Abduhllah,** a Malaccan contemporary of Stamford Raffles, wrote the first grammar book for the language. Because oral Bazar Malayan was a poor basis, he sought aid from elderly people who still had command of the ancient Malay language both written and spoken. Due to his ground-breaking efforts and the active support of the British colonial administration in the Straits Settlement, schools opened toward the end of the last century offering instruction in Malay.

In Malaya (up into the 20th century), as in the Dutch East Indies, Malay was written utilizing the Arabic alphabet. Even today, in conservative Islamic regions (Kelantan, Trengganu) this **Jawi** alphabet is still in use.

The use of Roman type only became popular in the 20th century. Today both Indonesia and Malaysia use the Roman alphabet.

The 1957 constitution of the Federation of Malaya declared Malayan to be 'Bahasa Kebangsaan' or the national language. In consideration of the large Chinese and Indian minorities, English was made a coequal administrative language for a period of ten years. **Bahasa Malaysia** has become the common means of communication between ethnic groups. Since 1984 it is used in all the schools, even the Chinese and Indian, as well as in the universities.

Few samples of writing exist from pre-Islamic times other than a few tomb inscriptions. Hindu and Buddhist influences, however, still abound in fairytales and fables. The Indian epics **Ramayana** and **Mahabharata** were translated into Malayan in the 15th century using Persian-Arabic characters. The greatest work of classical Malay literature is the **Sejarah Melayu**, the 'Malay Annals'. It tells the story of the rise and fall of Malacca. In Malacca's successor state, Johore-Riau, numerous historical studies were written by Raja Ali Haji during the early 19th century, but these can't be compared with the Sejarah Melayu.

The **Hikayat Hang Tuah** was probably written during the 17th century. It's the adventurous story of the noble warrior, Hang Tuah, in service to the Sultan of Malacca.

Generally the beginning of modern Malay literature dates from Munshi Abdullah (1796 - 1854). His autobiography **Hikayat Abdullah** made a break with classical literature by discussing everyday Malay life.

The first modern, Malay-language novel was published in 1928 by Sayyid Sheikh al-Hadi. **Faridah Hanum**, a love story, showed strong Egyptian influences. More recently, the novel **Salina** by Samad Said is considered a great work of Malayan literature.

Those interested in reading modern Malaysian literature, which is also published in Chinese, English and Tamil, should check the **Writing in Asia** catalogue (Heineman Educational Books Ltd., Singapore - Kuala Lumpur). The publisher provides a platform for many modern South-East Asian authors.

BAHASA MALAYSIA

PRONUNCIATION: Generally the words are pronounced the way they are written with a few exceptions:

(a)	sama – identical	like in father
(e)	meja – table	spoken quickly like dead
(i)	manis – sweet	like in seize
(o)	kotor – dirty	like in bought
(u)	minum – drink	like in pool
(ai)	sungai – river	separately spoken like in fine
(au)	pulau – island	like in now
(c)	candi – temple	like in chair
(j)	juta – million	like in judge
(kh)	khabar – news	like German Achtung
(ng)	bunga – flower	like in singer but never like in finger
(ny)	nyanyi – sing	very French champagne/come-on-ya-all
(r)	roti – bread	rolled like rrrrroom
(y)	yang – which	like in you

A SMALL DICTIONARY AND PRHASE GUIDE

During your travels you'll constantly be asked the same questions - a few suggested answers:

APA KHABAR? – How are you?   'KHABAR BAIK. – I'm fine'
SIAPA NAMA MU? – What's your name? 'NAMA SAYA.. – I'm..'

DARIMANA? – Where're you from? 'DARI BULAN. – The moon.' or 'DARI AMERIKA, DARI AUSTRALIA, DARI SELANDIA BARU.
(PERGI / MAU) KEMANA? – Where're you going? 'KE PANTAI. – To the beach.' Or 'JALAN-JALAN' and 'MAKAN ANGIN (to eat some wind)' i.e. 'take a walk'.
TINGGAL DIMANA? – Where're you staying? 'DI LOSMEN. – In a losmen.'

BERAPA LAMA DI MALAYSIA? – How long have you been in Malaysia? 'SUDAH LAMA. – Pretty long.' Or 'SATU HARI SAHAJA. – Just a day.' or 'SATU MINGGU. – One week.'
TAHU BERCAKAP BAHASA MALAYSIA? – Do you speak Malay? 'SEDIKIT – A bit.' or 'SAYA (TIDAK) MENGGERTI BAHASA MALAYSIA. – I can (can't) understand Malay.'

UMUR BERAPA? – How old are you? 'SATU TAHUN. – One.'
SUDAH KAWIN? – Are you married? And if yes the inevitable:
BERAPA ANAK-ANAK? – How many children? 3, 10 but never none! ...and don't forget that old English phrase: I want to practice my English.' So that the conversation isn't completely one-sided.

PEOPLE & COUNTRY

GREETINGS:
Always put the word 'SELAMAT' in front, such as:

SELAMAT PAGI! - Good morning!   SELAMAT MINUM ' Cheers!
SELAMAT TIDUR! - Sleep well! SELAMAT DATANG! - Welcome!

QUESTIONS:

APA	what	Apa ini? (What's this?)
SIAPA	who	Siapa nama mu? (What's your name?)
BERAPA	how much/	Berapa lama? (how long?)
	how many	Berapa jauh? (how far?)
BILA	when	Bila bas datang? (When is the bus coming?)

PERSONAL PRONOUNS:

SAYA / AKU	I	Nama saya... (My name is...)
ENCIK	you	more polite: Cik
DIA / IA	he, she, it	
KITA / KAMI*	we	*without the person addressed
MEREKA	they	plural

FORMS OF ADDRESS:

ENCHE	Mr. (formal)
TUAN	Mr. (traditional)
BAPAK/IBU/ABANG	father/mother/elder brother (to an elder - informal)
ADIK	younger brother

TIME:

PAGI / TENGAHARI / PETANG / MALAM	morning (till 11:00 h), noon, afternoon (till sunset), evening
HARI INI / BESOK / KELMARIN	today (this day), tomorrow yesterday

SEKARANG	now	SAKEJAP LAGI	soon
NANTI	later	BELUM	not yet
SUDAH	already	DAHULU	...ago

PUKUL BERAPA?   What time is it?

MINIT	minute	JAM	hour
HARI	day	MINGGU	week
BULAN	month	TAHUN	year

NUMBERS:
(1) SATU	(6) ENAM	(11) SEBELAS, (12) DUA BELAS...
(2) DUA	(7) TUJUH	(20) DUA PULUH, (30) TIGA PULUH
(3) TIGA	(8) DELAPAN	(45) EMPAT PULUH LIMA
(4) EMPAT	(9) SEMBILAN	(100) SERATUS, (200) DUA RATUS
(5) LIMA	(10) SEPULUH	(1000) SERIBU, (2000) DUA RIBU

SETENGAH	half	SEPEREMPAT	quarter
BANYAK	much, many	SEDIKIT	few, little
KURANG	less (-)	DITAMBAH	more (+)

SHOPPING:
(MEM)BELI	buy	(MEN)JUAL	sell
BERAPA HARGANYA?	How much?	(literally:	how much price)
MAHAL	expensive	MURAH	cheap
HARGA PASTI	set price	HARGA BIASA	real price

TRAVEL:
KEMANA	where to	(PERGI KEMANA? - Where're you going?
DARI MANA	where from	(DARI MANA DIA DATANG? - Where is he coming from?
DIMANA	where	(DIMANA ADA? - Where is?

KE / DI / DARI	to / in / from
SAYA PERGI KE...	I'm going to...
SAYA DATANG DARI...	I come from...
SAYA TINGGAL DI...	I live in...
TERUS straight	KIRI/KANAN left/right
UTARA/SELATAN north/south	TIMUR/BARAT east/west

ACCOMODATIONS:
DIMANA ADA LOSMEN/HOTEL?	Where is a losmen/hotel?
SAUDARA ADA KAMAR KOSONG?	Do you have a free room?
UNTUK 2/3 ORANG (MALAM)	for 2/3 people (nights)
BILIK (MANDI) room (bath)	KOSONG/PENUH empty/full
KUNCI key	NYAMUK mosquito

FOOD & DRINK:
MAKAN	eat (food)	MINUM	drink
MAKAN PAGI	breakfast	MAKAN SIANG	lunch
SAYA MAU MAKAN...		I want to eat...	
TEH / KOPI	tea/coffee	AIR BEKU	ice
AIR(MASAK)	boiled water	AIR LIMAU	lemon juice
HANGAT	hot	SEJUK	cold

PEOPLE & COUNTRY   49

PAHIT	bitter (=without milk and sugar) – TEH PAHIT		
MANIS	sweet (=with sugar) – TEH MANIS (sweet icetea)		
SUSU	milk (usually sweet canned milk)		

NASI PUTIH	boiled rice	MIE	noodles
ROTI	bread	KUIH	cake

DAGING   meat

LEMBU	beef	KERBAU	buffalo
BABI	pork	AYAM	chicken
KAMBING	goat	ITIK	duck
HATI LIMPA	liver	JANTUNG	heart
IKAN	fish	UDANG	shrimp
UDANG KARANG	lobster	KETAM	crab

SAYUR-SAYURAN   vegetables

UBI KENTANG	potato	KETIMUN	cucumber
TERONG	eggplant	SEJENIS BAYAM	spinach
BAWANG	onion	BAWANG PERAI	leeks
BUAH APUKADO	avocado	BUAH TOMATO	tomato
KOBIS	cabbage	KACANG	peas
KACANG KEDELAI	soy beans		

BUAH   fruit

NENAS	pineapple	KELAPA	coconut
MANGGA	mango	SEMANGKA	watermelon
NANGKAH	jackfruit	PISANG	banana

SURROUNDINGS:

KOTA	city	KAMPONG	village
PULAU	island	GUNUNG	mount
BUKIT	hill	HUTAN	forest
MATA AIR	well	AIR TERJUN	waterfall
DANAU	lake	SUNGAI	river
LAUT	sea/ocean	PANTAI	beach
KEBUN GETAH		rubber plantation	
LOMBONG BIJH TIMAH		tin mine	

TRANSPORTATION:

BAS	bus	BAS MALAM – night bus
		STESEN BAS – bus station
KAPALTERBANG	plane	LAPANGANTERBANG – airport
KAPAL LAUT	ship	PELABUHAN – harbor
KERETA API	train	STESEN KERETA API – train station
TEKSI	taxi	TEMPAT TEKSI – taxi stand
KELAS	class	POTONGAN discount
TEMPAT DUDUK	seat	CEPAT / PELAN fast / slow

HEALTH:

SAKIT	sick	SEHAT	healthy
JATUH SAKIT	getting sick	RUMAH SAKIT	hospital
UBAT	medicine	DOKTOR	doctor
DEMAM	fever	CIRIT	diarrhoea
JANGKITAN	infection	RUMAH UBAT	drugstore
(KAKI) PATAH	broken (leg)		

PARTS OF THE BODY:

KEPALA	head	LEHER	throat
MATA	eye	HIDUNG	nose
PERUT	stomach	LENGAN	arm
JARI	finger	KAKI	leg

CONVERSATION:

SAYA SUKA / MAU / BOLEH /HARUS   I like / want / can / must
TERIMA KASIH! - SAMA-SAMA! Thanks a lot (you're welcome!)

TOLONGLAH! / SILAHKAN!	Please! (asking / offering)
MAAFKAN SAYA!	Excuse me!
YA / TIDAK (BUKAN)	Yes / no (with a noun)

SELAMAT DATANG!	Welcome!
SELAMAT TINGGAL!	Good Bye! (to those staying)
SELAMAT JALAN!	Good Bye! (to those going)

BAIK / KABAR BAIK	good / I am fine!
BAGUS / LOSMEN INI BAGUS	good (OK) / This losmen is good.
SEDAP / MAKANAN SEDAP	tastes good / This food...
CANTIK / INDAH	good-looking(people)/pretty (things)
LELAH / LAPAR / HAUS	tired / hungry / thirsty
KOTOR / JELEK	dirty / ugly
JAUH / DEKAT / BESAR / KECIL	far / near / large / small
BAIKLAH!	Okay!

LEARNING:

SAYA BELAJAR BAHASA MALAYSIA	I'm learning Malaysian.
APAKAH SAUDARA BISA BAHASA INGGERIS?	Do you speak English?

BERCAPAK LAMBAT LAMBAT	Please speak slowly!
SAYA TIDAK FAHAM.	I don't understand!

APA INI? / APA ITU?	What's this / that?
APA NAMANYA DI BAHASA MELAYU?	What's this in Malay?
BOLEH FOTO?	May I take pictures?

THE MEDIA

Malaysia's population of 15 million has a choice of 50 newspapers, published in eight different languages. Around 2,200,000 copies are sold daily. Almost 3/4 of the total population can read Bahasa Malaysia and about half the newspapers sold are in the national language. English takes 35 % of the market, followed by Chinese with 16 % and Tamil with 1 %.

Berita Harian, founded back in 1957, is the number one paper with a circulation of 215,000. The second-highest Bahasa Malaysia circulation is claimed by **Utusan Malaysia**. Just 37,000 readers regularly enjoy the Jawi newspaper **Utusan Melayu**.

The most important English language paper is the **New Straits Times** with a circulation of almost 200,000. The **Malay Mail** and **The Star** are also published in English, but have more regional importance.

In Singapore, eleven papers are published daily in five languages. About half the total circulation is in Chinese. The most important English-language paper is **The Straits Times**, which was founded in 1845. Only in the 1970s did the KL edition become the 'New Straits Times', and thereby an independent newspaper. In 1982 a new afternoon paper started publication, **The Singapore Monitor.**

Singapore boasts two TV stations broadcasting in the four national languages. Using the American model, there're lots of advertising interruptions.

Malaysia has two state-owned TV stations (RTM), and since 1984, one private station (Third Channel) which can only be received in Selangor. According to press reports, about 70 % of the programming is of foreign (i.e. American) origin.

Generally, all the media in Malaysia, Singapore and Brunei are supportive of their governments. No newspaper in Singapore, for example, can afford too much criticism of the ruling PAP or Premier Lee Kuan Yew. So observers were a bit startled in early 1984 when critical voices were raised against Lee Kuan Yew's proposal that parents with university degrees should be encouraged to have more children, while lower class parents should be sterilized. There was a similar reaction in Malaysia when Premier Mahathir began talking about a future Malaysia saddled with 70 million Malaysians. The press in these countries sometimes appears to have more freedom than outsiders might like to admit.

ART & CULTURE

Malaysia, with its complex mixture of peoples and cultures, is a melting pot of several major cultural traditions. Some of these originate in the Malay archipelago, but others have roots in China, India, the Near East, and the Occident. During the first 1500 years AD, the Malay culture was primarily influenced by Indian and pre-Islamic elements. Thereafter, Islam became the guiding light. Since the 19th century, western ideas have influenced many aspects of Malayan life. Technology and science, the justice system, economy, and public administration are all based on western models.

Contemporary Malaysian society is very diverse. Its syncretism reconciles elements of Animism, Hinduism, Islam, and particularly in the cities - from the west. Only on the surface, can Islam be seen as the dominating element.

Unlike the merchants who once-upon-a-time resided in Malacca and Penang, the great majority of Chinese immigrants in the 19th and 20th century regarded Malaya just as a place to visit. They formed closed communities. Their present-day culture in Malaysia and Singapore has its roots in pre-revolutionary China, outside of a few local influences.

Much the same can be said for the ethnic Indian population. Neither the Indians nor the Chinese have been assimilated into or transferred their culture to the Malay population.

The tribal cultures of East Malaysia have no written heritage, nor is the architecture very developed. Art forms are expressed mostly in dance and handwork: the ikat work of the Iban tribe, the textiles of the Bajau, in rattan weaving, or woodcutting.

On Peninsular Malaysia you'll find flourishing examples of Malay art in dance, music, literature, and in handicrafts such as batik, silversmithing, kris (dagger) forging, woodcutting and weaving. Painting is poorly developed, a reflection of the Koran's prohibition against depictions of the human body.

In recent years, a number of Malaysian artists of various ethnic backgrounds have made names for themselves in literature, film, architecture and other persuasions. This shows the development of a new Malaysian art and culture utilizing the most diverse influences and traditions.

Here is a list of the most important forms of arts and crafts you'll find in Malaysia:

DANCE & THEATRE

The **Ronggeng,** probably the most popular traditional Malay dance, is assumed to have Portuguese roots. Young boys and girls stand in two rows facing each other and begin to recite poems. During the entire dance there is no touching. Several other forms of dance descend from the ronggeng.

Of Arabic origin is the **Hadzrah**, a slow dance performed only by men. Many Malay folk dances originate in village tradition and are performed on special occasions to celebrate the rice harvest, marriages, or for sorcery. The **Tarian Balai**, performed primarily in Trengganu, is marked by the finest of movements symbolizing the sowing of rice. The Kadazan in Sabah are famous for their festivities celebrating the rice harvest. Frequently they perform the **Sumazau.**

Wayang Kulit is the traditional Malay shadow play whose stories are taken from the two great Hindu epics, **Ramayana** and **Mahabharata.** The **dalang**, who serves as storyteller, puppeteer, and conductor of the accompanying orchestra, sits during the performance with a lamp above him which projects the shadows of the shadow-play figures (punched out of buffalo skin) on a white screen in front. Using various voices, he tells the story of heroes and beautiful women, keeping the audience in suspense. He moves the puppets around the screen, while a rattle, controlled by his feet, provides emphasis for the action-filled scenes.

But it's completely different at a **Chinese Opera.** Too loud and shrill for western ears to understand, performances are held on the city streets.

ENTERTAINMENT

Of interest are the **Main Gasing** (top-spinning contests) in the east-coast states of Malaysia. The tops can be as big round as a plate and weigh up to 5.5 kg. It requires great skill to get the things spinning. You use a rope about 1.5 cm in strength and between 3-4 m long. Then with the aid of a small wooden stick, the gasing is placed on a post on whose metal surface it can spin for up to two hours. Should the proper spirit (semangkat) take hold of the top, it might even spin for 24 hours. In simple competitions, the winner is the one whose top stays in motion the longest. Much more exciting are the competitions where two teams try to start their gasing in such a way as to tip over their opponent's.

Silat is the Malay art of unarmed self defence, which has taken on a form of almost stylistic dance. Accompanied by drums, gongs and flutes, the opponent is attacked with simulated 'karate' chops and kicks. Silat demands great self discipline from its adherents. Silat show fights are often held at weddings.

A national sport, particularly in Kelantan and Trengganu, is **kite flying.** The local language differentiates between two types of kites, the **layang layang** and the **wau.** Builders of the wau are specialists, designing their kites as works of art. The Layang layang, however, are simple children's toys made of paper and bamboo. Wau are known to have wingspans of 2 m. The most famous kite is the **wau bulan** (moon kite), which due to its special construction emits a humming tone while soaring in the wind. Experts fly their kites up to 450 m in altitude. In competitions, altitude is not the sole deciding factor. Points are also given for manoeuvrability.

ARTS & CRAFTS

Many of the ancient traditional arts and craft are still produced today, particularly in Kelantan and Trengganu. Batik making is largely confined to the east coast. **Malaysian batik** is quite different from that found on Java. Not only are the patterns larger and the colors louder, but it is almost exclusively stamp batik (using a stamp rather than hand painting). This is how it's produced: white cotton cloth is covered with wax on all the spots which should keep their original color (i.e. remain white). In Kelantan this is generally done with a stamp. Then the cloth is placed in the first vat of dye. Later, hot water is used to remove the wax. Then a new pattern of wax is applied as called for by the intended design. This process of waxing and dying can be repeated according to quality of design up to eight times. By the more expensive hand batik, the wax is applied with a brush or a small 'pot of wax'.

Kain Songket is woven on traditional looms, mostly as a cottage industry. Different patterns of gold and silver thread are woven into the silk. Kain songket is used for all kinds of clothing, such as evening dresses, scarves, or blouses. But traditionally the cloth is worn by both men and women as a sarong at very special occasions such as a wedding or state reception.

Only the Iban on Sarawak use the **ikat** technique to produce textiles. Better known is the ikat from Indonesia, particularly Sumba. Ikat is an ancient form of colored weaving that's very labor intensive. The technique requires that either the warp threads (those originally on the loom) or the weft threads (those woven through the warp) are wrapped with bast threads so that when dyed, parts of the cloth retain its original color. The wrapping creates a negative pattern. For the succeeding dips in other colors, the parts already dyed are wrapped. On special occasions, the Iban wear a 1.5 x 2 m long **pua kumbu** of ikat cloth containing rhombic patterns adorned with woven snakes, lizards, other animals and people.

Another centuries-old craft in the Malay region is **wood carving**. Craftsmen are commissioned by the nobility and sultans to decorate their palaces with carvings. Balustrades, door frames and window frames, along with window shutters are decorated with leaves, flowers, branches, but never with human or animal shapes.

Wood carving is also an ancient tradition among the proto-Malayan peoples of Sarawak and Sabah. Masks and figures up to 2 m long can be seen today in isolated longhouses. However, many old carvings have long since disappeared via tourist antique shops.

ENTRY FORMALITIES

MALAYSIA

To enter Malaysia you need a passport which is valid for at least one month longer than the time you plan to spend in the country. People from most western countries can stay for a maximum of three months without having to get a visa in advance.

Lately, particularly in West Malaysia, a three month residence permit is stamped in your passport upon entry. There are only problems if you've too little money to show, or if you're too shabbily dressed – you could even be turned back. It's best not to show up at the border with a large group of travellers. Sarawak and Sabah each issue their own separate visas.

Should you only get a two week visa, you'll have to apply for an extension at an immigration office. The offices are located in the state capitals and Kuala Lumpur. When filling out the form, be sure to give a registered hotel as your address.

BRUNEI

Most nationalities receive a visa for 15 days which is stamped in the passport. Some nationalities like the Japanese are required to apply for a visa in advance from a British consular office. Convenient is the British High Commission at Tanglin Circus in Singapore. Should you travel overland between Sabah and Sarawak, be sure you get your entry and exit stamps.

SINGAPORE

Most nationalities can spend up to three months without a visa in Singapore. Others just thirty days. Upon entry, a residence permit for 14 days is normally stamped in your passport. They might ask to see a ticket out and money. If you want to stay longer than 14 days, take a day trip to Johore Bharu. Or fill out an application at the Immigration Department, North Boat Quay, (tel 324031).

Well-kept appearance is very helpful upon entry. However, long hair is not normally a problem any more, though they could send you back if your hair goes over you collar, covers your ears, or gets in your eyes.

Be careful not to run foul of the strict drug laws in Singapore, Malaysia and Brunei – they begin at the border. Just a forgotten crumb from a Thai stick could put you in jail! Possession of any amount of marijuana or hashish is punishable, more than 15 grams is considered dealing. People are sentenced to death for more than 15 grams of heroin. We strongly urge you not to take drugs across the border! You can even have problems bringing sleeping pills or or other medication into Singapore which aren't locally approved. It's good to have a doctor's certification for medication.

MALAYSIAN EMBASSIES ABROAD

AUSTRALIA, 71 State Circle, Yarralumla, CANBERRA, ACT 2600.
CANADA, 60 Beteler Street, OTTAWA, Ontario KLN 8Y7.
HONG KONG, 24th Floor, Lap Heng House 47-5, Gloucester Road, Wanchai, HONG KONG.
NEW ZEALAND, Chase NBA House, 163 The Terrace, WELLINGTON.
UK, 45 Belgrave Square, LONDON SW1X 8QT.
UNITED STATES, 2401 Massachusetts Avenue, WASHINGTON, DC 20008.

SINGAPOREAN EMBASSIES ABROAD

AUSTRALIA, 81 Mugga Way, Red Hill, CANBERRA, ACT2603.
HONG KONG, 19th Floor, Wang Kee Building, 36 Connaught Road Central, HONG KONG.
NEW ZEALAND, 17 Kabul Street, Khandallah, WELLINGTON.
UK, 5 Chesham Street, LONDON SW1.
UNITED STATES, 1824R Street N.W., WASHINGTON DC20009.

EMBASSIES IN MALAYSIA

AUSTRALIA, 6 Jl.Yap Kwan Seng, KL, tel 423122.
CANADA, 5th Floor, AIA Building, Jl.Ampang, KL, tel 289722.
NEW ZEALAND, 193 Jl.Tun Razak, KL, tel 486422.
UNITED KINGDOM, 13th Floor, Wisma Damansara, 5 Jl. Semantan, KL, tel 941533. Consulates in Penang, Kuching and Kota Kinabalu.
UNITED STATES, 376 Jl.Tun Razak, KL, tel 489011.

EMBASSIES IN SINGAPORE

AUSTRALIA, 25 Napier Road, tel 7379311.
CANADA, 8th Floor Faber House, Orchard Road, tel 7371322.
NEW ZEALAND, 13 Nassim Road, tel 2359966.
UNITED KINGDOM, Tanglin Circus, tel 639333.
UNITED STATES, 30 Hill Street, tel 3380251.

EMBASSIES OF NEIGHBORING COUNTRIES IN MALAYSIA

INDONESIA, 233 Jl.Tun Razak, KL, tel 421011.
Consulate in Penang, 37 Jl.Northam, tel 25162 and in Kota Kinabalu, Wing On Life Bldg., 1 Jl.Sagunting, tel 54100.
INDIA, Visa Section, 32 Jl.Tun Perak, Oriental Bldg., 2nd floor, tel 280429.

THE PHILIPPINES, 1 Changkat Kia Peng., tel 484233.
SINGAPORE, 209 Jl.Tun Razak, tel 486377.
THAILAND, 206 Jl.Ampang, tel 488222.
Consulates in Penang, 1 Air Rajah Road, tel 63377 and in Kota Bharu, 4426 Jl.Pengkalan Chepa, tel 22545.

EMBASSIES OF NEIGHBORING COUNTRIES IN SINGAPORE
BURMA, 15 St.Martin's Drive, tel 2358763.
INDIA, 31 Grange Road, tel 7376809.
INDONESIA, 6-D Orange Grove Road, tel 7377422.
MALAYSIA, 301 Jervois Road, tel 2350111.
THE PHILIPPINES, 605, 6th floor, Thong Teck Building, Scotts Rd., tel 7373977.
THAILAND, 370 Orchard Road, tel 7372644.

In countries where Malaysia or Singapore don't have diplomatic missions, use the consulate of the other or the British Consulate.

CUSTOMS REGULATIONS
As usual you're allowed a carton of 200 cigarettes, 1 liter of alcohol, or a small amount of perfume. Any other gifts have to be declared.

Leave your dogs and cats at home. Otherwise you need a health certificate, plus an entry permit from the veterinary administration in Malaysia or Singapore; expect at least a month quarantine.

ENTRY REQUIREMENTS OF THE NEIGHBORING COUNTRIES
THAILAND: Without a visa you can stay for 15 days. If you've longer plans, apply for a 60 day visa which can be extended twice for 30 days.

INDONESIA: Upon entry you receive a visa for 60 days which can't be extended. This applies to most airports and harbors, but not for Tanjung Pinang (Riau) and all the borders to Kalimantan. Here you have to apply at a consulate in advance for a 30 day visa that can be extended for another 15 days.

BURMA: Visas valid for just seven days have to be applied for at a Burmese consulate in advance.

THE PHILIPPINES: If you're plans are for less than three weeks, you don't need a visa other than the 21 day stamp at the border. If you want to stay longer, apply for a visa in advance.

CLIMATE & TRAVEL SEASONS

Go where you like on the Malaysian Peninsula, in Singapore, East Malaysia or Brunei: you're in the tropics! The constant, intense sunlight creates **Temperatures** that remain consistently hot, particularly along the coast. They vary little over the course of the year, but rise and fall with the sun between 22° C and 32° C. During the dry season, temperatures go even a bit higher, but then it's cooler during the rainy season. The closer you get to the equator, the less temperature variation you'll find.

Deviations from the average of 27° C are only found in the hill stations (Cameron Highlands, Fraser's Hill) where it is much cooler. Here the mean daily temperature maximum is only around 22° C (in KL 32° C) and the mean temperature minimum 13° C (KL 23° C). Remember to take a jacket or sweater with you because after a couple weeks in the tropics, you'll freeze just like the locals. Come evening, the beautifully decorated English fireplaces take on a place of honor. In Sandakan the average daily high temperature ranges just between 29° and 31.7° C. The lowest temperature ever measured was 21° C. Other parts of the country have similar meteorological histories. The only exceptions are in the highlands, where it can get much cooler at night.

Seasons aren't determined by temperatures, rather by **precipitation.** Like in other South-East Asian countries, monsoons create regional wet and dry seasons which vary greatly from coast to coast. So if you know what you're doing, you can avoid the rains year round. But stay anywhere too long and you'll experience what flood is all about. Within one day more rain falls than in several wet European months put together. Stormy winds chop the seas, unpaved roads become impassible mud ruts, and whole parts of cities are flooded.

A trip to the east coast or the jungles of central Malaysia should be avoided between October and February - your whole trip could be drowned. Other parts of the country can be visited year round since the rainy season isn't as pronounced. Sabah and Sarawak get most of their rain from the Northeast monsoon. A typical example is Kuching where during the wettest month, January, 546 mm precipitation falls, while in the driest, July 173 mm still falls. You'll find similar conditions in Sandakan, Sabah.

Winds bring rain when they come across the ocean - when they come from across land, they're dry. From May to September the South-East Asia region is dominated by the southwest monsoon bringing high precipitation to the west coast of Sumatra, northwest Malaysia, Thailand and Burma. From November to March the northeast monsoon brings rains to the islands of Indonesia and the east coast of West Malaysia.

So make your **travel plans** with the rainy seasons in mind. Even if you can't expect to see sunny-blue skies every day during the dry season, at least floods and days of unending rains are unlikely. However, in recent years the rainy season has been delayed by up to a month.

PENINSULAR MALAYSIA
Three seasons can be defined, all based on the amount of rain:
From November to March the region is under the influence of the northeast monsoon. During this period the whole east coast receives heavy rains. From December to January, for example, the Taman Negara is closed because the rivers are too high.
From June to August is the season of the southwest monsoon.

Only Penang and several regions in northwest Malaysia, receive the full force of the rains however. The Peninsula is in the wind shadow of the mountainous island of Sumatra. April-May and September-October are months of high precipitation, but not caused by monsoons: rather by the rising of hot air into the cooler upper atmosphere.

Due to the influence of the different monsoons, there are four climatic regions on Peninsular Malaysia:

NORTHWEST (Alor Setar): Two periods of high precipitation (April-May, September-October) and at least two months of extremely low precipitation (January-February).
WEST (KL): Two short periods of high precipitation (April and October) but no real 'dry season'.
EAST COAST (Kota Bharu): One pronounced rainy season (October-January), low precipitation from June to August.
SOUTH (Johore Bharu): Precipitation is sprinkled equally over the course of the year.

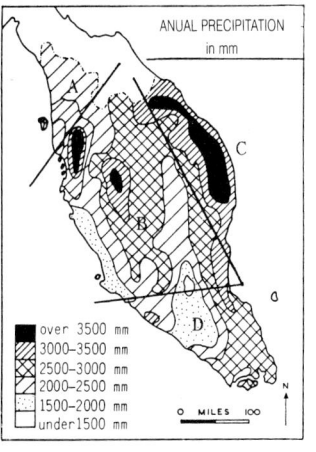

EAST MALAYSIA

Temperatures change little over the course of the year. The best travel season is the European summer. But that must be said with reservations. From the month of June to the beginning of the rainy season the rivers are very low. Many hard to reach areas then become inaccessible (or only with great difficulty). For example, in August we weren't able to get from Kapit to Belaga due to low water. If you want to go far inland, the best months are from March to June.

BRUNEI

Like Sarawak and Sabah, the highest precipitation is from September to November, the lowest in January and February.

SINGAPORE

The island is located just 180 km north of the equator, so as expected you have year round a tropical maritime climate. The average daily high temperature is 30° C year round. The city has never been cooler than 19° C. Even the precipitation is spread out evenly during the year. There's somewhat more rain from October to January. But there's still no real rainy season.

CRITERIA FOR PLANNING YOUR BEST TRAVEL SEASON

* Beach vacations, jungle tours and trips along the coast are best during the dry season. If you want to be real certain, then begin a full month after the end of the rainy season.

* Stay away from holiday resorts during school vacations. You're unlikely to find a room free (ferries and buses are booked out), particularly in the highlands and at the major beaches. Most schools have a long vacation in April, December-January (the Chinese New Year!) and at the end of Ramadan.

Avoid long bus and train rides on Sundays and holidays. At Hari Raya Puasa and the Chinese New Year, the whole country seems to be on the move.

During Ramadan, most restaurants in Brunei, Kelantan, Trengganu and other Muslim regions are closed during the day. This seems to put a damper on all public life. It's no reason not to travel, but it does make things less comfortable.

PLANE TICKETS

Newcomers may find confusing the myriad of prices and classes offered the international air traveller. No wonder, it is intended to be that way. **IATA** (International Air Traffic Association) is a cartel of airlines which sets the prices for all airline services (including plane tickets) artificially high. The theory is: no matter which airline you fly, you should be overcharged by the same amount.

In practice, fortunately, it is possible to find cheaper flights. Officially a one way ticket London-Bangkok costs 1261 £, buy your ticket in Bangkok and you'll only have to pay 380.-$. Even in Europe it is possible to find tickets on the 'Grey Market'. Check the travel agencies. They often have cheaper rates that they are not permitted to advertise, even with airlines that belong to IATA.
In general we recommend:

If you have a set itinerary: Buy a return ticket (round trip) at home to Kuala Lumpur or Singapore. Any tickets that you need within South-East Asia should be bought in Asia. Check the cheap travel agencies for worthwhile offerings. They can organize an itinerary to fit your wishes.

If you have no set plans: A one way ticket is best (except to Burma and Indonesia which require a ticket out for your entry visa). No matter where you end up, you can always get the tickets you need in Penang, Singapore, or KL.

If you are long on the road: Normally a plane ticket is good for one year. Check for "valid for one year" on your ticket. Many cheap flights offer limited services including restricted validity. Most student tickets are only good for six months along with being "non refundable" and "non endorsable". You're stuck with the ticket even if you don't use it. Sometimes you can still get money back if you agree to pay a cancellation fee.

If you are a student or have an International Student Identification Card (ISIC), you can get among other things cheaper plane tickets. Besides in the student travel agencies your card is honored by Malaysian Airlines, Thai Airways International, and Cathay Pacific. It is not certain, however, that all city offices of the airlines will offer the 25 % discount.

Normally people get their ISIC card because they are properly enrolled students somewhere no matter what their age. There are certain places in South-East Asia where non-students can buy the cards. Watch out for bad forgeries! Experts, such as the people in the travel agencies, recognize them immediately. If you want to buy a fake card then have a look at a real one beforehand. Otherwise...

ADDRESSES OF STUDENT TRAVEL AGENCIES IN ASIA

KUALA LUMPUR: MSL Travel, South East Asia Hotel, 69 Jl.Haji Hussein, tel 984132.
PENANG: MSL Travel, Hotel Merlin, 25A Farquhar Street, tel 24748.
SINGAPORE: STA Travel, Ming Court Hotel 02-17, tel 7345681.
BANGKOK: STA, Viengtai Hotel, 42 Tanee Road, tel 2828670. TTS, 2/9 Sribumphen Road, tel 2868609.
JAKARTA: Travair Buana P.T., Hotel Sabang Metropolitan, 11 Jl.Haji Agus Salim, tel 371479 ext 358.
BALI: STA, Kuta Beach Club, Kuta Beach, tel 5051 ext.80.
NEW DELHI: STIC Travels, Hotel Imperial, Janpath, tel 344789.
HONGKONG: KKFS-STB, 8/Fl., 130-132 Des Voeux Rd., Central Hongkong, tel 5-414841.
MANILA: YSTAPHIL, Room 104, Marietta Appartments, 1200 Jorge Bocabo Street, Ermita, tel 5210361.

Sample prices for **INTRA-ASIAN FLIGHTS** in US$. To compare we give the IATA price and in parenthesis the ISIC price. The cheap travel agencies are usually a bit above the ISIC prices.

KUALA LUMPUR: JAKARTA 177.-(105.-), MADRAS 351.-(237.-), MANILA 291.-(212.-), MEDAN 67.-(57.-), MELBOURNE 733.-(342.-), PERTH 611.-(237.-), SEOUL 624.-, SYDNEY 733.-(342.-), TAIPEI 460.- (261.-), TOKYO 607.-(330.-) US$.

SINGAPORE: JAKARTA 159.-(84.-), PENANG 69.-(50.-), PERTH 642.-(224.-), SYDNEY 779.-(317.-), TAIPEI 505.-(261.-), TOKYO 634.-(337.-) US$.

BANGKOK: BAHRAIN 741.-, CALCUTTA 235.-(117.-), COLOMBO 327.-(146.-), DHAKA 235.-(133.-), DELHI 327.-(164.-), HONGKONG 291.-(122.-), JAKARTA 381.-(128.-), KARACHI 405.-, KATHMANDU 315.-(184.-), KUALA LUMPUR 180.-(82.-), MANILA 342.-(173.-), MELBOURNE 1206.-(348.-), OSAKA 570.-(263.-), PENANG 139.-(78.-), RANGOON 106.-(66.-), SEOUL 570.-(263.-), SINGAPORE 223.-(119.-), SYDNEY 947.-(348.-), TAIPEI 384.-(185.-), TOKYO 570.-(263.-)US$.

HONGKONG: BAHRAIN 717.-(580.-), BRUNEI 252.-, DARWIN 654.-, DUBAI 709.-, JAKARTA 392.-(258.-), KAOHSIUNG 107.-, KOTA KINABALU 252.-, KUALA LUMPUR 286.-(188.-), MANILA 125.-(117.-), MELBOURNE 830.-, NAGOYA 289.-, OSAKA 285.-(180.-), PENANG 263.-, PERTH 831.-, PORT MORESBY 648.-, SEOUL 300.-(249.-), SINGAPORE 297.-(195.-), TAIPEI 126.-(85.-), TOKYO 289.-(208.-) US$.

These aren't all the flights in Asia, but you can get an idea as to the general cost. With an ISIC you can get your tickets at a student travel agency before leaving home.

STUDENT TRAVEL OFFICES OVERSEAS
AUSTRALIA
Adelaide: STA, Level 4, The Arcade, Union House, Adelaide University, South Australia 5000, tel 2236620.
Brisbane: STA, 40 Greek Street, tel 2219629.
Canberra: STA, Concessions Bldg., Australian National University, ACT 2600, tel 470800.
Melbourne: SSA/STA, 220 Faraday Street, Carlton, tel 3476911.
Perth: STA, Hackett Hall, University of Western Australia, Crawley, Western Australia 6009, tel 3802302.
Sydney: STA, 1a Lee Street, NSW 2000, tel 2121255.
CANADA
Montreal: Travel Cuts, Student Union Bldg., McGill University, 3450 McTavish, tel 8499201.
Ottawa: Travel Cuts, 60 Laurier Avenue E, tel 2388222.
Toronto: AOSC/Travel Cuts, 44 St.George Street, tel 9792406.
Vancouver: Travel Cuts, Student Union Bldg., University of BC, tel 22401111.
Winnipeg: Travel Cuts, University of Manitoba, tel 2699530.
NEW ZEALAND
Auckland: Student Travel, 61 Shortland Street, tel 399191.
Wellington: Student Travel, Courtenay Chambers, 15 Courtenay Place, tel 850561.
Christchurch: Campus Travel, First Floor, Students' Union, University of Canterbury, Ilam Road, tel 486507.
UNITED KINGDOM
Birmingham: Travel Bureau, Birmingham University, Edgbaston Park Road, tel 4724770.
London: ULU Travel, Malet Street, tel 6360221.
Oxford: Student Travel Centre, 13 High Street, tel 242067.
Cambridge: Zackarama Travel, 22 King Street, tel 314577.
UNITED STATES
New York: CIEE, 205 East 42nd Street, tel 6611414.
Berkeley: CIEE, 2511 Channing Way, tel 8488604.
Boston: CIEE, 729 Boylston Street, Suite 201, tel 4971497.
Los Angeles: CIEE, 1093 Broxton Ave., tel 2083551.
San Francisco: CIEE, 312 Sutter Street, tel 4213473.
Seattle: CIEE, 1314 Northeast 43rd Street, tel 6322448.

HEALTH

Most important for travel in South-East Asia is good physical health. To reduce the physical effects of sharp climatic changes and jet lag, take it easy just before and after flying. If you work overtime up to the last day and get little food and rest, you could spend your first week of vacation in bed with a fever or cold. Be especially careful if you come from a cold winter into the steaming tropics with only a plane ride for preparation. Try to sleep a lot the first couple days until your body has adjusted to the new environment.

Two or three months before you travel, start getting your inoculations. Check with a doctor who knows something about tropical medicine. Even better, go to a national inoculation center where advice is given on tropical illnesses or an institute for tropical medicine at a university hospital. Besides your shots, get prescriptions for the medication that you want to take with you, and ask about the latest inoculation requirements.

Each immunization must be registered in your **International Certificate of Vaccination** detailing place, date, signature of the doctor, and an official seal from the local health office.

SMALLPOX: This scourge was officially eradicated in 1979 according to WHO. WHO officials offer a US$ 1000 reward to anyone bringing a new case to their attention! You only need vaccination when visiting Chad and Campuchea.

CHOLERA: Officially you only need a cholera vaccine to visit Niger. The reality is, however, that cholera still thrives and is endemic in the overpopulated regions of Asia. For this reason get your shots, even if it doesn't offer absolute protection! Two shots within 14 days is good for six months; then you need one injection every half year thereafter.

TETANUS: There is always the possibility of injuring yourself somewhere on the road. For this reason get two inoculations four weeks apart, then one booster shot a year later. You should then be safe for eight to ten years.

POLIO: If you haven't had the Salk oral vaccine in the last four years, then check with your doctor. Allow several weeks!

HEPATITIS: There's an expensive new Swiss vaccine against the dangerous liver infection Hepatitis B (which over half the population of Asia is infected with). It's called HEVAC B and should be injected at intervals of four weeks, eight weeks and fifteen months. You won't need a renewal for five years. A similar vaccine available in the USA is called HEPTAVAX. You might still ask for the old fashioned GAMMAGLOBULIN shots which are designed to increase your resistance to all infectious diseases, but its benefits are not universally accepted. Whether the inoculation is at all necessary can be shown through an antibody test (costs about US$ 10).

TYPHOID/PARATYPHOID: The oral vaccination TYPHORAL L or a new Swiss product VIVOTIF (about 20 US$) is now offered. It is taken over a period of six days and lasts for two years. If you have to take the oral vaccination against Polio as well you must take it three days after typhoid. Allow three weeks if you do it the other way round.

MALARIA: According to WHO, malaria is making a comeback. All of South-East Asia is a malaria region - especially the tropical jungles and swamps. Maintaining a high level cloroquin in your blood can help prevent infection, but it is no guarantee. Most people take RESOCHIN (or CHLOROQUINE, NIVAQUINE, ARALEN), two tablets a week. In some areas the plasmodia (malaria carriers) are immune to RESOCHIN (East and West Malaysia, Burma, Thailand, especially Kanchanaburi area and Chanthaburi, Kalimantan, Sulawesi, Sumatra and the Moluccas). In these areas combine the RESOCHIN with one DARAPRIM tablet per week (the Sunday pill). Instead of this, you can get a prescription for FANSIDAR (one pill a week) but this shouldn't be taken by pregnant women. Start your medication one week before visiting these areas and continue for four weeks after your trip home (incubation period!).

If you have unusual spells of fever and aching joints even after your return home, go to a hospital immediately. **Tell your doctor that you were in a malaria region.** Symptoms are aches in your head, back and joints and high periodical fever. Many doctors will diagnose these symptoms as simple flu and give the wrong treatment. This has led to several deaths in Europe.

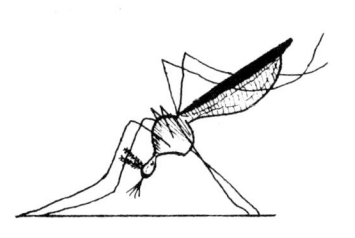

The malaria-carrying mosquito, Anopheles, usually bites between sunset and sunrise. Mosquitoes make the worst bedmates. In many areas, particularly around the cities, these beasts have been eradicated by stern measures. In the highlands, there isn't a problem because it's too cool. Protect yourself after sundown, particularly in moist areas, through the use of coils, nets, or insect repellent. Coils are green spirals which burn like incense, stinking the air. It is better to get used to the smell rather than to spend sleepless nights chasing mosquitos. The insect repellent AUTAN can be put on your skin, but it doesn't last very long. Watch out that your mosquito net doesn't contain a mosquito before you get inside. Even one mosquito can be a bad bed partner. Check it for holes and use tape to make sure it is secure.

WORM INFESTATIONS: It is possible to pick-up large and small varieties on any part of your body. Usually they are found weeks after returning home. Most are quite harmless and can be rid of with a simple treatment. Others are dangerous such as the infamous hookworm which bores its way through the soles of your feet. Therefore always wear sandals when walking on damp ground! After travel in outlying areas, try to have your bowel movement checked for worms in an institute for tropical medicine. This is a must if even a slight discomfort continues over a longer period of time.

SORES: Even scratched mosquito bites can develop into dangerous infections under unhygienic conditions if left untreated. Keep your wounds clean, perhaps using the spray-on-bandage ONDROPLAST along with a vitamin ointment.

SKIN DISEASES: Just by sweating you can pick-up an itchy fungus in the tropics. The warmer and damper the environment, the higher the parasite to host ratio. A hot and sweaty body is sure to attract fleas, lice, mites, and bedbugs. The best protection is two baths a day and frequent changes of clothing. Against skin fungus wear cotton clothes. Tiny guests can be dissuaded by smearing yourself with JACUTIN. The best bet against head lice is the American shampoo QUELL.

SNAKE AND SCORPION BITES: Here there is no real danger. There are few poisonous snakes in Malaysia, and those found, only attack when they feel threatened. The scorpions here are not deadly.

VENEREAL DISEASES: Gonorrhoea and the even more serious syphilis are ever present diseases in South-East Asia, especially among prostitutes. The Bangkok and Manila variety of gonorrhoea is no joke – it is resistant to penicillin. Go to a good hospital where they have the equipment to test which drugs are effective against your variety of VD. Only then should you let them pump you up with medication. If they give you the wrong stuff, they risk making the VD almost immune to all drugs. It is irresponsible to let yourself be a carrier – see a doctor.

Women are especially liable to fungus infections. Talk to your gynaecologist before you leave and get her/him to prescribe you some medication in advance. Cream is better than a suppository.

DIARRHOEA: Every Asian traveller can expect to experience the runs, especially in the beginning. It's so much a part of third world life that it goes by many imaginative names: Bali-belly, Rangoon-runs, Hongkong-dog, Ho-Chi-Minhs, Tokyo-trots, not to forget Mexico's Montezumas' Revenge.
If you're afflicted, you'll usually find that a coal-sulfanomide compound (FORMO CIBAZOL or FORBINA) will give you some relief. If necessary you can try combining it with IMMODIUM (but only in small doses) in order to relax your bowel functions. There are also the alternative 'Globetrotter tips' such as egg yolk mixed with nutmeg, or having a rice and tea day. Don't take stronger medications if the above doesn't work – see a doctor! You could have bacteriological or amoebic dysentery.

Simple diarrhoea can be caused by spoiled food, unpeeled fruits, and icecream. Microorganisms in water are also a major cause. You will have to decide how much of a risk you want to take by drinking the water. Mineral water is not available everywhere, and it is not always possible to have water boiled, filtered, or purified through the use of purification tablets such as MICROPUR. You should even think again about that foolhardy icecube in your coke! Outside of Singapore, never drink tap water! Drink tea. You don't have to use tea to brush your teeth though.
Even more common than the runs is constipation. This is easily taken care of by eating a few peeled fruits. Pineapple helps!

WHAT TO DO WHEN THE WATER IS QUESTIONABLE
BOIL IT: Certainly the safest way to be sure your water is germ-free, though it can take time and is a hassle

for large amounts of water. The water should actually boil for at least five minutes! Then even the most turbid water should be practically germ-free.

FILTER IT: This method of water purification has been making big inroads lately. The modern filters have a ceramic filter core with pores so small that water can get through but not its impurities, including bacteria (and even a few viruses!). The resulting water is free of floating particles and germs, and can be drunk right away. Use of the devise is quite simple, and there're even 700 g pocket filters for use by backpackers. Disadvantage: the devices aren't cheap. You have to pump or the water takes a long time. Plus the filter core has to be cleaned mechanically with a brush from time to time and thereby is used up.

MICROPUR (silver salts): Available in tablets or powder for use only in purifying clear tap water. Suspended particles in the water stop the germ-killing function of the silver ions. It takes at least an hour to work. This stuff is best used to help keep filtered or boiled water pure for an extended period of time.

IODINE: The use of iodine tablets or the old-time practice of adding two drops of iodine to each liter of water isn't recommended anymore. There've been too many cases of allergic reaction. It offers about the same convenience and water quality as clorification.

SUGGESTED FIRST AID KIT
(for more developed regions)
Bandages - elastic bandage
thermometer
TONOFTAL powder (or MONPHYTOL paint)
vitamin pills
ASPIRIN
vitamin ointment
coal sulphanilamides (diarrhoea)
JACUTIN
antihistamine (SYSTRAL ointment)
malaria pills.

If your insurance company back home won't pay for some of these things, remember that the above (and inoculations) are often cheaper in South-East Asia.

As a contraceptive on the road, the pill can be a problem (lack of new supplies, diarrhoea). It might be better to go with condoms or a coil.

HEALTH INSURANCE

Hopefully you have good health coverage which includes illnesses abroad. But to be sure ask your insurance company what they do not cover (such as emergency flights home) and what additional coverage you can get, over what time frame, and at what price. Compare companies and plans for extent of coverage and price. If you do have travel health insurance and are sick, you'll still probably have to pay the initial costs yourself right away. Back home give your insurance company the bills (have them written in English!) from the hospitals, doctors, drugstores etc. and you're reimbursed, according to theory anyway.

To avoid future problems, all bills presented to the insurance company should contain the following details: FAMILY NAME - FIRST NAME - PLACE OF TREATMENT - DATE - DIAGNOSIS - TREATMENT PERFORMED (medication, laboratory tests, injections, hospital stay, etc.) - THE DOCTOR'S SIGNATURE.

The forms presented should appear as 'official' as possible with a letterhead and stamp from the doctor. Have everything written in English, otherwise you'll have to get it translated. The costs should always be presented in local currency. But since the insurance company will check to find the official exchange rate, have the amount paid in US$ also clearly displayed.

Should you have particularly high costs (i.e. because of a hospital stay) be sure to establish contact with your local consulate; explain your case and ask for their help.

One tip for people with glasses: For a fraction the cost spent at home, you can get very stylish, high quality glasses made for you in Singapore. Be sure to bargain! And in some countries your insurance company at home will pick up at least part of the bill.

HEALTH CARE IN MALAYSIA AND SINGAPORE

The quality of the doctors and the hospitals in both countries is good. Even in smaller towns of Sarawak such as Kapit, there are hospitals with competent doctors. Due to the excellent infrastructure in West Malaysia, it is always possible to reach the next larger town quickly. Treatment in Malaysian public hospitals is free. It is not worth trying to find a private doctor: those in the hospitals are just as good. In Singapore you will have to pay for your treatment, but the fees in a super modern private clinic are much cheaper than in the west.

OUTFIT

Generally a tour of Malaysia requires more than a toothbrush and a checkbook. On the other hand, your hundredweight trunk belongs in the attic, not with your luggage. Avoid the extremes, here is our advice:

Many of your needs are best bought in Asia. Why not pick up snorkelling equipment and jungle boots in Singapore. Whether you fly into KL, Penang, or Singapore, you'll find the goods listed below with '*' cheaper than in the west. Caution: large sizes of shoes and clothes may be hard to find - maximum: jeans legs 32, or shoe size 8 (British), 42 (German), or 9 (American). In department stores you may have better luck, but prices are higher.

CLOTHES

SHOES: SHOES, SANDALS, BATHING SLIPPERS (rubber sandals for wear in bath house and toilet are a must. The staple footwear in Asia, they can be found in all sizes).

PANTS/SHIRTS: JEANS*, LONG COTTON PANTS (good for long bus rides if not too tight), SHORTS (women should not wear them off beach and men are always discouraged from their wear).

JACKET (cotton) / **SWEATER** (for those cool evenings) / **SHIRT*** / **BLOUSE*** / **T-SHIRTS*** (you'll have fun choosing the prints - definitely buy in Asia).

SUN WEAR: HAT / SUNGLASSES* / SUNTAN LOTION (in unbreakable container).

RAINWEAR: PONCHO* (can also be used as a tarp when your pack is on the roof of a bus) / UMBRELLA*.

UNDERWEAR: UNDERPANTS / 2 Pairs of SOCKS.

BATHINGSUIT/BIKINI: In conservative areas a one-piece suit is best - for example in Brunei bikinis are illegal. In back areas it is best for men and women to bath in a

SARONG* the local wraparound dress from one piece of cloth. In my opinion, this is the most important piece of clothing you'll be carrying. Besides bathing you can wear it as a dress or cover up. It is best not to wear this or any other peasant clothes in the cities. Not only will you be stamped as the lowest social level, you will also be a laughing stock in the western oriented metropolises.

OTHER NEEDS

TOWELS: one small and one large for bathing.

WASH KIT: SOAP in a breakproof holder / TOOTH BRUSH / TOOTH PASTE / SHAMPOO / NAIL SCISSORS / WET RAZOR (better than finding a fitting plug) / TAMPONS (difficult to get upcountry; in Sarawak/Sabah only to be found in expensive international hotels and supermarkets - much better than sanitary napkins in the tropical heat).

SEWING KIT: strong thread, needles, safety-pins, and string.

FLASHLIGHT / **POCKETKNIFE** / **PLASTIC BAGS** trashbags best, to keep your dirty laundry, protect camera equipment and bags during boat rides) / **WATER BOTTLE** / **TOILET PAPER** (replaces handkerchiefs) / **PLASTIC BRUSH** (for doing laundry, detergent*) / **ALARM CLOCK** (best is a watch with a built in alarm) / **AIR PILLOW** (to sit on during long bus rides and on hard wood benches on trains) / **PADLOCK** / **MOSQUITO NET** (for those who want to be as safe as possible - usually COILS* are enough - see HEALTH) / **FIRST AID KIT** (see HEALTH) / **NOTEBOOK** / **BALL POINT PEN** / **PRESENTS**.

VISIT MALAYA

VISIT THE ORIENT YEAR

all the magic of the East awaits you in MALAYA

Land of sunshine and laughter — that's Malaya. Of virgin jungles and bustling cities, palm-fringed beaches and air-conditioned hotels — that's Malaya too. Malaya is where the cultures of a dozen races have produced a unique society, a perfect pattern of social harmony.

Malaya is the Orient. Mysterious and exciting, gay and open-hearted. For that perfect story-book holiday in a tropical paradise come to lovely Malaya.

Your Travel Agent can tell you all about Malaya. For further details or for copies of brochures and leaflets write to:—

Federation of Malaya Embassy in Japan, 192, Sekiguchi-cho, Bunkyo-ku, Tokyo, Japan or write direct to:—

DEPARTMENT OF TOURISM
P.O. Box 328, Kuala Lumpur, Federation of Malaya.

DOCUMENTS AND MONEY: PASSPORT / INTERNATIONAL CERTIFICATE OF VACCINATION / ISIC (International Student Identity Card) / PHOTOCOPIES OF ALL OF THESE DOCUMENTS / CASH / TRAVELLER'S CHECKS / RECEIPT FOR CHECKS BOUGHT / PLANE TICKETS / MONEYBELT.

INFORMATION: TRAVEL GUIDE BOOK / MAPS / READING MATERIAL OF LOCAL FLAVOR.

If you are planning to do some mountain climbing or jungle trips the above list wouldn't be enough. In damp lowland jungles, proper shoes are a must. Jungle boots from Malaysian or Singaporean army surplus have shown their worth. They can be found in both countries. Whether you need to carry the extra weight of a tent or a sleeping bag depends on your intentions. Unless you are going to visit mountain areas a light sleeping bag or a sheet is enough.

Those with electric appliances in their travel kit should keep in mind the variety of electric plugs and voltage used in Malaysia and Singapore: 220 volt, 60 hertz. The best appliances are those which take both 220 V and 110 V as well as run on batteries. The right plug should be bought in Asia.

Photography buffs should check the photo section of this book.

When deciding on the clothes to take, remember that there are times when you may want to dress a little bit 'better' than otherwise. You may be invited to visit a family that places worth on appearance. Asian hosts should not be written off by travellers any more than the immigration authorities who have been known to turn away people at the border for wearing sandals. Borders are easier than they used to be, but don't take them for granted.

WHERE TO PUT THE STUFF?

BACKPACK: This is the most maneuverable means of transport for your things. But how much walking do you plan to do with your full kit?

TRAVEL BAG: For shorter trips or for people with fewer things a bag with a wide (and strong!) shoulder strap may be a good idea. The advantage: you won't be saddled with the negative image often associated with backpack tourists. They are also easier to stow away on public transport than the oversized backpacks.

VALUABLES

There's nothing more of a drag than to lose your valuables. Malaysia and Singapore may be considered relatively safe - when compared to neighboring Thailand or Indonesia, but still bags can be torn from your hands, rooms broken into, or someone might take off with your camera.

Who at home carries all of their possessions around with them? Because you are forced to do so when travelling, you face a higher risk of theft. There is no way to avoid all risks, but it is possible to reduce them.

*Carry as few valuables with you as possible!

Cash is much more sought after than checks; so cash only as many traveller's checks as you need to at one time. Expensive jewellery belongs at home. When staying at a hotel, stow your valuables in the hotel safe or give it for safekeeping in exchange for a receipt: especially when you're staying in a hut on the beach.

*Secure your room against prowlers!

A strong padlock is a must in your luggage. Sometimes hotel doors can be opened with simple tools so you need extra protection. Many hotel rooms can only be secured by a padlock. While you will usually get a lock, you never know who has the second key. In dormitories always secure your pack with a lock. Not every traveller is an honest bedmate!

*Keep valuables under your clothes!

Some people say your passport, traveller's checks and cash should be hung around your neck, bound to your body, or sewn into your clothes. We suggest a moneybelt large enough to hold all your essentials. As long as you are wearing pants it can always be hidden underneath. You can sew a wide cloth belt yourself. Use cotton (it soaks sweat best) and make several pockets, one of which must be large enough for your passport. Don't make it too tight, and protect your important papers including money and plane tickets from destructive sweat by keeping them in plastic.

No money should be carried in handbags or wallets. A few bank notes and some change should be kept in a deep pants pocket.

Cameras must be carried in a bag, but it shouldn't look as if it is holding something expensive. The bag should be of durable material (slit open!) and lockable.

*Secure your bags in bus and train!

When travelling it isn't always possible to keep an eye on things - especially on a train, bus or boat. So don't leave any valuables in your pack, and be sure to lock it with your padlock. Keep your handbag with you at all times. Seek out friendly seat mates; elderly local women are usually the friendliest and safest. If your pack is on the roof for a long bus ride use a chain to prevent it from falling off or being stolen.

*Friends and travel partners are important!

If you travel with a partner or friends you can take turns looking after your things. When you arrive in a new town one can find the best place to stay while the other keeps watch. Be careful when choosing travel companions, especially the "I want to practice my English"-types. Many 'nice' people have disappeared with all of their friends belongings.

*What to do if something happens?

Hotel room break-in: Call the police. If you are insured, you can only collect if you present a police report. If it isn't in English, then get it translated in Asia and notarized. Singapore has many inexpensive translation offices.

When traveller's checks are stolen:

You must always keep your receipt for the checks separate from the checks themselves. Only when you show the receipt, will the checks be replaced. American Express is the only company that offers immediate replacement.

If you lose your passport:

All of your important papers should be photocopied - copies should be kept separate, of course! It is then much easier to prove your identity at your nearest consulate.

If you are down to your underpants:

If your luck is really bad, you will be dependent on your fellow travellers at first. Go to the nearest police station and from there to the nearest consulate or embassy. Your consulate has to give you money for the trip home and a new passport.

Remember that thieves are only interested in your money and valuables. Don't struggle unless you know that you can get away. We know of many travellers who are dead now for this reason.

INSURING YOUR LUGGAGE

This a way to reduce your risk, but your coverage is frequently very restricted. Be sure to read the conditions exactly, particularly whether your camera equipment is insured and to what percent of value. It might be worth it to take out additional insurance to make up the difference. Anything which isn't insured should be kept in your hand luggage. The insurance should be valid anywhere in the world, for your entire stay abroad, and cover the full value of your things. Should you lose all your bags, it's good to have a checklist showing all the objects lost and their value.

MONEY

Traveller's checks in US$ or £ probably get the best exchange rate. Whereas banks generally only change traveller's checks, moneycangers accept banknotes too. Compare the rates and don't forget 'stamp duty' or 'commission' you often have to pay.

There isn't one good answer to the question 'How to carry your travel money?' If you're planning to travel in remote areas, without spending much time in the larger towns, then you'll need to carry a good amount US Dollars in cash. Even in the city a few dollar bills can be helpful - for a quick taxi from the airport, perhaps. Carrying large amounts of cash is risky: if you lose it, it's gone.

Your safest bet is **traveller's checks.** You can buy them at any bank for a one percent fee. **AMEXCO (American Express) traveller's checks** can be bought in several different currencies. If lost or stolen, they will be replaced at the nearest American Express office.

A good alternative for people with money is the **American Express Card.** Credit card privileges cost 60.-US$ initially plus 60.-US$ per year. With the credit card you can buy many things such as plane tickets without cash. Perhaps more important, every three weeks you can cash at your local American Express office a personal check for up to 650.-US$. The money is paid partly in local currency and partly in AE $-traveller's checks. Get more info at any AE office.

MONEY TRANSFER

If you are planning to travel for several months, don't carry all of your resources with you. Open an account with a major bank and have the money transferred to you when you need it. The major banks have offices (or at least correspondent banks) in major Asian cities to which the money can be transferred. Here is how it works:

You go to the bank where you want to receive the money. If you want the money fast, they will send a telex (before you leave home, note your bank's telex number along with your account number). Otherwise it is possible by mail. A specific amount of money from your account will be ordered transferred. It can be even faster if you telephone and have the money telegraphed. Your money will take two days to reach Singapore from Europe. If you have a friend at home with access to your money, then he or she can simply telegraph the money. Money transfers are recommended in Singapore, Kuala Lumpur or Penang.

FREE MARKET

To get the latest quotes on the official and unofficial exchange rates for South-East Asian currencies, check the latest edition of **Far Eastern Economic Review** or **Asiaweek**. They contain the 'free market' rates from Hongkong. There, as in Singapore, rates are set by supply and demand. Weaker currencies such as the Burmese Kyat or the Philippine Peso are always much cheaper than the official rate found in the country itself. The Singapore and Malaysian dollars, however, are very strong 'hard' currencies! **Newsweek** carries the official rates but no longer lists the unofficial ones.

MONEY FROM THE CONSULATE

In many cases, such as if you are robbed, you may be forced to get money from your consulate to keep you afloat until you can get a flight home. That is what the consulates are there for: to protect and support their citizens overseas. However, this service has been greatly overused by travellers in recent years. Consulates or embassies are no longer as friendly as they used to be. An example:

A cheap flight is cancelled, and with his money gone, P. goes to his consulate where they give him seven dollars to last for three days. A stamp is placed in P.'s passport with a brief handwritten explanation. When departing there is a hassle because the immigration authorities can't read the writing and think that the passport is void. At each stop enroute home the same hassles. Finally home, the stamp is never removed.

EXCHANGE RATES:

MALAYSIA:	1 US$	=	2.45 M$	1 M$	=	0.87 S$
	1 UK£	=	3.45 M$	1 A$	=	1.73 M$
BRUNEI:	1 US$	=	2.15 B$	1 B$	=	1.13 M$
	1 UK£	=	3.03 B$	1 A$	=	1.51 B$
SINGAPORE:	1 US$	=	2.14 S$	1 S$	=	1.14 M$
	1 UK£	=	3.01 S$	1 A$	=	1.51 S$

RATE OF INFLATION: (yearly rise in consumer prices)

MALAYSIA:	3.6 %
BRUNEI:	4.0 %
SINGAPORE:	6.3 %

MALAYSIA

The monetary unit is the Malaysian dollar with 100 cents. The name 'Ringgit', however, is becoming evermore popularly used. In circulation are banknote denominations of 1, 5, 10, 50, 100, and 1000 M$, along with coins of 1, 5, 10, 20, 50 cents (in Malay: sen) plus 1 and 5 M$.

The Malaysian dollar is one of the hardest currencies in Asia; consequently there's no black market exchange rate. Until just a few years ago the exchange rate to the Brunei and Singapore dollars was 1 : 1 : 1. Still the coins in Malaysia and Singapore are used interchangeably.

Upon entry you can import up to 10,000 M$. It's illegal to import more than 3000 Indonesian Rupiahs or 270 Indian Rupees. All other currencies can be imported and exported without restrictions. You're only allowed to export 5000 M$.

BRUNEI

The monetary unit is the Brunei dollar with 100 cents. In circulation are banknote denominations of 1, 5, 10, 50 and 100 B$, plus coins of 5, 10, 20, and 50 cents. Backed by extensive oil reserves, the Brunei dollar remains a stable currency roughly fixed to the Singapore dollar.

There are no restrictions on the import or export of the Brunei dollar or any other currency.

SINGAPORE

The monetary unit is the Singapore dollar with 100 cents. Circulating are banknotes denomination as 500, 100, 50, 10, 5, and 1 S$, plus coins of 50, 20, 10, 5, and 1 cents. The Singapore dollar is a very hard currency today, used as a basis of exchange throughout South-East Asia.

Both money and traveller's cheques can be imported and exported without restrictions.

INCOME AND COST OF LIVING
MALAYSIA

The monthly per capita income runs about 400 M$. But remember, as with all statistics, that there are a few who earn much more and a lot who earn much less. The earnings of most people engaged in agriculture are below the subsistence level of 348 M$ per 5-person family. For example, the monthly wage of a plantation worker on a palm-oil plantation in 1983 was about 215 M$; the foremen did a bit better. However, the weeders got just half this wage. And the female workers in the small batik factories of Kelantan do even worse. The official wage for an unskilled worker is 15 M$ per day.

BRUNEI

Due to it's tremendous income from oil, Brunei is one of the richest countries in the region. The people don't have to pay income taxes, and schools and hospitals are free. It seems that a large part of the population profits from the oil wealth.

SINGAPORE

The average monthly income is about 800 S$. An office worker with some working experience receives up to 1200 S$ monthly. A bus drivers gets an hourly wage of 5 S$ plus overtime. From gross income, wage earners have 22 % of their pay withheld by the Central Providence Fund. The Employer pays an equal amount into this social security and health insurance program.

TRAVEL COSTS

The average traveller who wants to go cheap, will have to calculate about 14 M$ per night for a double room. More expensive are the east coast of the Malay peninsula, East Malaysia, Singapore, and particularly Brunei. At certain times, you might not find a bed for less than 30 M$ per night.

Full meals at the food stalls or in cheap restaurants run around 3 M$. If you want to save, drink tea since soft drinks and alcoholic beverages are relatively expensive. In general calculate at least 25 to 35 M$ per day.

Compared to Indonesia, your transportation costs are more expensive too. But the distances aren't as great, and everything is much more efficient. Cheapest are the local buses. Hitchhiking is possible in West Malaysia, but we don't recommend it after dark. Overland taxis (almost twice as expensive as buses) are a quicker alternative for those with a bit more cash. In general, prices in Peninsular Malaysia are below those found in Sarawak, Sabah, Singapore, and Brunei. In East Malaysia, particularly, you have to deal with high transportation costs. Expensive flights are unavoidable, and getting out to the long houses (boats, guides) isn't cheap.

WEIGHTS & MEASURES

Malaysia and Singapore inherited British miles, pints and pounds. Recently the metric system was introduced. But still you'll see the old weights and measures in use.

Inches	0.39	1	2.54	Centimeter	Example:
Feet	3.28	1	0.30	Meter	1 cm = 0.39 inches,
Miles	0.62	1	1.61	Kilometer	1 inch = 2.54 cm
Miles/h	6.2	10	16.1	Kilometer/h	
Gallons	0.22	1	4.55	Liter	
Ounces	0.035	1	28.3	gram	
Pounds	2.2	1	0.45	kilogram	
Tahils	0.03	1	37.8	gram	THERMOMETER:
Katis	1.7	1	0.6	kilogram	Top °Celsius
					Bottom °Fahrenheit

MAIL & TELEPHONING

First hand experience has shown us that things sent to or from Singapore and Malaysia actually do arrive. And the telephone systems work well.

GETTING MAIL FROM HOME

There are many ways to receive mail from home while you are travelling. The simplest method, and the one we generally use, is to give your friends a rough idea of your itinerary. They can then send your mail to be called for (**poste restante, general delivery**) at the post office you name. In your letters home give the name of the next major town or city you plan to visit and let your mail pile up there until you arrive. This usually functions well. Air Mail to Singapore from Europe only takes three days. The larger the city and the better the air communications, the faster the mail. Sometimes letters get lost somewhere. This is especially true of letters with stamps worth collecting.
Your mail should be addressed as follows:

FIRST NAME   LAST NAME
CITY   COUNTRY
GENERAL POST OFFICE
POSTE RESTANTE

Upon presentation of your passport you can pick up your mail at the poste restante counter. Make sure in smaller towns that the teller checks for mail listed under your first name; the same goes for double names. Usually letters are kept for three months and sent back to the return address. Telegrams, however, are generally returned after four weeks. In some post offices telegrams must be picked up at a separate counter, or as in Singapore, they may only be listed in a special book.

If you are expecting mail, there is always the possibility of having it sent on to a forwarding address by filling out a form. The chances of success are only middling, however. The mail either stays put or follows your journey in eight week intervals.

An alternative is to have your mail addressed to your respective embassy in the country you are visiting. Addresses can be found in the section on Entry Formalities. In this case it is important that your letters be addressed: **C/O EMBASSY OF....**

Anyone carrying an **American Express Card**, or at least using American Express Traveller's Checks can use AE-offices as a mailing address. Be sure such letters contain: **C/O AMERICAN EXPRESS.**

SENDING MAIL HOME

During long trips you'll begin to collect a lot of things which you've bought along the way and which clutter up and weigh down your backpack. Send these things on home in a package. Remember that seamail will take several weeks, but it's much cheaper. Important pieces of mail should be sent registered. **Special Delivery** mail isn't handled any faster than regular mail in Malaysia or Singapore (only in the addressee country); if you want it to move faster, mail it from the largest city possible. Only valuable and light items such as slides are worth sending by airmail. **Never send undeveloped film from Singapore** in packages because the mail there is X-rayed before being sent. Singapore offers the best postal rates by far. The maximum weight for a package is 10 kg (22 lb).

POSTAL RATES

These are the rates from Malaysia to Europe. In parenthesis are the Singapore rates.

AEROGRAM	40 c (35 c)
AIR MAIL LETTER	80 c (75 c)
POST CARD - air mail	40 c (40 c)
REGISTERED LETTER	(+ 60 c)
PARCEL (max. 1 kg)	(1.80 S$)

PACKAGE: The maximum weight for packages is 10 kg! The cheapest rate is from Singapore.

FREIGHT

If you have bought something a bit larger, you will have to engage a shipping firm (expensive!), unless the seller is willing to make the arrangements (demand an exact receipt). The shipping costs are determined by the rate for shipping by sea to your nearest harbour plus the land rate to your home town from there. Expect the land rate to be higher.

OVERWEIGHT LUGGAGE

If you are exceeding your luggage limit for the flight home, it is cheapest to have part of your baggage go by sea. An alternative is to send your overweight case as **unaccompanied luggage** with the same airline with which you are flying. Your bag will arrive on the first flight with space available.

CUSTOMS

Everything that you send through customs must have a Customs Declaration Form attached. It will have to state worth, weight and other facts. The forms are in the local language and in French.

TELEPHONE

Calls from a phone booth cost 10 c in Malaysia. In Singapore, calls are free from private phones; phone booths cost 10 c for the first three minutes and another 10 c for each additional minute. In Malaysian telephone books, **people are listed under their first names** first - so look for Peter White under 'P' rather than 'W'. Long-distance calls are 50 % cheaper from 18:00 h to 07:00 h. Rates: for 10 c you can call up to 50 km for one minute, up to 150 km fro twenty seconds, up to 550 km for 7 1/2 seconds, and longer distances for four seconds.

AREA CODES

Singapore (02) - Kuala Lumpur, Petaling Jaya, Port Kelang (03) - Penang, Alor Setar, Kangar (04) - Ipoh, Taiping, Telok Intan (05) - Malacca, Negri Sembilan (06) - Johore Bharu, Mersing, Segamat, Batu Pahat (07) - Kuching (082) - Kapit, Sibu (084) - Miri, Niah (085) - Bintulu (086) - Labuan (087) - Kota Kinabalu (088) - Sandakan (089) - Kuala Lipis (093) - Jerantut (094) - Kuantan (095) - Kuala Trengganu (096) - Kota Bharu (097) - Bandar Seri Begawan (006732) - Seria, Kuala Belait (006733).

IMPORTANT PHONE NUMBERS

Valid in all parts of Malaysia (Singapore):

Emergency (Police, ambulance, Fire Department)	999 (999)
Operator assisted calls inside Malaysia	101
Operator assisted calls Singapore to West Malaysia	(109)
Information (local)	103 (106)
Information (long distance)	102 (909)
Information (international)	108 (104)
International self dialling	(162)
Telegram	104 (91151)
Time	105 (1711)

INTERNATIONAL CALLS

From Singapore most phones can direct dial any country on the international direct-dial system. In Malaysia only a few phones have direct dialling and not to all countries. International self dialling is much cheaper than an operator assisted call (rates are charged in blocks of six seconds).

Keep the time differences in mind when making phone calls. Your telephone partner may have trouble understanding everything within three minutes if you call at 4:am.

Major countries which you can dial direct from Singapore:

Country	Code	Cost (6 Sec.)	Time Difference
Australia	0061	42 c	0 - 2 hours
Austria	0043	57 c	7 hours
Belgium	0032	57 c	7 hours
Brunei	00673	28 c	
Denmark	0045	57 c	7 hours
Germany (West)	0049	57 c	7 hours
Great Britain	0044	44 c	8 hours
Hongkong	00852	28 c/21 c (evenings)	
Indonesia	0062	28 c	1 - 3 hours
Italy	0039	57 c	7 hours
Japan	0081	40 c	1 hour
Netherlands	0031	57 c	7 hours
New Zealand	0064	42 c	4 hours
The Philippines	0063	28 c	
Sweden	0046	57 c	7 hours
Switzerland	0041	57 c	7 hours
Taiwan	00886	40 c	
Thailand	0066	28 c	1 hour
USA	001	42 c	13 - 16 hours

Normally you'll make such calls from a telephone office (addresses in the local sections). You pay according to six second blocks, but the minimum charge is for three minutes (30 blocks!). From Singapore a 'station-to-station' call costs 22.50 S$, in Malaysia 27.-M$ (any further minute 9.-M$), 'person-to-person' calls cost 40.50 M$.

TIME DIFFERENCES

Malaysia, Singapore and Brunei are eight hours ahead of Greenwich Mean Time (GMT).

The American continent (New York = EST) is 13 - 16 hours behind the times of South-East Asia (with the same differences within the region). Australia lies in the same time zone. New Zealand is 5 1/2 to 3 hours ahead.

Malaysia*: 00:00 03:00 06:00 09:00 12:00 15:00 18:00 21:00 h.
GMT: 16:00 19:00 22:00 01:00 04:00 07:00 10:00 13:00 h.
EST: 11:00 14:00 17:00 20:00 23:00 02:00 05:00 08:00 h.

* Same time in Brunei, Singapore, Hongkong, Indonesia (Kalimantan, Nusa Tenggara, Sulawesi), the Philippines, Taiwan and China.

GETTING AROUND

In respect to infrastructure, Malaysia is the best developed country in South-East Asia. An excellent road system is complemented by a north-south rail line with a branch-off to the north east. Domestic flights are relatively cheap and of great importance for Sarawak and Sabah.

Since completion of the East-West Highway, you can circle the peninsula by bus, overland taxi, or rental car. The Trans-Sabah Highway connecting Kota Kinabalu and Tawau has been open since 1982, though only a small section is paved. In 1983 the last bit of the Sarawak Highway between Sibu and Bintulu was opened. Just a small section needs to be completed between Bandar Seri Begawan, Limbang and Lawas. Once both roads are finished, you'll be able to drive from Kuching to Tawau. Road building is going at such a fast pace in both states, these reports will soon be outdated.

During school vacation and important holidays (especially Chinese New Year, Hari Raya, Christmas), all means of transport are packed. So book your place in advance.

BUSES

By local bus you can reach any kampong on the peninsula fairly quickly. Even in East Malaysia, if there's a road, a bus can get you there - though slowly due to all the stops. Overland buses are faster, more reliable and quite cheap. MARA-Buses, which are air-conditioned, travel express between the major West Malaysian cities. Sometimes overpriced tickets are sold in front of the bus-company offices; be sure they aren't forged! In most towns the bus stations are centrally located and often also serve as terminals for

OVERLAND TAXIS

The fast taxis with the yellow roofs are permitted by law to take four people. For this reason you frequently have to wait at the taxi stand until four passengers are found going in the same direction. If you rent a taxi for two or three people, then you'll have to pay for the empty seats. The price for this comfortable and fast way to get around lies just above the rate for 2nd class train travel, though the local buses are much cheaper.

TRAINS

Back in 1884, Indian laborers completed the first 13 km rail line in the old Malaysian tin mining region between Taiping and Port Weld. The various branchlines built to

FEDERATED MALAY STATES RAILWAYS.

THROUGH EXPRESS SERVICE BETWEEN THE FEDERATED MALAY STATES AND BANGKOK.

A Fast Through Weekly Service is now in operation between the Federated Malay States and Bangkok, enabling travellers to cover the journey between

Penang and Bangkok in 34 hours.

Departure from Penang about 8.0 a.m.
Arrival in Bangkok evening of following day.
Well equipped Restaurant and Sleeping Cars run on these trains, ensuring a most comfortable journey.

For times of departure, see Pocket Time Table (on sale at all Bookstalls and Stationers) or enquire at any Station. Time Tables are supplied to passenger boats running to the Federated Malay States and Straits Settlements.

Through tickets issued from the principal Stations in Malaya

FEDERATED MALAY STATES RAILWAYS.

Visitors to the Far East should break the journey at Penang and travel through the Malay States, rejoining their steamer at Singapore.

A DAILY SERVICE

of Fast Through Trains is run between Penang, Ipoh, Kuala Lumpur, Seremban, Malacca and Singapore.

Twenty-four hours Through Railway Service between Penang and Singapore.

Restaurant and Sleeping Cars lighted by Electricity and fitted with Electric Fans are provided on these trains.

Luxurious Restaurant and Sleeping Cars on all Through Trains. : **Providing Comfort of Travel unsurpassed in the East.**

The Railway Hotels adjoin the Stations at Ipoh and Kuala Lumpur and provide First Class Accommodation at moderate cost.

THROUGH COMMUNICATION WITH SIAM.

For train service see the Railway Time Tables. The train journey from Penang to Bangkok (Siam) is accomplished in 34 hours.

For Maps, Time Tables or further particulars apply to :— *The Traffic Manager, F.M.S. Railways, Kuala Lumpur; the F.M.S. Information Agency, 88, Cannon Street, London, E.C.4; to Messrs. Thos. Cook & Sons, Ludgate Circus, London, E.C.; Branch Office, 6, Battery Road, Singapore; or to Aktiebolaget Nordisk Resebureau, Gothenburg.*

---

carry raw materials to the harbours began to be interconnected around the turn of the century. By 1923 it was possible to take a train from Singapore to Bangkok. A 1920s travel guide reported a 24-hour ride by rail from Singapore to Penang (today the Express Rakyat takes 13 - 15 hours) and another 34 hours from Penang to Bangkok (today about 28 hours!).

Except for a few short branch lines, only of interest today is the main north-south line from Singapore to KL, Butterworth, and Thailand; along with the jungle connection from Tumpat via Kuala Krai and Kuala Lipis to Gemas. The Ekspres Rakyat and Ekspres Sinaran on the main line only stop in a few places (i.e. they're faster) and only offer two classes. East Malaysia boasts just one line between Beaufort and Tenom (Sabah). Seats can be reserved, and you have a choice of with or without air conditioning.

In the express trains a bed (recommended!) in 2nd class costs between 4.-(top) and 6.-M$ (bottom), or in 1st class 15.-M$ (ac) or 7.50 M$ (non-ac). You can book your tickets up to 60 days in advance. Stopovers are only possible on trips of more than 200 km. Children between 4 and 11 years pay half price, younger children free. Baggage limit: 1st class 60 kg, 2nd class 35 kg, 3rd class 25 kg.

For 70 M$ (or 150 M$) you can buy a **Railpass** with which you can ride for 10 days (30 days) in every class on every train of the Malayan Railway. Available only at the train stations in Singapore, KL, Butterworth, Penang, Johore Bharu, Kelang, Rantau Panjang, Wakaf Bharu and Padang Besar.

If you want to book a ticket before your arrival in Malaysia, then contact:
MANSFIELD TRAVEL Pte. Ltd., Ocean Bldg., Singapore or Loke Yew Bldg., Kuala Lumpur or Chartered Bank Chambers, Penang.
THOMAS COOK OVERSEAS Ltd., Orchard Towers, Singapore or Damansara Office Complex, Kuala Lumpur.
HARPERS TRAVEL, Komplex Antarabangsa, Kuala Lumpur or Hongkong & Shanghai Bank Chambers, Penang or 2 Station Road, Taiping.

FLIGHTS
The era of passenger aviation came to Malaysia and Singapore in 1947 in the shape of an Airspeed Consul capable of carrying five passengers between Singapore, Kuala Lumpur, Ipoh and Penang. Shortly thereafter DC-3 aircraft provided domestic service, along with international connections to Jakarta, Palembang, Medan and Saigon. As the political situation changed, the airline's name changed in 1963 from Malayan Airways to Malaysian Airways. In 1966 it was rechristened Malaysia Singapore Airlines, only to spin off the two national air carriers in 1971: Malaysian Airline System (MAS) and Singapore International Airlines (SIA). Brunei has its own airline - Royal Brunei Airlines.

MAS (Malaysian Airline System - 'mas' in Malay also means 'gold') is the national carrier. Its inventory of aircraft include the tiny Britton Norman Islander, the Fokker Friendship, plus the DC-10, Boeing 747 and the Airbus. In Sarawak and Sabah, some routes are only served by the smaller planes. Domestic flight plans feature excellent Fokker Friendship aircraft (F 28), and the cheaper 'BN flights' with the smaller BN 2 aircraft. The main airport is the Subang International Airport in Kuala Lumpur (modernized in 1983). There's usually no waiting time at boarding, even of the larger planes (unless the computer has broken down again).

GENERAL INFORMATION 89

Singapore has one of the world's most modern airports. Changi Airport (opened in 1981) gives a first impression of the city's dynamism, and the six duty-free shops, open round the clock, insure that even on the shortest stopover, you can still spend some money. The Singapore Airlines fleet consists mostly of 747s, along with DC-10s, 727s and the Airbus.

Both airlines have extensive route systems within South-East Asia, but also serve London, Tokyo, and Sydney - on its Pacific route. SIA even flies into San Francisco. Both airlines offer excellent service on both their domestic and international routes.

Normally you're permitted 20 kg of baggage, on flights with smaller planes just 15 kg (Fokker) or 10 kg (BN2). Children under two years pay 10 % of the regular fare without entitlement to a seat of their own, children under 12 get a 50 % discount.
The airport tax for national flights is 7 M$, for flights to Singapore or Brunei 10 M$ and for international flights 15 M$.
Singapore International flights 12 S$, Malaysia and Brunei 5 S$. There's no airport tax in Brunei.

RENT A CARS

Malaysia is the perfect place to drive yourself. Large firms rent cars in Singapore which you can also drive into Malaysia and turn in there. AVIS, HERTZ and SINTAT all have different rates so compare prices. Watch out for special tariffs. There are special day or weekend rates with limited mileage or excursion rates with unlimited mileage. If you rent a car for a longer spell of time, a smaller one without ac may cost you as little as 1300 M$ per month (unlimited milage, including insurance) - provided you bargain.

Map out the route you want to drive before deciding which tariff is best. It is your choice as to which firm you choose. Only with the international companies are you guaranteed a good car.

If you want to leave from Singapore, you should check the prices of the respective offices in Johore Bahru (Malaysia) if possible. They are often cheaper, making it worth taking a bus across the causeway and renting the car there. And Singapore is a very expensive place to drive with tolls to enter the city center (CBD) and very expensive parking.

HERTZ: SINGAPORE, 33 Tanglin Rd., tel 7344646 - KL, 52 Jl. Ampang, tel 204830 - PENANG, 38 Farquar St., tel 375914 - KUANTAN, 22 Jl.Telok Sisek, tel 212015.

AVIS: SINGAPORE, Singapura Forum Hotel, tel 7377870 - KL, 64-B Jl.Kg. Attap, tel 443188 - PENANG, 38/6 Leboh Farquhar, tel 361685 - JOHORE BHARU, Tropical Inn, 15 Jl.Gereja, tel 221157 - KUANTAN, Loo Bros. Bldg., 59 Jl.Haji Abdul Aziz, tel 23659 - KUALA TRENGGANU, Hotel Warisan, tel 27654.
SINTAT: SINGAPORE, 50 Collyer Quay, tel 2244155 - KL, Holiday Inn, tel 482388 - PENANG, Lone Pine Hotel, Batu Ferringhi, tel 811101 - KUANTAN, Hotel Merlin, tel 24716.

Other offices at the arrival areas of the major airports. Local rent-a-car companies can be found in KL, Penang, or Singapore. With them, however, you have to turn in the car where you rented it, which isn't always convenient.

KL: MAYFLOWER ACME TOURS, 18 Jl.Segambut Pusat, tel 667011 - NATIONAL CAR RENTAL, G 10, Wisma Stephens, Jl.Raja Chulan, tel 489188 - SAN'S CAR RENTALS, Shop G 9, The Regent, Jl.Sultan Ismail, tel 480277 / 480350.
PENANG: MAYFLOWER ACME TOURS, 8 Greenhall, tel 368121 - LYE LYE SELF DRIVE, 110 Leboh Tek Soon, tel 64837 - NATIONAL CAR RENTAL, 24 Jl.Sultan Achmad Shah, tel 62454.

You can also rent a car in Bandar Seri Begawan: AVIS, Soon Thian Building, tel 24921, SHARIKAT YURAN, Jl.Chevalier 144, J.J. TOUR CAR HIRE, Jl.Kumbang Pasang, tel 24761, MORNI HIRE, Jl.Padang 23

Have a good look at the car before you rent; here's a checklist:

blinker	brakes
spare wheel	mileage
tyre profile	windscreen wipers
headlights	shock absorbers
full tank	tools
jack	insurance sticker
air conditioning	

In Singapore and Malaysia a national driver's license is enough to rent a car.
It's worth 7-10 M$ daily to get some extra insurance (collision damage waiver) removing your liability for damage up to 1000 M$ to the car.

Petrol in Malaysia costs about 1.10 M$ per liter (1985). Get yourself one of the good roadmaps provided by the major oil companies at just about every petrol station.

When planning your route, remember: rent-a-cars aren't landrovers and can't necessarily be used on every road shown on the map. Except for the first sections of the north-south line between KL and Seremban, there are no super highways. In addition you'll find completely different traffic conditions on Asian roads; so don't expect to cover any great distances in one day. While at home you may find a forest of signs warning of every possible road situation; in Asia be ready for surprises around every corner, whether it's a pot-hole or buffalo. During the rainy season, many roads are under water. These are specially marked on the Mobil maps. Expect unusual behavior by other drivers and pedestrians. Pedestrians always assume that they have enough time to make it over the street in front of your car; and drivers in the other direction naturally assume that you'll brake if they want to pass.

BOATS

In West Malaysia you'll rarely go by boat. Of interest are the connections into Taman Negara and to the offshore islands. Larger ships run to Langkawi, Pangkor and from Singapore to Indonesia (Riau). New ferry connections include Malacca - Dumai (Sumatra), Penang - Belawan (Sumatra), and Penang - Langkawi. During the rainy season, the smaller boats, discontinue service, particularly along the east coast.

Riverboats of various kinds and sizes are the most important means of transportation in Sarawak. All the major rivers are navigable, allowing you to reach the most isolated longhouse on the border to Indonesian Kalimantan. If there isn't a regular boat, you can either charter a boat (often very expensive), or you can wait by the jetty for a boat going in the right direction. This can require lots of time, but it's the best way to get into the interior. A prerequisite is a basic knowledge of the Malay language, the lingua franca in Borneo. Such boat trips into the blue are always the most interesting adventures.

Especially during the dry season when the rivers don't have much water in the upper courses, you'll have to walk with the boat along the riverbank pushing past rocks and shallows. At waterfalls, you'll even have to portage through the jungle.

During the rainy season, the rapids become dangerous, filled with the many uprooted trees carried down the river.

You can go by **coastal steamer** or other ships along the coast between Kuching and Tawau. There are a few speedboats. The regular connections are listed in the local sections.

ACCOMMODATIONS

WEST MALAYSIA
You'll find accommodations in all price classes and categories in West Malaysia. This book only mentions the international class hotels if they offer that something special outside the Hyatt/HiltonHoliday-Inn standard. Some Malaysian cities, along with Singapore, still have a few hotels offering a taste of the flair from the days of Somerset Maugham, Conrad and Kipling. The addresses of the international hotels can be found in any tourist brochure or the yellow pages of the phone book. The capacity of the more expensive hotels is ever increasing so there's rarely trouble finding a room.

It's much more difficult finding a hotel if you're on a limited budget. Many of the cheaper places are managed by Chinese. Since they're mostly located in older sections of town, new construction of banks, office buildings and shopping centres are closing them down. Some are slightly run down, but in general pretty clean. Always expect small bedmates, however; check your mattress in advance for bugs and take a couple of coils or a mosquito net with you.

In Chinese hotels the huge beds in single rooms are usually big enough for two people, or a double room for three people. So be sure to have a look before you check in.

On the beaches and in the kampongs, there're a number of cheap accommodations run by Malays. Sometimes you live in a house with your landlord including full board, and participation in family life. Usually, however, all you get is a simple hut furnished with little more than a mattress.

Bath tubs are only found in expensive hotels. The cheaper rooms usually have showers. If you use a common shower, we recommend you where rubber sandals to protect against athlete's foot. In the baths of some hotels you'll find a huge basin of cool water. From this **mandi**, you ladle water over your body. So that the water remains clean for the next person, never get into the mandi or wash your hands or clothes inside.

Most toilets contain no toilet paper. Instead, the Malays use water and their left hand to wipe themselves. If you don't want to follow this tradition, bring your own paper.

During the high season, and especially during Malaysian school holidays, telephone ahead to book your room - important if you're planning to arrive in the late afternoon or evening. Keep this in mind in KL, Penang, and along the east coast during turtle season.

Government Rest Houses are nice old relics from the past (in Malay: Rumah Persinggahan Kerajaan) and are often found in out of the way places. They could have the quality of a middle class hotel (Taiping), or just be very simple (Batu Rakit).

An English 'resident' or colonial official 'upcountry' during the days of Somerset Maugham used to look forward to the evening in the Rest House. After a hard day on the road it was wonderful to sit on the veranda sipping a gin or scotch while being fanned by the 'pukah boy' sitting quietly in the corner.

EAST MALAYSIA

Prices are generally a bit higher here than in the western part of the country. This is really noticeable in hotels. Expect to pay about 20 M$ for a double room. Places like Sandakan and Tawau are especially expensive.

What you pay in Iban or Kayan longhouses is up to you. Gifts are good, but leave the glass beads at home. The day when a cheap digital watch opened all doors is long gone, even in the most isolated parts of Borneo. Food is a much better gift than some inventions of modern man. Cigarettes and small amounts of money also have their place. If you're asked for medications, be sure to leave enough.

Hospitality is very important in many longhouses. Mass tourism has destroyed a lot, particularly along the Skrang River in Sarawak. The tourist industry picked this area to pipe its tourists through the long houses. The result is an example of how awful tourism can be. So try to behave such in a way that visitors in the future will still be welcome guests.

Don't make a lot of requests; just accept what you're offered. Never drink so much alcohol that you lose control. Have respect for other people living at the long houses. As soon as people start going to bed, reduce your volume, and head to sleep yourself. Ask about taboos and proper behavior right upon arrival. Respect their gods and obey the traditional rites, particularly when someone brings it to your attention.

And personal hygiene isn't up to western standards. There are few toilets, and bathing is done in the rivers. So don't forget your sarong.

BRUNEI

Hotel prices do honor to Brunei's reputation as an expensive country. Hotels are hard to find in Bandar Seri Begawan (BSB), Seria, or Kuala Belait for under 70.-B$. There aren't any cheap Chinese hotels. The only cheap place to stay is the Youth Centre (Pusat Belia). Should you get in there with some luck and fast talking, BSB can be OK.

SINGAPORE

In the city there's a tremendous selection of hotels of every price class and category. New luxury hotels are constantly being built. Still, if you arrive in the afternoon or late at night, you'll have a hard time finding a cheap room. Start telephoning from the airport or the nearest phone booth. For a fee of 10 S$, German Asian Travels will book a room and guarantee the advance payment to the hotel (without which no hotel here can be reserved).

We have established the following price categories (all double rooms):

	MALAYSIA	SINGAPORE	BRUNEI
*	up to 12 M$	up to 15 S$	up to 20 B$
**	up to 25 M$	up to 25 S$	up to 30 B$
***	up to 35 M$	up to 50 S$	up to 70 B$
****	over 35 M$	over 50 S$	over 70 B$

FOOD & DRINK

Malaysia has a lot to offer the culinary aware. As you'd expect, considering the multiracial population, there's no trouble finding Indian, Malay, Chinese and European food. Sometimes they have influenced each other, such as the **Nonya food** prepared by local Chinese: the way it's prepared is Chinese, the spices are hot like in Malay food, and it's not eaten with chopsticks, but with fork and spoon.

HOW TO EAT?

While in Malay restaurants you always eat with a fork and spoon, be prepared in rural areas to eat with your hand - like the Indians using only the right hand. The left hand is considered unclean and should never be used to touch food. It takes some practice to eat curry like an Indian from banana leaves. Almost all restaurants have basins where you can wash your hands before and after your meal. And you should learn how to use chop sticks. Most restaurants can provide you with silverware, but at foodstalls, chop sticks are all you'll find. Plus the Chinese will respect your attempts to join the local way of life.

WHERE TO EAT?

Numerous tiny foodstalls offer the thrifty traveller things to munch for friendly prices. It's no problem finding something to eat at any time of day, unless you happen to be in a strict Muslim region during Ramadan. Foodstalls are set up, generally evenings, on the streets around markets and squares. Wander about and order something here and there, prepared before your eyes. Other stands will be selling drinks and fresh juices so your tour can result in a complete meal. Some night markets (**gerai makan** = 'hawker centres') have permanent seating. Find a place at a table and order your meal from the surrounding stands. The bills will be calculated separately.

The cheapest food is served by the foodstalls, called **warung**. The **Kedai Kopi** (coffee shops) have inviting prices, unlike the expensive **Restoran** (restaurants).

WHAT TO EAT?

Since the sea is never far away, you'll find fantastic fish and seafood everywhere. The local palette ranges from hot fish curries or oyster omelettes at the night markets to lobster termidor, or delicately prepared shrimp in seafood restaurants by the beach. You'll rarely see a menu, and if you do, don't expect to find price information. Fresh fish is generally chosen right from an aquarium and paid for according to weight. Local people will know the prices. If you're still new and don't want a bad surprise, then ask about the price (per 100 g) before you order. If you like fish, you're in for a treat, because all the nationalities of Malaysia and Singapore prepare their fish differently.

MALAY FOOD

All over the country you'll find stalls selling **SATAY** - tiny pieces of meat coated in sugar and spices and grilled over charcoal. They are served with a spicy-sweet peanut sauce. The following meat **(DAGING)** is used: beef **(LEMBU)**, mutton or goat **(KAMBING)**, and less often chicken **(AYAM)**. What the Muslims hate and the Chinese love to use is pork **(BABI)**.

GADO GADO is a cold vegetable salad served with a peanut sauce dressing. If you have any suspicions as to the hygienic conditions, then forgo on the peanut sauce. **ROTI** is a general term for bread, usually flatbread.

The best known dish is **NASI GORENG** - fried rice mixed with white boiled rice **(NASI PUTIH)** and the following ingredients: egg **(TELUR)**, different vegetables **(SAYUR-SAYURAN)** and sometimes meat or shrimps **(UDANG)**. **NASI BERIANI** is an Indian variation of this dish served with hot curries. Nasi goreng in all its variations can be found at the foodstalls.

Besides fried rice, there's also fried noodles **(MIE GORENG)**, fried vegetables **(SAYUR GORENG)**, and of course for breakfast your fried egg **(TELUR GORENG)**.

LAKSA is a typical Malaysian type of thick noodle soup. A speciality is **PENANG LAKSA**, a noodle soup spiced with fish paste.

Really like your food? Then say: Makananmu enak sekali!

CHINESE FOOD

A must, when eating Chinese food, is mastery of chop sticks. You gain a lot of face if you show competence.
In Singapore you have a chance to try many regional varieties:

CANTONESE is the most prevalent, since most Chinese in South-East Asia originate from Guangdong Province. Dishes are only mildly spiced, using lots of ginger. Meat and vegetables are lightly fried in peanut oil. A speciality are the tiny stuffed dough balls, **DIM SUM,** which can either be steamed or quickly fried. You can hunt for your favorite types in bamboo baskets. A dim sum meal can take hours; in the end you only pay for what you actually ate.

SZECHUAN cooks use lots of garlic and chilli; food is generally heavier spiced. Try Szechuan duck or chilli chicken.

PEKING FOOD is that of the imperial court, with lots of Mongolian and Muslim influence. Instead of rice, dumplings and noodles are often served in the north. The main speciality is Peking duck. The delicacy is not in the meat, rather in the crisp, spicy brown skin with an underlayer of fat. It is prepared by blowing air under the skin of the roast.

SHANGHAI FOOD is a treat for stew lovers and people who appreciate fish dishes. The liberal use of soy sauce makes everything taste a bit sweet.

HAINAN FOOD from the large tropical island off Vietnam offers its own speciality: chicken rice - rice boiled in chicken broth and served with chilli, ginger, soy sauce and chicken.

HUNAN presents the delicacy, chor chong tung. It's made of small pieces of chicken served with big red chillies and various sauces. Hunan's native son, Mao Tse-tung, once said that all the true revolutionaries come from places where spicy food is appreciated: Spain, Mexico, Bengal and, of course, Hunan.

SPECIALITIES TO LOOK FOR:
   100 YEAR EGGS are actually only a couple of weeks old. Fresh duck eggs are laid in a mixture of earth, rice husk and ash. After fermentation the egg white is darker and the yoke dark red. Certainly an acquired taste.
   BIRD'S NEST isn't exactly like it sounds, just the edible threads swallows use to build their nests. It's an expensive delicacy served with quail eggs and chicken broth.
   SHARK'S FIN SOUP is made of well cooked fins mixed with chicken and shrimp - excellent.
   YAM POT is a hot, puff-paste pie which can be filled with fish, chicken, pork, shrimp or vegetables - wonderful.
   STEAMBOAT - this is most fun if you have at least four people; the raw ingredients (fish, shrimp, meat, liver, vegetables, etc.) are boiled in a pot of simmering broth placed on your table. Before eating you should dip them in chilli or soy sauce. For the topping, you drink the rich broth into

which egg has been beaten. Additionally, there are foodstalls offering steamboats. Complete skewers of seafood, entrails, quail's eggs, are steamed in brew.

Those who want to eat cheap at the foodstalls don't have to forgo the delicacies. Besides the egg rolls, Hainan chicken rice, dim sum from Canton, soups with meat, fish and vegetable bases, soybean curd and shrimp balls, you might go out of your way for:

HOKKIEN MEE, fried noodles according to a Hokkien Province recipe. The noodle soup is also excellent.
CARROT CAKE, a mushy mixture of radish and carrots baked with eggs – filling and tasty.
OYSTER OMELETTE, a very reasonably priced omelette featuring – you guessed it!
CHAR SIEW, grilled pork painted with a spicy hot, but sweet, sauce; served on rice with gravy.

Otherwise you'll find the typical Malay fried noodle dish **MEE GORENG**, and of course **NASI GORENG**, or the Indian stuffed pancakes **MURTABAH**. To wash it all down try freshly squeezed fruit juice. Especially refreshing is sugarcane juice.

INDIAN FOOD

Curries, typically the basic spice, are varyingly hot. A good curry should be made of at least 20 different spices – it isn't to be compared with the brown powder commercially available in western shops. The hottest curries are **CURRY MADRAS** and **CURRY CEYLON** – too hot for some Europeans. You can reduce the strength of any curry somewhat by mixing it with yoghurt or sugar. Novices at Indian cooking should order a **KOOMA** (sometimes written 'kormah') which is a mildly spiced curry dish.

Traditional curries are always made with vegetables, but you can also get lamb, chicken, crab, and beef (of course not from Hindus). It is served either with rice or bread. **CHAPATHIS** are breads made of wheat flour and water which are baked dry. **PARATHAS** are similar but baked with butter. **NAN** is the simplest kind of bread. Be sure to try **MURTABAH**, a kind of pancake with a spicy filling of onions, vegetables, egg and sometimes meat.

SNACKS AND SPECIALTIES

In cities and tourist centers you'll also find Japanese, Thai, Korean, and European restaurants, catering to well heeled tourists. Everyone else has the alternative of the multinational fast food chains and their local variations.

If you're not one of those tourists who stays at hotels offering extensive breakfasts, you still have some breakfast possibilities. Not everyone will want to order the rice soup with fish eaten by elderly Chinese for breakfast. On the other hand, stuffed dumplings, **dim sum**, do fit western taste. There's good tea in the Indian restaurants, best drunk with **roti** and curry sauce (the less adventurous can sprinkle their bread with sugar). Many restaurants (also **kedai kopi**) offer small cakes, sweet stuffed breads and bananas, all for just a few cents as a snack. And don't forget, traveller hotels serve breakfasts featuring ham and eggs, toast, porridge, pancakes, musli, milkshakes . . .

BEVERAGES

Any restaurant or hotel will serve you, **AIR** (boiled water), which you can drink without worry. **TEH** (tea) and **KOPI** (coffee) are generally served with milk and sugar. If you want it otherwise, say **TEH (KOPI) OH**. if you want only sugar say **TEH (KOPI) OH MANIS**. **SUSU** (milk) is usually canned. Fresh milk is relatively expensive and only available in city grocery stores. Chocolate milk, particularly by MILO and DUTCH BABY, is offered fresh everywhere. Convenient when travelling are the 0,2 l containers of (sorry very sweet) tea, chocolate milk, and fruit juices. They leave little trash and can be found in all grocery stores and restaurants. Then there're all the usual soft drinks, available to go with lots of ice in plastic cups. Foodstalls also sell in convenient plastic cups **soybean milk** and **CENDUL**, a type of sirup with dough-like strips floating in it.

Alcoholic beverages are only served in non-Muslim restaurants. The most common types of **BIR** (beer) are Tiger, Anchor and Guinness. Wines and foreign liquors are very expensive and hard to find. Other local drinks are **tuak** and **arak**, Chinese rice wine, and rice liquors.

The fruit juices offered everywhere are fantastic. Be sure to try sugarcane juice and the cooled milk of young coconuts, **kelapa muda**. The fruit juices are always served with ice, **AIR BATU** (means 'water stones').

FRUITS

CHIKU - an egg-shaped fruit with soft, slippery pulp under brown skin, slightly sweet.

DELIMA - pomegranate, a round fruit whose refreshing pulp is divided into several sections; yellow with a spotty brown skin.

DUKU - a brown, golfball size fruit whose pulp can be pressed out of the skin; the segmented white pulp is slightly sour, the green core can be bitter.

GENERAL INFORMATION 101

DURIAN - a green fruit with thorns the size of a watermelon containing a sticky yellow pulp around big kernels. Its strong musty odour (as fitting the 'queen of fruits') makes it less popular among westerners. DON'T MIX DURIAN WITH ALCOHOL.

JAMBU AIR - the waxy skin can be white, green or pink. The whole fruit is eaten along with a sweet, peppery soybean-chili sauce.

MANGO - a fruit of green or reddish coloring with a nutty taste that's sweet or sour depending on its ripeness.

MANGOSTEEN -the size of an apple and deep purple with sweet sour segments. The skin juices stain! Never sweeten with sugar!

NANGKA - 'Jack fruit', the green, oval fruit can weigh up to 20 kg, with its sweet, yellow, segmented pulp.

NENAS - pineapple, cheap to buy on market.

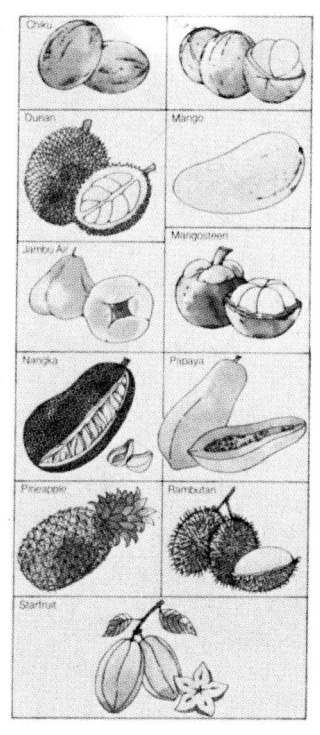

PAPAYA - a melon like yellow green fruit with an orange red interior, commonly served as desert.

PISANG - the general term for bananas of which there are several varieties for grilling, cooking, or eating as a fruit as we eat them. Especially tasty are the small bananas which you never see in Europe.

RAMBUTAN - hair (=rambut), the name is appropriate for this red-yellow fruit the size of a tennis ball under whose soft skin you'll find sweet white pulp.

STARFRUIT - a cross cutting of this long yellow-green fruit looks like a star. It can be sprinkled with salt or pressed into juice. Contains lots of water - thirst quenching.

FESTIVALS & HOLIDAYS

In the multi racial state of Malaysia, state holidays and official events take place according to the western Gregorian calendar. The **Islamic calendar** on the other hand begins with the flight of Mohammed from Mecca on the 16th of July 622 AD and is lunar based. This, however, is about 11 days shorter than the solar year causing each year to begin a bit earlier. Chinese holidays vary only within certain limits because their average year also has 365 days; only the beginning of each year is determined by the moon.

Sunday is a holiday in all states except Trengganu, Kelantan, Kedah and Johore where **Friday** is the official day of rest. However, in the other states of Malaysia, all government buildings (offices, museums, etc.) close on Friday afternoons. In Brunei both Fridays and Sundays are holidays.

Should a major holiday (such as the Chinese New Year) fall on a weekend, the next two workdays are declared holidays. Normally schools are closed between Christmas and the beginning of January, in April, in August, and at the end of Ramadan. In addition to the national holidays, there are state holidays on January 1st, December 25th, and the birthday of the King and the respective state's Sultan.

Many local festivals are mentioned in the regional sections. Here is a list of those festivities which are celebrated all over Malaysia:

The great Hindu festival, **THAIPUSAM**, is celebrated at the end of January or beginning of February at all temples in the country. The main festivities take place in Penang and in the Batu Caves near Kuala Lumpur, where the youngest son of Shiva, Subramaniam, is especially revered.

Before sunrise, thousands of believers collect at the foot of the mountain. Some have pierced their skin with steel needles from which they've hung tiny bells or peacock feathers. Long silver needles are stuck through the tongue or cheek without (it seems) causing any pain. Others carry heavy wooden bows, the **kavadi**, above their heads, held only by hooks digging into their flesh as they climb the steep steps. While the priests strike up religious songs, many Hindus fall into trance and dance through the crowd. In other places, people walk on glowing coals.

GENERAL INFORMATION

Every year between the 21st of January and the 20th of February the Chinese celebrate **CHINESE NEW YEAR**. The exact date is determined by the lunar calendar and is set on the first full moon. With a rhythm of 12 years, each year is named after an animal.

> So 1986 is the year of the **Tiger**, then follow the years of the **Cat, Dragon, Snake, Horse, Goat, Monkey, Rooster, Dog, Pig** (or Bear), **Rat,** and **Buffalo**.
> Days before the Chinese New Year, the shopping rush begins. A week before the new year, apartments and houses are cleaned since the god of the kitchen will make a report to heaven about every family. An especially sweet and sticky pastry made of molasses is baked so that the god has something sweet on his lips. Others say that the pastry makes his mouth so sticky that he can't say a thing. On the last evening of the year the whole family gets together for a huge meal. Children receive tiny red envelopes with money (ang pao). Considering the large size of many Chinese families, the New Year's partying can be quite expensive making the one, two or three months extra pay which workers receive at this time of year very handy.

Muslims celebrate **MANDI SAFAR**, originally a Hindu festival marking the first full moon of the rainy season, in the middle of April. Quotes from the Koran, written on pieces of paper are carried off by the waves and waters of the rivers, lakes or ocean. Afterwards people bathe symbolically in the water to wash away bad luck or 'malang'. A good place to see this is in Tanjung Keling near Malacca.

In the middle of May, all of Sabah goes wild - the Kadazan are celebrating **THANKSGIVING**. The ancient dance of the Kadazan - **Sumazau** - is one of the high points of the ceremonies.

In June, particularly in Kelantan, **BIRD SINGING CONTESTS** are held. The competing birds twitch and trill in their cages hanging on 8 m long poles. An expert jury judges according to traditional guidelines.

At the beginning of June (usually the 1st), Sarawak celebrates **GAWAI DAYAK**. After the rice harvest has been brought in, several days of thanksgiving can begin. Longhouse visitors take part in the enthralling festivities. '**Tuak**' flows in streams! Blowpipe shooting contests during 'Gaway Dayak' are probably the only occasion when the old fashioned weapons are used. A rifle is preferred for today's hunting. If you're lucky you might even get to see the old war dance '**ngajat**'.

> **TUAK** is a kind of rice beer, yellowish to dirty white in coloring. When offered, it should never be refused. Normally a young girl will offer the guest a full glass. Those in the know will only take a very small sip and give the girl back the glass. According to the ancient tradition, she must then drain it. The party becomes louder and louder, the gongs and drums sound, dancing begins. The guests, too, are required to dance. Thunder and laughter lasts into the early morning hours.

At the beginning or middle of June the **DRAGONBOAT FESTIVAL** is celebrated in many Chinese communities. In memory of the death of a famous Chinese poet who chose to be drowned rather than living a life of corruption. It is said that fishermen who saw his suicide threw rice cakes into the river and drummed madly in an attempt to prevent a dragon approaching the body. Try to see it in Penang or Singapore where boat races are held.

The most important festival in Malaysia is **HARI RAYA PUASA**, the end of Ramadan. For four long weeks, people fast between sunrise and sunset, and in the conservative Muslim states of Kelantan and Trengganu, this is strictly adhered. After days of preparation the festivities can only begin when at least three different villages have spotted the moon. Thanks is given to Allah that the command to fast during Ramadan could be obeyed. Then in two days everyone catches up with all that they missed during the period of fasting. In the mosques, verses from the Koran are recited, friends and neighbors are visited, presents are exchanged, and people are forgiven for mistakes of the past year.

On the 1st July in Keningkau, Sabah, a famous **TAMU** is held. Horse and buffalo races take place, and the most beautiful Murut and Kadazan girls are selected. There's also a large tamu in Kudat on the same day. Other important tamu are held on July 29th in Tuaran, end of August in Beaufort and the middle of September in Papar.

On the 9th August Singapore celebrates **NATIONAL DAY**: incredible parades were all the nationalities participate; military parades and dances including the famous Chinese dragon and lion dances.
On the 31st of August the Malaysian **NATIONAL DAY**, Hari Kebangsaan Malaysia, is celebrated. It'is in remembrance of the founding of Malaysia in 1957. Sarawak celebrates Malaysia's national holiday in a different division capital each year. This is a tremendous occasion for the

GENERAL INFORMATION

ulu-people, well worth a trip of several days. Iban and members of other tribes come down the rivers in their boats. They build small huts along the banks and wear their best clothes (mostly western) to show off a bit. The population of Simanggang, where we partied, quadrupled during the fun.

In the seventh month of the year, the souls of the dead return to the earth from purgatory. Through the **FESTIVAL OF THE HUNGRY GHOSTS**, an attempt is made to win their approval by putting tasty snacks everywhere.

In the middle of the eight month, when the moon is specially round, the **MOONCAKE FESTIVAL** is held in honor of a victory over the Mongol dynasty. Tiny round cakes are baked. On the night itself, incense is burned, and the children carry lanterns through the streets.

The second most important Hindu festival is **DEEPAVALI** celebrated in October or November. Literally translated it means 'deepa' lamp and 'vali' row by which they refer to the light which drives away darkness. On this day in all Hindu regions, flaming wreaths are hung.

Two popular legends tell of the creation of Deepavali. The first goes back to the Ramayana and tells of the triumphant return of Rama to Ayutthaya after 14 years of banishment in the jungle. The inhabitants greeted the returning hero with countless lanterns and torches to celebrate his victory of good over the evil Ravana.

The second legend tells of the victory of Krishna over the king Narakasura. He, it is said, had a harem of over 16,000, even the daughters of the gods weren't safe from him. While dying, he pleaded with Krishna to create a holiday for the people to honor him each year.

Twelve days after the Islamic New Year, **MUHARAM**, Muslims celebrate **MAULIDIN NABI**, the birthday of the prophet Mohammed, with prayers in the mosques and parades.

CHRISTMAS, the birthday festival of the founder of Christianity isn't celebrated just by Christians. Particularly in Singapore and the major cities of West Malaysia, Christmas shopping is big business. Present-laden Santa Clauses and cotton - snow - covered plastic flowers decorate store windows. Christmas music resounds from loudspeakers everywhere. Hotels offer special Christmas menues with all the trimmings.

PHOTOGRAPHY

There are many arguments for and against taking pictures when travelling. Just because of your camera, you will be viewed as a typical tourist.

We do think that it's worthwhile to take pictures, but leave your 25 lb. gadget bag at home. 'I was there' snapshots in front of monuments are equally useless. Look around for the landscapes, people and incidents which you will enjoy reliving through your photos.

If you do decide to take pictures, then do it properly and forget the instamatic. Your camera should have variable exposure setting - whether manual or automatic - sunny and cloudy are not enough. A camera with TTL (through the lens metering) is also helpful considering the sharp tropical contrasts of light and shadow.

Due to the variety of motifs you'll be interested in having several lenses. You can then get the whole temple in the picture and still be able to get some detail in other shots. Beginners should start with an inexpensive model from one of the major camera makers. Later when you move up to a better camera, you can still use your old lenses.

Should your **CAMERA** have automatic shutter speed control, automatic aperture or be fully automatic? You will have to decide this yourself depending on your interests. For landscapes and temple shots, automatic shutter speed is best because you can set the aperture to ensure good depth of field. If you are more interested in moving targets such as people, then you would want automatic aperture so that you can set the shutter speed to a fast level and get sharp pictures despite subject movement. If you are planning to do macrophotography, look into a camera with an adjustable flash where it is possible to step down the lens.

Another point of controversy concerns **LENSES.** Your basic lens should be a fast 50-55 mm so that you can do good available light photography when you use a fast film. For a telephoto you can use a zoom but be warned that zooms aren't very fast (f 3.5-4 at best). You will lose many pictures in the tropical shadows unless you get a faster lens. A 135 mm/2.8 or even a 200 mm/2.8 would be much better. For wide angles a zoom (28-70 mm or 28-50 mm) is ideal. Because buildings aren't going to walk away, you can use longer exposure times to get the pictures you want even in poor light.

GENERAL INFORMATION

SLIDES are your best bet for capturing the motley colors of the tropics. You can always have prints made of your best shots. Besides your standard 100 ASA film, also take along some of the faster 200 ASA. It is also a good idea to have a couple rolls of 400 ASA for poor light conditions. If need be, you can push a 400 ASA film to 800 or even 1600 ASA and forget your flash. Don't keep your film in a refrigerator! You will have trouble finding one, and when you remove the film it will be spoiled due to condensed water - watch out for air conditioners as well. Pack film in the middle of your pack. Be careful about X-ray searches at the airports. Keep your camera and lenses in your hand luggage, and try to protect them from dust and water in addition to bumps.

The price differences between Europe, the USA and Singapore are not what they used to be. So you're not much better off buying or developing film in Singapore any more. It's better to rely on your dealer at home where you know you get good quality and service. And you film won't be lying around in the heat.

Remember how you feel when someone aims a camera at you. Keep yourself in the background and don't be pushy just to get a good picture. It is their country and we are only guests. These are people who eat, sleep, pray and die. Let them live in peace without selling their souls for your picture album or slide show.

TOURIST INFORMATION

This book can't provide you with up to the second information. Some details, such as currency exchange rates and prices, are constantly changing. Other details can be changed at a whim, such as visa and entry requirements. So check at your nearest tourist office for the latest info before you go.

TOURIST DEVELOPMENT CORPORATION MALAYSIA
MELBOURNE, 250 Elizabeth St.; NEW YORK, 420 Lexington Ave.; LOS ANGELES, 510 West Sixth St.; SAN FRANCISCO, 600 Montgomery St.; LONDON, 17 Curzon St.

SINGAPORE TOURIST PROMOTION BOARD
SYDNEY, 1 Alfred St.; NEW YORK, 342 Madison Ave.; SAN FRANCISCO, 251 Post St.; LONDON, 33 Heddon St.

WOMEN BACKPACKERS

That weight which you are carrying isn't just your pack, it's the patriarchal world in which you travel. South-East Asia is distant not so much in air travel time as in the mentality of its people. Western moral standards are something South-East Asian people learn to a certain extent from contact with tourists, but even more so through Hollywood. Cheap films and television depict a world of assault and murder; sex and hate, where women throw themselves at the feet of the hero.

Think about the effect such films must have in Malaysia where some women are still veiled, male-female contact in public is taboo, and a bra is a must. Correct appearance is especially important. Emancipation hasn't had much success in this part of the world.

'White is beautiful' at least for South-East Asian men. Whereas during colonial times the white 'memsahib' was unapproachable, today sexually free western tourists are within grabbing distance. Considering the reputation western women have from Hollywood, there are sure to be problems. There is no sure-fire repellent such as for mosquitos or leeches to protect women from forward men. So no matter what you wear; bra, a long dress or a sweaty blouse won't protect you from the men who stare at you, speak rudely, and try to grab.

It is easy to avoid such people. All you have to do is to stay in big, international hotels. The more tourists, the more expensive and exclusive the atmosphere, the fewer contacts you will have with local men other than liftboys, waiters or chauffeurs. But not everyone will let themselves be imprisoned in the western enclaves. Outside of these protected areas, life is more complicated for everyone. But for women, especially those who travel alone, life is difficult.

Few women actually travel alone in South-East Asia. Sometimes women will travel in pairs, but usually women travel with a male partner. In tourist areas you will find quite a few women, but in outlying areas it is mostly men. Single women who survive on their own in spite of everything must be very independent. Those who don't really like to travel alone would find it torture.

For unusual trips it is best to find a partner. It'd be a shame to have your trip spoiled because of a few rude men. You might even be attacked; in which case it is always best not to be alone. Especially in rural areas, check out the attitude of the local men toward foreign women. It is not nice being treated as if you don't exist: No invitations to tea, or difficulties in finding a guide.

Don't let this hold you back, however, from discovering Malaysia, even without male escort. Many women who travel find that, while there were some problems, on the whole travelling alone can also be enjoyable.

How you should act when confronted by forward men depends on the situation. It is important to maintain your self-confidence and your humour. If you look as if you want something they will come running; if you give the masher a fictional description of the husband for whom you are waiting then he will lose his interest quickly. Of course it isn't always that simple - often you both don't even speak the same language.

You have to decide for yourself how you want to travel in Malaysia. There too, half of the people are women. Though local women are less likely than men to speak your language (less education), they are often happy to make you feel welcome. There are much fewer social pressures in the women's world, and it shouldn't be difficult for you to make friends and to learn something about the hidden world of Asian women.

ALIEN

A trip to Malaysia sure costs a lot of money. First you pay to get here, then you pay for your hotel. You can hire a guide to get you through the jungles of Borneo, or a becak driver for a city tour. But money can't buy friendship and courtesy. Your behavior alone will determine how people react to you. A trip to Malaysia, Singapore or Brunei is certainly incomplete if all you see are landscapes and buildings. If you want to get to know a country, then establish contact with its people.

Whether you consider yourself a tourist or a traveller, you are still a guest in a foreign country. Remember that your western mode of behavior doesn't always fit in.

Nothing is worse than loss of face. It is extremely impolite to lose your temper. Our everyday contacts and gestures can be greatly misunderstood. On the other hand, we can be confused by the Asian smile and struggle for harmony. Our individualistic lifestyle is completely contradictory to the Asian subordination of the individual to family, group and society.

Children are loved and worshipped - win their hearts and you'll easily establish contact with adults. But try not to praise the children all the time! An evil spirit might hear and spread a curse! And never stroke anybody's hair, because the head is the seat of spiritual strength, is holy, and should never be touched! You'll rarely see physical contact between men and women in public. But within the sexes, there's no shyness about touching. Whether you're visiting a mosque, temple, or church, be sure to dress properly and to take your shoes off if necessary. And stay in the background during religious ceremonies.

Malaysia, Singapore and Brunei are multi-ethnic countries where Malays, Chinese, Indians, and other ethnic groups with their own separate traditions, try to live together. Tolerance is necessary when Muslims, Hindus, Buddhists, and Christians live door to door.

Almost all parts of **Malay** life are influenced by Islam. Women have to cover themselves in public so that only the face, hands and feet can be seen. Only food prepared under Islamic rites, 'halal', can be eaten. Gambling, drinking alcohol, and eating pork are forbidden. And touching either the saliva or the excrement of dogs is taboo; which is why there're no dogs in Malay villages. When entering a Malay home, remove your shoes at the front door. Wait until you are shown a place to sit. If you're sitting on the floor, make sure your feet are never pointing at anyone. Be sure to walk behind anyone sitting, and never walk over anyone. If you bring a present, tradition holds that it should be opened only after you've left. Should you be offered something to eat or drink, never refuse completely, just try a small bite. Malays are very good hosts. If they sometimes seem to be too passive, remember that human harmony is much more important for them than material gain.

The family in a greater sense is the primary environment of the **Chinese**. Even today it's not unusual for the family to pick the marriage partner and determine how children should be raised. Decisions of the family elders are respected. Ancestors are worshipped in the temples and at home. You enter a temple through the door on the right and leave it through the door on the left. Should you be invited to visit a Chinese, don't dress in blue, black or white. Presents aren't usually given at the first visit. If you want to make a present to good friends, food - always two of everything - works out best. Eating together is very important and abundantly enjoyed. Never leave the last bit uneaten - it's considered a waste. The financial difficulties which forced the Chinese to leave their homeland, shows its effects here. Aiding the family to achieve affluence is the goal of many Chinese.

The **Indians** don't belong as a group to any one religious community. Some are Muslim, others are Hindu or members of various sects. Their lifestyles vary correspondingly. While Muslims refuse to eat pork, beef is taboo for the Hindu; other Indians are vegetarian. When visiting an Indian restaurant, wash your hands before eating, and only eat with your right hand.

Because you're foreigners, people will be tolerant when you break unspoken rules. But still they expect you to try to behave as well as possible. Don't be the typical 'white man' who thinks he knows all the answers. So what if everything works much better at home? And you don't need to exaggerate in order to make everything seem more believable. in comparison, the Asian way is to be politely reserved and to understate.

'Travelling cheap' or 'never getting saddled with the bill'

The food here is terrible again. But what do you expect at the cheapest joint in town. Hey, set me up another coke please! Wow, you sure can drink a lot in this heat. And coke is cheap, but beer? Man, come evening, I just can't make it without my beer, but it hits you. No not in the head; I can hold my liquor. In the wallet, understand? But the Chinese up the street sell beer for 20 c cheaper than here. That's where I end up in the evening.

By now I know my way around this place. I've been here, after all, for three days. Before here, I was in Phuket, everything's half as expensive there. Now I need a couple days rest. Man, the ride down here was a real stress. A whole day in the train, third class, completely packed; then three hours at the border. These people are really chaotic. Good thing that I stocked up on canned food in Thailand. The stuff they sell at the train stations is awful. When they see a white person, they charge twice as much. And nobody understands English either. I'd rather go to a supermarket. There at least, they don't cheat you. When I got here I was really dead and took a rickshaw to my hotel. Imagine, the guy really wanted 3 $. What a rip off. It took forever, but I bargained him down to 2 $. I could of course got him down to 1.50 $. Just frustration all day long. And the hotel? You can forget my travel guide - it says rooms for 9.80 $ - they want 10.20 $. I moved out the next day. They have cheaper rooms across the street. It doesn't have a window or a fan, but I'm generally here during the day anyway. This is where it's happening.

I've met a bunch of neat guys, like the Aussie. He manages to crash somewhere on the beach for free, and somehow he always finds a meal. Well, it's OK if you've been here that long. But I can't live like that. Tomorrow I'm headed for Malacca. Everything's supposed to be cheap there. Huts right on the beach, without electricity. You can live just like a native. See over there all the tourists. They sit in their air conditioned buses and have no idea what's going on. They stay in these super hotels, and are carted out to photograph one temple after the other. If they went by foot, they'd soon be sick of visiting temples. Another day is gone. Visited at least five travel agencies about my ticket to Malacca. After it cools down a bit, I'm going to check at the bus station. Tickets are supposed to be cheapest there.

KUALA LUMPUR

Malaysia's capital was originally founded in 1857 when 87 adventurous Chinese miners paddled up the **Klang River** looking for tin. In a malaria infested swamp at the confluence of the Gombak and the Klang, they built huts. After the first mines opened, new laborers and traders began to arrive. At first they named the spot Ampang. But conditions soon gave birth to a new name, Kuala Lumpur, meaning 'muddy estuary'. Despite epidemics, catastrophic fires, and floods, the tin mines were so lucrative that war broke out in the turmoil-ridden 1870s between Chinese and Malays. But the city's famous Yap Ah Loy, Captain China, was able to recapture a demolished town. The years of his rule (until 1884) were marked by deep-rooted change. Tin prices rose dramatically in 1878 leading to an increase in production. In 1880 native rulers gave way to the British resident. After a disastrous fire in 1881, that almost completely destroyed the town, Kuala Lumpur was systematically expanded into the capital of Selangor: in keeping with British interests. Just five years later the first railline was completed connecting KL (pronounced 'K''L') to the harbor at Port Kelang. In 1896 the city was declared the capital of the Federated Malay States.

Today the Malaysian capital is a modern city sporting everything from highways and shopping centers to sterile concrete and glass structures. In between, however, there's lots of green, and impressive relics of British colonial architecture. KL boasts one of the most beautiful train stations in the world (looks more like a mosque). But the old-fashioned, two-story, Chinese-owned shops are becoming fewer and fewer each year. Traditional business and residential quarters are being torn down to make room for tremendous banks and modern shopping centers. City renewal, as in Singapore, has taken on clean-sweep dimensions. On the other hand, there are attempts to create a new, syncretistic Malaysian architecture such as the new mosque and National Museum.

Unlike Penang, the nation's capital isn't a tourist Mecca. Still, there's enough to make a couple days stopover worthwhile. Take a rewarding walk through the tiny shops and markets in Chinatown and the Indian quarter near Jl. Tuanku Abdul Rahman. But KL's sticky humidity does stifle enthusiasm for long tours.

Begin your tour right at the river junction of Sungei Klang and Sungei Gombak. Here you'll find a red and yellow structure in oriental style: the **JAME MOSQUE** was once the national mosque. It's an exotic bit of color hemmed in by modern concrete architecture.

On Jl.Raja (Federal Secretariat) and Jl.Tun Perak (courthouse, townhall), the Malayan colonial past retains its lustre. The old administrative buildings (photo opportunity!) have been renovated as has the **SELANGOR CLUB**, a wee bit of England in Malaysia. The pinnacle of Malay society meets at the club, and on the Padang, the well-kept English lawn in front, an Indian cricket team trains every Sunday.

You'll enjoy a walk through **JALAN TUANKU ABDUL RAHMAN** - check it out if you aren't living there (see shopping). Find some exotic souvenirs in the small Indian and Chinese shops before they fall victim to a shopping-center's bulldozer.

East of the river, between Jl.Sultan, Jl.Petaling, Jl.Cecil and Jl.Sultan Mohammed is the old **CHINATOWN** or what's left of it. Life pulsates in this quarter during the late afternoon and evening: stands are set up everywhere, and the restaurants do great business. On the streets you can buy anything from cheap T-shirts to live pythons and Chinese medicines. When a paper airplane is burned on Jl.Petaling, it goes over into the great beyond where a deceased person might need it as a means of quick transport.

On Jl.Bandar you'll find the beautiful old **SRI MAHAMARIAMMAN TEMPLE**, decorated with numerous Hindu deities. At this Hindu temple, the festivities begin in January or February for the famous Thaipusam Festival.

One of the oldest Chinese temples is the **SEE YEOH TEMPLE** (Sze Ya) on Leboh Pudu (off Jl.Bandar near the central market). Decorated with countless paintings and gold--plated wood carvings, the temple was financed by the legendary Captain China, Yap Ah Loy, whose picture can be seen behind the altar. At religious festivals and when visiting temples, remember to keep out of the limelight and behave within the bounds of tradition!

Another tour takes you to sights in the south of town. On a hill is the **NATIONAL MOSQUE**. The minaret sits proudly aloft, 75 m above a pool of water. The main dome with 18 pointed stars symbolizes the 13 states of Malaysia and the five basic principles of Islam. The 48 smaller domes emulate the great mosque in Mecca. The mosque, one of the largest in South-East Asia, is open to visitors (proper dress required) daily, except Friday, from 09:00 - 17:00 h. Women have to use a separate entrance.

Not far from here is the **TRAIN STATION**, built in 1910 in a Moorish style. Facing it and fitting the colonial motif is the Malayan Railways Building. You can taste that old-time atmosphere at the Station Hotel.

The new **NATIONAL ART GALLERY** has taken up residence in the Majestic Hotel with 17,000 pieces of art on display in its permanent collection. Open daily except Sunday and public holidays from 10:00 to 18:00 h.

Another must visit is the **NATIONAL MUSEUM** (Muzium Negara), only 10 minutes from here by foot.

On the outer wall of this modern Malaysian building, you can see two huge murals depicting high and low points in Malaysian history and the making of traditional arts and crafts. On the ground floor is an ethnological exhibit featuring Malaysia's motley ethnic groups and the history of Malaysia's individual states. Check out the arts and crafts exhibits, such as the wayang kulit puppets from different regions presenting a comparison from all over the world. Just as informative is the exhibit on the Orang Asli. There is hardly anything representative of Sabah and Sarawak, however. (Go there yourself and check out the museum in Kuching.) Upstairs are fauna and flora, industry and transportation. Next to the main building in a small open-air museum are a longhouse and a few statues from East Malaysia.

Open: daily 9:00-18:00 h; closed Fri from 12:15-14:45 h; open during Ramadan only till 17:00 h. Admission free.

You can recover from that dose of museum culture in the nearby **LAKE GARDEN**. For 2 M$ per hour you might rent a rowboat on the artificial lake, Tasik Perdana. Or just wander through the hilly park. Elements of an English garden are combined with jungle.

In the northernmost part of the park are the **PARLIAMENT BUILDING** and the **NATIONAL MEMORIAL** built in remembrance of the state of emergency before 1960. Seven larger than life statues represent members of the Malay security forces in their fight with communist guerillas. Though the state of emergency was lifted in 1960, members of the illegal MCP were still active enough in 1975 to do damage to the memorial in a bomb attack.

KUALA LUMPUR

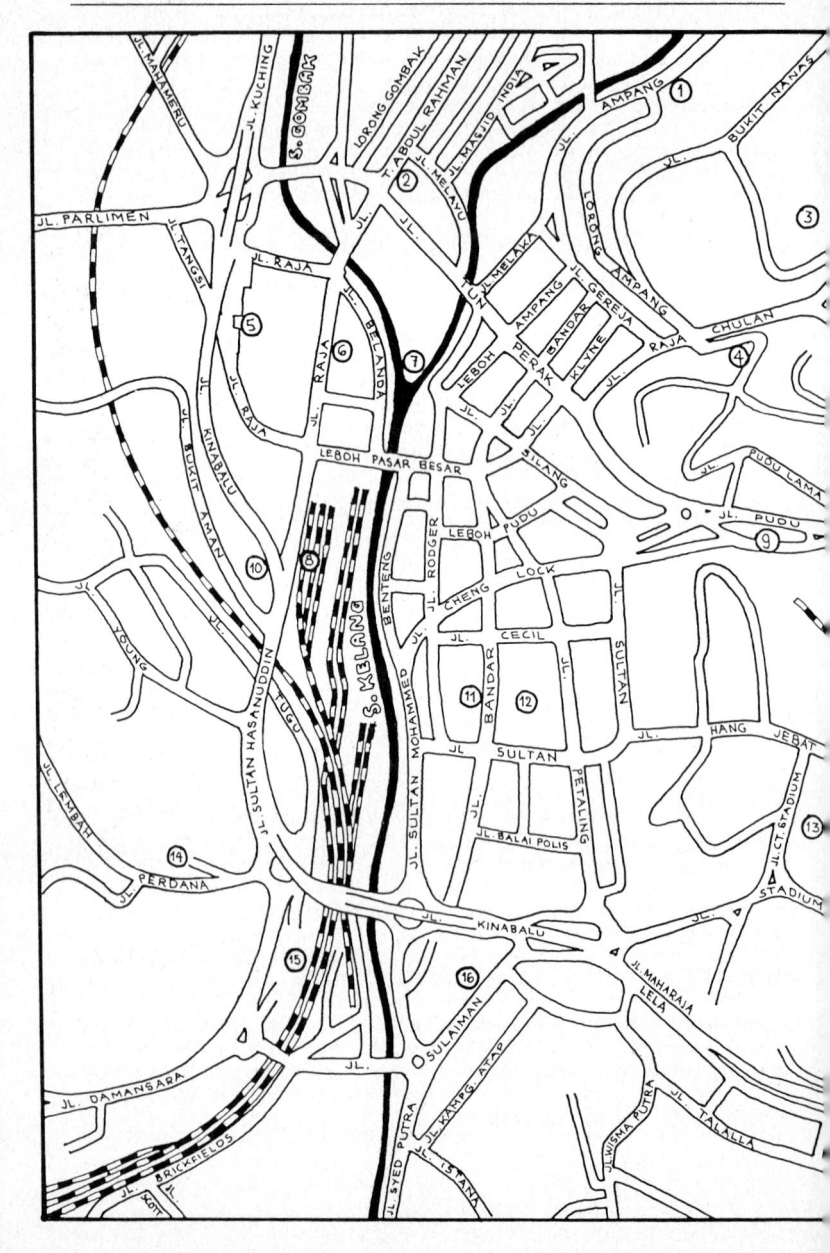

KUALA LUMPUR

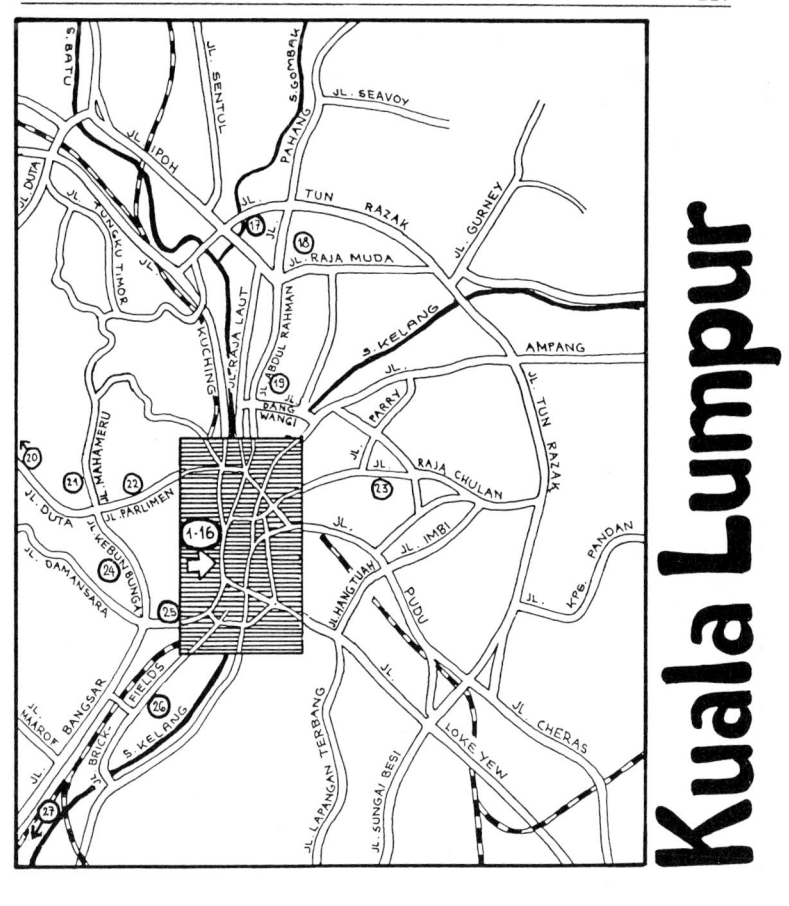

① A.I.A. Building U.S. Embassy / Canadian Emb.
② City Hall
③ Bukit Nanas
④ Telegraph Office
⑤ Selangor Club
⑥ Sultan Abd. Samad Buildg.
⑦ Jame Mosque
⑧ Post Office
⑨ Pudu Raya Bus & Taxi Station
⑩ British Council
⑪ Hindu-Temple
⑫ Chinatown (Hotels)
⑬ Stadium Negara
⑭ National Mosque
⑮ Railway Stn.
⑯ U.M.B.C. Building
⑰ Pahang Bus Station
⑱ General Hospital
⑲ Wisma Loke
⑳ Chief Game Warden
㉑ Parliament
㉒ National Monument
㉓ Tourist Office
㉔ Lake Garden
㉕ National Museum
㉖ Y.M.C.A.
㉗ Immigration Dept.

HOTELS

Since many houses - including numerous cheap hotels - on Jl.Tuanku Abdul Rahman have been razed, you may find it necessary to look for lodgings elsewhere. But, here is a list of hotels still standing: **COLISEUM****, no 98-100, tel 926270, an old hotel from the 1920s with huge rooms. **REX****, no 132-134, tel 983895, get a room on the first floor (the ground floor is too loud). Right next door is **NEW TIVOLI****, tel 924108. Besides that there're the **PARAMOUNT****, no 154, tel 927274, **KOWLOON*****, no 142-146, tel 926455, **HAN MING****, no 149, tel 985034. Parallel to Jl. Tuanku Abdul Rahman, on Jl.Rajah Laut, are several still cheaper hotels such as **BEE SENG****, no 60, tel 929584, **ALISAN*****, no 132 B, tel 986905. Many of the cheaper places are actually brothels paid for by the hour. More expensive and respectable are **SENTOSA******, no 316, tel 925644 or the **NEW CYLINMEN*****, no 110, tel 982088.

Near the last stop of the airport buses: **STARLIGHT HOTEL****, 90/92 Jl.Hang Kasturi (formerly Jl.Rodger), tel 21744. You're centrally located in Chinatown near the night market. **LEE MUN****, 9 Jl.Sultan, tel 282981, clean and pleasant, but loud. **COLONIAL****, 39-45 Jl.Sultan, tel 280336, a creaky old hotel, **LENG NAM****, 165-167 Jl. Bandar, tel 201489, or try **DUNIA*****, 142 Jl.Petaling, tel 283978.

Somewhat out of the way, but an alternative is the **YMCA**, Jl.Kandang Kerbau corner Jl.Brickfields, tel 441439. Dormitories with 6 beds*, single rooms*** with ac. If the Y is full, which isn't unusual, try one of the many hotels in the area. On a parallel street to Jl.Brickfields behind the Lido Cinema is Jl.Thambadillai: **WING HENG****, no 24, tel 441650, fan, shower and toilet, or **PENG AUN****, no 20, tel 441263.

The cheapest possibility is the **YOUTH HOSTEL**, Jl. Vethanavam near Jl.Ipoh (tel 672872), about 9 km from town. A bunk in the dormitory costs about 5 M$. Take bus 143 or minibus 11 from Jl.Rajah Laut. Give as your destination either 'Wisma Belia' (youth hostel) or 'Batu tiga stengah' (= 3 1/2 miles). Unfriendly!

Renovation is complete at the **STATION HOTEL****** right in the train station, tel 202250. They have 28 rooms with style for rates between 48-60 M$. Besides you'll find a large selection of international hotels in the upper price bracket.

KUALA LUMPUR

FOOD
In the **COLISEUM**, Jl.Tuanku Abdul Rahman, you can still get good and inexpensive steaks (10.-M$) served with a flourish. At the **GOLDEN ARROW RESTAURANT** in the Station Hotel, a full-course Malay lunch is served from Monday through Friday. The best area for food stalls is Jl.Benteng on the Klang River, across from Masjid Jame. During the day it's a big parking lot; in the evening they roll out the charcoal grills. Get there before sundown, when the old mosque is caught in the best light. Find exciting breadrolls for breakfast at Puduraya busstation gate 16 (**CHIEF'S CORNER**).

Chinese food is naturally best in Chinatown. In the evening at the night market, various snacks are offered. Try the sticky rice in banana leaves, or spicy, dried beef. Good steamboats at the foodstalls on Jl.Sultan or Jl.Cecil. You're presented with several skewers of ingredients at your table, each with their own price (ask!). Then just toss your choice in the boiling broth yourself. Right around the corner is **ENGLISH HOT BREADS**, Jl.Sultan 60, where besides pastry, they serve pizza and spaghetti. There is good Chinese vegetarian food at **FATT YOW YUEN**, Jl.Balai Polis.

Get hot Indian curries in **CEYLON**, Jl.Melayu. Much cheaper though are the Indian shops on Jl.Brickfields. We like the food best at **DEVI**. You eat with your right hand from palm leaves. You can watch how bread is baked. More expensive, with white tablecloths and ac, is **AKBAR**, Jl. Medan Tuanku. Across the way is **SHIRAZ**, next to the MARA building, serving Pakistani food.

SHOPPING
KL isn't a duty-free shopping center like Singapore or Hongkong, but you'll still be able to wet your palate with a large selection of arts and crafts and other typical Malaysian goods. The following list should help you in your search for souvenirs:

JALAN TUANKU ABDUL RAHMAN - especially on the northern part of the street, between Jl.Raja Muda and Jl.Raja Bot, there are many Chinese shops offering cheap textiles, woodcarvings and things made of rattan. The morning market on Jl.Chow Kit is quite good. Here you'll find home-made goods such as peasant hats and bamboo shopping baskets.

Near Jl.Medan Tuanku Abdul Rahman, in **WISMA LOKE**, you'll find antiques from all over Asia. While they aren't exactly cheap, it's worth visiting just to see the building, one of the oldest (built in 1904) and nicest in KL.

Near Jl.Campbell is the Pertama Shopping Complex offering just about everything you can imagine.

At the lower end of the street you'll find several bookstores and Indian shops offering everything from saris to religious literature (similar to comics) from the subcontinent. A good selection of travel guides is offered in MINERVA BOOKSHOP under the Kowloon Hotel. Other good bookshops: UNIVERSITY BOOK STORE off Jl.Ipoh at 34 Jl.Lumut, MPH and BERITA BOOK CENTER in Bukit Bintang Plaza, Jl.Bukit Bintang. MPH also has a bookstore in Petaling Jaya (Jaya Supermarket).

KARYANEKA HANDICRAFT CENTRE (JALAN RAJA CHULAN) – on Jl. Imbi 14 traditional Malay wooden houses have been built representing the 14 federal states of Malaysia. You can buy Malaysian arts and crafts: everything from batik to woodcarvings. Only interesting for people with little time to scout around Malaysia for themselves – moderate prices! On the stage, dance and cultural events are held on Friday and Saturday evenings. The centre is open daily, except official holidays, from 10:00 – 18:00 h. On Jl.Raja Chulan are two supermarkets (Fitzpatrick's and Irma) for those who miss cheese, bread, and wine after a long time on Asian fare.

Kuala Lumpur – early days.

KUALA LUMPUR

MARKETS - NIGHT MARKET in Chinatown at the corner of Jl. Cecil/Jl.Sultan. Music cassettes are reasonably priced (make them play it first!) and textiles ranging from cheap T-shirts to name-brand jeans for about 35 M$. Many street vendors sell antiques or things easily mistaken for such - be careful!

Every Saturday night the so called **Sunday Market** is held until very late in Kampong Baharu (Jl.Raja Muda Musa/Jl.Alang). You can combine eating and shopping, though it isn't all that great.

GENERAL INFORMATION
TOURIST INFORMATION - TDC (Tourist Development Corporation) has its information center in Wisma M.P.I. 17th/18th floor, Jl.Raja Chulan, tel 423033, open Mon to Fri 8:30-16:30 h, Sat 8:00-12:45 h - provides info on other Malaysian states including Sarawak and Sabah. Other information offices are at Subang Airport, tel 755707, open daily 9:00-22:30 h and in the train station, tel 281832, open Mon to Fri 8:30-16:30 h, Sat 8:30-12:30 h.

Pick up free of charge the brochure **'Kuala Lumpur - Penang This Month'** offering current info and practical tips.

IMMIGRATION - there's usually no problem getting visa extensions. The window for commonwealth citizens is always busy since many Indians don't have Malaysian passports. Address: Immigration Headquarters, Jl.Pantai Bharu, tel 578155.

POST OFFICE - the new General Post Office is on Jl.Raja, open daily except Sun from 8:00-19:00 h. The charges are generally reasonable, though parcels can be sent cheaper from Singapore. If you're expecting mail, have them check at the poste restante window under both your first name and last name.

TELEPHONE - calls within town cost 10 c. For international calls go to the Central Telegraph Office on Bukit Mahkamah off Jl.Raja Chulan: open round the clock. At the airport you can make international calls from 7:30-23:30 h. Connections are fairly quick. Some countries in Europe, United States and Australia can be dialled direct. For international information call 108. In the telephone book, everyone is listed under their first name, so Mr.Peter Murran would be listed under 'P'.

You can call everywhere in Malaysia without problem. It's cheapest between 18:00 and 7:00 h. Area codes for long distance calls: Singapore (02), Kuala Lumpur (03), Penang (04), Ipoh (05), Malacca (06), Taiping (044), Seremban (067), Kuantan (075), Kuala Trengganu (076), Kota Bharu (077).

BRITISH COUNCIL - has a good library, Jl.Hishamuddin /Jl. Aman.

BANKS - KL banks are open Mon to Fri 10:00-15:00 h; Sat 9:30-11:30 h. Most banks can be found in the administrative center around Masjid Jame.

CITY MAPS - the free city map is quite good and useful - found as a supplement to the brochure '**Kuala Lumpur - Penang This Month**'. The satellite city of Petaling Jaya is missing, however. For those who need a more detailed map, the TDC Road Map Kuala Lumpur/Petaling Jaya for 4.50 M$ is recommended.

MEDICAL HELP - the General Hospital is in the north of town between Jl.Tun Abdul Razak and Jl.Pahang. It is new with modern equipment, English speaking doctors, fast working labs and its own dispensary. Treatment is free of charge. In case of emergency dial: 999.

NEWSPAPERS - the most important English language newspaper is the NEW STRAITS TIMES. Though critical reports about Malaysia are generally missing, it's quite informative. Foreign language papers, magazines and books can be found in all the big hotels as well as the bookstores mentioned above.

DRUGS - even if things are somewhat relaxed in Thailand, watch out here! The jails are filled with tourists caught with small amounts, and death-penalty quantities are within every tourist's budget.

SWIMMING POOL - right in town on Jl.Raja Chulan near Jl. Perak, open daily 9:30-12:30, 14:00-16:30 and 19:30-21:00 h.

AMERICAN EXPRESS - main office on Jl.Raja Chulan in the Plaza See Hoy Chan Bldg. (tel 289911) - see them about credit cards, loss etc. Representatives in Malaysia are Mayflower Acme Tours, 18 Jl.Segambut Pusat (tel 667011). Buy Amexco checks at the Chase Manhattan Bank, 88 Jl.Raja Chulan (Wisma Stephens), tel 482011, or at Pacific Bank, 1 Jl.Cecil, tel 205033.

FESTIVALS - Numerous holidays are celebrated with splendor in the Malaysian capital. The high point of National Day on **August 31st** is the big parade in KL. In the Lake Garden there's music and dance, a soccer tournament is held in Merdeka Stadium, and at Changkrat Pavilion, a 'Made in Malaysia Fair' is held.

Equally splendid are the festivities honoring the **King's Birthday** on the field in front of Selangor Club, in the Lake Garden, at the Royal Palace, and in Merdeka Stadium. The faithful gather for prayers of thanksgiving at their mosques, temples and churches.

KL celebrates its founding on February 1st with parades and pageants.

The largest of all religious festivals is the Hindu **Thaipusam Festival**. The impressive parade runs from Sri Mahamariamman Temple in Chinatown to the Batu Caves.

GETTING AROUND KL
The olden days and rickshaws are gone: in KL today you use a taxi, minibus (bas mini) or full-size buses.

TAXIS
The drivers usually speak some English. Be sure that the meter is turned on. The charges for ac taxis are 1 M$ for the first mile (non ac 70 c) and 30 c for every further half

mile. The waiting charge is 20 c for every 8 minutes. It costs 10 c for every third or fourth passenger. Between 1:00 and 6:00 h there's a 50 % surcharge for night travel. Renting by the hour costs 10 M$ per hour.

MINIBUSES
All routes within town 40 c. Bas Mini 11 runs an important route from Jl.Raja to the youth hostel as well as to the Batu Caves. All minibus lines are listed in KL - Penang This Month.

BUSES
Several large, private companies run routes in KL. Here too, only the important lines: buses 170 and 177 (big bus) go to the National Zoo and the Aquarium from Leboh Ampang, across from the AIA Building. Len bus 70 leaves from Jl.Raja Laut to the Batu Caves. Len buses 66, 78, 83 and 72 leave from Puduraya bus station to Templer Park. Bus 19 and 20 go up Jl.Duta to the National Park Office (Taman Negara).

DAYTRIPS AROUND KL
BATU CAVES
Twelve kilometers north of KL, get bus 70 or Minibus 11 from Jl.Raja Laut, at the corner of Jl.Ampang. Spread over a square mile, steep limestone cliffs dominate the landscape. At the foot of the cliff a batik factory and numerous refreshment stands await the tourist buses. It's 245 steps up to the big caves. Occasionally you'll meet partially tame monkeys on the stairs begging for peanuts.

The largest cave is the almost eternally closed **DARK CAVE** - about 400 m long and 120 m high. It was first discovered by Europeans in 1879, though the

Orang Asli traditionally collected bat guano here - they weren't averse to the flesh either.

Via another 42 steps you reach the **LIGHT CAVE,** sometimes called the MAIN CAVE. It is about 120 m long and a central place of worship for Malaysian Hindus. A shrine to the Hindu god MURUGAN was built here in 1892. Every year in January/February, it plays a central role in the **THAIPUSAM FESTIVAL,** the largest Hindu festival outside of India where 70,000 people gather in front of the Batu Caves. For 20 c you can visit a museum cave exhibiting colorful Hindu sculptures.

TEMPLER PARK
On about 1600 ha of land, just 22 km north of KL, is this well preserved bit of the jungle equipped with walking paths. Get buses 66, 72, 78 or 83 from Puduraya bus station. Limestone cliffs tower 305 m, dominating the view. If you're not planning to trek through the Taman Negara, then use this opportunity to comfortably visit a tropical forest. The path up to the waterfall is very pretty. On weekends many people come here from the city, though most only picnic near the parking-lot.

In 1954 the National Park was opened and named for the last British High Commissioner of Malaya, Sir Gerald Templer. Thus a tiny piece of natural jungle was saved from the land-eating tin mines and rubber plantations along with as the constantly expanding city. Many types of butterflies, flying lizards, and other small wildlife thereby had a bit of their habitat saved.

NATIONAL ZOO/AQUARIUM
From Jl.Ampang take bus 170 or the big bus 177 to the zoo located 13 km out of town. The drive passes through rubber plantations; you can see how the trees are tapped. In the zoo there are 200 kinds of animals and many types of Malaysian plants. Those who weren't able to see any large animals in the Taman Negara can make up for it here. Open daily from 10:00-18:00 h, admission for the aquarium and zoo: adults 2.50 M$, children 1 M$.

PETALING JAYA
About 10 km south of town on the highway to Port Kelang is this town originally planned as a residential community. Get minibus 19 A right into the center, or Minibus 20A to the university. Independent of KL today, PJ is a city of its own with shopping and administrative centers, a university and lots of industry. Working, living and shopping all go hand in hand here. The town featuring streets running in half

circles and lots of greenery was designed on a drawing board, yet is not half as sterile as many of our suburban communities. It's also 'the' residential area for Europeans and rich Malaysians.

PORT KELANG
Parallel to the railline to Port Kelang (Malaysia's first railline), the Federal Highway heads west. About 24 km after the branch off to the AIRPORT is SHAH ALAM, the capital of Selangor. The sultan's seat in the state of Selangor, however, is Kelang, 32 km from KL. Worth a look are Istana Alam Shah and the royal mosque. Malaysia's most important harbor, Port Kelang (buses from Jl.Sultan Mohamed in KL for 1.30 M$ or get the train), is 8 km away. Even so, most of Malaysia's foreign trade passes through Singapore. Spend the night in Port Rest House, Jl.Watson, Port Kelang, tel 388534.

In Port Kelang, the Chidambaram, of the Shipping Corporation of India, lays anchor enroute to and from Madras. For bookings and information: UBAIDULLA & Co. Sdn. Bhd., KL, 18 Jl.Tun Perak, tel 920255.

LEAVING KL
INTERNATIONAL FLIGHTS
Subang International Airport is served by many airlines. Like Singapore, Bangkok and Penang, it is an important stop for cheap flights. The drive to Subang by taxi costs about 15 M$. It isn't easy to find a taxi because most drivers fear long waits at the airport. From Jl.Sultan Mohammed, across from the Toshiba Building, bus 47 leaves hourly from the airport for 1 M$. When you land in Subang and want to take a taxi into town, first get a coupon at the 'Taxi Coupon Booth'. You don't have to pay the driver anything else. The airport tax for international flights is 15 M$, for domestic flights 7 M$ and for flights to Brunei and Singapore 10 M$. The addresses of major airlines serving KL:

AEROFLOT, Yayasan Selangor, Jl.Bukit Bintang, tel 423231.
AIR INDIA, Bangunan Angkasa Raya, Jl.Ampang, tel 420166.
BIMAN, Bangunan Angkasa Raya, Jl.Ampang, tel 483765.
CATHAY PACIFIC, MUI Plaza, Jl.P.Ramlee, tel 433755.
CHINA AIRLINES, 64 Jl.Bukit Bintang, tel 427344.
CSA, 68 Bangunan GGI, Jl.Ampang, tel 280176.
GARUDA, Bangunan Angkasa Raya, 123 Jl.Ampang, tel 484072.
KOREAN AIRLINES, Wisma MPI, Jl.Raja Chulan, tel 428311.
PAKISTAN INTERNATIONAL, Bangunan Angkasa Raya,tel 425444.
PHILIPPINE AIRLINES, Wisma Stephens, Jl.Raja Chulan, tel 429040

QUANTAS, AIA Building, Jalan Ampang, tel 289133.
SINGAPORE AIRLINES, 2 Jl.Dang Wangi, tel 923122.
THAI INTERNATIONAL, Denmark House, Jl.Ampang, tel 223720.

Student tickets can be booked at: AUSST, c/o MSL Associates, 1st Floor, South East Asia Hotel, 69 Jl.Haji Hussein, tel 984132 / 989049 / 980961.
Here are SAMPLE PRICES in M$ to neighboring countries, in parenthesis the ISIC prices:

BANDAR SERI BEGAWAN 294.-, BANGKOK 403.-(198.-), HAADYAI 169.-, HONGKONG 821.-(454.-), JAKARTA 426.-(251.-), MADRAS 843.-(567.-), MANILA 699.-(507.-), SINGAPORE 130.- (nightflight: 113.-), TAIPEI 1105.-(631.-), TOKYO 1459.- (798.-) M$.

DOMESTIC FLIGHTS
MAS (Malaysian Airline System) is the national carrier. The main office is located at the UMBC-Building, Jl.Sulaiman, not far from the train station, tel 206633. From KL you can fly into just about every airport in West and East Malaysia. SAMPLE PRICES in M$, in parenthesis the price for nightflights:

ALOR SETAR 94.-, JOHORE BHARU 77.-(58.-), KOTA BHARU 86.- (61.-), KOTA KINABALU 380.-(266.-), KUALA TRENGGANU 86.-, KUANTAN 61.-, KUCHING 231.-(162.-), MALACCA 39.-, MIRI 367.-, PENANG 86.-(61.-) M$.

OVERLAND TAXIS
are used in Malaysia for the overland routes. Most leave from the new Bus-Taxi-Terminal at Jl.Pudu/Jl.Cheng Lock. Search for the right taxi on the first floor of the huge complex. Information at the following telephone numbers: 220821 and 225082. Ac taxis charge 20 % more. Always ask about the fare before getting into a taxi.

SAMPLE PRICES: ALOR SETAR 32.-, BUTTERWORTH 27.-, CAMERON HIGHLANDS 21.-, GENTING HIGHLANDS 6.-, IPOH 15.-, JERANTUT 16.-, JOHORE BHARU 31.-, KANGAR 36.-, KELANG 5.-, KOTA BHARU 42.-, KUALA KANGSAR 20.-, KUALA LIPIS 12.-, KUALA TRENGGANU 27.-, KUANTAN 19.-, MALACCA 13.-, PADANG BESAR 42.-, SEREMBAN 5.-, TAPAH 15.-, TAIPING 20.-, TEMERLOH 10.-M$.

OVERLAND BUSES
Most long-distance buses leave from the bus/taxi terminal Puduraya at the corner of Jl.Pudu and Jl.Cheng Lock. Some buses for Pahang leave in the morning from Pahang Busstation, Jl.Tun Razak (tel 631473).

Locations are served by several companies. The prices are usually the same, with slightly higher prices for air conditioned buses. The major companies have their offices in the Puduraya terminal: MARA EXPRESS, the largest company, serves most places in Malaysia, tel 286990; KUALA LUMPUR - SINGAPORE EXPRESS, tel 227553 and KUALA LUMPUR - MALACCA EXPRESS, tel 281578.

SAMPLE PRICES: ALOR SETAR 19.50 (ac 20.-), BUTTERWORTH 12.70 (ac 14.70), GERIK 11.50 (ac 14.-), IPOH 7.20 (ac 8.20) JERANTUT 12.-, JOHORE BHARU 15.50, KANGAR 21.50, KOTA BHARU 19.-(ac 24.-), KUALA KANGSAR 8.-, KUALA TRENGGANU 17.-(ac 20.-), KUANTAN (Dep. 10.30 h) 12.10, MALACCA 5.50 (ac 6.50), takes 3-3 1/2 hrs, PORT DICKSON 3.30, RAUB 7.-, SEGAMAT 8.50, SEREMBAN 3.-, SINGAPORE 15.50 (Nightexpress, ac, 17.50, best to book several days in advance), TANAH RATA 7.75, TAPAH 6.- (ac 7.20), 8:30 /14:30 h), TEMERLOH 4.90 M$.

HITCH-HIKING
To get out of town heading north take bus 70 (Len Company) to the branch-off for the Batu Caves. Heading south get a

GENERAL INFORMATION 129

bus from the Jl.Pudu bus terminal to Jl.Cheras/Jl.Peel roundabout. Important: after Seremban, the road splits to the south. One goes down the coast (Malacca) and then on along the sea to Ayer Hitam, where it rejoins the other road running from Seremban via Segamat to Johore Baru.

BY RAIL
The architecture of the train station is clearly one of a kind - or should we call it 'railroad mosque'. Latch on to a copy of the time table there (Malay: Jadual Waktu) for the Malayan Railway (Keretapi Tanah Melayu). For information, phone 282861.

KL is situated on the mainline from Singapore in the south and Butterworth (Penang) in the north. Some trains go on through to Bangkok (just Mon. Wed. and Fridays, **be sure you're in one of the few cars going through**, or change at Butterworth, takes about 1 1/2 days). If you want to go to the east coast (Kota Bharu), you have to go via the railroad junction, Gemas, south of KL. It'd be quicker though to take a taxi or bus to Kuala Lipis or Temerloh (the **Mentakab** train station is about 10 km to the west of Temerloh on the big east-west road) and get the train there.

For long trips, get your ticket in advance. For 1st and 2nd class you can book a month in advance. For night trains reserving a bed is recommended. Costs in 2nd class 4 M$ for the upper bed and 6 M$ for the bottom, in International Express trains: 7.30 M$ and 10.40 M$.
SAMPLE PRICES - oneway in 2nd cl. (3rd cl.):

ALOR SETAR 23.90 (15.-), BANGKOK 57.50, BUTTERWORTH 19.90 (12.50), HAAD YAI 28.80, IPOH 10.50 (6.60), JOHORE BAHRU 18.90 (11.90), KUALA LIPIS 20.40 (12.90), PADANG BESAR 26.90 (16.80), SEREMBAN 3.80 (2.40), SINGAPORE 19.90 (12.50), TAIPING 15.- (9.40), TAPAH 8.- (5.-), WAKAF BHARU (Kota Bharu) 34.30 (21.50) M$.

SAMPLE PRICES - express trains (in parenthesis ac compartments):
BUTTERWORTH 15.50 (26.-), JOHORE BAHRU 14.90 (25.-), KUALA KANGSAR 11.40 (20.-), SINGAPORE 15.50 (26.-), TAPAH 8.- (14.-) M$.

****
THERE MUST BE A MISTAKE IN THIS BOOK!
Write and tell us. What has changed? What have we missed?
****

FROM KL TO PENANG

A ride along the North-South Highway through industrialized Malaysia: truck-filled roads, industrial plants, tin mines, palm-oil and rubber plantations. Even 500 years ago, ore reserves and convenient harbors provided the basis for dynamic development of this region stretching from Malacca in the south to Penang in the north. The Portuguese, Dutch, and British all participated in the spoils. To work the plantations and mines, Chinese came by the thousands via the Straits Settlements. In Selangor, Chinese formed an ethnic majority already before the turn of the century. They were also profitably engaged as artisans and merchants, lending considerably to local development. Even today they dominate the cities. The rubber boom at the beginning of the century led to the rise of huge plantations in the tin mining region, attracting new ethnic groups to the area. Indians, particularly Tamils from the south of India, were considered by the British to be better suited for rubber-plantation labor than the hard to control Chinese. Even today, many Indians are employed on the plantations.

If you have enough time on the way from KL to Penang or Thailand, numerous sidetrips along the 464 km route invite you to get to know the region better. In the Cameron Highlands, one of the old British **Hillstations**, you can hike in the cool mountain air, visit a tea plantation, or watch vegetable farmers at work. Hardly anyone strays off to Fraser's Hill where the colonial elite once spent their holidays. If you're into sun, sea and sand, try Pangkor Island. And the almost completely Chinese towns of Ipoh, Kuala Kangsar and Taiping are certainly worth a brief stopover.

Fraser's Hill

Louis James Fraser was an English adventurer who around the turn of the century did a thriving trade in opium. He's reputed to have run an opium den at almost 1350 m above sea level! In 1916 Fraser suddenly disappeared, never to be seen again. Back then only a small path ran up the 7 km from The Gap. Today there's a thin road which is open in 40 minute cycles to one-way traffic in each direction.

Across from the Lodging House is the information center where they provide maps of Fraser's Hill. In the cool of the mountains you can take excellent walks, try the 5 km to **JERIAU WATERFALL**. The view of the Malay mountains covered by impassable forest is alone worth the drive. However, more and more luxury bungalows are being built. Fraser's Hill is a vacation area for rich local tourists who enjoy golf and tennis in the cool mountain air.

HOTELS

Right on the road at The Gap is the peaceful **GOVERNMENT RESTHOUSE****, for room reservations tel 071/382227. Nice, in the old-fashion English country home style, but the food's a bit dear. It's a 1 1/2 hour walk through the woods to the Hill - fascinating near dusk. At the top you've the new **MERLIN HOTEL******, tel 382274. There's no cheap place to stay. More reasonable are **FRASER'S HILL BUNGALOWS******, tel 093/382201, and **THE LODGING HOUSE******. Be sure to phone in advance!

HOW TO GET HERE

If you've rented a car, take the route **KL - KUALA KUBU BHARU** for about an hour, then it's another hour on the road to **RAUB**. Buses leave KL regularly for Kuala Kubu Bharu on the main North-South Highway. From there buses leave daily at 8:00 and 12:00 h direct to Fraser's Hill. Going back they leave at 10:00 and 14:00 h. For 4 M$ you can take an overland taxi from Kuala Kubu Bharu; from KL the whole taxi would be about 60 M$. Luxury buses direct to Fraser's Hill depart Tues, Wed, Thurs, Fri, and Sundays at 15:00 h from the Merlin Hotel in KL, plus Saturdays at 11:00 and 17:00 h. Costs 16.50 M$.

It's not as simple coming from Kuantan. In Temerloh, get a bus to Raub or Kuala Lipis via TERANUM. From here you can transfer to the Raub - KL bus departing at 12:00 and 15:00 h. This bus stops in The Gap next to the Resthouse on the main road.

Cameron Highlands

The Cameron Highlands in the State of Pahang offer a beautiful contrast to beach, palms and ocean. In 1885, William Cameron, a surveyor travelling under contract of the colonial authorities, discovered "a fine plateau with gentle slopes shut in by lofty mountains". Tea planters and vegetables farmers were quick to appreciate the climatic advantages of the up to 2200 m high plateau. Later a road was built, and the area became a favorite vacation place for the English suffering under the hot sun.

ORANG ASLI

About 50,000 people fit into the ethnic category called 'Orang Asli' (directly translated: 'native, original people'). They are jungle and coastal dwellers whose forefathers were here before the Malays. The term 'Orang Asli' is used to describe many very different ethnic groups including about 1800 **Negritoes,** the oldest population who are mostly settled in the northern jungle areas. Or the **proto-Malays** which include about 1800 **Orang Laut**, the sea people.

The largest group are the 30,000 **Senoi,** some of whose villages can be found in the forests of the Cameron Highlands. Many tribes such as the **Temiar, Semai, Mah Meri,** and the **Semok Beri** are sub-groups of the Senoi. They are said, like the Negritoes, to have migrated into the region 6-8000 years ago. Their skin, however, is lighter, and unlike the nomadic Negritoes, they live off slash and burn agriculture. They have been pushed back by the Malays into hard to reach jungle regions.

Some still live there today, completely cut off from civilization. Others, especially those living near the major cities and along the main transportation links, have largely taken on the life style of their former enemies. Many Senoi have opened themselves up to the influences of modern times. Some of their children go to schools, and small groups of Senoi work on the Highland tea plantations.

Their social structure is set up to avoid any kind of controversy or conflict. The traditional settlement is a longhouse inhabited by about 50 people, usually a clan with an old man as chief: the founder of the house or one of his sons. Decisions are made in collective discussions, the chief only taking the role of mediator. Visiting back and forth is a regular pastime, so you'll always find a number of guests.

Besides a blowpipe or rifle and a few durian trees, individuals have no private property. Every clan has its own carefully defined fishing grounds and a section of jungle which it works. The forest is usually cleared in a two year rhythm for the planting of mountain rice and tapioca. Only males are permitted to cut down trees; but at harvest time, the gathering of fruit and vegetables is women's work. Hunting and fishing is a privilege of adult males again. The bag is then divided

> among all members of the community. The traditional weapon, an over 2 meter long blowpipe with poisoned darts, is still commonly used.
>
> During the 'emergency' from from 1948 to 1960, the Orang Asli were courted by both the MCP and the British. They were the only people who knew their way around in the jungle. There is still a Senoi Pra'ak Regiment in the Field Force Police which is used against the MCP - even though 'war' and 'fight' are new concepts for the Senoi who traditionally seek compromise.

At first you pass through rubber plantations and rice fields; then the road becomes smaller and winds unendingly through the mountains. The vegetation changes as well - huge ferns and other mountain plants are typical of the evergreen tropical mountain forest. Occasionally you'll see scattered Orang Asli villages.

The Cameron Highlands are a good place to relax. Spend a week hiking in the fresh mountain climate, especially after a while in the tropics. The evenings and nights can get quite cool. The coldest temperature ever recorded in the Highlands was 2°C one January night.

If you're taking a rented car through the Highlands, stop at the 24 mile marker for a look at the **Malaysia Insect Museum**, costs 1.50 M$.

Three small villages form the center of the Cameron Highlands: **RINGLET** (disappointing, keep going!), **TANAH RATA** (the nicest!) and **BRINCHANG**.

On the road into Tanah Rata is an information office - though they only offer an old hotel directory and a map for 1 M$.

Here are some tips for your tours and hikes:
Jungle hikes and walks are much more comfortable in this climate than in the humid heat of lowland forests such as Taman Negara. The battalions of leeches are gone too! The beasts like less light and air (joy!). On longer trips, however, you should still wear sturdy shoes.

For getting started, try a walk along the paved path to **ROBINSON WATERFALL**, only 15 minutes from Tanah Rata. Afterwards try path 8 to **GUNUNG BEREMBAN**. This is the prettiest, but also the most strenuous jungle trek. By way of Path 3 you'll need at least three hours, and via Path 5 six hours.

Only a kilometer away on a Brinchang side street is **SAM POH TEMPLE**, a beautiful Chinese temple with huge, shiny, gold temple guardians (open just till 17:00 h). Path 2 heading south from here is quite difficult because it's so steep, running over trees and through streams - don't do it alone!

In the tropical mountain forest, Path 3 starts at the Golf Links. It's pretty steep, but the vegetation is incredible. For a 15 minute walk, try Path 4 starting behind the Garden Hotel.

Expect a five hour hike from Tanah Rata via the waterfall to **ROBINSON FALLS POWER STATION** and via **HABU POWER STATION** back to the main road. From there you can go by bus or hitchhike to the **BHARAT TEA ESTATE** and then back to Tanah Rata. This tea plantation is situated near the road to Ringlet, about 5 km south of Tanah Rata (bus 35 c) - easy to reach for the less active. You can follow the whole process of tea production from picking to packing.

EMAS TEA ESTATE is another tea plantation a bit further south, 3 km off the main road - closed Fridays. You can buy cheap tea to send home - but keep customs duties at home in mind!

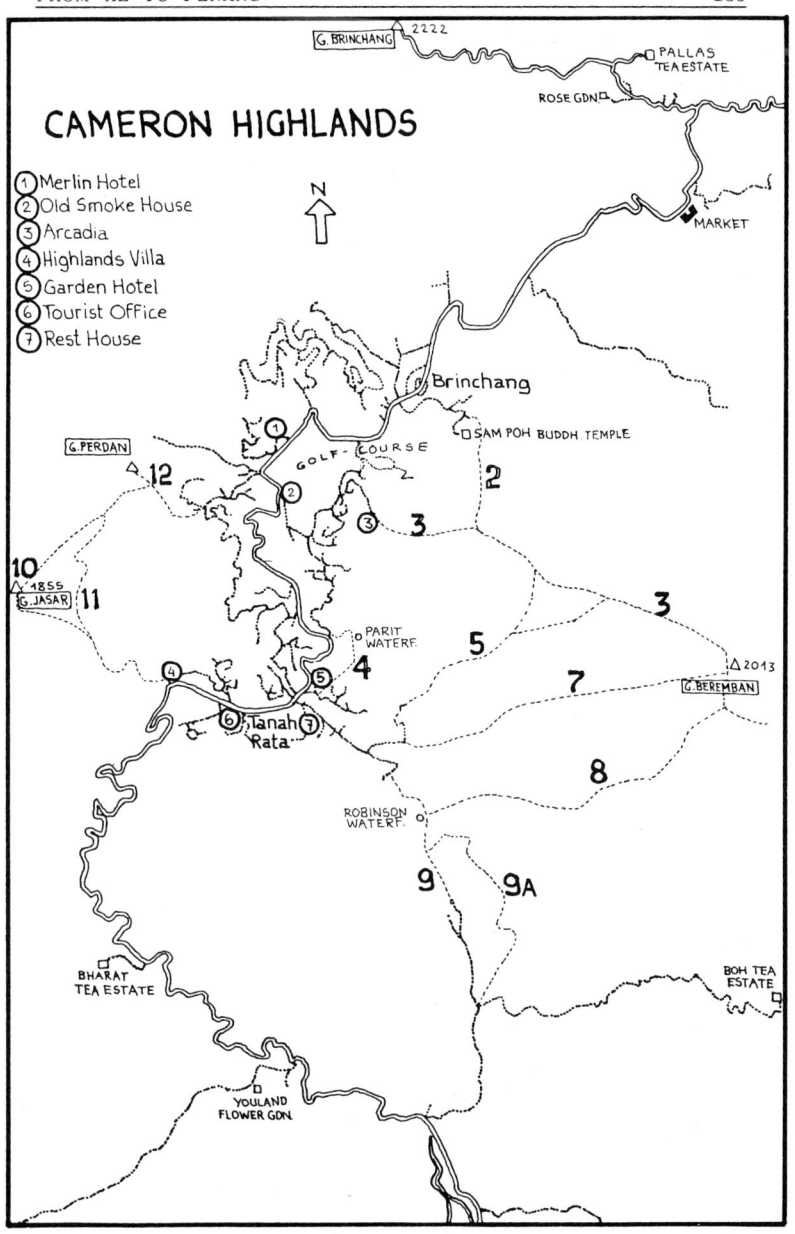

CAMERON HIGHLANDS

1. Merlin Hotel
2. Old Smoke House
3. Arcadia
4. Highlands Villa
5. Garden Hotel
6. Tourist Office
7. Rest House

In just 1 1/2 hours you can climb the 1855 m high **GUNUNG JASAR** - take path 10 from Tanah Rata (Highlands Villa). The path is a bit steep and partially overgrown. Take Path 12 back to Tanah Rata (one hour).

If you've got a car, be sure to drive up **GUNUNG BRINCHANG** (over 2200 m). If you're in a small group, you can rent a taxi - about 50-60 M$ to the top. To the foot of the mountain you'll only have to pay about 7 M$; however, you then face a 1 3/4 hour hike (beautiful country!).

TEA

Tea has been grown in the Cameron Highlands since 1926. The English started the first plantations with tea plants from Assam. The workers were mostly brought from southern India. They were considered to be the best plantation workers because they were more willing than the Chinese to obey the orders of white owners, and because they were used to working in a hot tropical climate. By 1938, when the emigration of unskilled labor to Malaya was prohibited by the Indian government, hundreds of thousands of immigrants (especially Tamils) had arrived. They form the majority of the plantation population. You can still frequently see barrack settlements for Indian workers on palm-oil, rubber and tea plantations, complete with tiny Hindu temples.

Tea processing takes time. Once every seven or eight days, the young, tender leaves are picked. It takes about five pounds of leaves to produce one pound of tea. A laborer can pick perhaps 90 pounds per day. At the factory, the leaves are spread out on troughlike screens, and huge fans get them half dry. Then the withered leaves are mechanically 'rolled'; meaning the remaining juices are allowed to ferment. This includes spreading the leaves on tables to ferment for several days covered by wet cloth. Thereby the tanning agents in the exiting juices are oxidized. Then the leaves are mechanically dried, giving them their familiar black color.

For green tea, the fresh leaves are briefly processed with hot steam, then rolled and dried with special machines. This way they keep their green coloring. At the end of the processing, the dried leaves are sorted according to quality, and all the threads and stems removed.

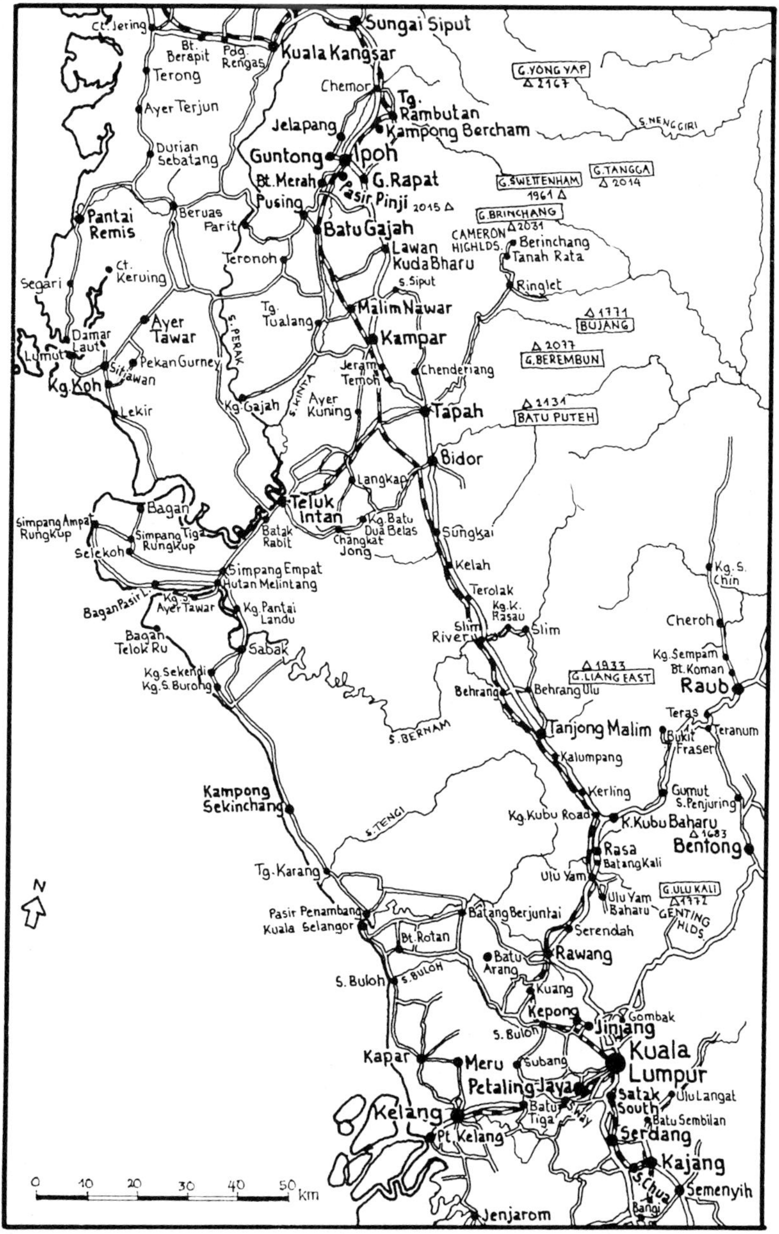

Ct. Jering
Bt. Berapit
Pdg. Rengas
Kuala Kangsar
Sungai Siput
Terong
Chemor
Tg. Rambutan
Ayer Terjun
Jelapang
Kampong Bercham
Durian Sebatang
Guntong
Ipoh
Bt. Merah
G. Rapat
Pasir Pinji
Pusing
Beruas
Parit
Pantai Remis
Batu Gajah
Teronoh
Lawan Kuda Bharu
Ct. Keruing
Segari
S. Siput
Tg. Tualang
Malim Nawar
Damar Laut
Lumut
Ayer Tawar
S. PERAK
Kampar
Pekan Gurney
Sitiawan
Kg. Koh
Jeram Temoh
Chenderiang
Lekir
Kg. Gajah
S. KINTA
Ayer Kuning
Tapah
Bidor
Langkap
Bagan
Teluk Intan
Simpang Ampat Rungkup
Simpang Tiga Rungkup
Batak Rabit
Kg. Batu Dua Belas
Changkat Jong
Sungkai
Selekoh
Simpang Empat
Hutan Melintang
Kelah
Bagan Pasir L.
Kg. S. Ayer Tawar
Kg. Pantai Landu
Terolak
Kg. K. Rasau
Bagan Telok Ru
Sabak
Slim River
Slim
Kg. Sekendi
Kg. S. Burong
Behrang
Behrang Ulu
S. BERNAM
Tanjong Malim
Kalumpang
Kampong Sekinchang
Kerling
S. TENGI
Kg. Kubu Road
K. Kubu Baharu
Rasa
Batang Kali
Tg. Karang
Ulu Yam
Ulu Yam Baharu
Pasir Penambang
Kuala Selangor
Batang Berjuntai
Serendah
Bt. Rotan
Batu Arang
Rawang
S. Buloh
S. BULOH
Kuang
Kepong
Gombak
Jinjang
S. Buloh
Kuala Lumpur
Kapar
Meru
Subang
Petaling Jaya
Satak South
Ulu Langat
Kelang
Batu Tiga
S. Way
Batu Sembilan
Pt. Kelang
Serdang
Kajang
S. Chua
Semenyih
Bangi
Jenjarom
G. YONG YAP
Δ 2167
S. NENGGIRI
G. SWETTENHAM
1961 Δ
G. TANGGA
Δ 2014
2015 Δ
G. BRINCHANG
Δ 2031
CAMERON HIGHLDS.
Berinchang
Tanah Rata
Ringlet
Δ 1771
BUJANG
Δ 2077
G. BEREMBUN
Δ 1131
BATU PUTEH
Kg. S. Chin
Cheroh
Kg. Sempam
Bt. Koman
Raub
Δ 1933
G. LIANG EAST
Teras
Bukit Fraser
Teranum
Gumut
S. Penjuring
Δ 1683
Bentong
G. ULU KALI
Δ 1772
GENTING HLDS.
N
0 10 20 30 40 50 km

From Tanah Rata the road leads to Brinchang, and there take a left, uphill (about 20 km from Tanah Rata). You pass through seemingly endless tea plantations and then through mountain jungle, up to the highest point in Malaysia accessible by car. On the top are a TV and radio station - the view in good weather is fantastic! In the west you can see down to the ocean, to the east are the jungle covered mountains of Malaysia.

On the way back stop a bit at **PALLAS TEA ESTATE** and have a talk with the Indian tea pickers. You can watch the tea leaves being processed. The factory is about a kilometer from the road. Daily at 11:30, 13:30 and 16:10 h, a bus leaves from Tanah Rata to the plantation entrance. The last bus back is at 15:30 h.

On the main road, just beyond the fork, a **FRUIT AND VEGETABLE MARKET** is held every day for produce grown further up the valley. Tourists seem willing to pay any price asked, at least the prices fit this pattern - so bargain! On the street, butterflies and other insects are sold in glass containers. You'll aid local conservation if you reduce demand for the Rajah Brookes and other butterflies - find another souvenir!

HOTELS

Reasonable priced is **WONG VILLA***, 113 Main Road, on the road out of Brinchang, tel 941145, simple rooms (hold up to four people) with a basin, like losmen in Indonesia. Next to the Hindu temple is the **JOLLY VILLA*** offering about the same. About 1.5 km above Tanah Rata travellers meet at **BALA'S CHALETS**, featuring a dormitory* and kitchen facilities. Food a bit expensive.

Otherwise Tanah Rata is a better place to stay. On the main road are lots of middle priced hotels, usually with a private bath and warm water: **SEAH MENG***, no 39, tel 941618; **HOLLYWOOD****, no 38, tel 941633; **TOWN HOUSE****, no 41, tel 941666 and others. Not bad is the **RESTHOUSE****, Jl.Tepi Sungei to the right off the main street, tel 941254. Those who want to spend more should try the **GARDEN HOTEL*****, tel 941911. Absolutely luxurious is **YE OLDE SMOKE HOUSE** near the golf course with rooms up to 250 M$.

FOOD

Get a cheap breakfast of local milk teas and sweet pastry at either of the Indian shops on Tanah Rata's main street. They also offer simple curries and flatbread. **SRI TANAH RATA** serves good food.

More expensive, but with excellent Chinese and western food is the restaurant in the **HOLLYWOOD HOTEL**. If there're three or four of you, try a steamboat, costs about 8 M$ per person. Meat and vegetables are cooked in a broth on the table, which later becomes a tasty soup. Good, but expensive, are strawberries from the surrounding fields.

Find long forgotten colonial atmosphere with English porcelain and silverware, antique furniture and plush (which of course you pay for!) in **YE OLDE SMOKEHOUSE INN**, about 3 km towards Brinchang by the golf course and in **FORSTER'S LAKEHOUSE** on the bridge between the two reservoirs.

HOW TO GET HERE
From KL there're direct MARA buses leaving at 8:30 and 14:30 h for 8.-M$. Taxis cost 21.-M$ per person. From TAPAH on the big North-South Highway, buses leave 7 times a day until 16:00 h for the two hour drive to TANAH RATA (3.-M$). To Tapah you have regular connections from IPOH, BUTTERWORTH and the south. From TANAH RATA (Townhouse Hotel) there's a daily bus for 7.75 M$ to KL - arrives at Puduraya at 19:00 h. If you come by train, get off at Tapah Road and then go either by taxi up into the mountains, or first by bus to Tapah and then as explained above.

Pulau Pangkor

Unlike the east coast, the west coast isn't blessed with sandy beaches, islands and coral reefs. Just 12 km long and 4 km wide, Pangkor Island is one of the few exceptions. All around the main island are smaller isles, easy to reach by fishing boat. Pangkor's inhabitants live mostly from fishing. Besides Malays, many Chinese and Indians live here making this one of the few places in Malaysia where you can find Malabari (Indian) fishing villages.

The island fits into an ancient legend: once upon a time a young warrior from Sumatra fell into eternal love with a princess whose hand he hoped to win. To prove himself in battle, he set sail upon the sea. The princess waited months for his return before finally deciding to go seek him. And so she landed on Pulau Pangkor where she learned of his death. When the villagers showed her his grave, she flung herself from a cliff in complete despair. Even today the beach still carries the princess' name, Pantai Puteri Dewi.

Most accommodations are in Pasir Bogak, facing the open sea. This village has been turned into a tourist center catering primarily to families. From the ferry landing, Kg.Pangkor, get a taxi for 3 M$.

A walk around the island takes five hours – leave early! From **PASIR BOGAK** you'll come upon two beautiful beaches about 3 km to the north, **PANTAI PUTERI DEWI**. Then cross the island. On the east coast further to the north, go to **GOLDEN SANDS**, where the ferries from Lumut dock. To **KAMPONG PANGKOR**, hike south through the jungle, where with some luck you'll see birds and monkeys. Another good walk might be south of Kg.Pangkor to **KOTA BELANDA**, the old Dutch fort. It was built in 1680 to protect Dutch tin traders from attack by Malay pirates. It was heavily fortified and its cannon could cover the whole Strait of Dinding. But in 1690 the Dutch were forced to abandon the fort after an attack by the Malays. The Dutch reoccupied the fort from 1745-1748.

If you've a group of 10-12 people, why not rent a fishing boat to visit off-shore island beaches, like **PULAU PANGKOR LAUT**. Snorkelling is best at **EMERALD BAY** but coral reefs are not to be compared to the east coast.

HOTELS

One of the first cheap places was **KHOO'S MINICAMP**. Mini is by now maxi and the whole beach is rather dirty. The business-minded Mr. Khoo has built an assortment of huts priced about 10 M$ per night. During school vacations, whole school classes terrorize his camp; bring your ear muffs! A pleasant alternative is the camp **PANGKOR ANCHOR****, run by Agnes Wong, offering much greater cleanliness for the same price. Take a walk on down the beach and after 10 minutes you arrive at the **GOVERNMENT RESTHOUSE**** (tel 939236). Each bungalow has two rooms with a shower and fan. First rights of habitation, however, go to cockroaches and bedbugs. New and priced over 50 M$ are the rooms and bungalows at the **BEACH HUTS HOTEL******, tel 939159, a bit to the south. Similarly priced is the **SEAVIEW HOTEL******, tel 939056. On the Golden Sands is the **PANGKOR BAY VILLAGE******, peacefully situated and serving excellent seafood. Reservations in Ipoh, 41 Jl.Tasek, Ipoh Garden, tel 557627.

HOW TO GET HERE

First head for LUMUT, the departure point for boats to Pangkor (see below). The ferry to KAMPONG PANGKOR costs 1 M$ and leaves every half an hour. The first boat from Lumut is

at 6:45 h and the last at 19:30 h. From Kampong Pangkor
the first boat is at 6:45 h and the last at 18:30 h. Plus
ferries serve GOLDEN SANDS BEACH for 1.20 M$ from Lumut at
8:30, 10:30, 13:30 and 16:15 h.

Lumut

A couple of years ago the town became a major base
for the Malaysian navy. From the ferry you can see quays,
wet docks, and warehouses. About 8 km south of town are
the beaches mostly used by Malaysians: **TELUK RUBIAH,
TELUK MURUK** and **TELUK BATIK.** On the last beach you can
rent simple bungalows. A major government project calls for

developing the beaches into tourist centers with a golf course, botanical garden, sports facilities, plus camping and picnic areas.

At the end of July, beginning of August, a three-day festival is held on the Lumut esplanade featuring sports competitions such as boat and go-cart races. And there're Chinese opera, dance and boxing matches.

HOTELS

If you miss the last ferry, then spend the night here. On the road to Ipoh is the **LUMUT HOTEL****. Somewhat better is the **PHIN LIM HOOI HOTEL****, 93 Jl.Titi Panjang, tel 935641. The **RESTHOUSE** can be reached at tel 935938.

HOW TO GET HERE

From Shell garage, not by bus station. $2.90

Buses leave from IPOH for LUMUT. Direct buses depart at 8:00, 10:30, 13:00 and 16:00 h for 4 M$. If they've already left, get a bus for 3.50 M$ to SITIAWAN (takes 45 minutes), and then for 1 M$ take the 15 minute ride to Lumut. Taxis charge about 6 M$ from Ipoh. An alternative is the bus from BUTTERWORTH for 8 M$. If you're coming from KL, go first to Ipoh. Get Murni Express from Malacca for 18.50 M$. Takes 7 1/2 hours.

7:30, 9:00
12:00, 13:00
16:00, 17:00

Ipoh

Ipoh is the capital of the state with the Malay name 'Perak', meaning silver. But it was another metal which brought wealth to this region. The world's largest tin reserves are located in Kinta Valley. Once upon a time, Ipoh was a mining settlement exploiting the coveted raw material. The town was called PALOH – 'Pool of Stagnant Water' – because fishermen dammed the flow of the Kinta River, and only here was the thick jungle cleared around the mines.

The profitability of tin can be seen in the town of Ipoh. Sometimes this place is called millionaire city: many of the one-time tin prospectors are now wealthy mine owners. You can see them on weekends at the race track.

The Kinta-River separates the old and new parts of Malaysia's third largest city (population 250,000). In the old town, which hasn't changed much in the last 60 years, you'll find the obligatory **CLOCKTOWER** and an incredible **TRAIN STATION** built in 1917. South of the station the **GPO**.

Hardly any other town in West Malaysia has so much greenery – with money you can do everything. In the biggest park, **TAMAN DR. SEENIVASAGAM**, is the town's last Ipoh tree from which the city got its name.

FROM KL TO PENANG 143

> Today you'll only find the once widely distributed
> **Ipoh tree** (antiaris toxicaria) in the jungle areas of
> Malaysia. At first glance it looks like any of the rubber
> trees on the plantations. The Orang Asli get a poison
> from the white latex which they use for their blow pipes
> darts. Fibre cloth is made from the bark.

The most interesting garden or park is the small
JAPANESE GARDEN on Jl.Tambun east of the city center.
Follow this road toward Tambun and within a few kilometers
you're in a bizarre limestone cliff landscape. Signs along
the road advertise the palm readers in business here.

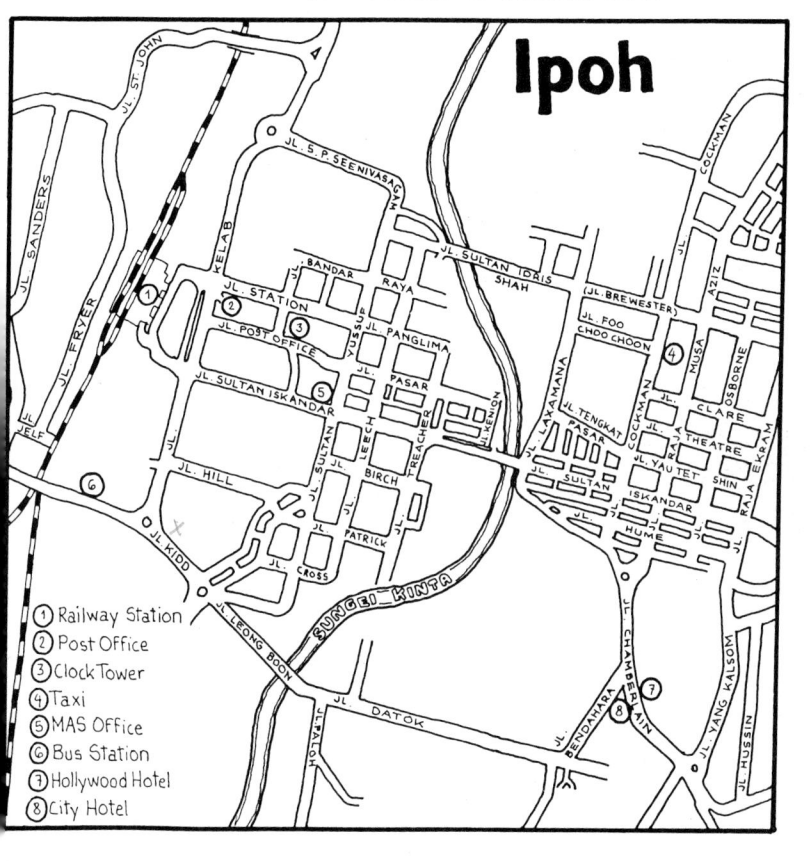

① Railway Station
② Post Office
③ Clock Tower
④ Taxi
⑤ MAS Office
⑥ Bus Station
⑦ Hollywood Hotel
⑧ City Hotel

TIN
With about sixty thousand tons annually, Malaysia is the world's largest tin producer. Mining was going on 500 years ago in the high quality, easily accessible, alluvial soil of western Malaya. But the country still has huge untapped reserves. The oldest and simplest method of mining ore near the surface is called 'dulang'. The tin-rich ore is washed with the aid of a 'bowl' in the river. Europeans began dredging in 1912. Huge floating steam shovels comb the muddy riverbed, leaving behind a huge desert. In smaller and uneven regions, the Chinese particularly utilized gravel pumping. The ore is washed out using water pressure and transported via a pipe system to 'palong' where the tin is filtered out. Only a few mines are operated underground.

Over a dozen temples, both large and small, have been established in caves in the limestone cliffs north and south of town.

6 km south of town along Jl.Gopeng (the main road to KL) are numerous cave temples. The prettiest is **SAM PO TONG**, just behind the cliff with the Mercedes star. In the main cave are several altars. To the right, a stairway leads to an open cave. Here, surrounded by high, steep limestone cliffs, a turtle pond has been built. Near Sam Po Tong, toward Ipoh, is the **NAM THIAN TONG** cave temple with a vegetarian restaurant. There's tin mining to the west of the road. Buses from Ipoh cost 50 c.

Be sure to take a tour 6 km north of town (Jl.Kuala Kangsar) to **PERAK TONG** - where Chinese immigrants built a temple in caves of a 120 m high limestone cliff. In front of the entrance are a pretty garden with a pond full of lotus blossoms and a restaurant. Climb to the top and you'll find a huge stalactite cave containing various Buddhist and Chinese deities. Towering above everything is a 12 m tall sitting Buddha. Wander about in the caves! Via a path behind the main altar, you can go deeper into the cliffs. Some steps lead 100 m to the top where you have a good view. Another stairs leads to a picture of the Goddess of Mercy. Take a bus from Ipoh to Kg.Tawas for 45 c.

HOTELS
Many of the hotels in this town (famous for its nightlife) are red light establishments. Colonial atmosphere (expen-

sive) at **STATION HOTEL****** in the train station, tel 512588. Many hotels are on Chamberlain Road. Relatively expensive are the big **CITY HOTEL******, no 79, tel 512911 and the **HOLLYWOOD HOTEL******, no 72-76, tel 515322. Cheaper are **CATHAY HOTEL*****, no 88-94, tel 513322 and **EMBASSY HOTEL*****, no 35. In the still cheaper category are the smaller Chinese hotels: **IPOH HOTEL****, 163 Jl.Sultan Idris Shah, tel 78663, **KUO MIN HOTEL****, 48 Jl.Cockman, tel 512087, **CONTINENTAL HOTEL****, 62 Cowan Street or **CHEW NANYANG HOTEL*****, 22-24 Jl.Yang Kalsom.

In the city are a number of interesting **Night Markets** with good food stands.

LEAVING IPOH
Quick flights which are seldom of interest: KOTA BHARU 113 M$, KL 55 M$, PENANG 41 M$.

Buses leave from Jl.Silibin: KL 7.20 M$ (ac 8.20 M$), MALACCA 11 M$ (ac 13 M$) SINGAPORE 20 M$ (ac 25 M$), JOHORE BAHRU 16 M$ (ac 20 M$), KAMPAR 1.55 M$, LUMUT 4 M$ (last bus leaves at 16:00 h), KUALA KANGSAR 2.50 M$, takes 1 1/2 hours stopping in every village.

Overland taxis leave from Jl.Kido across the busstation and cost 13.50 M$ to BUTTERWORTH and 15 M$ to KL.

Six trains leave daily for KL (3rd cl. 6.60 M$) or BUTTERWORTH (3rd cl. 5.80 M$). Information in the train station at tel 540481.

Kuala Kangsar

Perak's old sultan seat, a nice little town of less than 20,000, is situated about half way between Ipoh and Taiping. Check out the famous **UBUDIAH MOSQUE**, the most beautiful mosque in Malaysia with golden cupolas and thin minarets. Next to it are the graves of the royal family. You can get to the mosque by walking along the river from the town. After going through the big gate, it's another kilometer.

Just 500 m further is the majestic **SULTAN'S PALACE**, the Istana, sitting on a hill. Be sure to check out the woodcarvings on the light colored house a bit off to the side.

About half way between the mosque and the main road is the RESTHOUSE which has a great view of the Perak River.

Just behind it is an old Chinese cemetery.

HOTELS
Besides the beautifully situated, but not very clean, **REST-HOUSE****, tel 851699, there are several hotels in town. Near the bus station and movie theater on the road out of town is the **DOUBLE LION HOTEL****, 74 Jl.Kangsar, tel 851010, somewhat more expensive is the **TIN HEONG HOTEL**** on Jl.Raja Chulan, tel 851255.
Good **foodstalls** in town.

HOW TO GET HERE
A branch off the main KL - Penang road runs right into the center of town. The famous mosque is at the opposite end of town.
Bus connections from BUTTERWORTH 6.-, KL 8.-, TAPAH 5.20 M$. In Kuala Kangsar the road forks to the east; a bus leaves at 13:00 h to Gerik.

Taiping

In English Taiping means 'the city of everlasting peace'. One of the most ancient towns in the country was given this name in 1874 when the bloody feud between two Chinese secret societies, the Hai San and Ghee Hin found a peaceful settlement here. As just about everywhere else in Perak, the trouble (lasting 25 years) was over tin. Taiping is located in the oldest tin-mining region of Malaysia.

As early as 1890 a beautiful park - **LAKE GARDEN** - was set up on the site of an abandoned tin mine. The **PERAK MUSEUM**, right behind the prison, is the oldest in Malaysia. The exhibits include Malayan weapons, many types of kris, jewellery, tools of the Orang Asli and archaeological finds collected since the turn of the century. Plus there're a zoological section and a photo documentary of Perak's eventful history. Admission is free, open daily 09:00-17:00 h, closed Fridays from 12:00-14:30 h.

There are two temples to check out: Near the museum, a bit further out of town, is the **LING NAM TEMPLE** - the oldest Chinese temple in Perak. A hundred years ago many statues, urns and antique weapons were brought here from China - since then they have been gold plated. On the other side of the train tracks, on Station Street, is a **HINDU SHRINE** - the deities seem like a pyramid between the coconut palms.

HOTELS
The **RESTHOUSE****** is beautifully located, tel 822044, right on the slope with a view of the Lake Garden. By foot you'll need about 45 minutes, by taxi it's 2 M$ per person.
On Jl.Iskandar are two cheap hotels: the **CHEONG ONN HOTEL***, no 24, tel 822815 and at no 32 the **PEACE HOTEL****, tel 823397. Quite reasonable hotels can also be found near the market hall such as on Jl.Kota, **WAH BEE HOTEL***, no 62-64, tel 822065, and **TOWN HOTEL****, no 220, tel 821166. The best hotel in town is **MIRAMAR******, 30 Jl.Peng Loong, tel 821077.

HOW TO GET HERE
Taiping, 56 km south of Penang, is accessible by bus (3.- M$), overland taxi (7.25 M$), or by rail (4.90 M$ 2nd class or 3.10 M$ 3rd class).
There're regular connections to KL (by rail 15.-M$ 2nd class or 9.40 M$ 3rd class).
There are direct buses to Lumut.
Taiping is convenient to visit on Penang - Pangkor trips.

THE LARUT WARS
Besides the two most important Chinese secret societies in Malaya, behind the scenes participants in the conflict included the Malay sultans and their rivals, along with English traders and administrators. The Chinese, bound by origin to their secret societies, were fighting for economic power, ie the mines and water of Sungei Larut.

The diversion of river water, or just a gambling dispute, could lead to explosions in this tense atmosphere: villages burnt down and the inhabitants kidnapped, driven away or killed. The secret secret societies supported the Sungei Larut conflict with money, weapons and men from as far away as Penang, Singapore and China. The British began to fear an expansion of the conflict (which already consumed all of Perak) to the Straits Settlement, where their own economic interests could be jeopardized. Britain decided to get involved. The Malay sultans and their rivals, who at first used the conflict to expand their own power, also saw the danger of being overrun by the Chinese and looked to end the conflict. On Pangkor Island, Malay and Chinese leaders met in January 1874 under the direction of Britain's Sir Andrew Clarke to draw up a peace treaty. It solidified the power of the sultans and the influence of the appointed British resident.

MAXWELL HILL

Ten kilometers inland, at about 1000 m altitude, is the oldest 'hill station' in Malaysia, MAXWELL HILL. Called **Bukit Larut** today, it's situated on the slopes of Gunung Hijau (green mountain). From the highest point, The Cottage, you can on clear days see along the whole coastline from Pulau Pangkor up to Penang. Those looking to relax in a cool climate can find relatively reasonably priced bungalows. All bookings for Maxwell Hill should be made by phone with the Superintendent, tel 886241. There are 8 bungalows** for rent.

HOW TO GET HERE
The road built by Japanese prisoners after the 2nd World War is paved, but still so bad that only Landrovers spaced in hourlong, one-way cycles between 7:00 and 18:00 h are allowed up. The ten kilometers take more than 40 minutes. They leave from the end of the Lake Garden; it costs 2 M$ up the twisting road to the Cottage.

PENANG

The tourist center of Malaysia is Pulau Pinang – the 'island of the betel palms'. This is where package tourists relax in air-conditioned luxury hotels for a few days on the beach at Batu Ferringhi. Experienced travellers gather in the numerous Chinese hotels to exchange stories on the way between India and Indonesia. Your co-authors, Stefan and Renate, had the sudden hair-brained idea of getting married here while researching the SEA Handbook.

You can stretch out on a tropical beach (even if the beaches sag under the crush of mass tourism) or enjoy the bustle of a Chinese city (with some sprinklings of Malays and Indians). Check out the remains of British colonial atmosphere, magnificently colored temples, restaurants from all over the world (offering everything from curry to steak) and hundreds of tiny shops with a wide selection of wares. The staid modern banks and insurance companies keep a low profile – this town still has character.

Since September 15, 1985 the island is connected by a 13.5 km (8.4 km over water) long bridge to the mainland. It took 1600 South Korean and Malaysian workers 3 1/2 years to complete this masterpiece of bridge building.

Pulau Pinang, as the island is called in Malay, gained its importance when the Portuguese moved into Malacca in 1511. Penang, one of the largest islands in the Strait of Malacca, became a hide-a-way for pirates. Originally the island belonged to the Sultan of Kedah, but he restricted his activities to the mainland. The island was covered by jungle and practically uninhabited when **Francis Light** of the East India Company was looking for a suitable base, east of the Bay of Bengal. Company ships damaged by monsoons had at the time to sail all the way around the southern tip of India to Bombay for repairs. A typical colonial treaty was signed with the Sultan of Kedah: Pulau Pinang would be turned over to the English in exchange for the military protection of the British Empire.

On August 11, 1786 the Union Jack was raised, and work soon began on a wooden fortress. The sky threatening cannon on the walls of Fort Cornwallis date from that time. Light had captured them from the pirates in their hideout.

By 1804, Georgetown was one of the most cosmopolitan cities in South-East Asia. The governor of the day, **Sir George Leith**, wrote: "There is not, probably, any part of the world, where in so small a space, so many different people are assembled together, or so great a variety of languages spoken."

It's best to cover downtown on foot. You'll find lots of interest on the bustling streets. The colorful street markets are still here, fortune tellers read palms under the arcades of the old houses, rickshaw drivers offer their services, the food stalls simmer. Indian and Chinese families are forced onto the streets by lack of space, as are wares from the small shops; there's hardly any room anywhere.

Start your walk at the **TOURIST OFFICE**, an area where the colonial character of the city is best preserved. **FORT CORNWALLIS** now stands on the site of Sir Francis Light's old wooden fort. Prisoners built the stone walls and buildings at the beginning of the 19th century. The huge cannon is revered by women as a fertility symbol.

On Leboh Light, corner of Leboh Pantai (Beach Street), many old **ADMINISTRATION BUILDINGS** stand behind Victorian columns. Here is the immigration office and the registry office. Across the road near the sea is the **TOWN HALL** built in traditional colonial style. The inscription on the Town Hall has by now been translated into Malay. At sundown the square in front bustles with activity.

Other British built buildings are on Jl.Farquhar, such as the **SUPREME COURT**, the **MARINER'S CLUB**, and **ST. GEORGE'S CATHEDRAL**, which in 1817 was the first Anglican church in South-East Asia. A statue of Francis Light stands in front of the **MUSEUM** next door. It's the place for people interested in the history of the British Empire in South-East Asia. The building housed the first English language public school east of Suez, established in 1816. Admission free.

Those interested in learning more about Penang's history should check out the books and other material available in the **PENANG LIBRARY** located in Dewan Sri Penang, the modern all-purpose building behind the old town hall.

One of the few still inhabited Chinese houses dating from the 18th/19th century can be found on Leboh Leith across from the Cathay Hotel. It's assumed that there're only three such buildings to be found outside China (in Manila, Jakarta, and Penang). When visiting the **CHEONG FATT TZE**, remember that the house is inhabited and not a museum.

Down Leboh Pitt, you'll find the **GODDESS OF MERCY TEMPLE**, built in 1880, whose carved roof features a fire-breathing dragon. The best time to experience Chinese temple life is during the major holidays. Often in the evening, Chinese puppet theatre is performed in front of the temple.

Life in an Indian temple is much different. Visit **SRI MARIAMMAN TEMPLE** just before Chulia Street. A few steps further on the same street is one of the largest mosques in Malaysia, the **KAPITAN KLING MOSQUE**. Work was begun at the beginning of last century, financed by a merchant from southern India. Make a small donation to the mosque and they'll give you a tour of the building, and even pray for you.
Turn left just before Leboh Aceh into a small side street. There you'll see one of the most beautiful buildings in South-East Asia, the **KHOO KONGSI**. It was built in 1906 and completely renovated in 1955 - notice the roof with all those splendidly colored porcelain figures.
Other **'kongsi'** but by no means so impressive, can be found on Leboh Armenian (Yap Kongsi) and on Jl.Burma (Khaw Kongsi, Lee Kongsi) as well on the corner of Leboh Codrington (the kongsi of Chuah, Sin and Quah).

> **KONGSI** are clan houses, built by Chinese families sharing the same name and ancestry: if they have the money. The **Khoos** are one of the most prosperous families, as can be seen by the plaques of its ancestors. They studied at the world's greatest universities.

Those who enjoy temples can visit other holy places in the city:
Take bus 4 from Leboh Victoria to Anson Road. The stop is across from the **PENANG BUDDHIST ASSOCIATION** which you can visit. Inside the old villa you'll find Italian marble and Bohemian chandeliers. A Buddhist monk had it built at the end of the 1920s. He wanted a temple dedicated to simple Buddhist teaching rather than ancestor worship, without the usual gambling, palm reading and horoscopes.

One of the world's largest reclining Buddhas, 35 m long, can be found in the Thai temple, **WAT CHAI-YAMANGA-LARAM.** Two huge temple guardians keep watch over the entrance to the temple built completely in Thai style. Numerous other Buddhas surround the central figure.

Across the way is the only **BURMESE TEMPLE** on the island. You might combine visits to these temples with a trip to Batu Ferringhi or the Botanical Garden. Take a blue bus from Jl.Maxwell and get off at the Pulau Tikus police station. The temples are on Burmah Lane, near Jl.Kelawai. Take a walk around and have a look at the many old colonial-style villas.

(1) Thai Consulate & Botanical Gdn.	(8) Supreme Court	(15) Post Office Telephone	(22) MPPP Buses
(2) Indonesian Consulate	(9) Museum	(16) Hameediyah/ Meera Restaurants	(23) green, blue and yellow Buses
(3) E & O Hotel	(10) St. George's Cathedral	(17) Swiss Hotel	(24) Khoo Kongsi
(4) Youth Hostel	(11) Fort Cornwalles	(18) Market Hall	(25) Thai Airways International
(5) Town Hall	(12) Penang Tourist Office	(19) Tye Ann Hotel	(26) KOMTAR Bldg. MAS-Office Duty-Free Shop
(6) New China Hotel	(13) Immigration Office	(20) Kaptain Kling Mosque	(27) Butterworth Ferry
(7) Cathay Hotel	(14) Goddes of Mercy Temple	(21) Sri Mariamman Temple	

PENANG 153

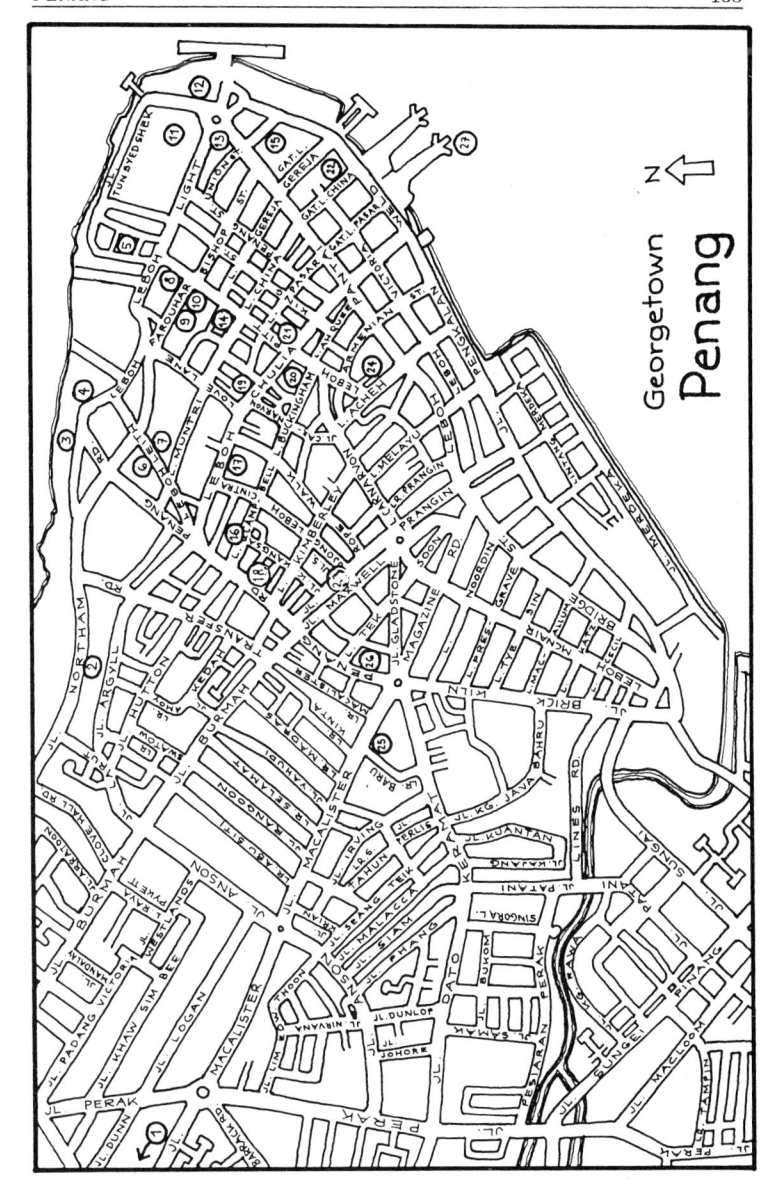

HOTELS

Hardly any other Asian city has so many hotels in every price class. According to statistics by 'International Tourist Promotion', there are 62 hotels for budget travellers and 21 for other tourists.

Most of the budget hotels are centrally located and a bit set back from the road so that they aren't too noisy. Some even have small gardens. On Leboh Chulia is the **SWISS HOTEL**** at no 431, tel 370133 or the old backpackers' hang-out **TYE ANN HOTEL****, no 282, though it's said to have run down a bit. **ENG AUN HOTEL****, no 380, tel 372333 is good. About the same is the **NOBLE HOTEL***, 36 Market Lane, tel 22372, behind the Tye Ann. Another backpacker's pitstop is the **NEW CHINA HOTEL***, 22 Leith Street, tel 61822.

Other cheap Chinese hotels are on Love Lane such as the very friendly **WAN HAI****(dorm*), no 35, tel 61421; **TEONG WAH****, no 23, tel 62057; and the good **PIN SENG HOTEL*****, no 82, tel 379004. There are many hotels on Penang Road (Jl.Pinang - don't confuse with Leboh Pinang = Penang Street), though they are pretty noisy being on a main road: **NAM KOK***, no 481B, tel 65363, **KING WAH****, no 99A, tel 62915, **WHITE HOUSE** **, no 72, tel 60142, **CAPITOL****, no 170, tel 21296 etc.

Those who want to spend more money can try **CATHAY HOTEL*****, 15 Leith Street, tel 26271, with large rooms and lots of atmosphere at affordable prices. Similar is **EMBASSY HOTEL**, a bit out of the way at 12 Burmah Road, tel 65145, an old mansion in the middle of rundown gardens.

Much has changed since the days of Somerset Maugham, though the colonial atmosphere remains (with servants in livery and dinner à la old-time England) in the **EASTERN & ORIENTAL HOTEL******, Farquhar Street, tel 63543. Rooms with a view of the sea cost about 150 M$. The old wing will be supplemented by a new building. Next to the E&O is the **YOUTH HOSTEL** where for the first night you pay 4 M$ and 3 M$ thereafter.

FOOD

Penang is probably the biggest food trip in Asia. You can eat Chinese one evening, Indian the next, Malay, Western, or even Nonya food at the urge. From the cheap foodstalls on the street to the luxury restaurants, there's something for every budget.

First the Indian for hot curry lovers: Excellent is the **HAMEEDIYAH**, 164A Leboh Campbell. We recommend the mild mutton kurma or the famous curry kapitan. Right next door is the **MEERA**, though it's not quite as good as its neighbor. On the corner of Jl.Pinang/Leboh Chulia is the **TAJ MAHAL**, a good and inexpensive establishment. A bit more expensive, though not quite as exclusive as its facade might indicate, is the **DAWOOD** at 63 Queen Street. Or try **RIO** at the corner King/Bishop Street. They have good lassi.

Everyone has their favorite among the countless Chinese restaurants. Vegetarians should check out **EE HOE CHAI**, 450 Dato Kramat Road. The **HSIANG YANG CHAP** is a good Kedai Kopi, below the Honpin Hotel on Chulia Street. Between Leboh Chulia and Campbell on Leboh Cintra is **HONGKONG**.

A fantastic mixture of Malay and Chinese food has been developed by the Nonyas or the South-East Asian Chinese. Be sure to give it a try, even if it isn't cheap, in **SUN HOE PENG**, 25 Leboh Light or **DRAGON KING**, 99 Leboh Bishop.

The typical Malay dish, Satay, can be found in many restaurants on Penang Road as well as at food stands in the **NIGHT MARKETS**. These are constantly changing their locations. During the day, many foodstalls can be found on Leboh Union by the post office as well as on Leboh Light between Penang Street and King Street. In the evening try the Esplanade, today Jl.Tun Syed Sheikh Barakbah, the square in front of the Town Hall, or Chulia Street /Jl.Campbell. A typical Penang speciality is Laksa, a clear noodle soup with a fish base and lots of fresh ingredients. Have them press you some fresh fruit juice to go with it - try something exotic like starfruit or sugarcane juice.

Another night market, rarely visited by tourists, is located a bit out of town on Gurney Drive near the circle at the end of Jl.Sultan Achmad Shah. Drinks and fruits are rather expensive, though.

Those who want to rough it up with sailors and Australian RAAF will find lots of pubs, such as the **HONGKONG BAR**, 371 Leboh Chulia or the **BOSTON PUB**, 477 Penang Road.

SHOPPING

Penang is no longer the duty free shopping paradise of days gone by. Even so you'll find a huge selection of goods; have a look for things typically Asian. Handicrafts and other Malaysian products are much more expensive in Penang than where they are made. On the other hand you'll find everything here in one place, and the selection is much larger than anywhere else.

On **JALAN PINANG**, Chinese shops, one after the other, offer everything of possible tourist interest, whether antiques or pewter products from Selangor. Mixed in you'll find Indian tailors ready to take your measure for a suit of Malay batik or Chinese silk. There are western style department stores as well as market halls for local foodstuffs (Chowrasta Food Market). And almost next door on the corner of Jl.Maxwell is a Chinese emporium offering all kinds of goods from the People's Republic of China. Next to it, street dealers offer cheap cassette recordings (make them play it first) and colorful printed T-shirts. This is one place where you really have to bargain. At the end of Penang Road is a modern Shopping Centre à la Singapore. In Kompleks Tun Abdul Razak, or **KOMTAR** for short, you'll find modern boutiques, electronic and western goods shops as well as many services. Another department store featuring a western food department is GAMA at the roundabout, 1 Jl.Dato Kramat.

The scene in the **INDIAN QUARTER** is completely different. You'll find fewer things offered, but it's no less interesting. There're crazy shops on Leboh Gereja, Leboh Pinang and Leboh Bishop. Have a look on Leboh Light, Leboh Kimberley and on Rope Walk.

Tourists can under certain conditions make duty free purchases. You must, however, leave Malaysia within two weeks, and only open the sealed packages outside the country. About 40 shops in Penang call themselves **'DUTY-FREE SHOPS'**, offering electronic goods and appliances in addition to liquors and cigarettes.

Photographers will be disappointed because **FILM** isn't a 'duty-free good' and is more expensive in Penang than elsewhere. The only possibility is a duty-free purchase when leaving the country at the airport. They don't always have adequate stores of film on hand, so check in advance with the TDC Shop, KOMTAR Building, tel 361133.

Besides the bookshop in the E&O, the English literature scene is pretty dreary. However, there are a bunch of small bookshops on Leboh Chulia near the Swiss Hotel and on Jl.Macalister dealing mostly in second hand books!

GENERAL INFORMATION
TOURIST INFORMATION - at the Tourist Office, 10 Jl.Tun Syed Sheikh Barakbah, tel 369067. There're lots of shiny brochures, plus the monthly **'Penang Tourist Tips'** and **'Penang for the Visitor'**. But there's little useful info for people on a budget.

IMMIGRATION – not as busy as in KL, nice people. Office on Leboh Pantai, corner of Union Street, tel 365122.

POST OFFICE – General Post Office on Leboh Downing, tel 366461, open Mon to Sat from 8:00 to 18:00 h. Pickpockets in the city have one nice trait: if your valuables have been stolen there's a good chance that your passport will end up in one of the city mail boxes. Check at the GPO!

TELEPHONE – the area code of Penang, Butterworth, Alor Setar, and Kangar is (04), for other regions see KL or chapter 'Mail & Telephone'. Overseas calls from the Telegraph Office (Pejabat Taligerap), tel 23492, on Leboh Downing next to the GPO, open round the clock.

BANKS – most banks are in the old administrative quarter around the GPO. Don't just compare the exchange rate, check the charges too. Some banks charge up to 6 M$ per check! Open from Mon to Fri 10:00 to 15:00 h, Sat from 10:00 to 11:30 h. Often you'll get a better rate at the

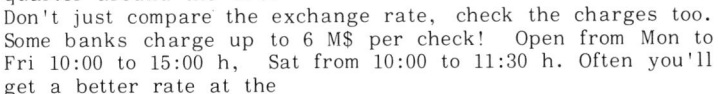

MONEY CHANGER – usually Indian, they're found mostly in the banking quarter and on Leboh Pitt. Unlike the banks, they're almost always open, and they change cash. You can bargain for the exchange rate, especially for large notes and amounts. Be sure to check in advance the rates in the newspaper and at the banks. Of interest might be the purchase of so-called weak currencies, mainly the Indian Rupee and the Indonesian Rupiah. Both countries have import restrictions on their own currencies so watch out!

AMERICAN EXPRESS – office at 8 Green Hall, Unit 2, off Leboh Light behind the Town Hall, tel 23724.

FIRST AID for police ambulance or fire department call 999 In case of emergency you ll be brought to the General Hospital on Western Road (near the pologrounds)

Otherwise there are a number of private clinics such as Medical Centre 1 Jl Pangkor tel 20731 Adventist Hospital 465 Jl Burmah tel 24134 or Mt Miramar Hospital Jl Bulan tel 366201

CONSULATES – most important for you is the Thai consulate which you have to visit for a visa The Thais want 3 passport pictures and 15 M$ Germans get their visa free
For Indonesia it s a bit more complicated For your entry via MEDAN or BELAWAN you don't need to apply for a visa in advance. Otherwise: 2 passport pictures, 200 US$ to show and a return ticket – takes one to two days for Germans it's free, all other nationalities have to pay 10 M$.

ROYAL THAI CONSULATE 1 Ayer Rajah Road tel 63377 (Bus 7). open Mon – Fri from 9:00-12:00 h and from 14:00-16:00 h.

INDONESIAN CONSULATE 37 Jl Sultan Achmad Shah tel 25162/3 (blue bus) open Mon Fri 9 00 12:00 and 14:00-16:00 h.

About the return ticket Without presenting a return ticket you will have problems getting a visa in Penang or entering Indonesia via Medan If you know your itinerary and want say to hit Lake Toba on Sumatra before returning to Penang then buy a round-trip ticket at a cheap travel agency or at AUSST with an ISIC. But if you plan to leave Indonesia by ship from Pekanbaru via Tanjung Pinang/Batam to Singapore and later return to Penang then turn in your return ticket for a refund upon return. AUSST charges 5 US$.

If you don't know what your travel plans are buy a normal return ticket to Medan in a MAS office and get it refunded later in any MAS office.

DRUGS – if you're offered hard or soft drugs on the street don't let yourself be tempted here. Many a rickshaw driver who seems to have everything from grass to skag – even in kilo quantities – reveals himself as an informant! Since drug laws in Malaysia were hardened, the death penalty has become quite frequent. So stay away from the stuff here – jail is always a bad trip

FESTIVALS – the Chinese festivals are particularly splendid in Penang. In January or February you can enjoy the CHINESE NEW YEAR including all its hectic preparations. Plus all the major temples have their own TEMPLE FESTIVALS in honor of their namesakes. The Indian THAIPUSAM celebrations provide another good reason to visit Penang in January or February. There's a colorful program during the whole month of December The high point of the PESTA PULAU PINANG are the dragonboat races. At the tourist office pick up a copy of the brochure Penang for the Visitor featuring detailed descriptions of the above festivals along with the exact dates for the coming year (moon calendar holidays vary from year to year). Walk the streets in the evening and you'll witness some family and temple festivals which are no less splendidly celebrated. Chinese opera. puppet theatre, dance and music keep the guests happy.

GETTING AROUND PENANG
Most of the time you'll be in the city center where you can get everywhere by foot. But some places do lie a bit out of the way so you'll need to use public transportation.

TRISHAWS – the bicycle rickshaws are the perfect way to get around downtown – you sit in front of the driver and have a perfect view of the road including all its dangers. Bargain for the price in advance because the first one offered is always too high! Foreigners seem to have a hard time here. A ride should cost about 1.20 M$ per kilometer. A full hour should cost 6.-M$.

TAXIS – though most vehicles have a meter installed, it's almost always said to be broken. The first mile costs 70 c, each additional half mile is 30 c. Waiting is set at 20 c for each 8 minutes. If you rent a taxi, the rate is 4 M$ for the first half hour and 1 M$ for each additional 15 minutes.

BUSES – five different bus companies serve the city and island. The MPPP buses all leave from Leboh Victoria except buses 8, 12, and 13. Take bus 7 to the Botanical Garden, bus 8 to Penang Hill. and bus 11 to the Aquarium. An exact listing of the bus routes can be found in **KL** – **Penang This Month'** or **'Penang for the Visitor'**. Prices vary according to distance from 15 c and 85 c.

Green, blue and yellow buses leave from Jl.Maxwell. You can catch the blue to Batu Ferringhi and Telok Bahang. The yellow go south to the airport, Snake Temple etc.

RENTAL CARS / MOTORBIKES
It's worth getting three or four people together to split costs and rent a car for a tour of the island, if you've the nerve to steer a car through the bustling streets of Penang. Those with some cash can even rent a car in Penang to tour Malaysia and return it in Singapore.

Here is a list of companies:
AVIS, Penang Bowl Bldg., 38/6 Leboh Farquhar, tel 361685.
HERTZ, 38/7 Leboh Farquar, tel 375914.
ISLAND TAXI & TOUR AGENCY, 40 Leboh Ah Quee, tel 372481.
MAYFLOWER ACME TOURS, 8 Green Hall, tel 23724.
SINTAT, Lone Pine Hotel, Batu Ferringhi, tel 811101.

Ask about special rates and compare prices. Hertz offers a weekend rate (Fri 17:00 h till Mon 08:00 h plus 200 km) for 125.-M$ in a Suzuki SS80.

Rent motorbikes for about 25 M$ a day in the Wan Hai Hotel or other hotels.

FERRIES - although the impressive bridge to the mainland is completed, ferries still scurry round the clock between Penang and Butterworth.

During the day they come and go every 7-10 minutes, in the night between 24:00 and 7:00 h they leave less frequently. The ferry from Butterworth to Penang is free of charge. Going back you pay 40 c, cars cost 4 to 6 M$ according to size.
The dock is at Pengkalan Weld. Long distance buses and trains leave right from the dock in Butterworth.

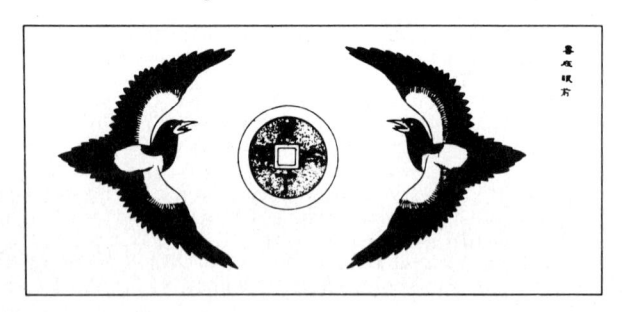

DAYTRIPS AROUND GEORGETOWN
PENANG HILL
Take bus 91 from Maxwell Road for 50 c to the end station AYER ITAM. On the way you pass the corner of Jl.Ayer Itam and Green Lane and the **MOSQUE** of the State of Penang, well constructed in a modern style. You have a good view from the top of its 57 m high minaret.
From Ayer Itam, take bus 8 (25 c) to the funicular railway station (Lower Station). Every half hour the car leaves on the 24 minute trip up 817 m. A return ticket costs

3 M$. Paths and stairs will take you even further up PENANG HILL.

You have a beautiful view of Georgetown, the island of Penang and in good weather even of the mountains of Kedah and Pahang. Twice a week the funicular railway runs late into the night. It's worth it to stay and check out the night-time panorama. At the top are a restaurant and hotel. It is 6° C cooler than in the city – the wonderfully colored vegetation reflects this.

A well-marked footpath leads down the other side to the Botanical Garden – takes about 1 hour. Nice countryside!

KEK LOK SI TEMPLE

From the Lower Station, you can go by foot to KEK LOK SI TEMPLE. The pagoda of the ten thousand Buddhas dominates the village of Ayer Itam. However, most of these Buddhas are only pictures on the wall tiles. A donation is often expected at the temple.

The temple complex is one of the most important Buddhist monasteries in Malaysia. The abbot of the Goddess of Mercy Temple on Leboh Pitt came from China in 1885; the Ayer Itam landscape reminded him of his homeland. He began collecting money from rich Chinese merchants. With it the huge terraced temple was built. On the way up you pass a turtle pond. Hundreds of turtles stick out their long necks and wait for 'kangkong' – a green vegetable, sold by dealers nearby. For the Chinese, the turtle is a symbol of long life.

The pagoda is built in three different styles: the lower according to Chinese design, the middle section is Thai-Buddhist, and the upper level's spiral shape is Burmese. In the upper section, which is closed to visitors, real treasure is guarded including a Buddha relic, a statue made of pure gold, diamonds and silver coins.

BOTANICAL GARDEN

Take bus 7, leaves every 30 minutes from Leboh Victoria. On the way you pass through the colonial villa quarter.

The BOTANICAL GARDEN is a popular place, and the crowds reflect this on weekends. It is situated in a valley surrounded by jungle covered hills. Right at the entrance, a huge pack of monkeys waits for you to buy a packet of peanuts which they'll quickly rid you of. Greenhorns will enjoy the walk through the small natural jungle section! Plus, there is a tiny zoo with three sun bears and some deer.

NATTUKOTTAI CHETTIAR TEMPLE

About a kilometer before the Botanical Garden on Waterfall Road is the NATTUKOTTAI CHETTIAR TEMPLE. It's the largest and most famous Hindu temple on the island. The Thaipusam festival in February is celebrated here in style. The ceilings are decorated with numerous Indian pictures.

ROUND TRIP OF THE ISLAND

For just 4 M$ you can cover the whole 74 km route around Pulau Pinang. Unless you make a long stop, the round trip should take about 4-5 hours. If there's a group of you, you could rent a car and split the expenses.

The counter-clockwise tour: First take a blue bus to **BATU FERRINGHI** (mile 10) and then transfer onto another blue bus to
TELOK BAHANG (mile 12). From here there are relatively few buses to
BALIK PULAU (mile 25). If it's not running, you could try hitchhiking. From here, there are also yellow buses 65c and 66 via
TELOK KUMBAR (mile 33), past
BAYAN LEPAS AIRPORT (mile 35), and the
SNAKE TEMPLE (mile 37) back to Georgetown.

And the less travelled clockwise tour:

Start on the yellow bus 66 or 65c to the **SNAKE TEMPLE**, easily recognized by the souvenir stands. The snake temple was built in 1850. Snakes were said to be the disciples of the god Chor Soo Kong, to whom the temple is dedicated. Very poisonous wagler pit vipers dazed by incense laze around sleepily in the temple - don't touch! Just for the tourists, a few of the snakes have had their fangs pulled, convenient for photo opportunities.

At the **BAYAN LEPAS AIRPORT** a road cuts off left to the fishing village of **BATU MAUNG** where you can enjoy excellent seafood. Otherwise there's a foot print of the famous Chinese admiral Cheng Ho who is said to have landed here and to whom a small shrine is dedicated. The yellow buses serve this village as well.

In **TELOK KUMBAR**, take the branch off to **GERTAK SANGGOL**, bus 78 and 80. There are beaches here, but they are packed on weekends and most of the time dirty. Nice hike from here to **PULAU BETONG** on the west coast of the island. Take yellow bus back to Balik Pulau.

PENANG 163

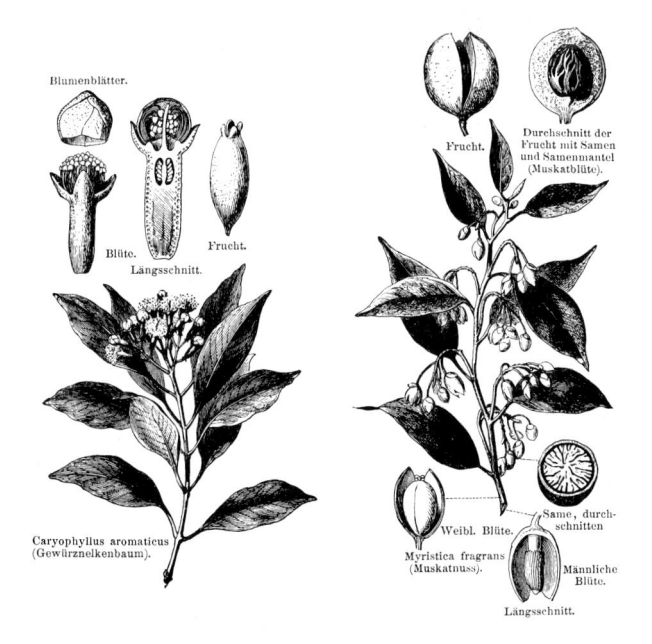

Back to Telok Kumbar - the road winds up into the mountains with its terrific landscape and wonderful views. On the slopes, cloves and nutmeg are planted. Across the way are rubber plantations.

BALIK PULAU is the last stop for the yellow bus. Only four or five times a day, the last at 16:00 h, bus 76 goes up to Telok Bahang.

Another sideroad goes down to **PANTAI ACEH** (bus 75), a small fishing village. A few kilometers beyond the branch-off, you can bathe under the **TITI KRAWAN WATERFALL** - but don't expect anything overwhelming!

TELOK BAHANG is a village inhabited mainly by Malabar fishermen. At the western end of the village there's a footpath to **MUKAH HEAD**, the northwestern tip of the island. A number of fishing boats are tied up to a jetty stretching far out to sea. Notice how the catch is unloaded! If you don't mind the smell of fish, you might even find a room here.

Just beyond the crossroads to Balik Pulau on the right is a Malay kampong where batik is made and sold at inflated prices to tourists. Across the way is an orchid nursery (1 M$ admission).

Nearby, about 100 ha of forest has been declared a nature preserve because numerous types of Malay trees which grow here. Great museum! **(MUZIUM PERHUTANAN)** There're several pools in a stream where you can swim, plus marked hiking paths. Then go on with the blue bus.

BATU FERRINGHI, meaning 'Portuguese rock', is the tourist center of Penang today. Highrise hotels plaster the area; just look at the travel brochures. And ughh, the prices! At least the beach is several kilometers long. Relatively cheap, meaning not quite 100.-M$, are the rooms in LONE PINE HOTEL, tel 811511. The top hotels are RASA SAYANG, GOLDEN SANDS, and HOLIDAY INN. In the hotel restaurants you can enjoy international fare from steaks to seafood, as far as your budget will stretch. Between the Holiday Inn and Casuarina Hotel you'll find reasonably priced foodstalls and restaurants. Or stay in ALI'S GUESTHOUSE** right on the beach. They serve good and cheap food too.

The last village before Georgetown is **TANJONG BUNGAH**. We can't recommend the beach, but there are a few cheap hotels and good seafood restaurants, try EDEN HOTEL**.

LEAVING PENANG
INTERNATIONAL FLIGHTS
Bayan Lepas Airport is about 18 km south of town. Yellow buses leave from Jl.Maxwell for 85 c; a coupon-taxi costs 13.50 M$. The airport tax is 15 M$ for international flights, 10 M$ to Singapore and Brunei, and 7 M$ for domestic flights.
SAMPLE PRICES for flights to neighboring countries:
THAILAND: (MAS or Thai Airways) HAADYAI 83.-, PHUKET 106.-, BANGKOK 304.-M$.
INDONESIA: (MAS and GARUDA) MEDAN tickets for the half hour long flight cost about 110 M$.

Flights from Penang to Europe and Australia are relatively cheap. Check in the cheap travel agencies, be sure to ask about student discounts and compare prices!
If you have an International Student Identity Card (ISIC), you can save even more at: AUSST, c/o MSL-Travel, Hotel Merlin, 25A Leboh Farquhar, tel 24748/49.

Here's a list of the most important airline offices:
CATHAY PACIFIC, AIA Bldg., 88 Leboh Bishop, tel 370411.
GARUDA, Mandarin Arcade, 202 Jl.Macalister, tel 365257.
MAS, KOMTAR-Bldg., Jalan Pinang, tel 21403.
THAI AIRWAYS INTER, Wisma Central, Jl.Macalister, tel 64848.
THAI AIRWAYS CO.LTD., 9 Pengkalan Weld, tel 67633.
SIA, Wisma Penang Garden, 42 Jl.Sultan Achmad Shah, tel 363201.

DOMESTIC FLIGHTS
Only of interest to East Malaysia and for those in a real hurry:
IPOH 41.-, KOTA BHARU 72.-, KL 86.- (61.-), SINGAPORE 150.-, KUALA TRENGGANU 80.- (3x a week), LANGKAWI 65.-M$.

BY TRAIN
Trains leave from Butterworth Railway Station. You can get tickets in Penang at the ferry terminal (Railway Booking

Station - tel 360290) or at Butterworth Station, tel 342274.
Six trains leave daily to KL. To the north there's an international express to Bangkok on Mon, Wed, and Fri and from Bangkok on Mon, Wed, and Sat. In addition there's a regular train at 6:00 h to Haad Yai (arrival 11:35 h).

Sample one-way prices second class (third class):
TAIPING 4.90 (3.10), IPOH 9.20 (5.80), KL 19.90 (12.50), JOHORE BHARU 38.30 (24.-), SINGAPORE 39.30 (24.60), KUALA LIPIS 39.80 (24.90), HAAD YAI 10.60, BANGKOK 39.30 M$.

Ekspres Rakyat/Ekspress Sinaran (dept. 7:30 h and 15:00 h) cost 15.50/26.-ac M$.

OVERLAND BUSES / OVERLAND TAXIS

They all leave from Butterworth bus station where the ferry docks. You can get your tickets in advance to KL or Singapore at a travel agency or a hotel in Penang. When booking in Penang, you'll sometimes be charged a 5.-M$ commission. The local buses leave quite often making advance bookings unnecessary.

SAMPLE PRICES for buses and (overland taxis):
KL 12.70, ac 14.70 (27.-), SINGAPORE 30.-, JOHORE BHARU 29.- (60.-), ALOR STAR 3.25 (7.80), TAIPING 3.50 (7.25), IPOH 5.50 (13.50), MALACCA 17.50, ac 21.40, KUALA KANGSAR 4.- (9.40), KUALA PERLIS 6.- (12.-), LUMUT 8.- (15.25), PADANG BESAR (14.50), KOTA BHARU (daily 9:30 and 10:00 h with MARA) 18.- (36.-) M$.

Several times a week there're direct buses via HAADYAI (20.-) to KO SAMUI (48.-) and PHUKET (42.-). Get your ticket in one of the backpacker's hotels.

BY SHIP

One last passenger ship, the CHIDAMBARAM, leaves regularly from here for the 5 day run to MADRAS, and sometimes on to TRINCOMALEE (Sri Lanka). It docks every three weeks in Penang and normally follows the course Madras - Nagappattinam - Trincomalee - Penang - Port Kelang - Singapore - Penang and back. If you're planning this trip, get further information in advance from the agent of the Shipping Corporation of India Ltd.: R.Jumabhoy & Sons, 39 Green Hall, tel 363616.

The GADIS LANGKASUKA is a new ship, leaving at Swettenham Pier in Georgetown for PULAU LANGKAWI (prices: 35.-M$ per person, 10.-M$ motorbike, 100.-M$ car up to a length of 5 m) and since 1985 also to BELAWAN (Sumatra) and PHUKET. Check it with the travel agents in Penang.

FROM PENANG TO PADANG BESAR

The two northernmost states in Malaysia, **Kedah** and **Perlis**, are generally just pitstops for travellers on the road between Haad Yai and Penang. Together these two states are the rice basket of Malaysia. The plain encompassing Alor Setar and Kangar is situated just a couple meters above sea level. Originally this was swamp and mangrove country. But after the turn of the century, countless dams and canals dried things out making it suitable for planting wet rice. In the mountainous areas further inland, the rubber plantations begin again. In Perlis, near the Thai border, the climate is greatly influenced by the monsoons, meaning pronounced dry and rainy seasons.

Archaeological finds confirm the existence of a Buddhist, Indian empire here between the 2nd and 10th century AD. **Langkasuka** stretched right across the Malay Peninsula. Within its sphere of influence lay one of the earliest trade routes between the Bay of Bengal and the Gulf of Thailand. But unlike its geographical neighbors, Malaysia boasts few cultural monuments, intwining the lost kingdom in fairytale and legend.

BUTTERWORTH
A less than interesting harbor town with lots of industry. There's a Royal Australian Airforce base, which under terms of the Five Power Defence Agreement (Singapore, Malaysia, Australia, New Zealand, UK) is home to two squadrons of Mirage fighters. For this reason you meet a lot of Australians, especially in the bars and pubs of Georgetown. Should you want to spend the night here, you'll find a cheap (but not very good) hotel at the circle about five minutes from the station.

For connections to and from Butterworth, see 'Penang' above. Just outside of Butterworth you'll see the first signs for a branch off the new East-West Highway. The first stretch, along narrow secondary roads (follow the signs), runs through a thickly populated rice-growing region and lots of rubber plantations.

SUNGEI PATANI
36 km to the north, right on the main road. In Sungei Patani the real main road branching off the East-West Highway

begins, leading also to Yala and Patani in Thailand. Notice the clock tower downtown. Otherwise there's little to see.

PANTAI MERDEKA
West of Sungei Patani is a lovely beach. Malay families like to picnic under the casuarina trees and enjoy the cool breeze. No public transport comes out here. If you've got a car or motorbike, take the branch off the main road in Tikam Batu toward Kampong Kuala Muda. The 13 km ride runs through pretty Malay kampongs and past seemingly endless rice fields.

Gunung Jerai

A few miles north of Sungei Patani, 40 km south of Alor Setar, the 1330 m high Gunung Jerai towers over the flatlands. On the slopes of this limestone mountain, archaeological finds have been made leading to inferences about the Langkasuka Kingdom. Excavations of a number of temples, forts and audience halls began in 1936 on the banks of the Sungei Bujang, a tributary the Sungei Merbok. The finds show both Hindu and Buddhist influences and can be seen at the National Museum in KL as well as in the tiny **MUSEUM** at the foot of the mountain. The new museum with explanations in both English and Malay is open daily from 10:00 to 17:00 h, but closed on Friday during prayer time from 12:45 to 14:45 h, admission free.

The best known site is **CANDI BUKIT BATU PAHAT**, just above the museum. There was a Shiva temple here during the 7th or 8th century near the waterfall, which was probably a holy spot to bathe. In the temple, a bronze Shiva statue and silver caskets full of sapphires and rubies were discovered. Plus there are the remains of several other temples, some of which have been brought here from other sites. Don't expect finds on the scale seen in Java or Thailand; it's really just the foundation ruins. Get a Mara bus for 1.30 M$ from Sungei Patani to **KG.MEROBOK**. From there, taxis to the museum cost 1.80 M$. It's located about 2 1/2 km north of the village on the slope of Gunung Jerai.

The peak of Gunung Jerai can best be reached from the northeast. A few kilometers north of **GURUN**, on the main Sungei Patani - Alor Setar road , there's a winding 11 km road to the top. Beautiful mountain forest! Try to get a lift with one of the Landrovers which drive from the bottom to the resthouse. A night's rest costs 90 M$ or 100.-M$ in the

new bungalows. But there's only room for 8 people. To register write:
Perbadanan Kemajuan Negeri Kedah (Kedah State Development Corporation), Bangunan UKIR, Jl.Tunku Ibrahim, Peti Surat 140, Alor Setar, Kedah, tel 722455 or 722636.

When the weather's good, you've a great view of the northern coastal plains and the sea. About 2 km below the resthouse, you can do some hiking on the well-marked paths over the slopes - very pleasant in the cool high-altitude climate.

Keroh

Located just 4 km from the border to Thailand, this is the Malaysian checkpoint. The border region is still an area of guerilla activity by the MCP (Malayan Communist Party). Fighting across the border in Thailand are Muslim separatists as well as units of the Communist Party of Thailand. When things get hot they can always slip cross the border into the neighboring country. Under a treaty signed in 1975, the security forces of both countries are permitted to cross the border.

You have to check for yourself the momentary situation for travel into the interior. The road from **YALA** to **BETONG** in Thailand and on to Keroh is open during the day and used by taxis. You'll probably have to spend the night in Keroh if you want to take this unusual route into Thailand. There is a RESTHOUSE**, tel 23722 and some cheap hotels.

Another road, also within the MCP activity range, runs south from Keroh to the big North-South-Road just before Kuala Kangsar. Until Gerik, 50 km south of Keroh, the road is in very poor condition and winding. Then the road goes on through jungles and mountains (one bus daily) to **TASEK CHENDEROH**. The lake, formed by the Perak River, is a poor place to bathe due to its overgrown, swampy banks. In the background are the high, jungle-covered mountains, with now and again a fishing boat - wonderful scenery!

Gerik

Gerik, with its market, numerous shops, and the last gas station before the highway, is the most important town on the route. In the area are several Orang Asli villages which, however, you can't visit on your own. North of town, the East-West-Highway branches off to Kota Bharu, a route which is finally finished after many years of construction.

HOTELS
For those wanting to spend the night, **ROME****, 1 Jl.Tan Saban, tel 885242 is the most expensive place. Everything else is*, such as **BEE LOON** at no 3 and others on Jl.Takong Datoh. **ENG WAH** at no 7 serves good food.

HOW TO GET HERE
All together, 10 years were spent building this road connecting the east and west of Malaysia. Construction equipment was frequently blown up, and guerilla attacks on work teams weren't uncommon. The costs ran to 360 million M$, and are certain to rise since repairs are constantly necessary. It was built with a total disregard for the facts of nature, right through the jungle - whole mountains were torn down and huge breakfires set. Its importance for the infrastructure of the country is enormous. Before completion, in order to get from Penang to Kota Bharu, one had to make a tremendous detour via KL and Kuantan - all together more than 1000 km. That's now been cut to 365 km.

Even today the route isn't completely void of danger, which is why the road's western entrance is closed after

FROM PENANG TO PADANG BESAR   171

16:00 h. A section of the road between Gerik and Jeli, which
is only open to traffic from 07:00 to 19:00 h, is protected by
military encampments every five miles.

   A taxi to Kota Bharu costs 16 M$ per person.   The bus
to KL costs 11.50 M$ (ac 14 M$).   Mara express offers a
direct connection daily to PENANG - KOTA BHARU.

Alor Setar

This sultan's seat and capital of Kedah has developed in the
last few years into the business and trading center of

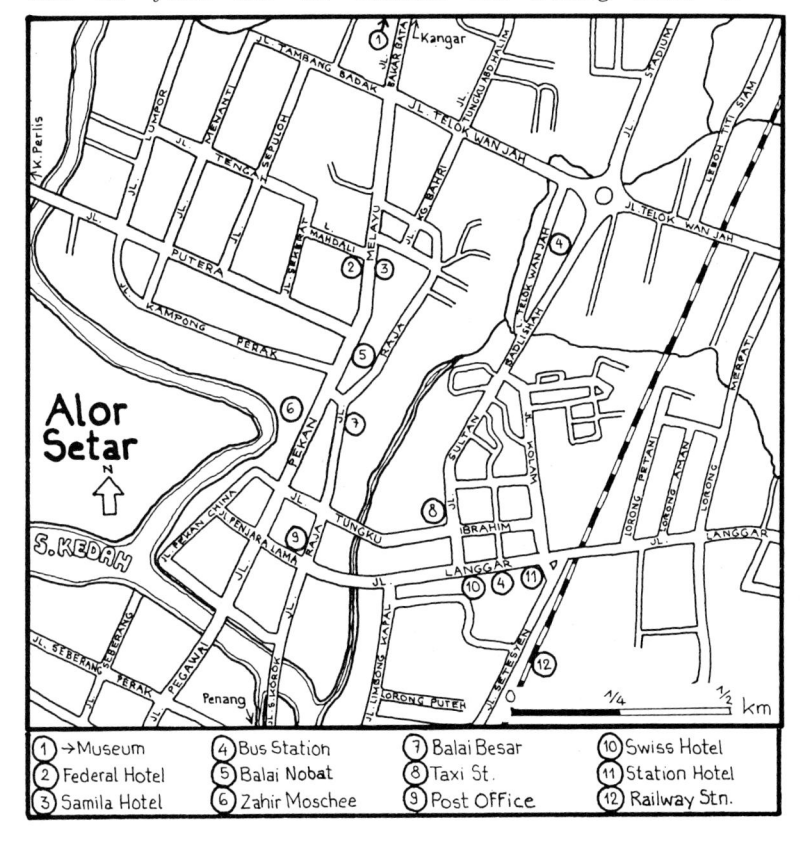

```
① → Museum      ④ Bus Station    ⑦ Balai Besar    ⑩ Swiss Hotel
② Federal Hotel ⑤ Balai Nobat    ⑧ Taxi St.       ⑪ Station Hotel
③ Samila Hotel  ⑥ Zahir Moschee  ⑨ Post Office    ⑫ Railway Stn.
```

northwest Malaysia. Like the rest of the west coast, the ethnic Chinese can be seen at a glance to form the majority of the city population.

Most important buildings surround the main square: the **ZAHIR MOSQUE** is, next to Kuala Kangsar, probably the most beautiful oriental mosque in the country; the **BALAI BESAR**, meaning 'the great hall', where still today the sultan holds audiences on special occasions; and the **BALAI NOBAT**, which is 400 years old and the home of the royal orchestra. Its instruments consist of drums, kettle drums, gongs and a trumpet. Be sure to check out the small **MUSEUM** on the main road to the north built in the same style as the Balai Besar. The exhibits include a large collection of archaeological finds from around Kedah.

If you have the time, you might make an excursion to **KUALA KEDAH**. Buses and taxis leave regularly. The city (!) at the mouth of the Kedah River was already an important port for trade with India a thousand years ago. The ruins of an old fort, built between 1771 and 1780, can be seen. Kuala Kedah is well known for its many, reasonably priced, seafood restaurants.

HOTELS

On the side streets between the taxi stand and the bus station are many cheap Chinese hotels. **SWISS HOTEL*** is cheap, but loud and infested. You're better off in **STATION HOTEL****, Jl.Langgar, tel 723855; or in **LIM KUNG***, 36A Jl.Langgar, tel 722459. On Jl.Kancut there are two more expensive establishments: **FEDERAL HOTEL*****, no 429 and the rather filthy **SAMILA HOTEL******, no 27, tel 722344. You can eat cheaply in the Indian shops on Jl. Langgar and in the foodstalls behind the bus station.

LEAVING ALOR SETAR

From the Central Bus Station you have connections in all directions: bus to PENANG for 3.25 (ac 7.80); 1 1/2 hours, KL 19.50 (ac 20.-), SINGAPORE 34.-(ac 40.-), KUALA PERLIS 2.20, IPOH 10.-M$.

The taxis are faster and more comfortable. Price: PENANG 7.80, KL 32.-, KUALA PERLIS 3.50, KOTA BHARU via Gerik 26.-M$.

The train station is on Jl.Setesen corner of Jl.Langgar., tel 731798. The express train from Bangkok to Butterworth stops here as well. In addition there's a daily train to Haad Yai in Thailand. Stopping also in Padang Besar, the

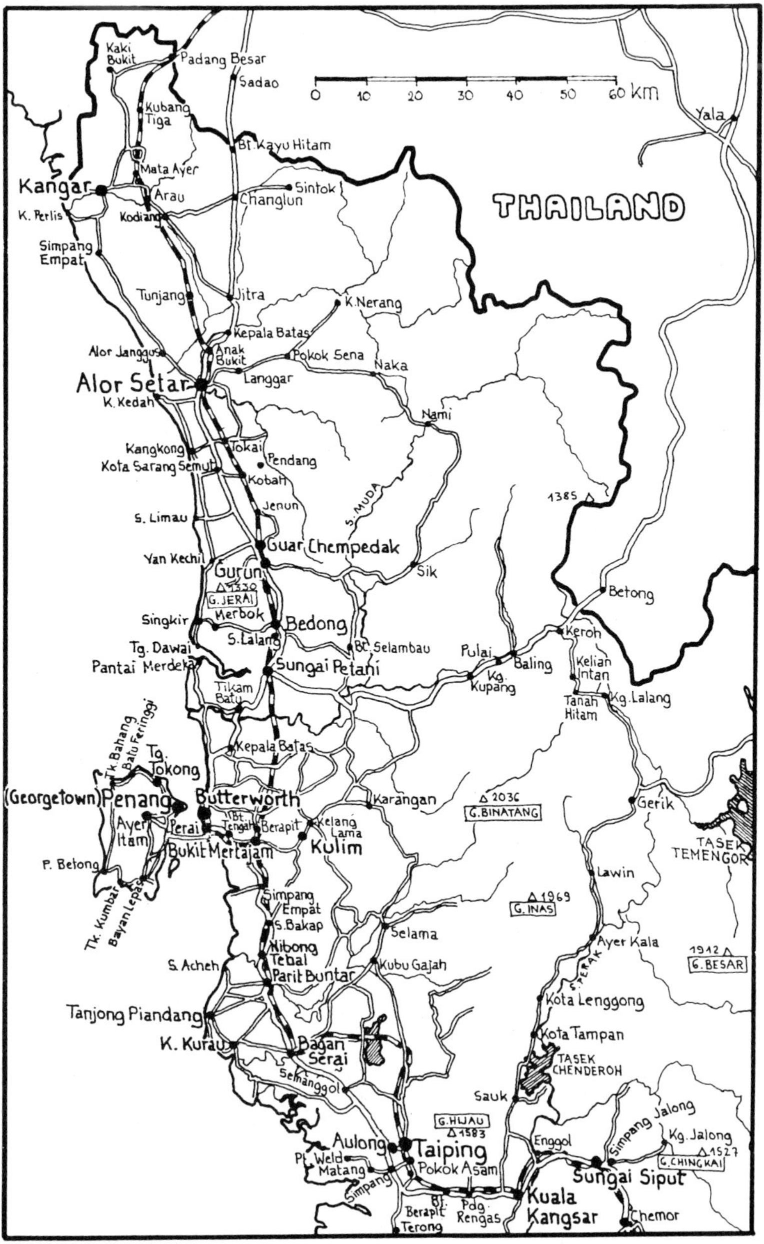
THAILAND
0 10 20 30 40 50 60 KM
Kaki Bukit
Padang Besar
Sadao
Kubang Tiga
Bt. Kayu Hitam
Yala
Mata Ayer
Kangar
Arau
Sintok
Changlun
K. Perlis
Kodiang
Simpang Empat
Tunjang
Jitra
K. Nerang
Kepala Batas
Alor Janggus
Anak Bukit
Pokok Sena
Naka
Alor Setar
Langgar
K. Kedah
Nami
Kangkong
Tokai
Pendang
Kota Sarang Semut
Kobah
1385
Jenun
S. MUDA
S. Limau
Guar Chempedak
Yan Kechil
Gurun
Sik
1330
G. JERAI
Betong
Merbok
Singkir
Bedong
Keroh
S. Lalang
Tg. Dawai
Bt. Selambau
Pulai
Baling
Pantai Merdeka
Sungai Petani
Kelian Intan
Kg. Kupang
Tikam Batu
Tanah Hitam
Kg. Lalang
Tk. Bahang
Batu Feringgi
Kepala Batas
Tg. Tokong
(Georgetown) Penang
Butterworth
Karangan
2036
G. BINATANG
Gerik
Bt. Tengah
Ayer Itam
Perai
Berapit
Kelang Lama
Kulim
Bukit Mertajam
TASEK TEMENGOR
P. Betong
Lawin
Tk. Kumbar
Bayan Lepas
Simpang Empat
1969
G. INAS
S. Bakap
Selama
Nibong Tebal
Ayer Kala
1912
G. BESAR
S. Acheh
Kubu Gajah
S. PERAK
Parit Buntar
Kota Lenggong
Tanjong Piandang
Kota Tampan
K. Kurau
Bagan Serai
TASEK CHENDEROH
Semanggol
Sauk
G. HIJAU
1583
Simpang Jalong
Aulong
Taiping
Enggol
Kg. Jalong
1527
Pt. Weld
G. CHINGKAI
Matang
Pokok Asam
Sungai Siput
Simpang
Bt. Berapit
Pdg. Rengas
Kuala Kangsar
Terong
Chemor

train leaves at 8:38 h (fare: 2nd/3rd cl. - 5.10 or 3.20 M$).
In the opposite direction to Butterworth the train departs at
16:55 h.

From the airport 11 km away, you can get flights to
KOTA BHARU 59.-, KL 94.-M$.

KANGAR
The capital of the smallest sultanate in Malaysia, **Perlis** -
806 km^2, 147,000 inhabitants. This is a sleepy nest without a
lot to offer. You could take a trip to **ARAU**, the sultan's
seat, and check out the Istana and royal mosque. If you
want to spend the night, an alternative to the hotels is the
RESTHOUSE****, Jl.Kangar, tel 751183. Cheaper, however, are
BAN CHEONG***, 79A Main Road, tel 751074 and the HOTEL
KANGAR*, near the bus station.

Several times a day longboats leave from KUALA PERLIS to
SATUN in South Thailand. It takes 1 1/2 hours and costs
3 M$.

Pulau Langkawi

This island group in the northwest of Malaysia consists of 99
tiny islands. The largest is **Pulau Langkawi**, twice as large
as Penang with a port at **Kuah**. On the island are many
rubber plantations, tropical forests, fishing villages and
sandy beaches - in short a miniature Malaysia. Some of the
tiny islands are really just coral reefs; others with limestone cliffs are covered by jungle. Most have beautiful sandy
beaches and are unpopulated. Langkawi is a good place to
kick back and relax. This knowledge has got around among
overworked Malaysians, so during school vacations it's hard
to find an empty room. Outside the high season, there's no
problem.

The island figures in many tales and legends. Including a curse by Princess Mahsuri upon being condemned to
death: "For seven generations this island shall not prosper!"
Seven generations have long since passed, but even the construction of Langkawi Country Club hasn't brought prosperity. But that's due to change. In a major effort by the government and a number of private companies, the island will
be transformed into a tourist center. Construction began in
1983. Plans call for airport expansion, a hospital, several
hotels and a new center of town, all for just 3 billion M$.

FROM PENANG TO PADANG BESAR 175

KUAH
The largest town on the island with about 2000 inhabitants consists of a collection of apartment buildings, shops, and hotels along the main road running parallel to the coast. This is a sleepy little harbor, until the construction boom arrived. It's your departure point for tours of the island and ferries to other islands.

HOTELS
Not far from the ferry is the **LANGKAWI COUNTRY CLUB****, tel 749209, rooms however run 70 M$ and up. The prices seem to reflect the comfort offered. On the way to Kuah, you'll pass the **RESTHOUSE**** at the entrance to the village next to the mosque, right on the sea. The village has three hotels: **LANGKAWI HOTEL**** (tel 749248), **HOTEL ASIA**** (tel 749216) and **FAIRWINDS HOTEL****, all with about the same standard. At the end of town there's a cheapie. It is, however, 3 km from the ferry, so you'll have to take the bus for 40 c. Tell the busdriver to stop in Pokok Assam. **MOTEL MALAYSIA*** is on the right side. Mr. Velu, the owner, is very helpful. Good food! He rents bicycles, organizes cheap taxis as well as boat trips to the outlying islands. During your round trip of the island you might also ask in the villages about some accomodations offered there.

FOOD
Mr. Velu (mentioned above) serves excellent Indian food. There are also Indian foodstalls and other foods at the food market on the main road. Many hotel restaurants serve Chinese food.

GETTING AROUND LANGKAWI
BY BUS - quite irregular and undependable. Four buses daily starting at 9:00 h leave Kuah for Tanjung Rhu. Costs 1.15 M$. Last bus back at 19:00 h.

BY TAXI - about 40 taxis drive on the 100 km of paved road. They charge 8 M$ per hour or 30 M$ per day. If there's four of you, it's a good deal.

BY MOTORBIKE - the perfect way to get around. The roads are well paved and there's hardly any traffic. Careful you don't run down one of the huge monitor lizards which sprawl on the road sunning themselves. Small Honda 75 or 90s can be rented for 15 M$ per day at a shop (hairdresser's) near the three hotels.

BY BICYCLE - costs 2.50 M$ per day. Pick it up the night before, so that you can head out early, since you should rest during the heat of the day; the shop doesn't open till 9:30 h. You can cover the all paved roads by bike in 3 or 4 days. Although the highest mountain, Gunung Raya, is almost 1000 m high, there are hardly any really steep stretches on the few paved roads.

BY BOAT - to snoop around the other islands you can rent a boat at the village jetty for the whole day (10:00 to 18:00 h). After a lot of bargaining, expect to pay about 90 M$. Carries up to 20 people. So try to get all of the travellers to go in with you. At the Langkawi Country Club, horrendous prices are charged for boat trips.

To get to know Pulau Langkawi, you shouldn't just hang around Kuah, which is pretty much always the same. Here are some ideas for excursions:

ROUND TRIP OF THE ISLAND
A round trip of the island can be done in one day on a Honda. By bicycle, of course, think two days. If you've got some time, do some excursions to the various beaches.

PANTAI TENGAH - 18 km from Kuah, is the nearest beach at the southwest of the island. Take the road to the west and

FROM PENANG TO PADANG BESAR 177

go left at the golf course. After about 14 km, a road branches off to TEMONYONG, a small dreary fishing village at the southern tip of the island. To the right of the road, about 1 km from town, there's a beautiful white sandy beach featuring offshore islands. The fishermen rent bungalows. Get there by bus right to the branch-off or straight to TEMONYONG.

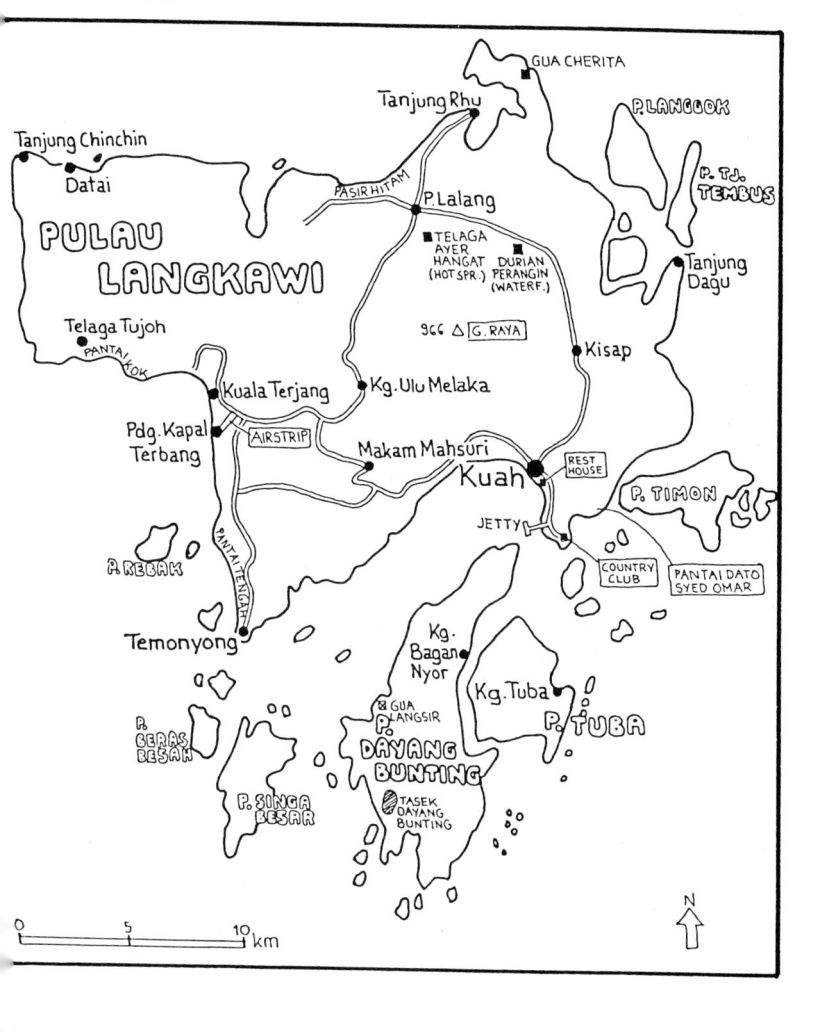

About 400 m north of Pantai Tengah round the cliff is PANTAI CENANG - nice sandy beach

MAHSURI TOMB (MAKAM MAHSURI) - 11 km from Kuah, take a right at the golf course. In the village is the grave of a Muslim woman with the typical flat, curved tombstone and a memorial plaque.

PADAN MATSIRAT - 7 km up the road, was once the main village on the island. Burned rice is still found in excavations, where the inhabitants once buried their entire rice harvest. Ask the way to **PADANG BERAS TERBAKAR** - the place of the burned rice.

> Princess Mahsuri was condemned to death for alleged adultery. Her husband was often away on trips, and the beautiful princess became friends with a young poet. For this reason her mother-in-law had her charged with adultery. Though she always protested her innocence, she was sentenced to death. On the 22nd of January 1355, she was executed, as you can read on her tombstone. Her curse, that the island would suffer seven generations of poverty, soon became reality: The Thais attacked the island, killing, plundering and burning. They burned Matsirat and razed the village to the ground.

KUALA TERIANG - 22 km from Kuah is a small fishing village. Here too is the island's airport. From Kuala Teriang, you can take a hike to the seven springs **(TELAGA TUJUH)**. Take along something to drink on the 8 km hike. A small pond splatters into seven tiny pools lying one after the other. From Kuala Teriang, head right across the island, north, past the 'burned rice', through the lovely jungle.

PANTAI HITAM (the BLACK BEACH) - at the completely unexpected roundabout, take a left. After 3 km you reach the beach which has little to offer other than black sand.

TANJUN RHU - 23 km from Kuah, head north at the roundabout, at the end of the road is a beautiful beach with lots of casuarina trees. When the tide's out, you can walk over to the island - remember to head back in time! At high tide in the evening they get big waves on the beach. Careful when swimming; the currents are dangerous. At the beach are the bungalows of Tanjong Rhu Merlin and a restaurant. If at the roundabout you were to take a right, you'd pass through rubber plantations and past Indian worker's houses on your way back to Kuah.

EXCURSIONS TO THE NEIGHBORING ISLANDS
PULAU DAYANG BUNTING - the 'Island of the Pregnant Girl' - you can get to the second largest island by rented boat in about 45 minutes. There's a beautiful fresh water lake, not far from the beach, where it's said a girl who'd long remained childless became pregnant after bathing in the waters.

PULAU SINGA BESAR - **PULAU BERAS BESAH** - there are good coral reefs between the two islands. The beaches are second to none and unspoiled - right behind them it's jungle.

LEAVING LANGKAWI
To the ferry in Kuah, you'll have to take the bus for 40 c or walk 2 km. The ferry leaves twice a day from Kuah to Kuala Perlis, during high season more often. Departure time in Kuah is at 8:00, 10:00, 10:30, 11:30, 12:15 and 13:30 h and in Kuala Perlis at 9:00, 10:30, 12:00, 14:00, 15:00 h and 15:30 h - price depends on the kind of boat, 5.- to 10.-M$. From Kuala Perlis, take a bus (2.20 M$) or a taxi (3.50 M$) to Alor Setar or Kangar. A taxi to Padang Besar (the border) costs 3.50 M$.

MAC (Malaysia Air Charter) flies from KL (139.-) and PENANG (74.-M$). Info at MAC, KL, Subang Airport, tel 769822 or at travel agencies.

Since April 1984 a new ship the GADIS LANGKASUKA sails between Penang and Langkawi. Price: 35.-M$ adult. Ther're daily ferries from Teluk Ewa in the north of the island to SATUN in Thailand. Costs 6 M$. Immigration and tickets in Teluk Ewa.

PADANG BESAR
This is the border town to Thailand, accessible by bus, taxi or train. You can change money in the train station building or in the coffee shop at the bus station. But they don't give a very good exchange rate. Overland taxis leave from the train station. The cheapest way into Thailand is to walk up the street to the Malaysian checkpoint, get the necessary stamp in your passport, and then go up the bit of no-man's-land along the road to the Thai border station. An alternative is going across by motorbike. On the Thai side are buses for 15 Baht to Haad Yai.

FROM KL TO JOHORE BHARU

It is possible to go right from KL to Malacca or even Singapore. Places like Seremban, Kuala Pilah and Port Dickson can't boast of their sights. But they are very Malaysian and rarely visited by tourists, making them certainly worth a stopover.

Minangkabau immigrants from West Sumatra introduced wet rice in Negri Sembilan and Malacca before the Portuguese arrived. The original Malay population at the time lived largely from small trade and fishing. The Minangkabau maintain to this day their matrilineal social structure (Adat Perpateh).

For mile after incredible mile heading south, you pass seemingly endless palm-oil and rubber plantations. Once upon a time they were owned by large English companies. Today, production of rubber gives increasing way to palm oil. Still, numerous, but inconspicuous, small farms maintain the undemanding rubber trees in addition to coconut palms and rice. Like north of KL, the cities and markets are dominated by Chinese while the kampongs are Malay. The Sultanate of Johore breaks the pattern however; a large portion of Johore's village population is Chinese. Their forefathers moved out of Singapore onto the land during the 1930s depression. Today they provide the city markets with fresh meat, fruit and vegetables.

Seremban

This is the most important town in the state of Negri Sembilan (means 'nine countries'). Before the creation of this state by the British in 1895, there were nine different kingdoms here.

Between the 15th and 17th centuries, numerous Minangkabau settled in Negri Sembilan. Their architecture is characterized by the pointed roofs of their buildings, remindful of buffalo horns. The Minangkabau (the name means 'buffalo horns') are a Malay tribe, principally settled today on West Sumatra.

Not far from the bus station, in the southeast of town, is the **LAKE GARDEN** (Taman Tasek Negri). The modern **NEW MOSQUE** is mirrored by the lake. It stands on nine pillars representing the nine countries, Negri Sembilan.

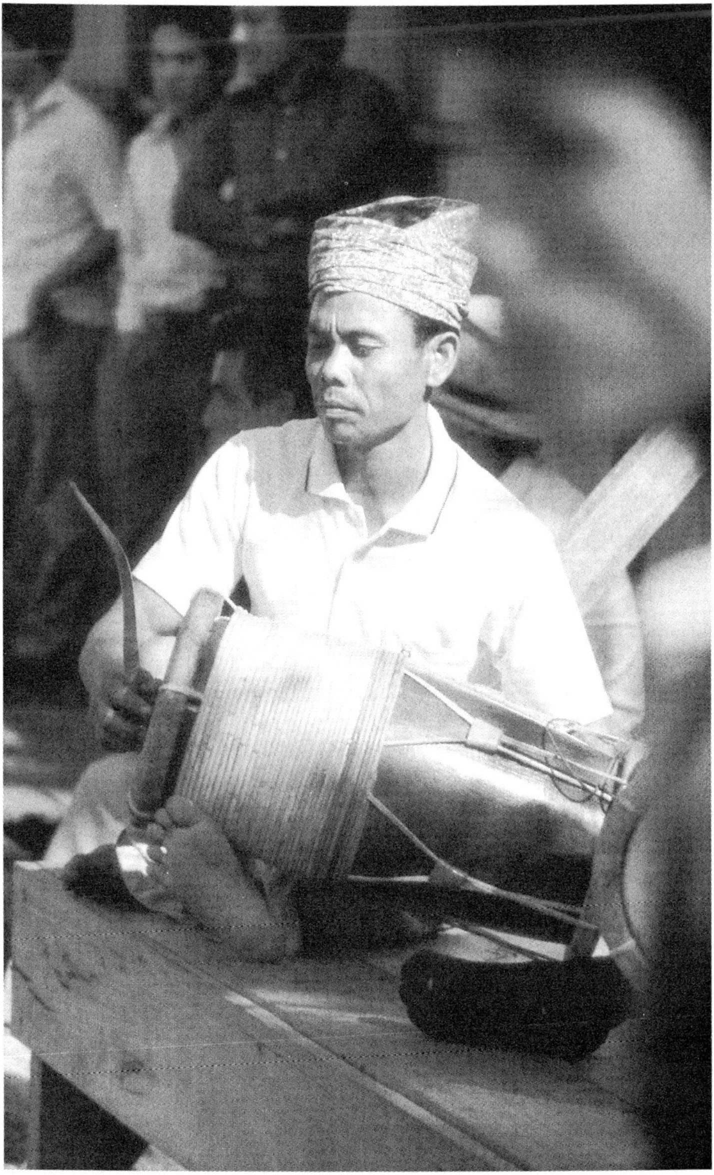

THE MINANGKABAU

'**Minang**' (sometimes 'menang') means victory; '**kabau**' (today usually 'kerbau') means buffalo. An old legend tells how the 3 million Minangkabau acquired their name. A Javanese army wanted to conquer the land. There were so many soldiers that whole rocks disappeared when they sharpened their swords. The king of the Minangkabau made an agreement with his Javanese counterpart. Two buffalos should fight to settle the matter peaceably. The Minangkabau let a young calf hunger for a long time before fastening a spearhead to its nose. The thirsty calf jumped to milk a bewildered opponent, thereby disembowelling it. The Javanese buffalo died.

It is interesting to observe the mixing of two such contradictory cultures: Islam which emphasizes the male role in society and the traditional Minangkabau culture with its matrilineal social structure. Matrilineal doesn't necessarily mean matriarchate or the domination of women, rather a female line of ancestral descent. The paddy fields and houses are owned by the Minangkabau women.

The unwritten laws and traditions called '**adat**' determine one's entire life. For a young boy the most important male relative is not the father rather the mother's eldest brother. Until marriage he remains in his mother's home where he is raised by his mother's relatives. After marriage he moves in with his wife and mother in law.

The Minangkabau civil and social system is quite complex. Four clans **(suku)** are considered today to be the oldest population groups: the **bodi, caniago, koto,** and **piliang**. They are distributed throughout the entire region. The next highest civil unit is the villaga with its fields **(nagari)**. A 'nagari' is only complete when it contains people from all four 'suku'.

The inheritance system, both materially and spiritually (passing down of names etc.) goes from mother to daughter. Men according to 'adat' are there to defend the system. At his wife's home the man is a guest. He must fulfill work obligations to both his mother and his wife. He is only entitled to a part of his mother's proceeds as determined by 'adat'. The fruits of the work

> he provides for his wife is for her and the children alone. The eldest son manages the estate of the mother.
>
> Decisions are first discussed separately in the family council which includes both sexes, everyone has the right to speak. The eldest family member (whether male or female) then announces the decisions of the council.
>
> According to 'adat' there is no repression of males. But the monopoly of decision making and ownership by males as found in our western patriarchy has been withdrawn.

A prince once resided in the old Minangkabau palace which today houses the **MUSEUM**. The 19th century structure originally stood in Ampang Tinggi. It was built of wood without the use of a single metal nail. During reconstruction in Seremban, however, they weren't able to completely follow the original instructions. In 1984, the structure was once again taken apart and moved from the Lake Garden to its present location on Jl.Sungei Ujong (the feeder road to KL Highway), about 3 km out of town.

HOTELS
Cheap is the **ORIENTAL HOTEL****, 11 Jl.Lemon, tel 713069. Several hotels can be found in the parallel street, Jl.Birch, try **TONG FONG****, no 104, tel 713022 or **WAH SONG CHAN***, no 111, tel 714334. Otherwise there are cheap Chinese places on the side streets Jl.Cameron and Jl.Tuan Sheikh. Somewhat better is the **CARLTON HOTEL***** at no 47 Jl.Tuan Sheikh, tel 725336. Most expensive place is **RIA HOTEL******, Jl.Tetamu on the Lake Garden, tel 719440.

HOW TO GET HERE
The bus and taxi station is at Jl.Labu/Jl.Lemon. Sample Prices (in parenthesis taxi): KL 2.40(5.-), MALACCA 2.85 (5.-), PORT DICKSON 1.30, BAHAU 1.90 (5.-), KUALA PILAH 1.20(3.-), KELANG 3.50, GEMAS 3.60, SINGAPORE 16.-, JOHORE BHARU 12.-(23.-M$).

Seremban

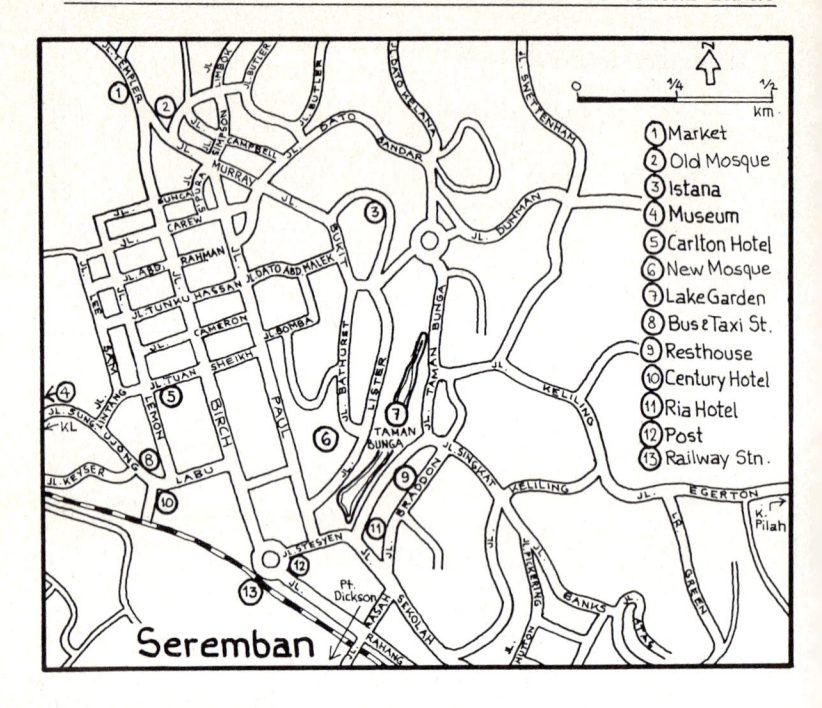

Map legend:
1. Market
2. Old Mosque
3. Istana
4. Museum
5. Carlton Hotel
6. New Mosque
7. Lake Garden
8. Bus & Taxi St.
9. Resthouse
10. Century Hotel
11. Ria Hotel
12. Post
13. Railway Stn.

There are six trains daily to KL (2nd/3rd class: 3.80/2.40 M$), Ekspres Rakyat/Sinarang 5.40/10.-M$.

KUALA PILAH
Located 37 km east of Seremban. The scenic jungle-covered mountains and rice fields are indeed remindful of West Sumatra. After about 25 km, you come to **ULU BENDOL**, a popular picnic spot by a forest stream. A path leads upstream to a rubber plantation.

On Jl.Lister, near the bus station is an ancient Chinese temple. From Kuala Pilah you have a connection to Bahau – buses every 20 minutes. From there you can go on to Tasek Bera or up to Temerloh.

SERI MENANTI
Get a bus from Kuala Pilah to Seri Menanti, a royal seat, takes 45 minutes, costs 50 c. Check out the **ISTANA LAMA**,

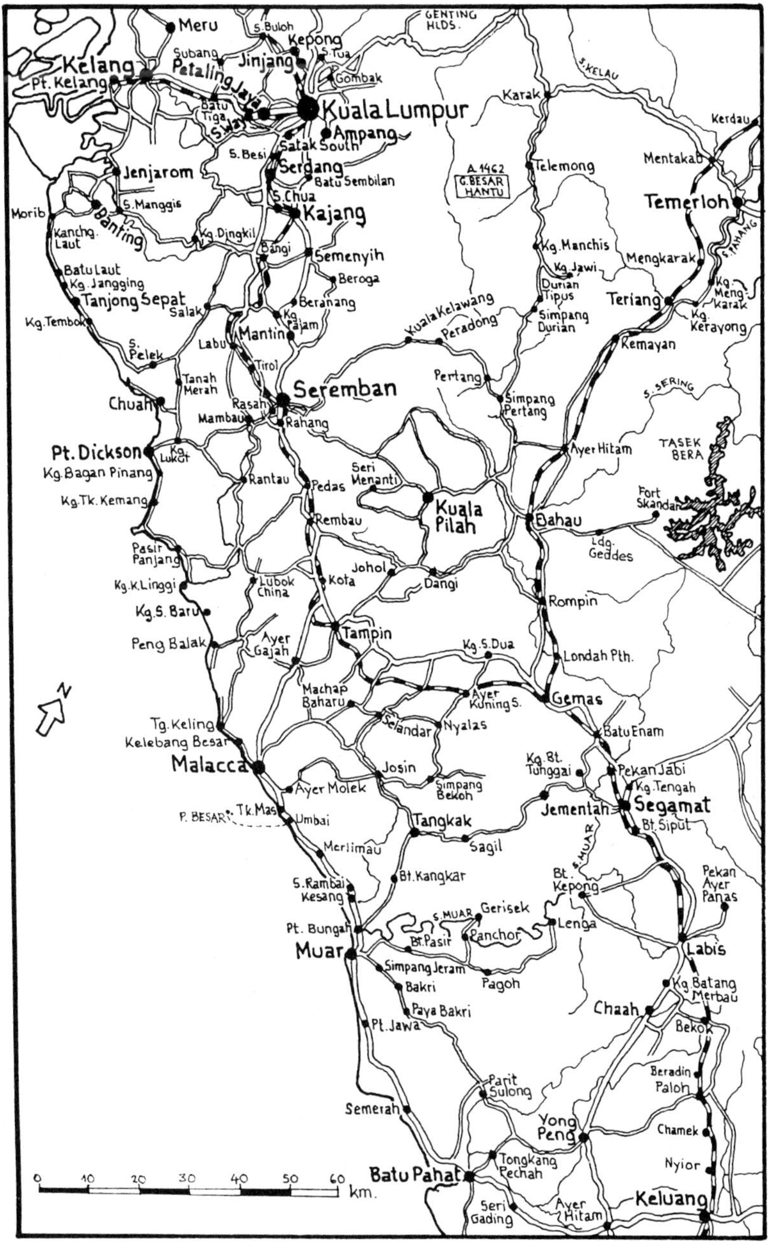
Meru
GENTING HLDS.
S. Buloh
Kepong
Subang
Jinjang
S. Tua
Kelang
Petaling Jaya
Gombak
Pt. Kelang
S. KELAU
Karak
Batu Tiga
Kuala Lumpur
S'Way
Ampang
Kerdau
Satak South
S. Besi
Mentakab
Sergang
A 1462
G. BESAR HANTU
Telemong
Jenjarom
Batu Sembilan
S. Chua
Temerloh
S. Manggis
Kajang
Morib
Banting
Kanchg. Laut
Kg. Dingkil
S. PAHANG
Bangi
Kg. Manchis
Semenyih
Mengkarak
Kg. Jawi
Batu Laut
Beroga
Kg. Jangging
Durian Tipus
Kg. Meng-karak
Tanjong Sepat
Beranang
Teriang
Kuala Kelawang
Salak
Simpang Durian
Kg. Kerayong
Kg. Tembok
Kg. Rajam
Peradong
Labu
Mantin
Kemayan
S. Pelek
Tirol
Pertang
S. SERING
Tanah Merah
Seremban
Simpang Pertang
Chuah
Rasah
Mambau
Rahang
TASEK BERA
Pt. Dickson
Kg. Lukut
Ayer Hitam
Kg. Bagan Pinang
Seri Menanti
Rantau
Pedas
Fort Skandar
Kg. Tk. Kemang
Kuala Pilah
Rembau
Bahau
Ldg. Geddes
Pasir Panjang
Johol
Kg. K. Linggi
Lubok China
Kota
Dangi
Rompin
Kg. S. Baru
Tampin
Ayer Gajah
Peng Balak
Kg. S. Dua
Londah Pth.
Machap Baharu
Ayer Kuning S.
Gemas
Tg. Keling
Selandar
Nyalas
Batu Enam
Kelebang Besar
Malacca
Josin
Kg. Bt. Tunggai
Pekan Jabi
Ayer Molek
Simpang Bekoh
Kg. Tengah
P. BESAR
Tk. Mas
Segamat
Umbai
Jementah
Tangkak
Bt. Siput
Sagil
Merlimau
S. MUAR
Bt. Kangkar
Pekan Ayer Panas
S. Rambai
Kesang
Bt. Kepong
Gerisek
S. MUAR
Pt. Bungah
Lenga
Panchor
Bt. Pasir
Muar
Labis
Simpang Jeram
Pagoh
Bakri
Kg. Batang Merbau
Chaah
Paya Bakri
Pt. Jawa
Bekok
Beradin
Parit Sulong
Paloh
Semerah
Chamek
Yong Peng
Tongkang Pechah
Nyior
0 10 20 30 40 50 60 km.
Batu Pahat
Keluang
Seri Gading
Ayer Hitam
N

built in 1908 and a good example of traditional Minangkabau
architecture. The road to the west, starting under the great
archway, leads first past the Royal Mosque. Then the road
curves to the right. There you'll find the former Istana. The
road ends at the new palace.

Port Dickson

Port Dickson has little in common with a large and busy port
despite its name - to the contrary. Stretching out south of
the village for 18 km is one of the most popular beaches on
the west coast of Malaysia. On weekends and during school
vacations, people pour onto the beach from west coast cities
to relax in the sun, sand and sea. Everywhere are weekend
houses, hotels and bungalow settlements. Those who'd like
for a change to see how Malaysians relax should check out
the beach for a couple of days.

This is the narrowest point on the Straits of Malacca;
Sumatra is only 60 km away. In good weather you can see it
from Cape Rachado lighthouse.

The Lighthouse was built in the 16th century by the
Portuguese. Sailing ships on the way to Malacca (then the
most important trading port in South East Asia) were dependent on it. From the Blue Lagoon Village a road leads about
half a kilometer up, then it's another 65 steps through the
jungle. In the end you're 180 m above sea level.

Off Blue Lagoon Village is a coral reef. But the water
is sometimes very dirty. Remember the Straits of Malacca are
packed with little fishing boats and huge oil tankers, not to
mention tiny offerings from the bathers - there isn't any
sewage treatment.

HOTELS

Along the beach you'll find many hotels (included are respective milestones showing distance from Port Dickson). In
the town itself, there's among others, **HAPPY CITY
HOTEL****, 26 Jl.Raja Aman Shah, tel 405183. Otherwise try
the **RESTHOUSE****, tel 405149. After three miles you come to
FAIRWINDS HOTEL**, tel 405657 and after another half a
mile there's the **YOUTH HOSTEL***. At the 8 and 9 mile
markers, most of the hotels are between the beach and the
road: **LIDO HOTEL*****, tel 405273, **KONG MING HOTEL***, with
shower in the courtyard, tel 405239, **GOLDEN SANDS
HOTEL****, tel 405284, **PANTAI MOTEL****** offers bungalows
of varying quality, tel 405265. After 10 1/2 miles you
reach the **METHODIST CENTRE HOSTEL****, bungalows****,
dormitory*, tel 405229.

FROM KL TO JOHORE BHARU

LEAVING PORT DICKSON
Every 30 minutes bus 67 (Utan Singh Bus Company) will take you to SEREMBAN for 1.30 M$. There's an hourly bus for 1 M$ to PENGKALAN KEMPAS and four times a day to PORT KELANG for 3.50 M$ (beautiful route all along the coast). Barat Express will take you for 3 M$ at 8:30, 10:30, 14:00 and 16:00 h to MALACCA.

Malacca

Certainly no other city in Malaysia has so fascinating a history as Malacca (see HISTORY). Arabs, Chinese, Portuguese, Dutch, British and others have all left a mark here. Seafarers of centuries past, whose sailing ships plied the routes between India and China, Europe and the East Indies, appreciated the port city's convenient location at the transition point between the northeast and southwest monsoon regions. Trade with gold and silk, spices and opium created a cosmopolitan city over 500 years ago. It was a center of political conflict. In 1511 the Portuguese drove out the Malay ruler by force of arms. But the rich merchants remained to exploit the new market. After a number of unsuccessful attacks, the city fell 130 years later to Dutch might. But it wasn't Malacca, rather Batavia (today Jakarta), which became the center of East Indies trade. In 1824, the British took control of a sleepy, very Dutch town.

Malacca is no longer a metropolis; its former grandeur has disappeared. Instead of modern office buildings and international shops, modest Chinese shops fill the picture. But each of the countries involved in its past has left a trace. You'll find the mixture of western and oriental tradition very interesting.

Begin your tour of Malacca's (Malay = Melaka) history at the Sungei Melaka. This is the 'Red Square' of the city. The **STADTHUYS** (town hall) is the oldest remaining Dutch building in Asia. It was built between 1641 and 1660 and today contains the **MELAKA MUZIUM**. It features an excellent exhibit on the history of the city, mostly in old engravings and pictures, as well as everyday objects of the former inhabitants (Malay and Chinese) and their conquerors. Admission is free.

Right next door is the massive **CHRIST CHURCH** built in 1753. Even bricks and roof tiles were brought from Holland. You can take the best photos from the terrace of the tourist office.

On Jl.Kota, which runs in a great curve around **ST. PAUL'S HILL**, you'll find the last remains of Portugal's greatest fortress in Asia. **PORTA DE SANTIAGO** was the eastern gate of the fortress, La Famosa. Albuquerque had the fort built in just a few months with the aid of hundreds of the sultan's slaves and many Portuguese. The fort withstood 24 attacks by Malays from Johore, Acehnese and the Dutch before falling in 1641.

Behind the Porta de Santiago a path leads uphill to the ruins of the Portuguese **ST.PAUL'S CHURCH**. The gravestones set in the ruin are of interest to the history minded. Think of the predicament faced by Dutch or Portuguese adventurers in the 17th and 18th centuries. Their journey to the east lasted many months; then they were completely cut off from their homelands. They were forced to survive in an unfamiliar tropical climate and frequently faced deadly diseases. Adventure, profit and power were sought by many!

In front of the church ruins is a memorial to **ST.FRANCIS XAVIER**. In 1541, he left Lisbon and spent the next 11 years on missionary trips. He charted 38,000 miles, before dying in 1552 on a tiny island off the coast of China. In 1553 his remains were brought back to Malacca and buried in St.Paul's Church. However, after just three months, he was again exhumed for transport to Goa.

Back on Jl.Kota, when circling the hill, you'll come to an old **ENGLISH CEMETERY**, now returning to the wild! Buried here are English and Dutch, most of whom fell in the Sungei Ujong war.

Still standing today, on Jl.Tun Tan Cheng Lock and Jl.Temple, are probably the most beautiful, well preserved old Chinese buildings in Asia. **CHEN HOON TENG TEMPLE** was built way back in 1644, making it the oldest Chinese temple in Malaysia.

Try to visit **ST.PETER'S CHURCH** (Jl.Tun Sri Lanang) on Good Friday! It is the center of the catholic church in Malaysia. The Easter processions, here in the middle of Asia, are a once in a lifetime experience more reminiscent of Spain or Portugal than Malaya. The church was built in 1710 when the Dutch reinstituted religious freedom. The architecture is similar to that of churches in Goa and Macau.

BUKIT CHINA is the largest Chinese cemetery outside the Middle Kingdom. It has an interesting history: In the 15th century a tribute delegation of the then Sultan Mansur Shah returned from the Ming Royal Court. As a "gift" it brought back the Princess Hang Li Po. She was accompanied by 500 "girls of great beauty" as one can read in the old annals. The princess and her royal household were given the hill (bukit = hill) as a residence. There's nothing left to be seen of the buildings today.

At the foot of the hill, near the **POH SAN TENG TEMPLE**, you'll find the Asian version of the Fontana di Trevi, the **SULTAN'S WELL**.

An excursion along the coast to the south will bring you to the **PORTUGUESE SETTLEMENT** on Jl.Albuquerque. About 2000 people, most of them fishermen, live here and speak Portuguese.

A Portuguese community has managed to survive here for 450 years. It speaks its own dialect similar to the otherwise forgotten, medieval language spoken in Cristao, southeast Portugal, hundreds of years ago. One of the reasons for the existence of this language and cultural island is the policy of the former colonial power. Unlike the Dutch or British, intermarriage was never ruled out. Marriages between Portuguese men and Malay women or even between Malay men and Portuguese women were common practice. So you can still find Portuguese speaking Eurasians on Jl.Albuquerque, all strict catholics, of course!

After the Portuguese conquered Malacca in 1511, they made the city not just their trading and military base of operations, but also their religious center in the far east. Thousands of missionaries spread out from here to preach their beliefs throughout South-East Asia. Most famous of these was Francis Xavier. Congregations belonging to the Malacca diocese can be found in present-day Malaysia, Indonesia, Thailand, Burma, China, and Japan.

By the way, should you ever be in Malacca in June, (and find a vacant hotel room) be sure to take part in the **FESTA DE SAN PEDRO** (a festival in honor of St.Peter, the patron saint of fishermen). Music blaring from countless loudspeakers will guide you to the festival grounds near the sea. You'll find booths with games and foodstalls serving tasty, but hotly spiced, seafood - try the 'devil curry'. Come evening, singers and dancers get on stage in Portuguese costumes to perform as best they can the old-fashioned songs and dance. On the last day, a priest blesses the fishing boats in a ceremonial mass. The colorfully decorated boats are then awarded prizes.

On your way back to Malacca, make a stop at **ST. JOHN'S HILL**. Originally just a Portuguese chapel stood on the hill. Later the Dutch built a fort; have a look at the remains.

FROM KL TO JOHORE BHARU 191

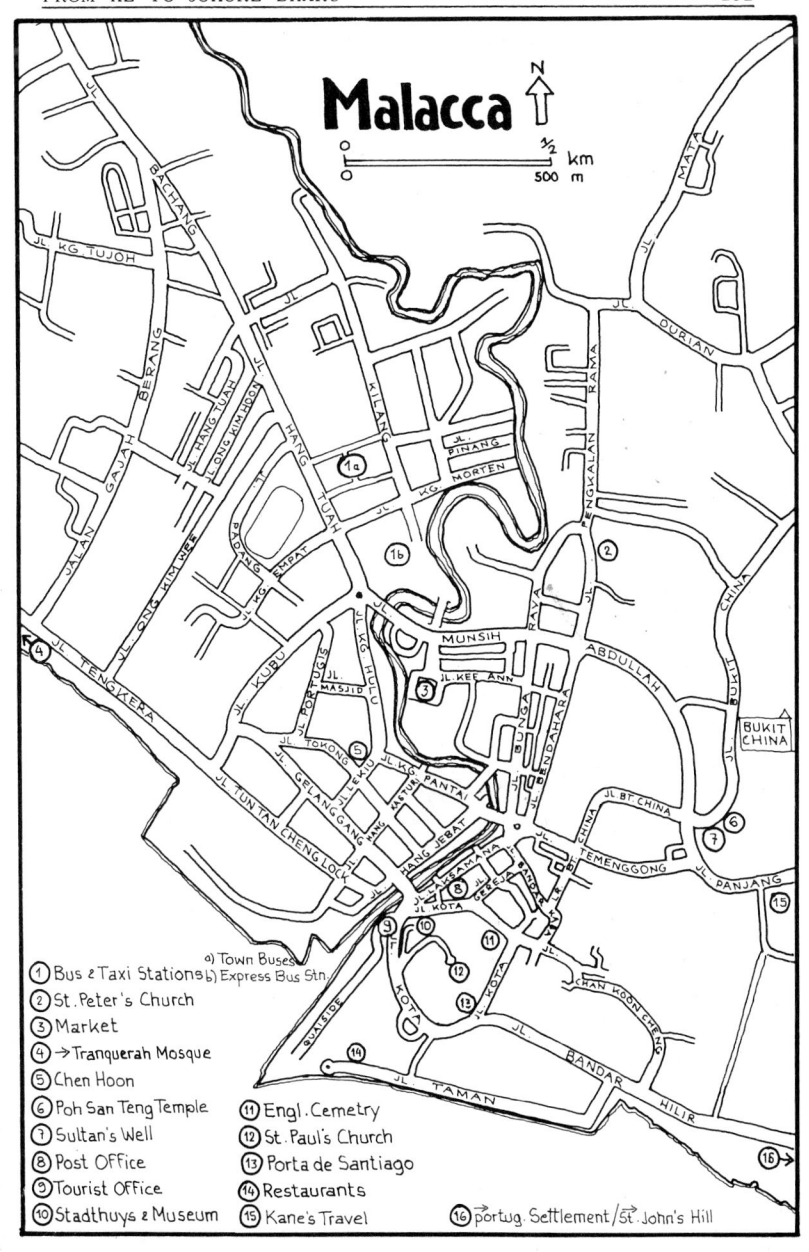

Malacca

1. Bus & Taxi Stations a) Town Buses b) Express Bus Stn.
2. St. Peter's Church
3. Market
4. → Tranquerah Mosque
5. Chen Hoon
6. Poh San Teng Temple
7. Sultan's Well
8. Post Office
9. Tourist Office
10. Stadthuys & Museum
11. Engl. Cemetry
12. St. Paul's Church
13. Porta de Santiago
14. Restaurants
15. Kane's Travel
16. → Portug. Settlement / St. John's Hill

Worth checking out is an interesting example of Malay architecture on Jl.Tranquerah. The **TRANQUERAH MOSQUE** is about 150 years old. Sumatra visitors will find many parallels; the minaret and the ornamentation on the roof show Chinese influence. Here too is the grave of Hussein Shah, Sultan of Johore, who in 1819 was party to the famous treaty with Stamford Raffles signing over the island of Singapore.

HOTELS

Don't let yourself get picked up by a trishaw driver (he is only out for a commission at your expense).

In TANJUNG KELING on PANTAI KUNDUR, about 10 km north of town are cheap backpacker's accommodations. Get bus 51 from the bus station (Jl.Hang Tuah) for 85 c. Though the beach can't be compared to the east coast - i.e. oil refinery nearby - everyone gets together here. Right on the beach are the huts of **SHM'S*** (Slow Harmonic Motion). If you stay here, hang an umbrella above your mosquito net. Still, it's a friendly place! At SHM'S, Nora is an excellent cook, but have a little patience, the kitchen's small and travellers abound. Next door are the huts of **RASA SAYANG*** (not so good), **SUNSET*** and a bit further north **HAWAI***. Like any happening place, there's bound to be drugs about. As the police know best; there's nothing unusual about undercover agents or police raids. Those who prefer more comfort can try **MOTEL TANJUNG KELING***** (tel 280652), on the beach with a palm garden and restaurant.

In the city itself there're hotels of every category, size and shape. Try Jl.Bunga Raya: **NG FOOK****, no 154; **CHIN NAM****, no 49 or **CATHAY****, no 100-104. Lots of atmosphere in **MAJESTIC****, no 188 (tel 222455). On Jl.Kee Ann, a side street off Bunga Raya: **NEW LONDON HOTEL****, no 54 (somewhat loud mornings - market!) or **TONG AH***, no 16. Quieter are **EASTERN***, 85 Jl.Bendahara, tel 223483, **CHONG HOE****, Jl.Tukang Emas (clean) and **KANE'S PLACE**** (dorm*), 107 Jl.Chan Koon Cheng (main road to Singapore). Very clean, Frankee has lots of valuable tips since he runs a travel agency too. He offers interesting tours. Address: 136A/1 Jl.Panjang, tel 315124.

FOOD

A whole row of different restaurants can be found by the sea on Jl.Taman. If there's no menu, check prices before you order! No longer to be recommended are the two restaurants in the Portuguese settlement! Still around is **UE TEA HOUSE** at Lorong Bukit China 20. Try Indian food in

MAJEEDIE, 96 Jl.Bendahara. Good Malay food in **NORLIAH**, 8 Jl.Hang Tuah. Chinese in **DODONG SAYANG**, 54 Jl. Laksamana. Beneath the Paris Hotel on Jl.Kee Ann, there's a baker selling hot bread.

SHOPPING – the antique shops on Jl.Hang Jebat (formerly Jonker Street) have become too expensive due to tourism – only for well-heeled travellers. The cramped, overstocked shops contain treasures left behind by the city's late inhabitants. Arabian oil lamps and Indian silver share space in the dusty shelves with Dutch and Chinese porcelain.

At the end of Jl.Kee Ann is the local market. On the streets leading in are lots of stands. On Temple Street you'll find many shops offering Chinese temple articles.

GENERAL INFORMATION
TOURIST INFO – Tourist Center on Jl.Kota, tel 225895 – a good source.

IMMIGRATION – in the big new administration building on the corner of Jl.Kubu/Jl.Hang Tuah.

POST OFFICE – GPO on Jl.Laksamana.

LEAVING MALACCA
BY AIR
MAS office at 238 Taman Melaka Jaya, tel 315722/23. Daily flights to KL for 39 M$. Of interest is the Fri flight with Pan Malaysia Air Carriers to PEKANBARU (Sumatra), costs 146 M$. This is the most reasonable way to get to Sumatra (Bukittinggi) by air. From Singapore it costs 172 M$. Book at: Atlas Travel Service, 5 Jl.Hang Jebat, tel 220777 (near the river). Airport tax: 15 M$.

BY SHIP
Since September 1983 there's a ferry every Sun, Wed and Fri between MALACCA and DUMAI (Sumatra). Price: 80 M$ one way, return every Tues, Thurs and Sat. Departure 10:00 h, arrival 12:00 h. You need an entry visa for Dumai, get it in KL or Singapore.

OVERLAND BUSES AND TAXIS
All long-distance buses depart from the central bus station on Jl.Kilang. Taxis depart from next to the bus station.

SAMPLE PRICES (taxis in brackets): AIR HITAM (10.-), BATU PAHAT (7.-), BUTTERWORTH 17.50, ac 21.40 with MARA Express, tel 220687, dep 21:00 h, IPOH (30.-), JOHORE BHARU 9.-(17.-), KELUANG 6.-(12.-), KOTA BHARU 25.- ac 29.- with Bumi Express, dep 19:30, arr 8:30 h, KL 5.50 ac 6.50 with Malacca-KL Express, Jebat Ekspres goes along the coast in 3 1/2 hours (13.-), KUANTAN 11.- 2xdaily with Cepat Ekspres, tel 249126, via Mount Ophir, PENGKALAN KEMPAS 1.05, PORT DICKSON 3.20, 4xdaily, (5.-), SEREMBAN 2.85 every 30 minutes, (6.60), SINGAPORE 8.50 ac 11.-with Malacca-Singapore Express, tel 224470 (22.-), TAPAH 14.50, TAMPIN (connection to the North-South Railline) 1.50, MUAR 1.80 (3.50) M$.

If you're on your way to Singapore and aren't in a hurry, here are some possibilities:

PULAU BESAR
A bit further south (take bus 2) at **KG.UMBAI** (about 10 km towards Muar), get a boat over to PULAU BESAR for 4 M$. This is a beautiful island with bungalows** and well-preserved buildings from a German development aid project gone bad. Lack of water killed the livestock production, along with the animals. Local inhabitants are quite superstitious and avoid the property. On Sat/Sun there's a boat for 8.-M$ return from Quayside Malacca.

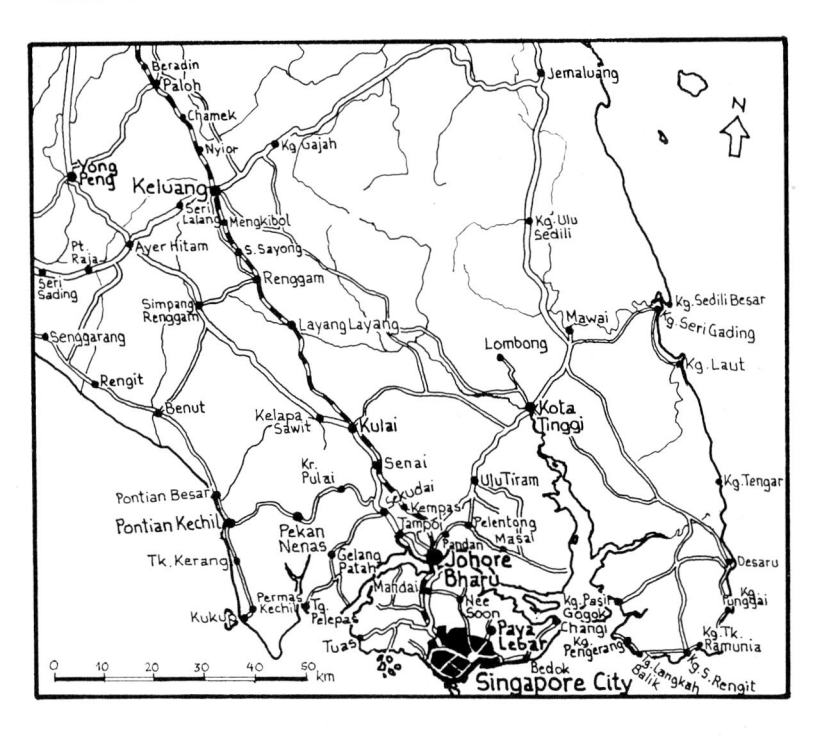

KG.MERLIMAU
In a small village on the road to Muar is one of the best preserved, traditional Malacca-style houses. Ask the way to the 90-year-old house of the 'Bendahara' - reputedly haunted by a ghost. Another nice Malacca-style house can be found across from Shahs Beach Motel in Tanjung Keling.

MUAR
There're lots of kampongs, rice fields, and rubber or pineapple plantations on the road heading south. After 38 km you come to Muar, the second largest town in the Sultanate of Johore. There's a beautifully situated RESTHOUSE**** (tel 932306) in Jl.Sultanah. Other hotels**. The bus station is on the river in the center of town. Buses leave for Malacca every half hour for 1.80 M$ (taxi 3.50 M$); to Batu Pahat also 1.80 M$.

BATU PAHAT
After another 55 km you come to this very Chinese town with lots of nightlife. Men come here from Singapore to grovel on the cheap. On weekends it's impossible to get a room. Batu Pahut is known for its numerous 'Kopek Korek' (coffee shops) where you're served a coffee or tea for 30 c by beautiful waitresses. Have a look during the week! Buses to Johore Bharu take 2 1/2 hours and cost 4.- or 5.50 M$ ac.

HOTELS
Reasonable is **VALERIE HOTEL****, 104 Jl.Rahmat (tel 441367) or **KHIAW ANN HOTEL****, 21A Jl.Jenang (tel 441330). Somewhat more expensive is **FAIRYLAND*****, 91-92A Jl.Rahmat (tel 441777).

KUKUP
Several buses leave daily to PONTIAN KECHIL, a small, quiet town. Make a trip from here to KUKUP, a fishing village across from **Pulau Kukup**. Excellent seafood! The last time we were in Kukup, there weren't any sleeping accommodations. Get a bus back to Pontian Kechil for 1 M$ (taxi 6 M$) and then on to Johore Bharu for 2.20 (taxi 5 M$).

SEGAMAT (MOUNT OPHIR)
The second possibility is to go from MUAR up to the almost 90 km distant SEGAMAT. The town is located on both the great North-South Highway and the railroad. After 45 km, just beyond SAGIL, **Mount Ophir** (1400 m) rises up suddenly dominating the landscape (Malay: Gunung Ledang). There are many legends about the mountain - including a fairy princess residing in an invisible palace at the top. The mountain was climbed, however, in 1854 by the great English naturalist Wallace during his study of Malay flora and fauna. If you're considering a climb, you'll need permission from the District Office (Pejabat Daerah) in Muar.

HOTELS
There're lots of cheap hotels in town such as **TAI AH****, 42 Jl.Genuang (tel 911709), **KEE SIANG***, 13-15 Jl.Mentol (tel 912443) or **NEW EUROPE***, 1-2 Jl.Leong Yong. Somewhat more expensive is the **RESTHOUSE*****, 750 Jl.Buluh Kasap (tel 914566).

HOW TO GET THERE
From KOTA BHARU, get the 'jungle train' from WAKAF BHARU or PASIR MAS every morning to GEMAS. After midnight there are two trains from Segamat to GEMAS heading north. From

there, you have a connection at 3:30 h to KOTA BHARU (takes about 14 hours and costs 15.90 M$ 3rd class). There are several trains daily to KL (6.60 M$, 3rd class) and to Singapore (6.10 M$ 3rd class).

AYER HITAM
The third possibility is to head direct from Malacca to the east coast (Mersing). Overland taxis from Malacca to KELUANG cost 10 M$. Or take a bus from Batu Pahat to AYER HITAM, a small village, little more than a few houses on an important crossroads. This is where the heavily travelled North-South Highway hits one of the few east-west connections. A few kilometers south in KG. MACAP, you can visit the most famous Chinese pottery workshop in Malaysia.

KELUANG
Overland taxis from Muar to Keluang cost 7.50 M$, buses from Malacca 7.-M$. Keluang is the center of the timber industry and less than interesting. If you have to stay here anyway, you'll find lots of cheap hotels. There is another connection here on to the North-South Railway or you can take a bus (8x daily, 5 M$) or taxi (8.20 M$) to Mersing. A good part of the trip runs through a forest reserve boasting lovely jungle, few villages, little traffic and an occasional mountain.

Johore Bharu

Not until 1866 did this town become the Sultan of Johore's royal seat. The sultanate, however, was established back in 1564, when the son of the last Sultan of Malacca retreated to the Johore River. By the end of the 17th century, Johore was the heir to Malacca. Except a small area around the city of Malacca, held by the Dutch, Johore controlled most of the old kingdom.

Before 1866, Johore was called 'Ujung Tanah', which means land's end,

Elaeis guineensis (Ölpalme);
a männlicher Blütenstand, b weibliche Blüten.

since this is the actual end of the Eurasian land mass. Today a causeway connects Johore Bharu with the island of Singapore. Foreign tourists hardly ever stop in JB, though Singapore's sister city has maintained much of its charm while developing into the industrial center of southern Malaysia.

On **BUKIT SERENE**, way outside town, is the Sultan's private residence featuring a 33 m high tower. The **ISTANA BESAR** and the palace garden can be visited daily except Fri from 9:00 to 12:00 h. You must, however, register in advance with the tourist office. The architecture shows strong Victorian influence. Sultan Abu Bakar had the tremendous Istana built in 1866. It contains the crown jewels and royal insignia as well as other works of art. Not far away on a hill is the picturesque **ABU BAKAR MOSQUE**, large enough to hold 2500 worshippers.

HOTELS
If you've got a long wait in Singapore and are low on money, the hotels in JB present a good alternative. After all, the border to Singapore is open round the clock. You'll find the cheapest hotels on Jl.Ah Fook and Jl.Meldrum. **TONG FONG****, 5 Jl.Ah Fook or on Jl.Meldrum: **TONG HONG****, no 37-39 or **FOOK LOY****, no 5A. Medium priced: **MALAYA HOTEL*****, 20 Jl.Bukit Meldrum, tel 221691; **FIRST HOTEL*****, Jl.Station, tel 222888 or **HONGKONG*****, 31A Jl.Meldrum, tel 223816.

LEAVING JOHORE BHARU
BY AIR
The MAS office is in the AZIZA Building on Jl.Wong Ah Fook (tel 220888). Singapore visitors should certainly consider the flights to Kuching and Kota Kinabalu. The flights from Senai Airport (20 km north of JB) are domestic and therefore cheaper. The Malaysian government plans to make the airport competitive with Singapore.
SAMPLE PRICES: KOTA KINABALU 301.- (night flight 256.-; from SGP 346.-), KUCHING 147.- (night flight 125.-; from SGP 170.-), KL 70.- (from SGP 103.-M$). MAS provides buses to the airport for some flights - ask at the MAS office in JB, Taxis charge 15.-M$ per person to Senai.
MAS buses leave from Singapore City Terminal, Singapore Shopping Centre, 190 Clemenceau Ave. tel 3366566, for 6.-S$.

OVERLAND BUSES AND TAXIS
Buses and taxis leave from Jl.Terus. SAMPLE PRICES (taxi prices in parenthesis):

FROM KL TO JOHORE BHARU

Johore Bharu

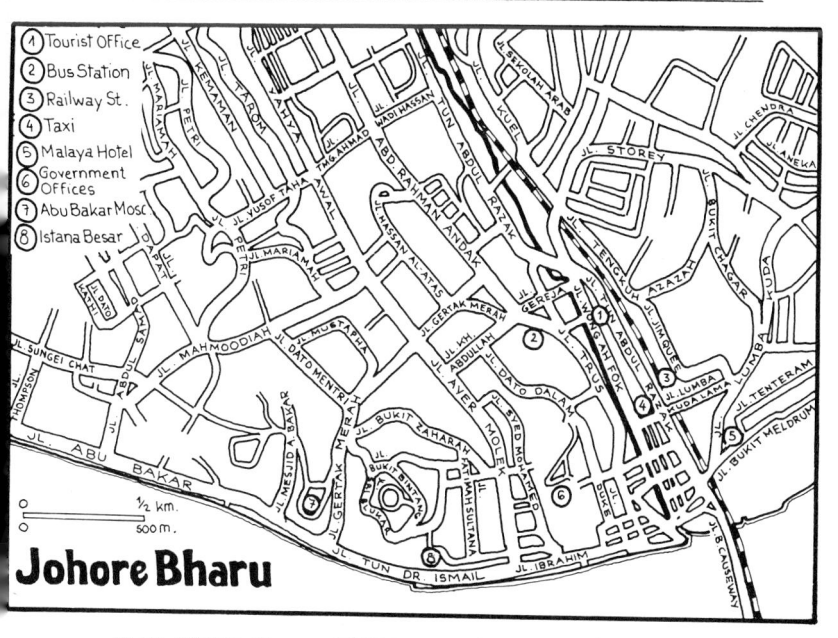

1. Tourist Office
2. Bus Station
3. Railway St.
4. Taxi
5. Malaya Hotel
6. Government Offices
7. Abu Bakar Mosc
8. Istana Besar

ALOR SETAR 33.-, BUTTERWORTH 29.-(60.-), IPOH 24.-, KOTA BHARU 25.- ac 30.-, KOTA TINGGI 2.-(3.-), KL 15.50(31.-), KUALA TRENGGANU 17.- ac 23.-(52.-), KUANTAN 12.50 ac 16.-(27.-), MALACCA 9.-(17.50), MERSING 5.-(10.85), SINGAPORE 80 c (3.-)M$).

BY RAIL
The train station is on Jl.Campbell, not far from the Causeway. For information call 224727. The Malayan Railways will take you to Singapore in half an hour, costs 90 c. SAMPLE PRICES: KUALA LUMPUR 18.90(11.90), BUTTERWORTH 38.30(24.-), SEREMBAN 15.20(9.40), IPOH 29.10(18.10), WAKAF BHARU 35.50(22.20). All quotations 2nd class, in parenthesis 3rd class. If you want to transfer in GEMAS to the jungle railway, take the 20:34 h or the 22:34 h train out of JB.

DAY TRIPS AROUND JOHORE BHARU
GUNUNG MUNTAHAK
On the way from JB to the east coast of Malaysia, try a stop in KOTA TINGGI, buses from JB for 2 M$, taxis 3 M$. From here you can get a bus to GUNUNG MUNTAHAK, 15 km to the north, for 80 c. Several waterfalls have cut the cliffs smooth

and formed natural swimming pools. Up to five people can rent a bungalow - costs 30 M$ with kitchenette, refrigerator etc. Lovely jungle walks! Up to now there's only one restaurant (which is priced that way!). So bring food from Kota Tinggi. On weekends the place is packed with people from Singapore and JB. We didn't find it all that great!

KOTA JOHORE LAMA
In Kota Tinggi you can charter a boat and sail down the Johore River. About 15 km to the south are the by now somewhat restored ruins of KOTA JOHORE LAMA, the sultanate's first capital between 1547 and 1587. Later the fortress was razed by the Portuguese. In KAMPONG MAKAM, just 1 1/2 km south of Kota Tinggi, is the royal mausoleum, where in 15 tombs, most Sultans of Johore are buried. You can spend the night in Kota Tinggi. Two cheap Chinese hotels are on Jl.Teo Kwee Cheo (FONG YENG HOTEL and PANG YIN HOTEL).

FROM JOHORE BHARU TO KUANTAN

The southern part of West Malaysia's east coast is less touristy than the strip between Kuantan and the Thai border. This is where stress-suffering Singaporeans spend their brief, hard-earned vacations. During the months from November to January, however, the sea is quite rough, making swimming and diving dangerous.

Off the coast is an archipelago of about 60 inhabited and uninhabited volcanic islands, several of which are ringed by coral reefs. Beyond the coast road, tremendous tropical forests and mangrove swamps abound. If you've the organizational talent and the endurance, you might journey up one of the huge rivers. It's sometimes difficult, however, to find an outboarder.

Desaru

This holiday resort south of Kota Tinggi is rarely shown on road maps. To date, several large hotels and a bungalow settlement have opened; others are being built. Planned is a holiday resort for rich Singaporeans, with some lower price accommodations on the side. The facilities are partly surrounded by jungle, and set on a long, white, sandy beach. The next village is several kilometers away. Just a couple years ago this whole area was covered by jungle. Then

FROM JOHORE BHARU TO KUANTAN

300,000 ha of forest were logged over to make room for huge plantations. Today the scenery is dominated by kilometer-long rows of palm-oil trees.

HOTELS

Worth recommending is the **DESARU HOLIDAY RESORT** (tel 838211). Up to now there are 35 chalets (60-75 M$ / 4 people) and two dormitories (10 M$). Several huts (dangkau) are planned which will cost 16 M$. An additional 2 M$ is charged for a mattress. Try to get a discount with your ISIC if you're planning to stay a while! The restaurant, which you can't really avoid, is pretty expensive, unless you do your own cooking. The camping area is loud. Coils or a mosquito net are an absolute necessity. Two other hotels been built: **DESARU MERLIN INN******, tel 838101, and **DESARU VIEW HOTEL******, tel 838221. Both run between 105.- and 190.-M$ per night.

HOW TO GET HERE

Take bus 41 or taxi from Johore Bharu to KOTA TINGGI and then a taxi for 5 M$ per person to DESARU. There are daily buses at 12:30 h and 15:00 h to KG.RAMUNIA. You can also come direct from SINGAPORE. Take a ferry from Changi Point to KG.PENGGERANG, and then a taxi for 4 M$ per person to Desaru.

Mersing

This port town is only important as a departure point for trips to the islands. If you're forced to spend a day here, take a walk to the **MOSQUE** or go to a beach. Take a right 10 km to the north (towards Endau) where you see the sign 'Pantai'. Just another 3 km and you're at the beach **KG. KAYU PAPAN**. The branch off leads through several coconut groves, small kampongs, and over two ancient wooden bridges. You can see **PULAU SETINDIAN** from the long white beach. By the way, when the tide's out, you might walk over to the island. A quicker way to the water is by taking the Mersing - Endau road before the branch off.

Another 10 km long beach can be found at **TELOK MAHKOTA** (Jason's Bay) south of Mersing, on the road to Kota Tinggi. The road is quite poor.

HOTELS

Beautifully situated on a hill, but unfortunately too expensive, is the **RESTHOUSE****** (tel 791101), 490 Jl. Ismail. The small hotels in town are much more reasonable, try large and restful rooms in **MERSING***, 1 Jl.Dato Timor (tel 791004). The restaurant is good too. Near the bus station and taxi stand at 53 Jl.Abu Bakar, you'll find the cheapest double room in Mersing in **TONG AH LODGING HOUSE***. Other cheap hotels: **MERDEKA***, 12 Jl. Sulaiman (tel 791231); **GOLDEN CITY****, 23 Jl.Abu Bakar; **EMBASSY****, 2 Jl.Ismail (tel 791302).

LEAVING MERSING

Taxis and buses leave from the bus stop:
JOHORE BHARU 5.50 (10.50), KELUANG 5.-(7.40), ENDAU 2.-(3.-), KOTA TINGGI 3.50 (7.40), KUANTAN 11.-(15.-), KUALA ROMPIN (5.-), KUALA TRENGGANU (33.-), SINGAPORE 7.30 M$).

If you want to visit some of the islands on your own, find a fishing boat. Upon arrival you're sure to be approached by touts offering boats. PULAU RAWA always has to be booked in advance, and you're expected to use the Rawa boat. The Tioman Office, 5 Jl.Abu Bakar, tel 791772, has one boat a day. BABI BESAR charges 18 M$ one-way, TIOMAN 29 M$. It's cheaper to Tioman via Wonderland Tour (near the bus station), tel 791229), only 20.-M$. Package tours are also organized to the other islands, i.e. to PULAU PEMANGGIL (3-day trip including boat ride, accommodations in the guesthouse, meals, a daytrip to PULAU AUR) for just 100.-M$ per person.

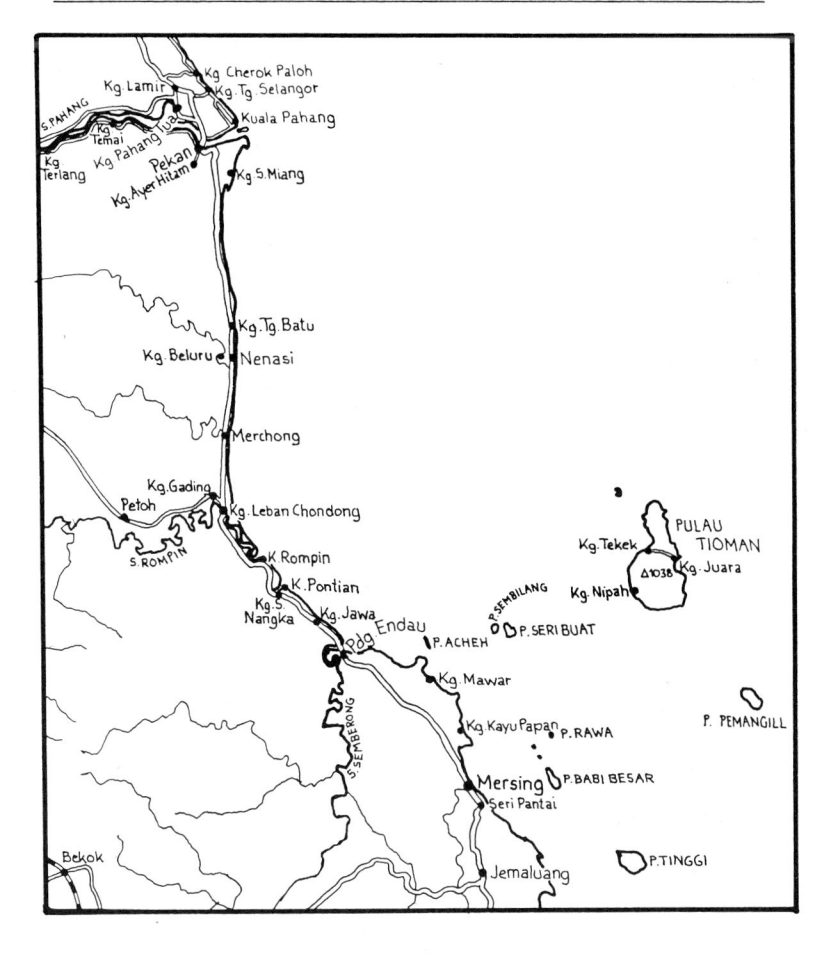

Pulau Rawa

The island is privately owned by a nephew of the Sultan of Johore. The youthful Tengku Mohammed Archibald Ibni Temenggong Achmad is quite a businessman, and his small bungalow village on the otherwise unpopulated island is usually booked up. The only place to eat is in the restaurant, which isn't the cheapest in the world. But to compensate, just jump from your hut over the sandy beach into that fantastic coral reef full of fish. A snorkel and mask rent for 10 M$ per day (you can buy both for that price in Singapore). Small bungalows cost 48 M$ for two people, larger ones with a shower go for 53 M$.

HOW TO GET HERE
Book at Rawa Safari well in advance, tel 791204. The office is on the river, almost at the mouth. For the hour long ride over you pay 14 M$ (round trip).

Pulau Tioman

The largest island in the archipelago - about 39 km long and 19 km wide. Arab and Chinese seafarers were aware of the island 2000 years ago. It offered a good anchorage and, more important, fresh water. About 1960 years later, Tioman was selected as the location for the Roger & Hammerstein musical 'South Pacific'.

Of the 10 tiny kampongs on the island, **KG.TEKEK** and **KG.JUARA** are of most interest to you. The island is mountainous with lots of jungle. **Gunung Kajang** is over 1000 m high. There's plenty of coral reef around Pulau Tioman; why not do some deep-sea diving (equipment at Merlin costs 45 M$, boats 150 M$). In addition there's great hiking! A walk across the island through the jungle from Tekek to Juara takes about three hours. It's hot and muggy on the east end of the island. The fine sandy beaches are often infested with sand fleas. Or get a boat to a peaceful beach near the village of **SALANG**.

HOTELS
Tourists with cash stay in the luxurious **MERLIN SAMUDRA HOTEL****. Prices range from 70 to 150 M$. Book rooms in advance at tel 791772. The Samudra is booked up for weeks during school holidays. The rooms are quite simple despite the price.

Freaks like to crash in **KG.TEKEK**. Most of the simple huts cost 3-5 M$ per person per night. A nice place but not the cheapest is **NAZRI**'s camp on a nice sandy beach, 45 minutes from the Tekek landing, with 10 huts and a restaurant. Once a week he takes his boat to 'Robinson island' for excellent snorkeling. Costs 15 M$. A bit more expensive is the **RESTHOUSE****. An alternative to Kg.Tekek is Kg.Juara. Bring your own fruit and cookies from Mersing; everything's expensive on the island where only bananas and coconuts grow.

FROM JOHORE BHARU TO KUANTAN

HOW TO GET HERE
The Merlin boat leaves daily at 12:00 h and charges 29 M$ one-way. Depending on the boat, the ride over takes 2 1/2 to 5 hours (slow fishing boat for 15 M$). People with little time and a lot of money can fly with Malaysia Air Charter from KL (Fridays, 125.-M$), Mersing (72.-M$), or Singapore.

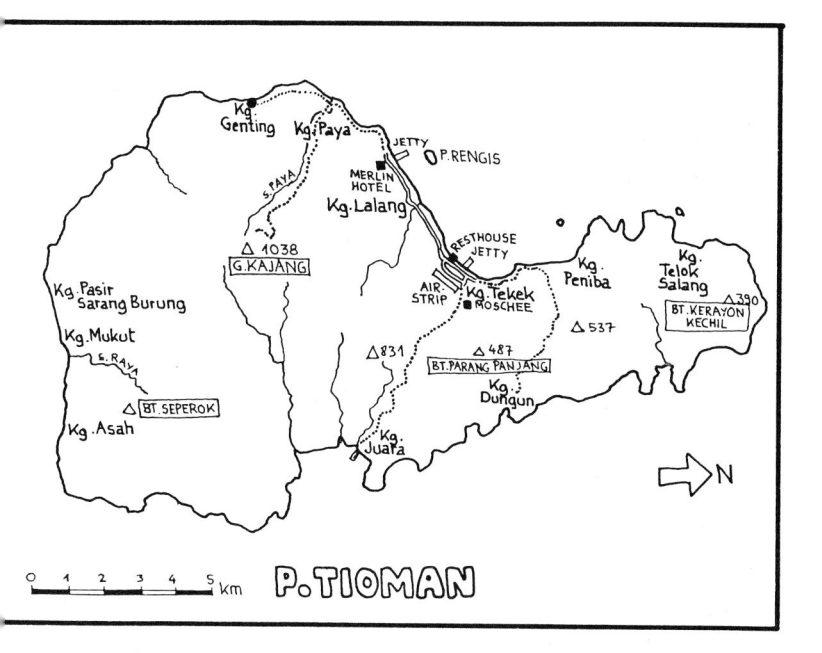

Endau

For a princely sum (about 120 M$ plus expenses), you can rent an outboarder in Endau to take up to 10 people on a trip up the **Sungei Endau** to **KG.PUNAN**. The trip can last 8 hours. Another 38 km further upstream is **KG.PATAH**. After that there're only Orang Asli villages, and you'll have to accept sleeping in the jungle.

Three-day tours are organized by Giamso Safari, 27A Jl.Abu Bakar, Mersing, tel 791636. We've heard that no women are allowed. Perhaps you can show the boys at Giamso

Safari who the real weaklings are. You go by boat on the Sungei Endau first to KG.PUNAN and then visit two Orang Asli villages: KG.PATAH and KG.JASIN. It's possible to trek between these two villages. Costs 100.-M$; you have to bring your own food. Giamso will arrange for the permit from the Forestry Department. A new National Park is planned for 48,000 ha between the Rompin (Pahang) and Endau (Johore) rivers. According to estimates, between 20 and 25 Sumatra Rhinoceros live in the area, the largest population in Peninsular Malaysia.

HOTELS
The only place to spend the night (till now) is in KUALA ROMPIN's **RESTHOUSE****, tel 095/65245 (good food!). Located on the road to Nenasi about 2 km from the bus station.

HOW TO GET HERE
Buses run several times a day between the towns (Endau-KR 1.60 M$; KR-Nenasi 2 M$). There's an express bus from RANTAU ABANG for 10.60 M$. Buses from KUANTAN to ENDAU 7.- (taxi 12.-); taxi from KR to MERSING 5.-M$.

The SUMATRA RHINOCEROS
(rhinocerus sumatrensis, Badak Sumatra)

The 'Illustrated Guide to the Federated Malay States' (1923), the earliest travel guide we've seen to Malaya, dedicated 31 pages to big-game shooting. By 'big-game', they meant primarily the elephant, seladang, rhinoceros, and tiger. Today all of these animals are threatened by extinction, due, in no small measure, to unlicensed shooting thru the 1930s. To quote: "But...those who are prepared to face a certain amount of inconvenience...should be able to obtain trophies that will repay them for the hard work, energy, and time expended."

Malaysian zoologists estimate the entire population in West Malaysia of this endangered species to be between 50 and 70 head. The one-horned Java rhinoceros is already extinct on the Malay peninsula. The largest (20-30 head) population of rhinos lives in the region of the planned Endau-Rompin National Park. Another 10-16 of the animals are spread out over the entire Taman Negara. The Department of Wildlife and National parks plans to resettle the rest of Malaysia's rhinos into these two regions.

Pekan

Just 47 km south of Kuantan, 142 km north of Mersing, you come to the sultan's seat of Pahang, which actually consists of several small kampongs. Only the bus station lends Pekan a bit of city character. During the Malacca Sultanate in 1470, there was mention of the town when Sultan Mansur Shah sent his son to Pekan to act as regent of Pahang.

Worth a look is the modern **ISTANA ABU BAKAR**. Because the sultan is an enthusiastic polo player, a polo ground has been set up next to the Istana. On Sungei Pahang are **ABDULLAH MOSQUE** (masjid lama) and the new **ABU BAKAR MOSQUE**. Both are interesting examples of Malay-Islamic architecture. Check out the **ABU BAKAR MUSEUM** (open daily except Fri from 9:30 to 17:00 h).

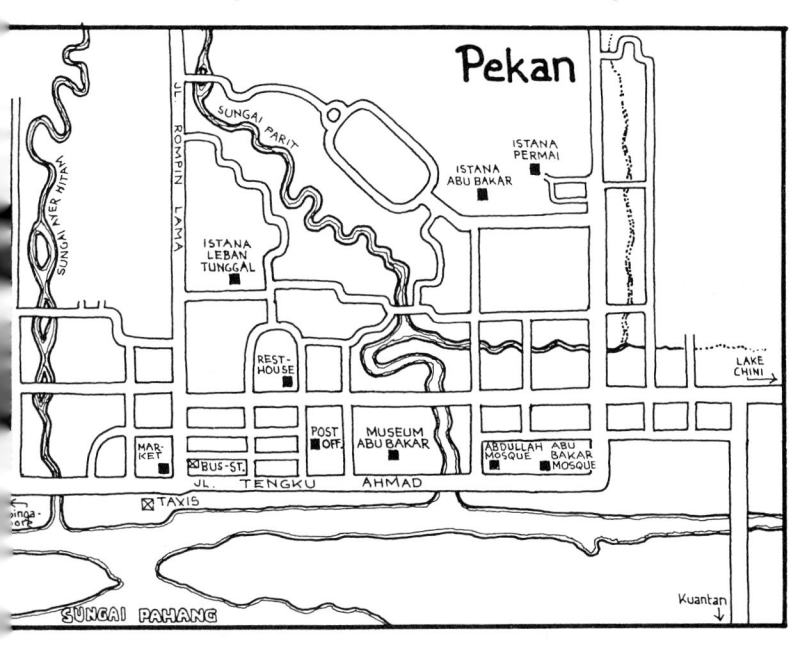

For 30 c, you can get a bus to **KG.PULAU KELADI**. Wonderful sarongs are made here on the Pahang River in a one-story wooden house. During our last visit, however, in 1984, the house was empty and in poor condition due to high water. Ask the bus driver for the 'Pahang Silk Weaving Center' or in Malay 'Tenunan Sutra Pahang'. Traditional silk sarong for men are woven her (70-90 M$).

HOTELS

Wonderfully situated is the **RESTHOUSE**** (tel 71240), book ahead by phone! The **PEKAN HOTEL**** (tel 71378 at 60 Jl. Tengku offers the Chinese alternative.

Kuantan

The capital of the state of Pahang is a boom town which is evolving into the economic capital of the whole east coast. Tourism, too, has really cranked up. On the beach at **Telok Chempedak** are two huge hotels - the Merlin and the Hyatt. Decide for yourself if the city fits your fancy. It is important to you, however, as traffic junction and as a base for excursions into the surrounding countryside. There's no way to avoid Kuantan.

CHANGING MONEY - best rates at People's Bank. Jl.Mahota.

TOURIST INFORMATION - good info about Pahang, as well as tips for excursions around Kuantan, in the **TOURIST OFFICE**, Jl.Hj.A.Aziz next to the MAS office.

HOTELS

Most travellers stay outside town at the beach. You'll find lots of cheap hotels on Jl.Telok Sisek and Jl.Besar. Try **EMBASSY****, 60 Jl.Telok Sisek; **MOONLIGHT****, no 50 (clean, friendly owner, good restaurant); **PLANET****, no 32. The **MIN HENG HOTEL*** on 22 Jl.Mahkota is a bit cheaper but very run down.

PANTAI TELOK CHEMPEDAK

Take bus 39 for 50 c to the beach, the last leaves at 16:00 h and the first back to Kuantan is at 7:00 h.

The beach itself is nothing tremendous. All that's breathtaking is the 140.-M$ for a room in the HYATT HOTEL. A bit further south in the MERLIN, the doors open for about 100.-M$. To the right, behind the row of restaurants and nightclubs, smart Chinese businessmen rent rooms in single family homes - costs between 6 and 15 M$. A four-bed room runs about 20 M$. Good, but unfortunately too expensive is the small, pleasant KUANTAN HOTEL**** (tel 24755). To the

FROM JOHORE BHARU TO KUANTAN

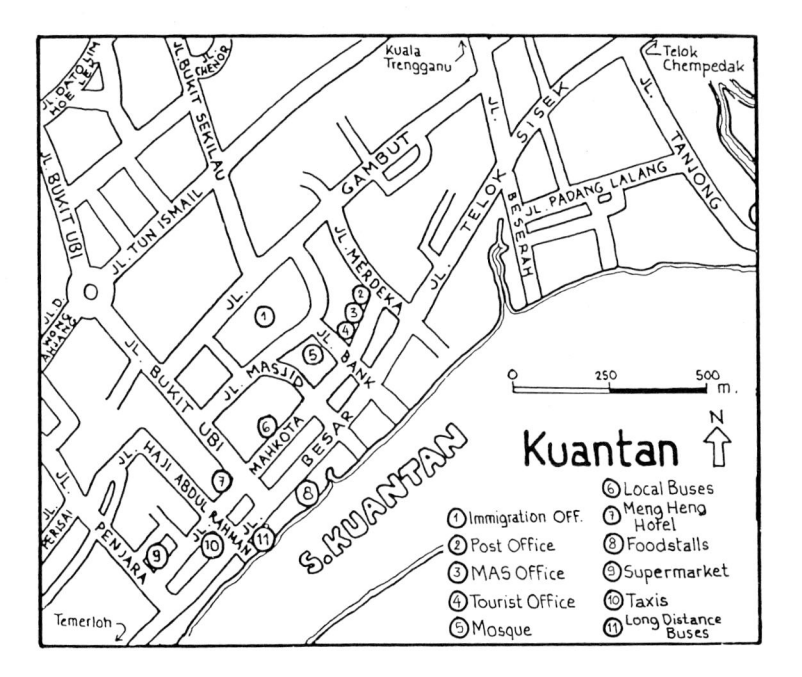

Map of Kuantan with legend:
1. Immigration Off.
2. Post Office
3. MAS Office
4. Tourist Office
5. Mosque
6. Local Buses
7. Meng Heng Hotel
8. Foodstalls
9. Supermarket
10. Taxis
11. Long Distance Buses

right of the Merlin is the ASRAMA BENDAHARA* featuring a Malay restaurant. You can eat outside, right on the beach. On the peninsula between the beach and the resthouse, you can hike along marked paths through the jungle – but nothing outstanding!

DAY TRIPS AROUND KUANTAN
SUNGEI LEMBING
Buses to Sungei Lembing, 43 km to the northwest, cost 1.60 M$. Here is one of the largest tin mines in Malaysia, more than 1000 m deep. Get permission in advance, and you can look inside – but women aren't allowed down.

PANCING
On the way back, make a stop in Pancing. Right in the middle of a rubber plantation is a limestone cliff. In the huge **CHARAH CAVE**, a Buddhist monk from Thailand has erected a 10 m long reclining Buddha. To climb the cliff you have to use the slippery stairs.

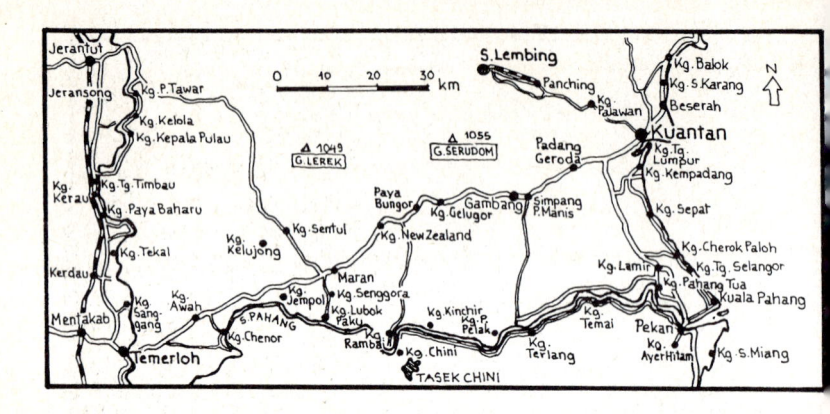

LEAVING KUANTAN
BY AIR
MAS office is at 25 Jl.Hj.A.Aziz (tel 21218). SAMPLE PRICES: JB 77.-, PENANG 141.-, KL 61.-, SINGAPORE 120.-M$. The airport is about 16 km to the west on the road to Temerloh.

OVERLAND BUSES / TAXIS
The bus station is by the market on Jl.Besar. Taxis depart from Jl.Mahkota (next to the Rex Cinema).

SAMPLE PRICES: ALOR SETAR 24.- ac 28.-, BENTONG (14.-), BUTTERWORTH 20.50 ac 24.50, ENDAU 7.-(12.-), JERANTUT 6.40(14.-), JOHORE BHARU 12.- ac 15.-,(25.-), KG.LUBOK PAKU 4.50, KOTA BHARU 13.-(22.-), KUALA LIPIS 10.40(24.-), KUALA DUNGUN (9.50), KL 9.- ac 10.25(20.-), KUALA TRENGGANU 7.-(15.-), MELAKA 10.80, MENTAKAB 4.-(10.-), MERSING 10.25(14.-), PEKAN 2.20(3.50), ROMPIN 7.-(9.50), SEGAMAT (14.-), SINGAPORE 17.- ac 22.-, TEMERLOH 4.30(8.50) M$.

****
THIS TRAVEL GUIDE IS ALIVE
Travellers need the latest information, but no book can keep pace with fast-moving Asia. That's why we completely revise our books annually. You too as readers can participate.
Write to us!
What we missed?
What has changed?
What is new?
****

KELANTAN

This is the part of the east coast most visited by tourists, 380 km long; just one sandy beach. The soil of the thin, agricultural portion of the coastal plain isn't very fertile keeping the state's population small. The dry and rainy seasons are much more pronounced here than on the west coast.

In those areas where agriculture is economical - particularly the delta of the Kelantan River - you'll notice the arrow-straight rows of trees on the rubber plantations. And there's the green of the rice paddies on the northern coastal plain. In most areas, the rice is planted in September and harvested at the end of the rainy season in February or March. Where irrigation has been installed, two crops per year are possible. The further south you go, the more the rice gives way to sand and swamps. You pass increasingly through villages dependent on fishing as their solitary income. Unlike the large fishingboats found on the west coast, the Malay fishermen here work with less effective, small boats. This isn't a place you get rich fishing. During the rainy season, the men can't go out on the stormy sea at all. And there's no convenient major city where large supplies of fish could be marketed.

Poor road connections along the east coast and to the major cities of the west coast have intensified the isolation of the local Malay population. The states of Kelantan and Trengganu are conservative, orthodox Muslim. Friday is the official day of rest. During Ramadan you can get food during daylight hours only from Chinese in the towns, everyone fasts in the kampongs. The quiet village life on the east coast is a nice change from the bustling (Chinese) west coast. Enjoy it before the oil industry destroys it.

This is a good place to try and adjust to the Islamic lifestyle. Don't walk through the village in your bathing suit. Women should never lie around topless on the beach. That's only accepted in the closed off Club Mediterranée. Malays are wonderful people and hosts, but some kinds of "openness" are just beyond their comprehension. Don't accuse us of being moralistic, rather try to understand Islam - thank you!

Kota Bharu

The capital of Kelantan is only a few miles from the Thai border. Till now, few travellers have used this border crossing, but with the opening of the big East-West Highway, there's no hassle getting to or from the west coast cities. Additionally, Kota Bharu is your departure point for an east-coast tour and a trip on the jungle train.

When the city was founded over 200 years ago, it lay right on the sea. But steady sand deposits at the mouth of the Kelantan River have pushed the sea back. The former harbor is now over 12 km inland and only accessible to small ships.

On Merdeka Square is the **MOSQUE** and the fenced in **ISTANA BALAI BESAR** - 'palace with the huge hall of audience'. It also houses the throne room and reception hall. The Istana was built in 1844 for Sultan Mohammed II. Today it is only used for royal ceremonies. Right next to it is the **ISTANA JAHAR** with the Kelantan State Museum. Interesting exhibits! Open daily except Wed from 10:30-18:00 h. Admission free.

In the center of town is **PASAR BESAR**, a big market located in a pretty new building, divided into several sect-

KELANTAN 213

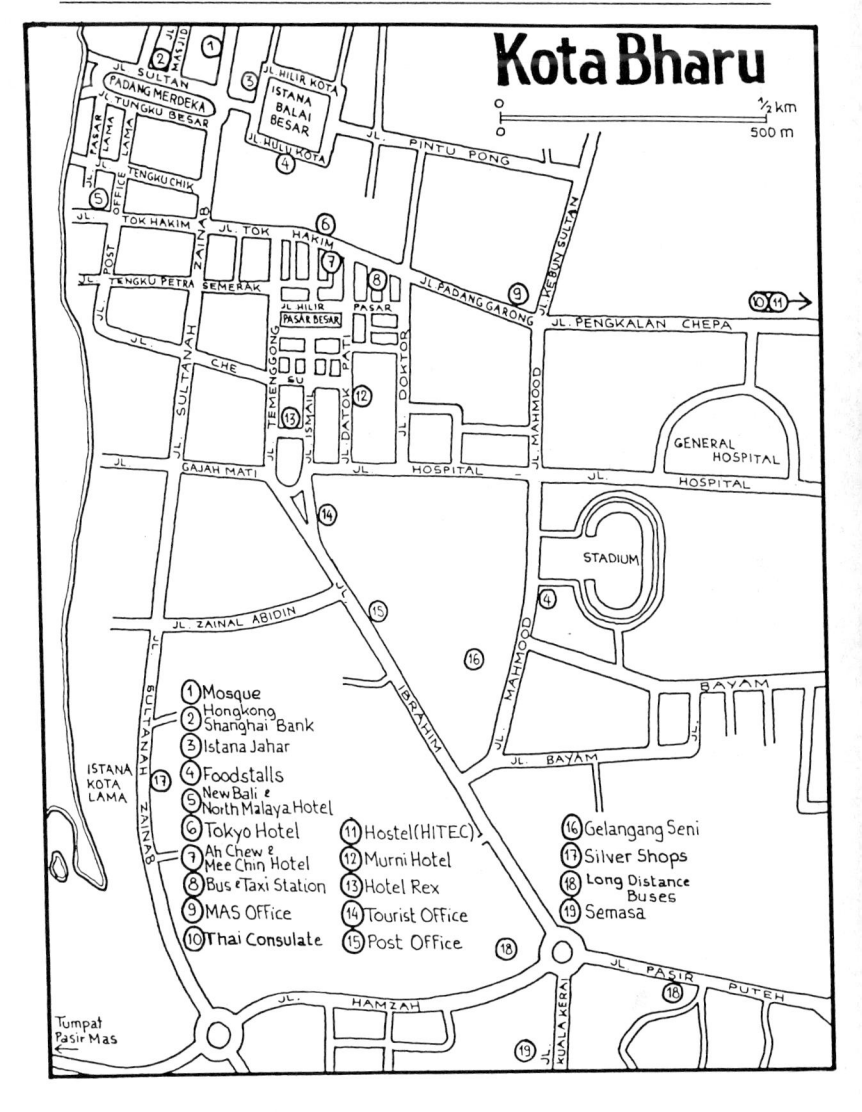

Kota Bharu

1. Mosque
2. Hongkong & Shanghai Bank
3. Istana Jahar
4. Foodstalls
5. New Bali & North Malaya Hotel
6. Tokyo Hotel
7. Ah Chew & Mee Chin Hotel
8. Bus & Taxi Station
9. MAS Office
10. Thai Consulate
11. Hostel (HITEC)
12. Murni Hotel
13. Hotel Rex
14. Tourist Office
15. Post Office
16. Gelangang Seni
17. Silver Shops
18. Long Distance Buses
19. Semasa

ions. You'll find wares such as fresh seasonal fruit and vegetables, cloth, batik, meat, and fish, cakes, baskets and mats. But notice too the women who run the market. Many wear expensive jewelery; a few plaster themselves with make-up.

HOTELS

Sometimes the whole city is booked out. The cheapest roof in KB is the **HITEC HOSTEL***, 4423 Jl.Pengkalan Chepa, next to the Thai consulate. Take bus 4 about 1 1/2 km towards the airport. Opposite is **MUMMY'S HITEC HOSTEL*** (no 4398). Great atmosphere! Several new places have opened up recently in the area. Check **RAINBOW INN*** managed by four young people. Readers recommend **TOWN GUESTHOUSE*** at 2921 Jl.Pintu Pong. Nice hotel in town is **TOKYO HOTEL****, 3945 Jl.Tok Hakim, tel 22466, right behind the bus station. Run by young people, the hotel's best rooms are upstairs off the huge terrace. In the same street but cheaper are the **NORTH MALAYA HOTEL****, no 3856, tel 22171 and the smaller **NEW BALI HOTEL****, no 3655, tel 22686. Also cheap is the **MEE CHIN HOTEL****, especially when four people share a room. **REX HOTEL**** is a bit run down, Jl.Temenggong, right on the square, tel 21419.

FOOD

There are lots of foodstalls near the bus station. Get cheap Indian food across from the Rex on Jl.Temenggong. Good food at the **MEE CHIN HOTEL**. Chinese businessmen amuse themselves in **HOTEL MURNI**, where a nightclub offers hostess service. Good Chinese food at **LOK KAU HOCK**, Jl.Kebun Sultan. Breakfast bread, excellent in Asian terms, can be found in the bakeries, try **MAJU ROTI** near the bus station. Good nasi padang in the corner shop at the bus station. Many foodstalls on the eastern part of the Merdeka Square and at Jl.Mahmud corner of Jl.Bayam.

SHOPPING

SILVER - in Jl.Sultanah Zainab, right after Jl.Zaimal Abidin, are several shops selling Kelantan silver - not cheap, though!

BATIK - if you're looking for batik and other souvenirs, have a look around the shops in Wisma Iktisad, the modern building on Jl.Maju. In the south of town, on the road to Kuala Krai (beyond Jl.Kg.Putih and just before Lee Motors), you'll find a large selection of batik at Batik Samasa. You can also watch how the batik is made. Another place to shop is on Jl.Pantai Cinta Berahi, the road to the 'Beach of Pas-

KELANTAN 215

sionate Love'. Get off the bus in KAMPONG PENAMBANG and have a look at the batik workshops, songket weavers and the kite-maker's houses. You can watch the people working, but you can't always buy. There are a number of small shops on the road heading to the beach.

WOOD CARVINGS - on Jl.Pengkalan Chepa, just beyond Jl.Dusan Muda, you'll find a number of woodcarvers at work (Ukiran Kayu Traditional).

GENERAL INFORMATION
TOURIST INFORMATION - Jl.Sultan Ibrahim (next to Majlis Perbandaran). The information on cultural events includes the BIRD SINGING CONTEST in June. Very eager to help. Open Sun to Wed 8:30-16:00, Thurs 8:30-13:15 h.

IMMIGRATION OFFICE - Jl.Dusun Muda near Jl.Bayam.

THAI CONSULATE - 4426 Jl.Pengkalan Chepa, tel 22545. Open Sun to Thurs 9:00-16:00 h. Two check points for crossing the border into Thailand: **Sungei Golok - Rantau Panjang** and **Kg.Pengkalan Kubor - Tak Bai**.

GELENGGANG SENI - cultural center off Jl.Mahmud; performances of traditional dances and plays every Sat and Wed during the months from February to October with the exception of Ramadan.

Wed 15:30 - 17:30 h top spinning (gasing uri) and self defence (bersilat); 21:00 - 24:00 h the WAYANG KULIT (Shadow Play).

Sat 15:30 - 17:30 h drum performance (rebana ubi), top spinning, kite flying (wau) and self defence. Further info at the Tourist Office.

DAY TRIPS AROUND KOTA BHARU
PANTAI CINTA BERAHI
The Beach of Passionate Love (bus 10 from Kota Bharu, 60 c) is definitely not one of the most picturesque beaches on the east coast, despite its name. Of interest is the 11 km long road leading out to the beach. The kampong atmosphere is filled with batik, souvenirs, songket, and kite shops, (and workshops!) along the street. SRI DESA RESORT offers rooms*** or bungalows****. Much more expensive is RESORT CINTA BERAHI (tel 097 21307). Very new is LONGHOUSE BEACH MOTEL (tel 740090). Double rooms cost between 20.- and 40.-, dorm 5.-M$.

PANTAI DASAR SABAK
Another beach is Pantai Dasar (Sabak), 13 km north of town. Here and further to the north, Japanese troops landed in December 1941. They made their way south in part on bicycle. Two months later, Singapore surrendered. South of the beach is a large fishing village. Of the 2000-odd inhabitants, a surprising number have reached prosperity. Cars are parked in front of wooden homes; videos and TVs are not uncommon. Sabak delivers to the fish market in Kota Bharu. Take bus 9 out to Sabak in the evening and watch the fishermen returning in their colorfully painted and carved boats. If you just want to use the beach, get off at the branch-off before the village. In the fields, the local type of tobacco is grown.

MASJID KAMPONG LAUT
The oldest mosque in Malaysia is located in KG.NILAM PURI, about 10 km south of KB. Around 300 years ago it was built by Javanese in emulation of the great mosque of Demak. It is built completely of wood without the use of metal nails. Originally the structure stood at Kg.Laut on the Kelantan River, but in 1968 it was taken apart and reconstructed here. The very high waters during the annual monsoon season had damaged it greatly.

PASIR MAS
The village on the opposite bank of the Kelantan River boasts a lovely local market. It is on the way to RANTAU PANJANG, the border crossing to Thailand. A small river, the Sungei Golok, forms the border. There are plenty of opportunities for smugglers.

TUMPAT
This is the end of the rail line, 13 km from Kota Bharu, get bus 19 from KB. Tumpat is primarily of interest as a departure point for river trips on the Sungei Kelantan. Boats can

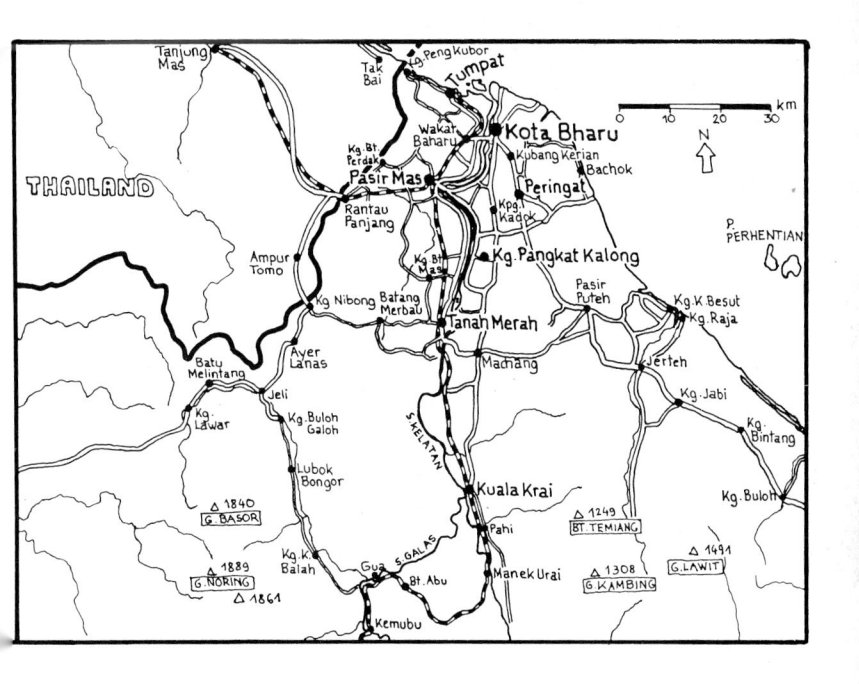

be rented at the dock in Tumpat, costs about 30.-M$ per hour.
    On an island in the Kelantan Delta (Pulau Jong, Junk Island), boats are built using old-fashioned methods. Many are used in the yearly regatta to celebrate the Sultan's Birthday (March 30th-31st).

WAT PHOTHIVIHAN
The longest reclining Buddha in South-East Asia (40 m, 9 m wide, and 11 m high) can be found in Kg.Jambu, a village populated by ethnic Thais. Get bus 19 or 27 to Tumpat and get off at the branch-off 'Cabang Empat Tok Mengah'. From there you've a short 2 km walk.
    Until 1909, Kelantan, along with Perlis, Kedah, and Trengganu were under Thai rule. Then the sultanates came under the British sphere of influence. Only the border region of Kelantan has maintained a meaningful Thai minority. Kg.Jambu has about 200 inhabitants known officially as 'Malaysian Thai'.

LEAVING KOTA BHARU
BY AIR
Sultan Ismail Detra Airport is 10 km out of town. MAS office in Jl.Padang Garong, Hotel Kesian Bharu (tel 743144). Daily flights to KL 86.-(61.-), PENANG 72.-, JOHORE BHARU 163.- and ALOR SETAR 59.-M$.

BY RAIL
The rail line runs west of the river. If you want to take the jungle railroad to KL or Singapore, you'll have to go to PASIR MAS (bus 24) or WAKAF BHARU (bus 19, 27). If you're coming from Thailand, you can hop aboard a rattling train at RANTAU PANJANG. However, for the short stretch to Pasir Mas, you'll need 35 minutes!

A train leaves Wakaf Bharu daily at 8:28 h to GEMAS where you change for SINGAPORE. Takes about 20 hours, price 79.20 M$ 1st, 37.30 M$ 2nd, and 23.40 M$ 3rd class. Be sure to get a berth for that long trip, costs in 2nd class 4.- or 6.-M$.

If you only want to go as far as KUALA LIPIS, you can take the train at 6:43 h, allow 9 hours. Another whistle-stopper leaves at 13:30 h for KUALA KRAI. Offering only 3rd class, it costs 3 M$ from Wakaf Bharu and takes 2 hours. Bus 5 is faster over the 70 km stretch and only costs 1.80 M$. From Kuala Krai there's another train at 6:05 h to Kuala Lipis. There're a number of cheap Chinese hotels* right by the train station in Krai. There aren't any accommodations in Pasir Mas, so be sure to stay in Kota Bharu.

OVERLAND BUSES/TAXIS
Local buses and taxis depart from Jl.Pendek. Long distance buses to Johore Bharu, Singapore and ac buses to KL from Langgar bus station, other buses from Jl.Hamzah.
  SAMPLE PRICES: KUALA TRENGGANU 6.-(12.-), KUALA DUNGUN 11.-(17.-), KUANTAN 16.-(23.-), KL 21.-(42.-), JOHORE BHARU 22.- ac 27.-(50.-), GERIK (via East-West Highway) by taxi 16.-, MALACCA 22.-, SINGAPORE 31.-, BUTTERWORTH 18.-(36.-), PENANG 18.- (30.-), PASIR MAS 1.50(5.-), KUALA KRAI 3.-, PASIR PUTEH 2.50, JERTEH 4.-M$.

Those crossing the border to Thailand can take bus 29 for 1.80 M$ right to RANTAU PANJANG. First bus leaves at 6:30 h. A taxi costs 3 M$. Ther're no hotels in town, sleep in SUNGEI GOLOK. A bridge leads right across the river to a border post, but it's only open until 18:30 h. First train to Haad Yai leaves at 9:00 h.

PULAU PERHENTIAN
The two islands are 2 hours from **KUALA BESUT**. On **PULAU PERHENTIAN BESAR** (=big), there's a resthouse with several bungalows, costs about 10 M$. A fisherman has set up eight huts which he rents for 5 M$. On a lonely beach with lots of coral, you can go diving and see the sharks and sea turtles. For a meal, ride over to **PULAU PERHENTIAN KECHIL** (=small) and eat in the kampong. We recommend you bring your own food and drink, however. After arrival on Pulau Kechil ask for Hashem who owns the 8 huts on the other island. He takes you over.

HOW TO GET HERE
Get a taxi from KUALA TRENGGANU to JERTEH for 7.-M$ or bus 3 from KB for 4.-M$ (leaves every half hour). Then get a bus to KUALA BESUT, where you have to register your trip to the island at the District Office (Pejabat Daerah) and pay for your stay at the Resthouse in advance. Boats cost 5 M$ per person if other people share the ride. Otherwise it's more expensive! As there are only four rooms for rent in the two bungalows on the island, better make a call (097 72328) before, than risk making the laborious trip to Kuala Besut in vain. You can spend the night in KG.RAJA in the Resthouse on the other side of the river. It isn't worth a long stay though - the beach is treeless, and the river water's dirty. There is a bridge between Besut and Kg.Raja.

TRENGGANU

PULAU REDANG
Those who find the east coast too touristy should visit Pulau Redang. The island - a marine national park - is situated 40 km off the mainland and boasts a beautiful coral reef.

HOW TO GET THERE
The normal way is to go to KUALA BESUT, register at the Pejabat Daerah and reserve a room in the Resthouse (costs about 20 M$). A chartered boat, however, could run you up to 100 M$. The cheapest time to come is Thursday or Friday when lots of boats are returning to the island from the market. Those who can speak a bit of Malay might try talking to the fishermen in the kampongs between BATU RAKIT and PENAREK. Maybe they'd be cheaper! Spend a night in one of the kampongs on Pulau Redang - a great way to improve your Malay.

KG. PENAREK
The east coast road heading south runs inland through the rice fields. Not until Kampong Bulah does a branch-off bring you back to the sea at Kampong Penarek. If you're travelling by car, take the road up to Merang. In 1983 the road wasn't paved, but it was passable.

KG. MERANG
There is no place to stay along the kilometers of white, sandy beach. The old Resthouse, a bit north of the village, is still occupied by police and military personnel, assigned to watch the coast and deter further refugee landings. Just off the coast, you can see **PULAU BIDONG**. 40,000 Vietnamese made do on this island during the high point of boat people activity in 1979.

BATU RAKIT
A couple kilometers north of KT, on a beach in the middle of a kampong, is a Resthouse asking only 15.-M$ for one of its three rooms. Other than the manager's daughter, nobody speaks any English. They serve breakfast and dinner. Good and cheap food in the kampong. The sunrises on this part of the coast are particularly nice. At the beach you'll find many fishingboats and yesterday's catch left out to dry.

HOW TO GET HERE
Hourly buses head south along the coast road from Kuala Trengganu to Batu Rakit and Merang.

Kuala Trengganu

The sultan's seat of Trengganu is situated at the mouth of the Trengganu River. The harbor, however, is very shallow and only of limited use. The road system has always been poor. There weren't any roads at all in the sultanate until the 1930s. Even today the town seems pretty sleepy. A couple modern 20th century buildings haven't changed things much. However, with the large offshore oilfields, Trengganu will soon learn to bustle.

Take a walk along **JALAN BANDAR** (formerly Jl.Kampong China). Many houses are more than 100 years old. At the end of the street is **PASAR BESAR**, the big market, located in a modern building, but still charming. On the ground floor and in the courtyard you'll find the staples of Malay village life; upstairs is the more "sophisticated" stuff such as ex-

Kuala Trengganu

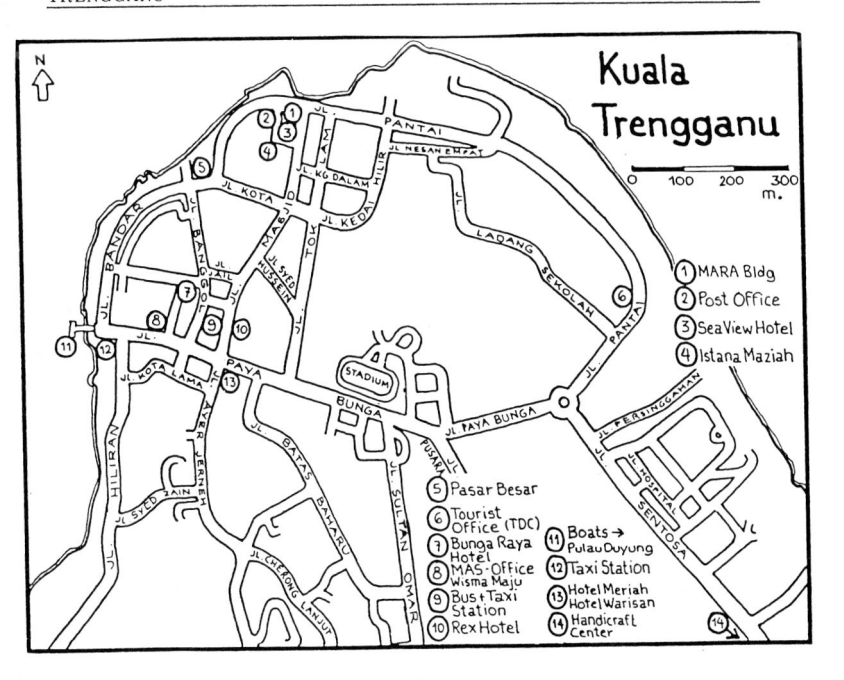

1. MARA Bldg
2. Post Office
3. Sea View Hotel
4. Istana Maziah
5. Pasar Besar
6. Tourist Office (TDC)
7. Bunga Raya Hotel
8. MAS-Office Wisma Maju
9. Bus + Taxi Station
10. Rex Hotel
11. Boats → Pulau Duyung
12. Taxi Station
13. Hotel Meriah / Hotel Warisan
14. Handicraft Center

pensive batik. Go early in the morning when the fishermen are bringing in their catch! Right around the corner is the at first glance fairly modest **ISTANA MAZIAH**. On closer examination, you'll see that the window frames of this completely wooden structure are covered with Arabic quotes from the Koran.

Take a trip to **PULAU DUYUNG**, the largest of the 13 islands lying at the mouth of the Sungei Trengganu. Boats leave regularly for 50 c from the jetty near the taxi station (Jl.Bandar/Jl.Paya Bunga). Malay prahus are still built there today. Ask for Awee and Roheny; the latter is a French woman who married a Malay. They'll put you up for 15 M$ per night, including meals, in their 'yellow house'.

About 4 km to the south on the road to Kuantan is the new **ISTANA BADARIAH** - diagonally across from part of the old istana which was dismantled and moved here. The beach, **PANTAI BATU BUROK**, begins behind the golf course across the street. It isn't a good place to swim because of the dangerous currents. Every year in May, the three-day beach festival, 'Main Pantai', is held featuring stands, shows, and demonstrations of 'silat' (the traditional art of self defence).

In **CHENERING** (921 Taman Peumint Jaya), several kilometers south of town, you'll find the **HANDICRAFT CENTER** (Kraftangan Malaysia). Various Malay crafts are practised in the village. The area might seem sterile, but it's worth a look, as is the exhibition room. A mile further is the salesroom.

HOTELS

There are several reasonable hotels on Jl.Masjid Abidin: **REX****, no 112 (tel 21384), **SEAVIEW****, no 18A (tel 21911) as well as on Jl.Banggol: **MALI****, no 78 (tel 23278) - pretty loud downstairs but ok on the upper floors - **CITY****, no 97-99 (tel 21481), **BUNGA RAYA****, no 105-11 (tel 21166) or **GOLDEN CITY****, no 101-103 (tel 21777). A few other hotels can be found on Jl.Paya Bunga such as **LIDO**** at no 62 or for those looking for more comfort: **MERIAH*****, no 67 (tel 22655) or **WARISAN******, no 65 (tel 22688).

DAY TRIPS AROUND KUALA TRENGGANU
KUALA BERANG

Go by bus for 1.50 M$. The village boasts a hotel and a Resthouse. Across a new bridge an access road runs to Ulu Trengganu. We were told, however, that boat trips to 'Ulu' are better made from Dungun. Take the branch-off left, and it's just a couple kilometers to KENYIR DAM. The huge dam appears without warning in the narrow valley. The artificial lake, which was being filled during our last visit in early 1984, runs all the way back to Taman Negara. At Kg.Dua Empat (branch-off to Sekayu), motorboat rides on the lake were already being offered, costs about 200.-M$ per day.

The famous Trengganu stone with Arabic-Malay inscriptions dating from 1303 was discovered near Kuala Berang. It is considered to be the oldest evidence of Islamic presence in Malaysia. However, Trengganu at that time wasn't an Islamic state. It was under the sovereignty of the Majapahit Empire. The stone can be seen today in the Muzium Negara in KL.

SEKAYU

You can get a bus from Kuala Berang to Sekayu (16 km). There are many waterfalls to visit in the jungle - great hiking! Lots of butterflies! At the bottom of a cascade-like waterfall are bungalows (35 M$) and dormitories. Reservations are necessary. The last bus back to KT leaves at about 17:00 h.

KG.PULAU RUSA
This is about three miles upstream from KT on the road to
Kota Bharu. You can get a ride up by boat for 3.- to 5.-M$
or go by bus. In the village are batik and songket workshops. Two batik factories can be found set back a little
from the main road; a songket workshop is right on the main
road.

LEAVING KUALA TRENGGANU
There are daily flights to KL (80.-), PENANG (80.-) and JO-
HORE BHARU (157.-) M$. MAS office: Wisma Maju, Jl.Paya
Bunga (tel 22266). Telega Batin Airport is situated about
14 km north of town on the road to Merang.

Some taxis leave from the taxi stand on the river
(Jl.Bandar/Jl.Paya Bunga); others leave from the bus station
Jl.Masjid/Jl.Banggol. SAMPLE PRICES:
KUALA DUNGUN 3.60(6.-), KOTA BHARU 6.-(12.-), KUAN-
TAN 7.-(15.-), KL 17.-, ac 20.-(27.-), RANTAU ABANG
3.50 M$.

Marang

Situated south of KT, you might stop off on the way in **KG.
RUSILA** where they've made a name for themselves weaving
mats, hats, baskets and handbags out of palm leaves (men-
kuang). In Marang stay at **IBI'S GUESTHOUSE** (B-283 Kampong
Paya). Ibrahim Muhamad offers a dormitory* plus several
rooms** and for a small surcharge will make you a real
breakfast. Since he's a native of Kuala Trengganu, he knows
the area well, and he'll let you know what's happening and
what to see - nice place!

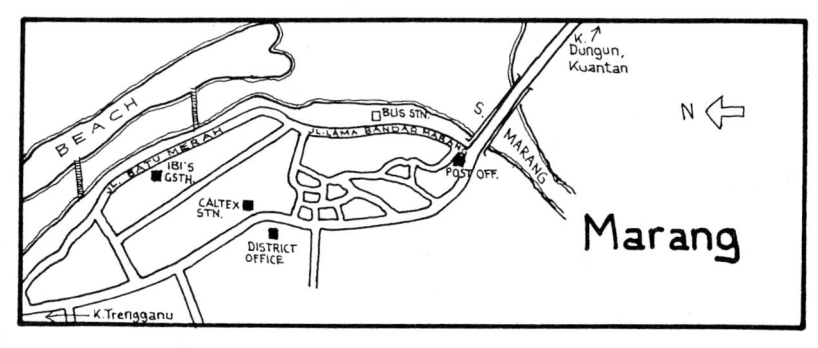

From Marang, you can cross over to **PULAU KAPAS**, a small unpopulated island with a beautiful coral reef. Unfortunately, a boat costs about 150 M$, holds up to 15 people. Three passengers (with hard bargaining) still have to pay 30 to 35.-M$ per person. Ibi can organize a boat for you, or on Jl.Lama Bandar Marang ask in the 'Tana Wangsa' shop for Malik (tel 628832). He is quite elderly and learned his English under British colonial rule.

South of the Sungei Marang, fishing boats are built in **KG.RHU MUDA**. The village is also famous for its dried fish and krupuk.

In **KG.PULAU KERENGGA**, 26 km south of Trengganu, bungalows are available for 50.-M$ at SRI MARANG HOTEL (tel 32566).

Rantau Abang

56 km south of Trengganu, and a couple of kilometers north of Dungun, is the best known spot on the east coast of Malaysia due to the giant sea turtles.

HOTELS
You can stay the night right on the beach next to the breeding station. **YEN & HAKIM** are the owners of a bungalow village (tel 096/41711), costs 8 M$. Next door are **AWANG'S BUNGALOWS** at the same price. During the turtle season prices soar up to 25.-M$. Rantau Abang has developed into a freak hang-out complete with hippie-food restaurants. This should be contrasted with facilities at the **RANTAU ABANG VISITOR CENTRE**, tel 841533, where 20 bungalows rent for 90.-M$. The hotel also has an exhibit about the sea turtles. The complex is run by the Tanjong Jara Beach Hotel, located further south.

Between May and September, and especially in August, over 1000 huge **Leatherback Turtles** (dermochelys coriacea) land yearly to bury their eggs in the sand. They live in the ocean, but go ashore on a few select tropical beaches to lay their eggs in the warm sand. The turtles are known to reach 2 m in length and weigh up to 600 kg. Unlike the other types of turtles, they lack a hard armour shell, and have an almost smooth leathery skin. Leatherback turtles also have real fins rather than claws on their feet. They drag their tremendous weight up the beach looking for the right place to bury their eggs. The fins are used to dig a nest in the sand where up to 100 eggs are laid. All the while they sob and sigh, sometimes you can see real tears running from their eyes (tears also help rinse sand from their eyes). Afterwards, sand is pushed back over the eggs, and the turtle disappears into the ocean.

Particularly in Rantau Abang, the creatures are marketed as a tourist attraction. Whole swarms of visitors invade the beach at night armed with flashlights and cameras. When a turtle appears out of the water, it is pestered with a circle of noise and flashing lights as it makes its torturous way dragging across the sand its tremendous body, which was designed for a life at sea. As they lay their eggs, the crowd of curiosity seekers grows closer and closer. It's no wonder that many of the leatherbacks are driven by the circus back into the sea without laying their eggs.

The Department of Fisheries has set up a hatchery in Rantau Abang to save the leatherback turtle (an endangered species) from extinction. The turtles themselves aren't hunted, but the eggs often end up on the stove. They are sought after not for their protein, but because they're considered an aphrodisiac. The eggs are collected and reburied on the beach in a fenced in area where the turtles can be hatched and tagged. After about 10 weeks the 10 cm long leatherbacks hatch from their eggs and by instinct head for the open sea. Most of them, however, fall victim to crabs, fish, and other hungry creatures. The tiny newborns which you see at the breeding center are therefore taken out to sea by boat for release.

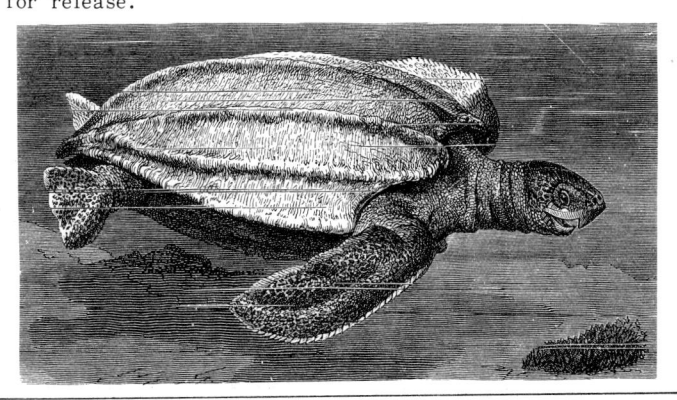

HOW TO GET HERE
Regular buses from KUALA TRENGGANU stop on the main road, costs 3.60 M$. Buses from ROMPIN cost 10.60 M$. Trips by boat out to PULAU TENGGOL are also organized from here.

Kuala Dungun

The town at the mouth of the Dungun River was once important for the shipping of iron ore mined at Batu Besi, one of the largest mines in South-East Asia. The ore was transported to Dungun via a 28 km rail line, where it was loaded into small ships for transfer to larger ships waiting at anchor off shore. Today the ore is moved by truck, and the town again lives from fishing. Everything is very peaceful; check out the nice morning market.

HOTELS
KASANYA**, 225-227 Jl.Tambun (tel 841704) offers reasonable rooms with fans. **SIN CHEW****, 10 K Jl.Besar (tel 841412) is about the same. Cheaper is the **SEAVIEW***, 222 Jl.Lim Teck Wan, tel 841891 or **MEDO****, 146-147 Jl.Tambun (tel 841246). As you'd expect, there's good seafood in town. Try the chilied shrimp in the Mali Hotel restaurant (huge servings!). Or try **TIEN TIEN LAI** on the same street, running from the highway into town. There're foodstalls on the highway. More good food at **BOBBY WANG**, next to the hospital.

A couple kilometers north of town, the most expensive hotel on the entire east coast has been built. If you're up for a night in the **TANJONG JARA BEACH HOTEL** (tel 841801), you'll need 150.-M$ for a double. But it's a nice hotel in Malay kampong style.

HOW TO GET THERE
Between Kuala Trengganu and Kuala Dungun are two roads: one runs right along the coast, the second road branches off to the south 8 km before Kuala Berang and runs inland to Kuantan. At Bukit Besi a road branches off to KUALA DUNGUN. Huge sections of jungle have been logged over. All that's left are buttress roots in the often barren soil.

Taxis leave from the stop behind the market by the harbor (KUANTAN 9.50, KUALA TRENGGANU 6.-M$). Long distance buses from KT-Kuantan Highway, local buses from the main road. Last bus to Rantau Abang leaves at 18:00 h.

PULAU TENGGOL

For about 150.-M$ you can rent a boat out to the island. It's situated about 2 1/2 hours from Dungun. Great coral diving and deep-sea fishing. Huge sharks have been reported. There are only two beaches on the unpopulated island. Trips are organized by Abi, who manages the boathouse at the Tanjong Jara Beach Hotel. If several people go, the trip will run each 35.-M$. Masks, snorkels, and fins cost another 8.-M$.

SUNGEI DUNGUN

We know of people who've taken the SUNGEI DUNGUN upstream and reached the Taman Negara in 10 days. That kind of jungle trek is only for fans of blood-sucking leeches and exhausting day-long marches. A shorter alternative runs via the Sungei Loh. Your departure point is JERANGAU, from where you first head up the Dungun River and then the Loh River. Boats can be chartered to the upper reaches of the Loh (KG.PASIR RAJA) for 200.-M$. Orang Asli guides will then bring you across the watershed on Gunung

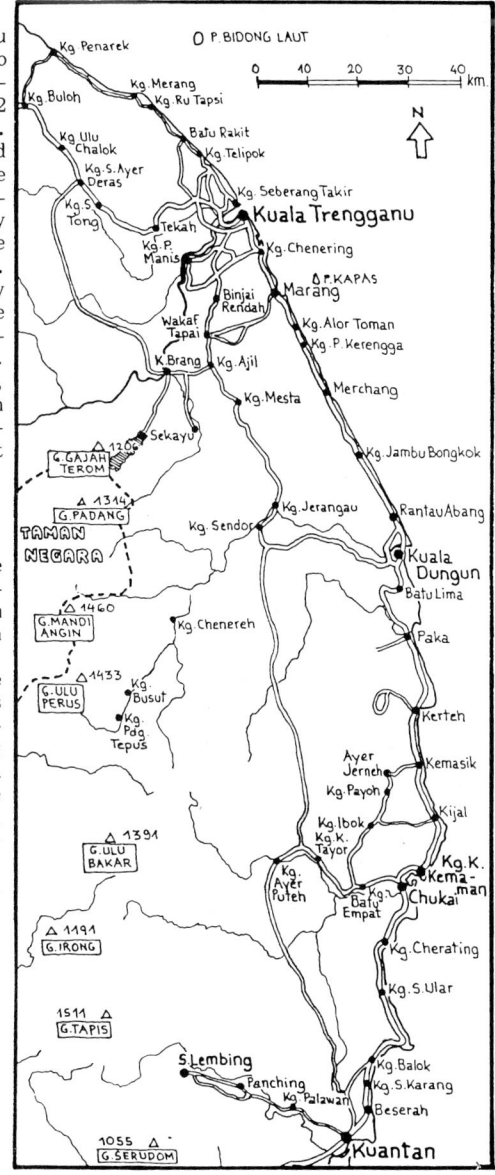

Mandi Angin. Takes at least two days including one night in
the jungle. At the first river, rafts are built which drift
down to KUALA TAHAN. Think in terms of 150.-M$ for the
guide and raft construction. **A guide is a must.** Get info
again from Abi at the boat house.

KEMAMAN
Four or five years ago, the prettiest beaches on the east
coast could be found south of Kuala Dungun. In wake of the
huge oil reserves discovered offshore, the industrialization of
Trengganu has begun. A gigantic electric power plant, complete with oil refinery has been thrown up in PAKA. KERTEH
is now the headquarters of the state oil company, PETRONAS.
A few kilometers south of KIJAL, work began in 1984 to construct a large deep-sea harbor, steel works and a huge LNG
plant. Even KEMASIK, a small fishing village with lovely
beaches, that had been spared until recently has now been
invaded by lots of Petronas bungalows.

CHUKAI
is the business center of Kemaman. It's a good base for excursions to regional beaches where you can watch turtles in
August/September.
   Be sure to have a bite at TONG YUAN* in Jl.Sulaiman.
Try stuffed crab for 9.50 M$ or other seafood. You can stay
the night here, too. If the Tong Yuan is full, go to the
RESTHOUSE** across the road.

Kampong Cherating

is another spot to spend a couple quick days. It's about
28 miles north of Kuantan. Sand deposits have turned the
harbor of this former fishing village into a beach. You can
stay the night with some of the villagers such as MAK DE
SEMAH (3 meals and a bed for 12 M$) or at the MAK LONG
TEH GUESTHOUSE - good seafood. Or try COCONUT INN**, 35
Jl.Cherating Lama. They rent canoes for river trips too.
Cherating has become another freak hang-out.

   A mile north of town is CHENDOR MOTEL (tel 095 591369)
- doubles without ac run 36 M$. Here, too, you can see the
turtles laying their eggs.
   Right next door, by the way, is the first Club Mediterranée in Asia! It was built with wooden Malay-style houses
at the end of the 1970s. Club life, not unintentionally, takes
place behind guarded barricades, away from Malay villages.
But the beach isn't closed off so you can walk for miles.

TRENGGANU

KG.SUNGEI ULAR

North of Kg.Sungei Ular you might try the TITIK INN****, no restaurant. From here and the village, trips are organized out to the Twin Islands, costs between 40.- and 70.-M$. In the village fine pandan mats, fans and baskets are produced. The road runs further inland.

Near TANJUNG GELANG, on the headland, is one of the biggest deep-sea harbors on the east coast.

BESERAH

Located just 5 miles north of Kuantan. You can spend the night in the kampong at YAFFAR'S HOUSE* although it's rather simple. At milestone 5 take a walk inland for about 8 minutes. Up to 8 travellers stay out there.

Have a look around. Notice how the fishermen process their catch into dried fish and crab bread. Watch the villagers make batik and carve wood. This is a great place to observe Malay village life - with some luck, there'll be a festival complete with traditional dancing and top spinning contests.

FROM KUANTAN TO KL

An important road runs from the very agrarian east coast, across impassable mountains, to the thickly populated west coast. Separating peaceful Malay villages and bustling Chinese towns is an insurmountable barrier of tropical rain forest covering more than half the country. This is the home of the Orang Asli, the 'jungle nomads'. Particularly north of the Kuantan-KL Road, the central region is mountainous and thinly populated. During the rainy season the eastern region receives so much precipitation that access is difficult from October through January. South of the road, the country is mostly flat and boasts better transportation infrastructure.

Tremendous projects are underway to open a million hectares of land to agriculture by the year 1990. But there are ecological and sociological problems created by the clearing of the jungle for replacement by monoculture agriculture (rubber or palm oil), and the resettlement of landless settlers who have to give up their traditional lifestyle and livelihood.

Take side trips left or right of the road and discover a completely different Malaysia: the jungles of the tremendous national park, Taman Negara; and two inland lakes, Tasek Chini and Tasek Bera (though they're hard to reach). Most of the route runs through the state of Pahang - with 35,932 km^2 the largest state in West-Malaysia.

Tasek Chini

During the summer, the lake is a sea of lotus blossoms! According to ancient legend, a Loch Ness type monster inhabits the lake. The Orang Asli swear to it! Others tell of a sunken city in the Tasek Chini. You can make a day trip from Kuantan to the lake, rent a boat (costs 80 M$ in **KG. BELIMBING**) or spend a night in a raft-house on the river.

HOW TO GET HERE
About 56 km down the Kuantan - Temerloh road (between PAYA BUNGOR and KG.NEW ZEALAND) there's a road heading off to the left to KG.RAMBAI and KG.BELIMBING. 28 km along, you come to Belimbing on the Pahang River. There isn't much traffic on the road. As far as we know there isn't a bus to Belimbing. So take a taxi or try to get a lift from the branch-off.

A second possibility: take the KL-Kuantan bus to the crossroads after the village of MARAN; off to the left is a 10 km long road leading to KG.LUBOK PAKU. Three buses daily run from Maran for 65 c. There are also direct buses from Kuantan at 8:30 and 11:00 h for 4.50 M$. In Lubok Paku is a Government Halting Bungalow charging about 5 M$ per night. Boats from here to Tasek Chini cost about 80 M$, takes two hours.

Temerloh

The largest and most important city between KL and Kuantan. Visit the weekly market, Sun mornings on a side street near the mosque. Village people come down the river to sell their produce. Great atmosphere!
 The town is situated on the Sungei Pahang, but unfortunately one can't sail the river down to Pekan any longer.

HOTELS
 The **RESTHOUSE**** (tel 51254) is beautifully located with a view of the Sungei Pahang. In town are many cheap Chi-

nese hotels: **FUDO***, 132 Jl.Mentakab; **BAN HIN****, 40 Jl. Tengku Besar; **SWISS HOTEL****, 57-58 Jl.Mentakab. Two middle class hotels: **HOTEL TEMERLOH******, 29-30 Jl. Kuantan (tel 51499) and **TROPICANA*****, A73 Jl.Sultan Ahmad Shah (tel 51095).

HOW TO GET HERE
Frequent buses/taxis from BENTONG, JERANTUT 2.60, KOTA BHARU 8.75(33.-) and KUANTAN 4.30(8.50) M$. There is a train station in MENTAKAB, about 10 km to the west.

Tasek Bera

A very special route leads south from Temerloh to TASEK BERA. This is also of interest for people who want to go direct from Kuantan to Malacca. If you want to stop off in Tasek Bera, you first have to get a permit from the Department of Aboriginal Affairs in Temerloh (behind the Temerloh Hotel). Only then are you permitted to spend the night in the Asli villages around **FORT SKANDA**.

'Tasek Bera' means "lake of changing colors". It's not really what we'd call a lake, rather a maze of canals connecting smaller lakes or ponds. The "lake" is about 5 km wide and 27 km long. FORT SKANDA is the only market far and wide. This is Orang Asli country. They belong to the 900 strong Semai tribe. Fishing is the most important source of livelihood. Transistor radios are the extent of civilization's invasion up to this point. By the way, during your visit to Fort Skanda, be sure to bring your own food.

HOW TO GET HERE
Take the two hour bus ride from TEMERLOH (Jl.Ibrahim) to BAHAU (2.50 M$). From there, go to SEREMBAN (1.90, 2 1/2 hours) - you can get from Seremban to Malacca for 2.85 M$ (see 'From KL to JB'). From Bahau you can get to LADANG GEDDES for 60 c. Then go on by motorbike taxi for 15 M$ to Fort Skanda, takes over an hour on the poor, dusty roads. Expect a long wait, sometimes no bikes at all are going. Then just get a taxi. It'll cost 30.-M$ per person, try to bargain. Rent a boat in Fort Skanda (costs 22 M$ per day).

During your East-West trip between KL and Kuantan or side trip into Taman Negara or Tasek Bera, it's possible you'll be forced to spend a night in a town where tourists are rarely seen. Sometimes the last bus or train has left when you arrive from Taman, or the boat heading there is

Kuala Lipis

The end of the road, heading north, you have to go by rail through the rubber plantations and thinly settled jungle. A lovely situated town boasting a number of old houses. Look for Johnny Tan Bon Tok (try around the station) who organizes jungle tours. A typical three-day-trek costs about 60 M$ per person.

HOTELS
Nice **RESTHOUSE**** (tel 311267). Lots of hotels on the main street: **PARIS*** (tel 311136); **TONG KOK***; **GIN HAI***; or the **CENTRAL***, Jl.Besar, tel 311207. Or try the very clean **SRI LIPIS**** across the railline.

HOW TO GET HERE
Three trains leave daily for KUALA KRAI at 7:30, 9:51, and 14:00 h. Prices: 1st cl. 23.20, 2nd cl. 10.90, 3rd cl. 6.90 M$. If you're travelling by rent-a-car, you can take it with you on the train, costs 120 M$. Telephone your reservation in advance with the stationmaster: 093 311341.
Buses/taxis to KL cost 6.-(12.-), KUANTAN 10.40(24.-M$).

Raub

In Malay the village's name means "digging with the hands". Up until 1955, quite a bit of gold was found in the area, much of it lying on the surface. They didn't even have to use a pick and shovel. Once a week there's a big market!

HOTELS
The most reasonable is the **RESTHOUSE**** (tel 51850). Otherwise there are several other hotels: **RAUB HOTEL****, 57 Jl.Lipis (tel 51288); **DRAGON HOTEL****, 1-3 Jl.Tras (tel 51321). Two others are on Jl.Mason.

HOW TO GET THERE
There's a bus connection every half hour to BENTONG (1.50 M$), for 7 M$ you can go all the way to KL. Taxis and buses go to KUALA KUBU BHARU via FRASER'S HILL (The Gap).

Jerantut

Only important when travelling to Taman Negara.

HOTELS
You're best off in the **RESTHOUSE**** (tel 62257). It's right behind the train tracks on the way to Raub. In town try **JERANTUT HOTEL****, 36 Jl.Besar or **SRI DAMAK*****.

HOW TO GET HERE
Buses to KUANTAN 6.40, to KL 12.-; taxis to KUANTAN 14.-, KL 16.-M$. The road between Jerantut and Raub or Kuala Lipis seems to be guerilla territory. You aren't allowed to drive at night. The 54 miles to MARAN on the Kuantan - KL highway leads through jungle, once in a while plantations, lumber camps and market towns, wild west in style. Partly very bad road!

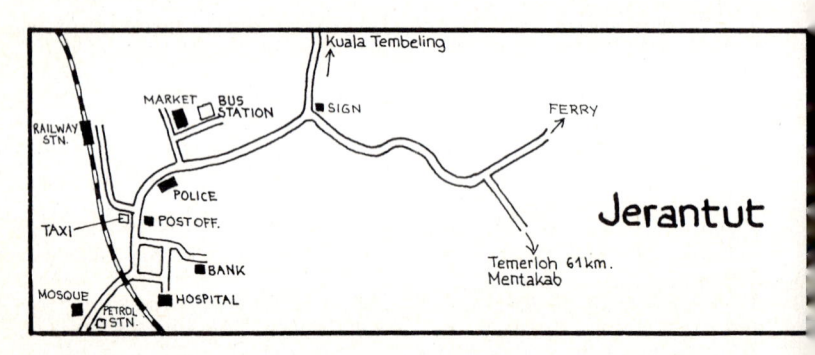

Taman Negara

The average traveller looking to spend a few days in the jungle will need to hire a local guide in most parts of South-East Asia. The cost of guides, boat rentals, accommodations, food, etc. can easily exceed a traveller's budget. The Taman Negara, Malaysia's national park, offers one of the best chances to experience the flora and fauna of a tropical rain forest without breaking your budget. The national park is largely situated in Pahang, but parts stretch into Kelantan and Trengganu. Marked paths of varying difficulty allow you to take short hikes or tours of several days without a guide. **Gunung Tahan**, in the northwestern-most corner, is the highest mountain in West-Malaysia at 2187 m. People in good shape can hike to Tahan, but be sure to get one of the various "visitor's books" in the park headquarters and make sure you are really up to it. There aren't any roads at all in Taman Negara. The only way to get around is on the rivers and jungle trails.

The jungle region of central Malaysia is roughly 130 million years old. This means that while other parts of the world were wrought by the forces of the ice ages or changes in water level and climate, nothing much has changed here climate-wise. The tropical rain forest is a focal point of botanical and zoological evolution: it's one of the oldest forest areas in the world.

A trip to the Taman Negara is very rewarding. Be sure to come in good shape and bring the proper equipment, plus a desire for adventure. The costs are really minimal, despite what you might read in other travel guides. People without much time should try to set aside at least 3 to 4 days. With less than that there's not much point. Just the trip in or back takes a whole day.

During the 60 km boat ride to the headquarters you get your first impression of the jungle. After about two hours, near KUALA ATOK, the national park begins on the left-hand side of the river: thick jungle down to the river, an occasional kingfisher flying overhead, much less often a rhinoceros bird, giant lizards or varan (not crocodiles!), and grey-brown monkeys (macaque).

Upon arrival head for the office where you register (1.-M$ for the **INFORMATION SHEET** and 5.-M$ for a photo license) and are assigned quarters.

ACCOMMODATIONS
Up to now the park headquarters in Kuala Tahan is only able to harbor a maximum of 100 visitors at a time. Many of these tourists never take any hikes at all - we can remember one group of Hongkong Chinese who on their first ten minute expedition were down right ambushed by blood-sucking leeches and never again ventured from the well-tended lawns of Kuala Tahan!

A night's rest in the hostel costs 3.30 M$, in the bungalows or at the Resthouse you pay 15.-M$ for a double. A night in one of the raised hides (blinds) costs 2.50 M$.

FOOD
A meal in the restaurant costs between 3 and 7 M$. We recommend that you prepare your own food, in Kuala Tahan there's a shop offering a small selection of groceries. Everything's cheaper in Jerantut, though; be sure to bring lots of fruit since the prices in the park are influenced by scarcity.

If you plan some trekking, take provisions which are light as possible, quick and simple to prepare, and don't leave much trash (cans, plastic, etc.). We recommend instant noodles, dried foods (soups, fish, vegetables, fruits, nuts), cookies, powdered milk, milo, tea, coffee, salt, oil...

INFORMATION
Pick up the **INFORMATION SHEET** when you book your reservations in KL (sometimes they've it in Kuala Tahan). You'll find general info along with detailed trail descriptions. On the basis of this info, you should be able to plan your activities during the visit.

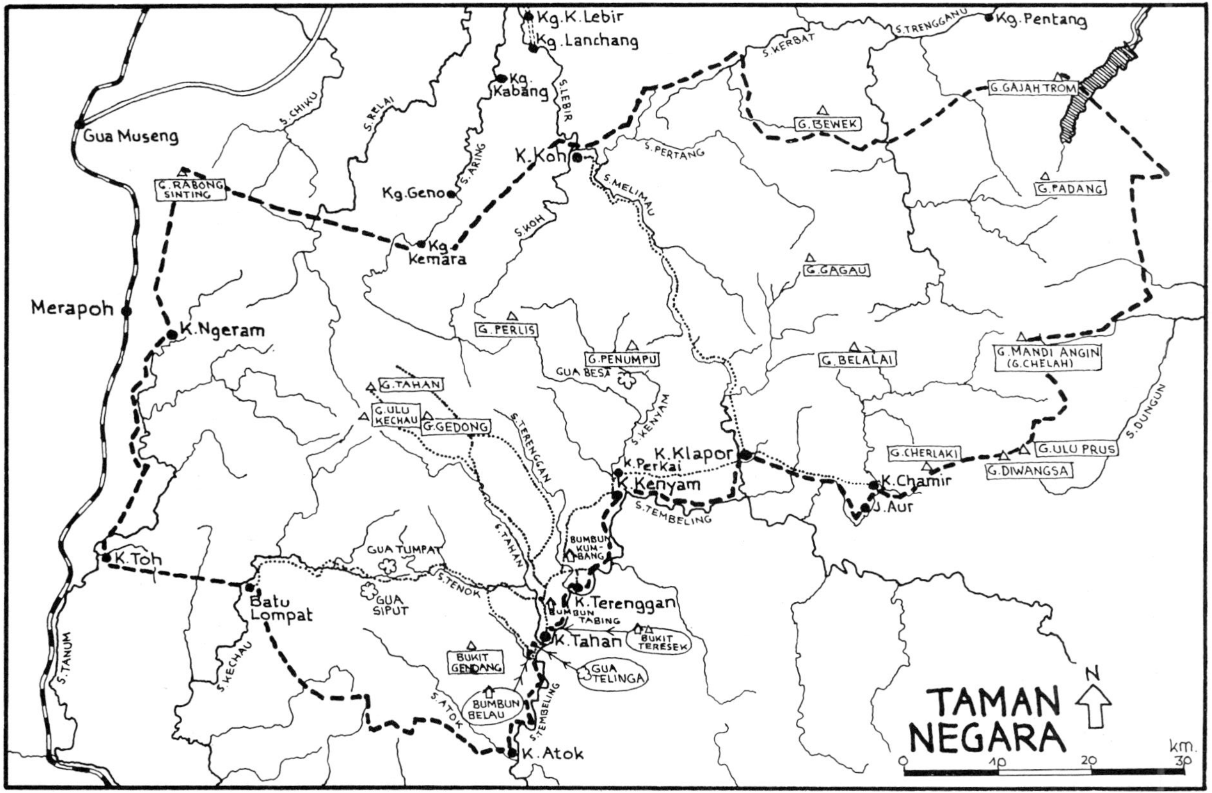
TAMAN NEGARA
N
km.
0
10
20
30
Kg. K. Lebir
Kg. Lanchang
Kg. Kabang
Kg. Pentang
S. TRENGGANU
S. KERBAT
G. GAJAH TROM
G. BEWEK
G. PADANG
S. PERTANG
S. MELIMAU
S. LEBIR
K. Koh
S. CHIKU
S. RELAI
S. ARING
Kg. Geno
S. KOH
Kg. Kemara
Gua Museng
G. RABONG SINTING
Merapoh
K. Ngeram
G. GAGAU
G. PERLIS
G. PENUMPU
GUA BESA
G. BELALAI
G. MANDI ANGIN (G. CHELAH)
S. DUNGUN
G. TAHAN
G. ULU KECHAU
G. GEDONG
S. TERENGGAN
S. KENYAM
K. Klapor
K. PerKai
K. Kenyam
G. CHERLAKI
G. ULU PRUS
G. DIWANGSA
K. Chamir
J. Aur
S. TEMBELING
BUMBUN KUMBANG
GUA TUMPAT
S. TAHAN
K. Toh
S. TENOK
Batu Lompat
GUA SIPUT
K. Terenggan
BUMBUN TABING
BUKIT TERESEK
K. Tahan
BUKIT GENDANG
GUA TELINGA
S. TANUM
S. KECHAU
S. ATOK
BUMBUN BELAU
S. TEMBELING
K. Atok

An excellent source of information is the **Guide To Taman Negara,** published in 1971 (no 3+4) in the MALAYAN NATURE JOURNAL. It is now available as a reprint for 1.50 M$ (Malayan Nature Journal, Petaling Jaya, no 17, SS 2/53). We weren't able to find the guide in any bookstore in Singapore or Malaysia, but it was available in the Penang Museum. Zoologists and botanists won't be able to do without reading its essay: **THE DISTRIBUTION OF LARGE ANIMALS IN TAMAN NEGARA.**

Another source of info are the many guest books lying around in the restaurant. They offer great reading along with many practical tips.

JUNGLE TREKS

This is the high point of any Taman Negara Trip! Choices range from a short excursion around the headquarters to 7 or 10 day treks to Gunung Tahan. Particularly near Kuala Tahan, the trails are well marked and easy to find with the aid of the maps in the Information Sheet. We've found the trail descriptions and warnings of special difficulties to be dependable. For up to the minute information (water level in the rivers, available hides, weather), ask one of the park rangers.

Before you go on a long trek, try a couple of short day tours to get used to jungle conditions: little light; endless green; damp, stinking heat; and ill-definable noises (particularly at sunrise and sunset).

A well-laid path leads up to **BUKIT TERESEK**, an instructional botanical trail, featuring 22 trees with English-language descriptions. Start out right at dawn in order to hear the jungle noises, and so you can see from the top how the morning fog rises over the forest.

A good four hours trek leads you from Tabing Hide via Bukit Teresek and Muda salt lick back to Kuala Tahan.

Other paths lead along the river banks to **SUNGEI TEMBELING** and **SUNGEI TAHAN**. You'll find special tips for fishermen in the Information Sheets. On some of the tours you can rent a boat with several other people and do part of the trip by river. For example, a ride with a small outboarder on Sungei Tembeling from Kuala Tahan to Kuala Trenggan runs 40.-M$ per boat (4-6 people).

Short tours are also possible on the other side of the river. A boat can take you across to the Orang Asli village.

The first part of the way is very steep in spots. A good hike is to **GUA TELINGA**, a bat cave. Those who aren't deterred by knee-deep stagnant water and tons of stinking guano (in order to creep through the cave passages and observe bats in their everyday surroundings) should carry a good flashlight and follow the markings.

The trail then leads on to **BUMBUN BELAU** hide, where, as at **BUMBUN KUMBANG** (near Kuala Trenggan) you can stay for the night if you register in advance in Kuala Tahan. The hides are equipped with several beds and have a window from which in the night you can watch a clearing (salt lick) to see what animals come. Prerequisites are lots of patience, quiet, and a powerful flashlight with which you can floodlight the clearing from time to time. Sometimes you'll surprise a tapir, there's little chance of stumbling across a tiger or elephant. Probably the only animals you'll get to see are the jungle rats which invade the hides at night looking for food.

EQUIPMENT
An absolute necessity on jungle tours are sturdy, comfortable shoes. Outside of the dry season, wear boots. You'll find a lot of different opinions as to which boots are best. We found the locally produced jungle boots ideal. They are made of canvas and have a thick, well-tread rubber sole. In addition you need to wear a pair of thick woollen socks or two pairs of thinner socks. Your long pants should be tied inside the boots to protect against leeches. If you didn't purchase them in KL (Ngoh Kiong & Co. Sdn. Bhd., 264 Jalan Ipoh). Or get them in Penang or Singapore for about 15 M$.

Cotton clothes are best. Wear a wide hat (really nice when it rains!). When it rains a bit harder (and when doesn't it rain in the jungle?), you should have a plastic tarp which you can also use as a poncho. When folded up, such tarps take up almost no space. On higher altitude tours (Gunung Tahan), it can get very cold at night - bring a windbreaker and a thick sweater.

For longer trips, you'll also need a small tent. A camping package (tent, cooking utensils, knife, water bottle etc.) can be rented for 2.50 M$ per day. A backpack (not very good) rents for another 2.50 M$. You'll also need a sleeping bag or blankets in case you sleep outside the hides. Blankets are available in the hides (don't expect clean ones), but the idea is to stay awake and experience a jungle night.

It's a real luxury to have warm clothes to change into in the evening. Since everything is wet in the jungle, change back into you wet clothes in the morning. Use any lengthy stopovers at a river to dry your clothes.

You'll also need toilet articles, matches, insect spray (against leeches), salt tablets, first-aid kit with lots of bandages, a sharp knife, and a strong flashlight. Take enough food, and particularly drinking water. Many of the rivers, which are shown on the Information Sheet, contain drinkable water. Boil it or use halozone tablets.

LEECHES

Generally leeches are pretty harmless creatures which lay along jungle paths and wait for a warm-blooded animal it can latch onto. Usually they crawl into your boots or up your pants' leg. With their suckers they fasten themselves to your skin and draw blood. At the same time they secrete an enzyme which keeps your blood from clotting for a while. When they're nice and fat, they fall off. If, however, they've crawled through your boots and socks, down to your feet, and have tanked up there, then they won't be able to get back out again due to their increased volume. So don't be surprised if your feet are coated with blood.

Preventive measures: Tie your pants into your boots, and spray your boots with one or more rounds of insect repellent (such as Johnson's OFF). The leeches are then dissuaded at least for a while. Smokers seem, by the way, to be better off than nonsmokers (try rubbing your feet with tobacco!).

In the evening or during a break, you can remove the leeches - but don't rip them off. It is much better to get them to loosen themselves first with a glowing cigarette or a bit of salt. The bleeding wounds should then be washed and covered with a bandage.

We found these unpleasant creatures only on the ground in the Taman Negara. In other South-East Asian tropical forests they fall out of the trees onto you. The only way to be completely safe is to remain on the headquarter's lawn.

HOW TO GET HERE

Since accommodations are limited, be sure to book well in advance. Single travellers, possibly even a couple, might

FROM KUANTAN TO KL 241

head for Kuala Tembeling without an advance booking and
hope to get a place in an unfilled boat. You're better off,
however, registering in KL. Normally you make an advance
payment which is credited against your final bill in Kuala
Tahan. You can also register by phone. The address in KL:
CHIEF GAME WARDEN, Block K19, Government Offices Building,
Jl.Duta, tel 941110, 941466 (from the city take bus 19 or 20).

From KL, take bus or taxi via TEMERLOH to JERANTUT 12.-
(16.-M$) - the local bus from Temerloh to Jerantut costs
2.60 M$. If you're coming from the north, get a bus
(4 hours) or taxi (1 1/2 hours, 7.-M$) from KUALA LIPIS. If
you're coming from KUANTAN, take a bus (6.40) or taxi
(14.-M$) to Jerantut. If you're coming from SINGAPORE or KO-
TA BHARU, take the train to TEMBELING HALT, but make sure
you inform the conductor to stop there. From here, it's just
half an hour by foot to where the boats dock. The trains always stop in Jerantut.

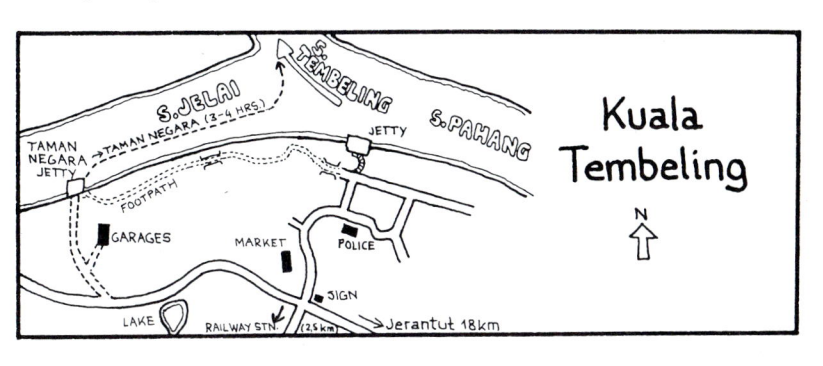

There are taxis from Jerantut charging 3 M$ for a ride on
the newly paved road to **KUALA TEMBELING.** At 10:30, 11:30
and 12:30 h there's also a bus charging 2.-M$. Around
14:00 h, sometimes a bit earlier, the boats depart for KUALA
TAHAN. The boat ride to KUALA TAHAN costs between 8 and
15.-M$ per person. The price depends on the size of the boat
and the number of passengers.

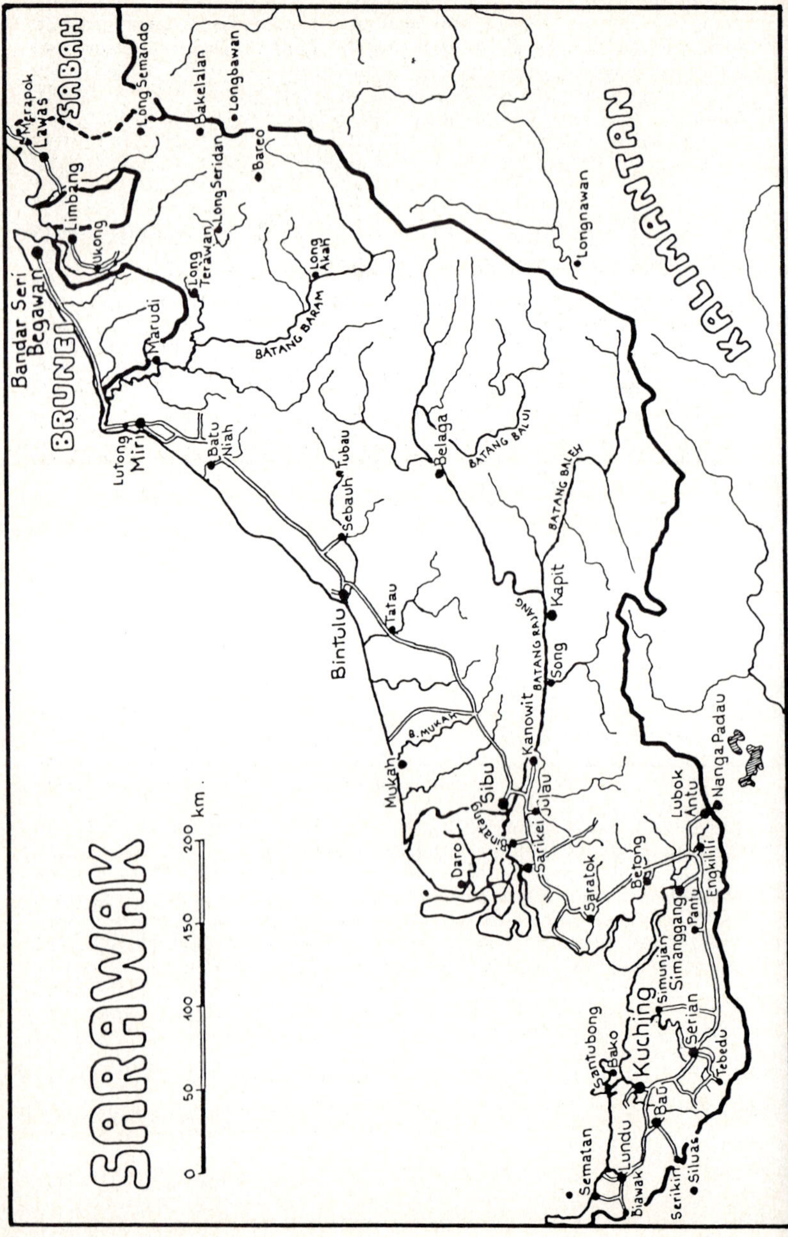
SARAWAK
0
50
100
150
200 km
SABAH
KALIMANTAN
BRUNEI
Bandar Seri Begawan
Merapok
Lawas
Limbang
Ukong
Long Semando
Bakelalan
Longbawan
Long Seridan
Bareo
Long Terawan
Long Akah
Marudi
BATANG BARAM
Lutong
Miri
Batu Niah
Tubau
Sebauh
Belaga
BATANG BALUI
BATANG BALEH
Longnawan
Bintulu
Tatau
Kapit
BATANG RAJANG
Song
Kanowit
B. MUKAH
Mukah
Sibu
Binatang
Julau
Sarikei
Daro
Saratok
Betong
Lubok Antu
Nanga Padau
Engkilili
Pantu
Simanggang
Simunjan
Kuching
Serian
Tebedu
Santubong
Bako
Bau
Lundu
Sematan
Biawak
Serikin
Siluas

SARAWAK

Malaysia's largest state is located on the world's third largest island. Plans for an extensive road system are still in their infancy, though the Trans-Sarawak Highway is now open from end to end. The primary arteries, however, remain the rivers.

Sarawak - 'land of the head-hunters': glossy ads entice civilization-weary adventure seekers. A river trip through the tremendous jungle sampling several tribal longhouses is part of the standard program for both group and individual tourists. According to taste, some people like rigidly organized tours up the Skrang River, an area set up to handle massive storms of visitors. Others go by boat for several days in the hope of reaching an almost inaccessible village, where 'no tourist has ever been'.

Conflicts are unavoidable where people are treated as tourist attractions. The Iban, Kayan or Kenyah, who live in Sarawak as well as on the Indonesian side of the island, are traditionally open to guests – but not to western tourists with their high expectations: snooping into even the most intimate corners of the longhouse; demanding meat on the table, and come evening, the tuak in rivers – but nice and primitive, please! Who stops to think that the people living here also have a need for privacy; that food stocks aren't easy to refill; and that for some people a good tin roof during the rainy season is the ultimate in comfort.

Kuching

Sarawak's capital, on the southern bank of the Sungei Sarawak, is only 20 km from the South China Sea. Even today, despite the Holiday Inn, you'll feel like you're in a Joseph Conrad novel instead of a modern metropolis. 'Kuching', by the way, is the Malay word for 'cat'; here's how it came about: When James Brooke landed here for the first time he pointed towards the village from the harbor and asked one of the natives the name. The native, however, thought that Brooke was pointing at a cat which chanced to be walking by and wanted to know the Malay word for 'cat'. So he told him 'kuching'.

The town's biggest attraction is the **SARAWAK MUSEUM** (open Mon-Thurs 9:15-17:15 h, Sat and Sun until 18:00 h). Admission is free. It holds the largest collection of archaeological and cultural artifacts in all of Borneo. The old museum houses the natural science exhibits, while the new Dewan Tun Abdul Razak harbors the ethnological and historical departments. You'll also find several cult objects in the huge garden. Plus, you can study the flora and fauna of Sarawak.

The museum was founded by the second Raja Brooke in 1888, probably with Alfred Russel Wallace, the discoverer of the dividing line of the same name, offering a few ideas. The Wallace line runs between Bali and Lombok and further to the north between Kalimantan and Sulawesi – to the west are Asian flora and fauna, to the east the Australian-Melanese varieties begin. Today, the Sarawak Museum is certainly one of the greatest museums in South-East Asia; the annual budget runs about 1.7 million M$.

On the corner of Courthouse Road/Main Bazar is the **SUPREME COURT BUILDING**, built in 1874. Its thick Victorian columns just don't seem to fit in on Borneo. In front is a **MEMORIAL** to the second Raja, Sir Charles Brooke. At each corner is a bronze relief representing the four main ethnic groups in Sarawak: Iban, Malay, Chinese, and Kayan.

SARAWAK 245

Kuching

Map Legend:
1. Istana
2. Fort Margharita
3. Long Jetty → Santubong → Bako
4. Syn Ah Hotel
5. National Mosque
6. Bus Terminal
7. Electra Building
8. Court House
9. Post Office
10. Jetty → Sibu
11. Holiday Inn
12. Kuching Hotel
13. Odeon Hotel
14. Sarawak Tourist Ass.
15. Sarawak Museum
16. Indones. Consulate
17. Immigration Dept.

The city is dominated by the **MASJID NEGARA**, the new national mosque with its golden dome.

On the other side of the river (20 c by boat) is the **ISTANA**, also built by the second Raja. Today it's the residence of the Sarawak governor. A bit further upstream is another structure testifying to the former strength of the White Raja. **FORT MARGHERITA**, named for the Raja's second wife, is a police museum today. Between the istana and the old fort is a Brooke family cemetery.

A new local landmark is the super-modern Sarawak Parliament Building **(COUNCIL NEGERI KOMPLEKS)**. Be sure to have a look across the river.

HOTELS

Good is the **KUCHING HOTEL****, 6 Temple Street. About the same, **KHIAW HIN**** at no 52 (tel 23708). Otherwise there's **SYN AH***, 16 Market Street (tel 21459). Other cheapies: **AH CHEW****, 3 Java Street or **NG CHEW***, 16-17 Courthouse Road. There aren't any middle class hotels under 20 M$. In the higher bracket you're best off at **KAPIT HOTEL******, 59 Jl.Padungan (tel 24179). Or try on the same street the **SARAWAK HOTEL*****, no 196 (tel 21547). Cheap dorm in the **HOSTEL*** at the St.Thomas' Cathedral in Jl.Tun Haji Openg between GPO and Aurora Hotel. The Hostel is right in the back. If you're weighted with cash, there's the **HOLIDAY INN****** offering double rooms for 170.-M$.

FOOD

Indian-Malay food can be found on Jl.India. In Carpenter Street there's a big Chinese place squashed between two temples. Nobody speaks any English though! Between the Electra Building (great view from the roof!) and the bus station are lots of foodstalls. Nasi goreng or mee goreng are served for as little as 1.20 M$. Get excellent Chinese food at **MANDARIN** in the Odeon Hotel on Jl.Padungan. A bit cheaper is **FOOK HOI** opposite the GPO.

GENERAL INFORMATION

TOURIST INFORMATION - good information available from the SARAWAK TOURIST ASSOCIATION in Temple Street. TDC office at the AIA Building, Jl.Song Thian Cheock, open Mon-Fri 9:00-16:30 h, Sat 9:00-12:00 h.

IMMIGRATION - Jl.Song Thian Cheock, open Mon-Fri 9:00-16:30 h, Sat 9:00-12:00 h.

BOOKS - a good bookstore in town is **REX BOOKSTORE** on Khoo Hun Yeang Street. Besides literature about Borneo, you can also get the two part Sarawak map providing a scale of 1:500,000. It's the best Sarawak map you can buy. We weren't been able to find this map anywhere else.

Lots of books about Borneo in the **SARAWAK STATE LIBRARY** on Jl.Java.

INDONESIA CONSULATE - 19 Jl.Deshon, tel 20551. **Pontianak is not a visa-free point of entry.**

DAY TRIPS AROUND KUCHING
SANTUBONG
is set on the sea about 30 km from Kuching and a popular place to swim. Between 7:00 and 8:00 h in the morning, a boat will take you down the river for 2.50 M$. The boats tie up at Long Jetty (Jl.Gambier). Don't miss your ride back - leaves around 14:00 h, check! Beautiful countryside! In the background is the 800 m high **Gunung Santubong.** Once this was a major trading center. Nearby excavations show contacts with the Chinese empire between 700 and 1200 AD. But a trip to Santubong is only worth it for people who've been dreaming of a beach for a long time!

BAU
is a tiny village west of Kuching. Gold prospectors were active here until 1890. Today the huge excavations have been flooded, and **Tasek Biru** (blue lake) is the town's main attraction. Only a few tourists make it here to swim in the fresh water and enjoy cheap lake-side food prices. For 1.85 M$, you can get a Bau Transport Co. bus at the bus terminal.

LUNDU / SEMATAN
From Bau you can get to the two villages and their beaches. From Bau, a bus leaves every 1 1/2 hours until 15:00 h to Lundu for 2.80 M$. Siar Beach is about 10 km from town. In Lundu stay at CHENG HAK BOARDING HOUSE**.

From Lundu, STC buses leave regularly for 1.95 M$ to Sematan, located at the western-most tip of Sarawak. Right on the beach are the bungalows of the THOMAS LAI SEASIDE RESORT, cost 25.-M$. Often booked out so reserve in advance from Doris Lai in Kuching, Jl.Bidayuh, tel 21810. Another hotel on the main street charges 20.-M$. Foreign tourists rarely make it out here.

KG.SEGU BENUK
If you don't have a lot of time and still want to visit a Land Dayak longhouse, here's your chance: About 35 km away is Kampong Segu Benuk. Take bus 6 (STC) from the bus station - leaves around 11:00 h, for 1.65 M$. Don't miss the last bus back! Less than recommendable - the longhouse is very touristy. If possible, organize your own visit to a longhouse further inland. Travel agencies in Kuching will sell you a trip to Segu Benuk for several times the bus fare.

LEAVING KUCHING
DOMESTIC FLIGHTS
Kuching Airport is about 10 km south of town, bus 12 from 6:25 h until midnight leaves every 25 minutes for 70 c, a taxi costs 18 M$.
MAS office in Ban Hock Road, shop no 6, tel 57210. Daily flights to West Malaysia, Singapore, and within East Malaysia.

SAMPLE PRICES: BANDAR SERI BEGAWAN 172.-, BINTULU 97.-, KOTA KINABALU 198.-, LABUAN 173.-, MIRI 136.-, SIBU 60.-, JOHORE BHARU 147.-(nightflight 125.-), KUALA LUMPUR 231.- (nightflight 162.-), SINGAPORE 187.-M$.

In addition there are the so-called BN-flights (Britton Norman Islander Flights), with which you can reach just about every tiny place in Sarawak, though sometimes only once a week.

INTERNATIONAL FLIGHTS
The fastest way to Indonesian Kalimantan is by the Merpati flights to Pontianak on Friday at 12:00 h for 84.-M$. Agent in Kuching: Sin Hua Travel, 8 Temple Street, tel 23276.

OVERLAND TO INDONESIA
The overland border between Sarawak and Indonesia is generally closed to foreigners. This is not the case, however, for the land border between Sabah and Indonesia. Our experience is this:

Travellers who travel from Kalimantan to Sarawak via the land border, and use an official border crossing point open for local border traffic, don't receive an entry stamp in their passport from the Malaysians. At the border, instead, they are issued a letter to be immediately presented in Kuching to the Sarawak Immigration Office. What happens next nobody knows. They probably won't send you back; at worst deport you. A lot depends on your tact and ability to talk.

An official departure from Sarawak via this border to Kalimantan is not permitted. Since there aren't any border posts in the middle of the jungle, there's really only the Indonesian authorities to stop you. It's much easier to deal with them than the Malaysians.

Here is a list of the immigration offices in Sarawak: Central office in KUCHING; Division Offices in SRI AMAN, SIBU, MIRI, LIMBANG, SARIKEI and KAPIT; Branch offices in BAU, SERIAN, LUNDU, ENGKILILI, BINTULU, MARUDI, LAWAS and SUNDAR; border posts in SEMATAN, BIAWAK, SERIKIN, BUNAN GEGA PADAWAN, LUBOK ANTU, BATU LINTANG and SUNGEI TUJUH.

SARAWAK   249

BY BUS
The local bus station is on Market Street near the Electra
Building. Buses 17 and 1 go to PENDING and the Jet terminal for ships to Sibu.
    Long-distance buses depart from Leboh Jawa by the
Long Jetty. SAMPLE PRICES: BAU 1.85, LUNDU 6.20, SERIAN
4.-, BANDAR SRI AMAN (Simanggang) 12.20 (leaves at
08:00 h), SARATOK 17.20 M$.

BY SHIP
Coastal ships regularly traverse all of Sarawak's coastline.
Daily at 8:00 h either the M.V.MAS JAYA 1 or 2 or the M.V.
CONCORD leave Kuching for SARIKEI. Change here for another
boat to SIBU. Costs 33.-M$, takes 6-7 hours. The departure
point is the Marine Base (Jl.Pending, bus 17 from Main Bazaar).
    Every Wed and Sat at 18:00 h the M.V.HONG LEE leaves
on the same route, taking 18 hours for 18.-M$ (deck) or
29.-M$ (cabin). The agent is Ramin Shipping Sdn. Bhd.,
Chan Chin Ann Road, tel 57043.
    Sibu is also the port of call for the M.V.RAJAH MAS
which leaves Mon and Thurs at 18:00 h. The agent is South
East Asia Shipping Bhd., Lot 175, Jl.Chan Chin Ann, tel
22966.
    Irregular freight/passenger ships sail the entire coast
making stops in Bintulu, Miri, Marudi, Limbang and up to
Lawas. Get more info at the Siam Company, 28 Main Bazar,
tel 22832.

PROBOSCIS MONKEY (nasalis larvatus, Bekantan)

Proboscis monkeys only live in
the low-land swamps and mangrove forests of Borneo. Their
most prominent feature is the
long nose, giving rise to the
Malay name 'orang Belanda' or
Dutchman. The monkeys are
daytime animals and can frequently be found in large
groups along the rivers. They
are excellent swimmers and
skindivers, and dives from over
15 m height into the water are
not uncommon.
In Bako National Park the proboscis monkeys generally clan in groups of 4 to 8 monkeys, that are difficult
to spot, because they mostly stay in the treetops. You
might spot them in the mangroves at Telok Delima.

Bako National Park

The 26 km² national park, situated on an ocean peninsula, is a place to relax, hike and study the flora. There isn't an awful lot of fauna. But you can still see sambar deer, wild pigs, and once in a while a proboscis monkey which the Malays call 'orang belanda' or 'Dutchman' because they have long noses. There're 30 km of well-marked paths taking you through a variety of vegetation. This ranges from rain forest, to mangove swamps to bush steppe. The longest path takes you in about 8 hours to **TELOK LIMAU**. Spend the night either in your own tent, or arrange in advance for a boat to bring you back. We recommend the red-marked circular tour past Bukit Tambi, takes about 4 hours.

You can spend the night quite cheap in **TELOK ASSAM** in a kind of hostel for 1.50 M$ or even cheaper with an ISIC. The two resthouses only have two and three rooms, sleeping six people each, and cost about 22.-M$ per resthouse. Tents can be rented for 1.10 M$.

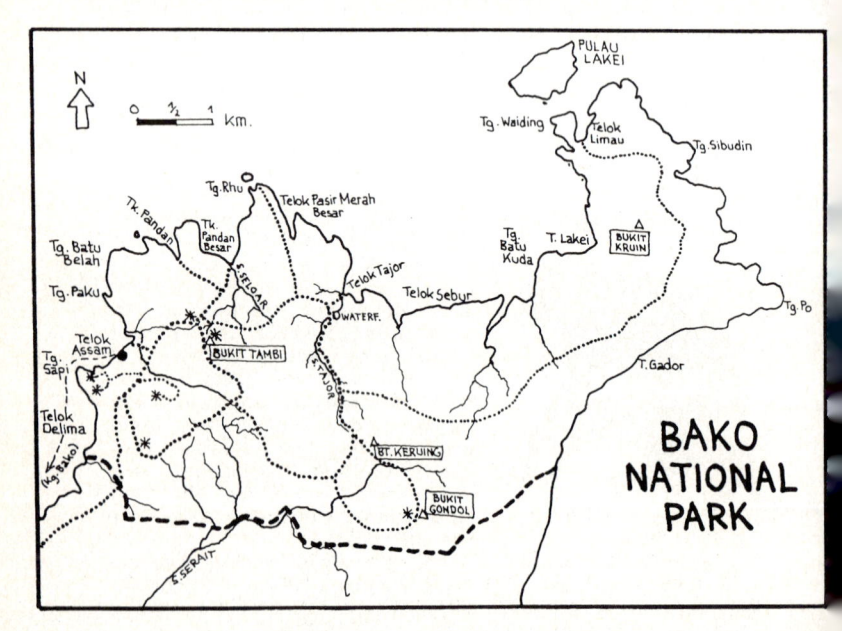

HOW TO GET HERE
You'll have to organize your excursion before leaving Kuching. The address: Office of National Parks (in the forestry department), Jl.Gartek, tel 24474. The cheapest transportation leaves between 7:00 and 9:00 h from Long Jetty, Jl.Gambier, for 2 M$ with the M.L.JUNO to KG.BAKO. Go from there by chartered boat to Telok Assam (about 6 M$).

From Kuching to Brunei

This huge region includes all the divisions with the exception of the fifth (Limbang). Tourists who make it here - and that's more than a few - aren't greeted by sights and romantic scenery. Your first objective, after a tiring boat or bus tour, is often a dreary market. The further you get from the few roads, the more the eternal green of the tropical rain forest takes hold. Occasionally the wilderness is broken by a longhouse surrounded by fields of pepper and rubber trees. However, primary jungle is only to be found in the national parks and hard to reach regions. Still, civilization weary travellers come here to rediscover nature. You'll never forget the jungle treks and nights spent in a longhouse as guests of the Iban, Kayan or Kenyah.

There are endless possibilities for river trips - it depends only on your sense of adventure and gift for language to get you going. Don't begin with a difficult jungle trek. There are too many incalculable risks. Remnants of communist guerillas still remain along the border to Indonesia. And you'll need a silver tongue when dealing with Malaysian and Indonesian officials. The further you get from villages with an airstrip or a hospital, the greater the risk to your health.

On the other hand, a trip through Sarawak's jungle is a one of a kind experience. Our friend Paul Mindon from New Zealand, who gained the relevant experience in the army, helped us put together a few ideas.

TIPS FOR JUNGLE TREKS
Don't go on a real jungle trip alone, rather find partners in equally good condition and with similar goals to your own. Three to five people are ideal numbers.
Advance preparation is very important; learn as much as you can about the area you plan to visit. All kinds of information (literature, maps, discussions, addresses, interviews etc.) should be collected in advance.

Resign yourself to doing without a lot of things we are all pretty used to: i.e. electricity, convenient transportation, food variety, toilets, super hygiene, or a place to be alone.

In most cases you'll cover long distances by boat. Hiking over rough territory, you'll hardly make 500 m per hour. If it's swampy, you'll make even worse time. Those who aren't used to the endless green and dimness of a tropical rainforest can easily go into a rage.

OUTFIT

For day long hikes through the jungle, the right equipment is very important. Even a daytrip to a longhouse can lead to your demise if the country is rough and you have the wrong shoes. Here are just a few of the most obvious pieces of equipment you'll need (which, depending on the region, you'll have to add to):

* Jungle boots with heavy traction, though not normal leather boots, which become too heavy when soaked with water. Besides they take too long to dry.
* Good cotton socks (and a second pair to change).
* Sandals, rubber thongs are best, so your feet can have a rest from the boots.
* Pants with lots of pockets and a belt from which you can hang your canteen, parang and other things.
* Bathing suit or sarong especially for women.
* Long sleeve shirts with button-down pockets, and T-shirts.
* A wide-brimmed hat against rain.
* A small plastic tarp which you can also use as a poncho.
* A small backpack - 12 kg could be the end of the world.
* Compass.
* Small tent - but it isn't always necessary since you'll be mostly going from longhouse to longhouse.
* First aid kit.
* Pocket knife with a can opener.
* Food - a bit of rice to offer your hosts and some canned goods.
* Wash kit including a small towel to wipe rain and sweat during the hike.
* Cooking utensils, including a good supply of matches and lighters which should be kept in a waterproof container.

SARAWAK 253

UNPLEASANT ENCOUNTERS
There are dangers everywhere - on the road as well as in the jungle. But you don't have to worry about an orangutan à la King Kong, you'd be lucky just to see one. Any animal hearing you tramp along the path will disappear. Much worse are the tiny members of the jungle population. You'll just have to accept leeches (see the section on TAMAN NEGARA in the West Malaysia chapter).

And here's a word about the much maligned snakes. Very few are actually poisonous. It is important, however, to go through the jungle with your eyes open. If you do step on a snake, it will feel threatened and bite. Should it be poisonous, the amount of poison you receive depends on when the snake last bit. In case of the worst, the only help is treatment with serum, a commodity found only in hospital refrigerators. Paul's advice:

Make sure that the poison doesn't get into the bloodstream. Cut open the two teeth marks with a sterile knife parallel to the arteries. Let it bleed as much as possible; suck out the blood or squeeze it out. The victim should lie as still as possible. The shock and fear, of the bitten as well as his or her partners, requires calm. Remember that snake bites are seldom deadly. Some people have even been bitten by a cobra and survived.

Insects such as wasps and hornets can be much more dangerous. Their nests are hung on trees or tree trunks and look like clumps of greyish brown clay. If you bump into a nest, clear out of the area as fast as possible. The bites of scorpions, centipedes and millepedes can also be dangerous.

Stories about the evil wilderness and head-hunters with poisoned blow-pipe darts are products of white colonialist brains.

We have decided not to mention any special village, region for you to see or river to travel on. Organize such a trip yourself - since all the tourists started going up and down the Sungei Skrang on completely organized trips, an awful lot has changed. We don't want to play a part in making that happen to other regions.

Bandar Sri Aman

The town was named BANDAR SRI AMAN in 1978 (formerly SIM-ANGGANG). In October 1973, the surrender of 482 communist guerillas under the leadership of Political Commissar Bong Kee Chok took place here. This event led to the renaming of the 70,000 strong town five years later.

It takes about four hours to drive the 135 km from Kuching to Sri Aman. The way to the administrative capital of the 2nd Division leads through a number of pepper plantations as well as many 'new villages'. During the high point of the communist guerilla activity in the 1960s, whole villages were uprooted and placed in these fenced and guarded camps. Most of the people are and were Chinese. There are still communist guerillas in the 1st and 2nd Divisions. Wanted posters can be found in many public buildings.

HOTELS
In Sri Aman you can choose between three hotels. The best is **HOOVER******, 125 Club Road (tel 2173). Right around the corner are two other hotels: **ALISHAN**** and **TAIWAN*****. In Alishan they serve very good, reasonably priced Chinese food.

DAY TRIPS AROUND BANDAR SRI AMAN
SELEPONG / GUA
You can visit a number of longhouses in quick sidetrips off the Sri Aman - Kuching road. Just outside Sri Aman is SELEPONG, a longhouse right on the road. A bit further toward Kuching is the longhouse GUA. It is an interesting example

of a traditional longhouse that's been modernized with glass windows, electricity, and gas stoves. Despite 20th-century influences, the old-fashioned village social structure remains.

EMPLANJAU / PANTU
A bit further along the paved road to Kuching, head right on the road to EMPLANJAU, a wonderful old Land Dayak longhouse. Skulls from head-hunting days still have an honored place in this household. After another 8 km you reach the road to PANTU, a typical market town. Here we saw a tame hornbill running around.

LUBOK ANTU
Another excursion might be to LUBOK ANTU (about 70 km, bus leaves five times daily for 6.-M$). Lubok Antu is an important border crossing point to Indonesia. Indonesians come across the border to buy, or better said, barter pepper or latex for hard ringgit. You can stay in the RESTHOUSE*.

The largest hydro-electric project in Malaysia is being built on the central reaches of the Batang Ai. Someday, electricity will be transmitted to Peninsular Malaysia via an underwater high-voltage cable. Numerous longhouses and lots of forest are do to be submerged in the artificial lake.

Once upon a time, this was the departure point for a real adventure trip to Indonesia. It's only a two hour hike to NANGAPADAU. From there you can go by boat down to SEMITAU where you can get the regular Kapuas riverboat to PONTIANAK or PUTUSSIBAU.

LEAVING SRI AMAN
To Kuching, there's a daily bus for 12.20 M$. Get a bus to **SARIKEI** (leaves daily at 7:30 and 13:30 h for 12.80 M$). Often the buses are booked up in advance. In that case take the STC bus to **SARATOK** (8:00 and 14:00 h, 9.20 M$) and from there the local bus to Sarikei for 4.20 M$. There are three hotels in Saratok (HOOVER, AMBASSADOR and GOLDEN CITY). Other buses to BATU LINTANG 2.80, ENGKILILI 2.80, BETONG 5.60 M$.

SARIKEI
Hourly from 7:00 to 16:00 h, a riverboat departs Sarikei for SIBU (5 M$), takes 2 1/2 hours. If you miss the last boat, you can spend the night in town. The cheapest accommodations are in RAJANG**, 1 Berjaya Road. A bit better is SARIKEI HOTEL***, 11 Wharf Road or SOUTHERN HOTEL***, 21 Repok Road.

HEAD-HUNTING

Dusty, smoked skulls of enemies killed still hang above many a 'ruai' (longhouse community porch). The newest specimens probably date from WWII when the British declared open season on Japanese skulls. Many longhouses boast up to 30 skulls in big rattan nets. Single skulls are hung in small, woven rattan baskets.

Even today there's lots of scientific controversy over the phenomenon 'head-hunting'. It has been established, however, that belief in an immortal spiritual power residing in the human head plays a key role in the ritual. Originally, it was the responsibility of every young Dayak to capture the skull of an enemy in order to prove his manhood. At the same time he gained possession of the spirit or soul of his enemy. Carry this idea a bit further, and the entire longhouse gained a portion of the collective power of their enemy's skulls.

At the time of the arrival of the first Europeans on Borneo, the ritual had become an end in itself. Heads were taken at any price. Even the heads of children or old women were acceptable. No wonder every colonial administration employed harsh measures against the ritual of head-hunting.

Sibu

Bustling Chinese merchants keep Sarawak's second-largest town lively. Although situated 130 km inland, the town is a major port. The Rajang River here is still big enough even for good size ships. The town is the center of Sarawak's timber industry and important in the pepper and rubber trade. Countless sailors enjoy the nightlife! Interesting books and information at the market in the Longhouse Arts & Crafts shop.

HOTELS
Some hotels, cheap in Sibu terms, can be found on Kg.Nyabor Road: **TODAY HOTEL*****, no 40 (tel 36499); **DIMAN HOTEL*****, no 27 (tel 36853) or **PENINSULA*****, no 8 (tel 22299). Or go to the **REX HOTEL****, 32 Cross Road. Also good is **HOOVER GUESTHOUSE***, Island Road at the church.

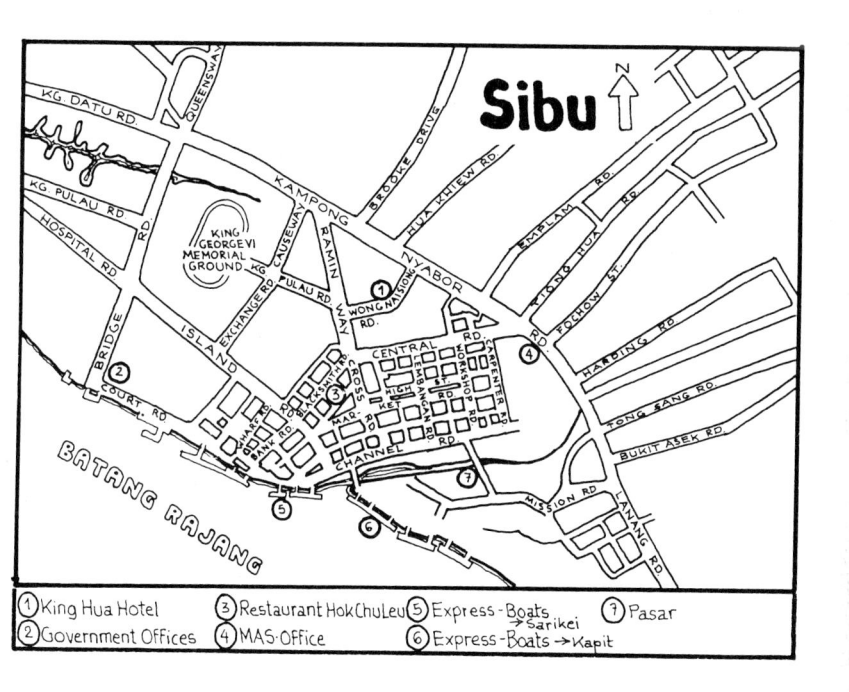

① King Hua Hotel ③ Restaurant HokChuLeu ⑤ Express-Boats →Sarikei ⑦ Pasar
② Government Offices ④ MAS·Office ⑥ Express-Boats →Kapit

LEAVING SIBU
BY AIR
MAS office is in 58 Jl.Kg.Nyabor, tel 21515. The airport is located 6 km north of town; get bus 1 for 50 c from the bus station on Cross Road.
SAMPLE PRICES: BELAGA 76.-, BINTULU 53.-, KAPIT 48.-, KUCHING 60.-, KOTA KINABALU 156.-, LABUAN 130.-, and MIRI 75.-M$.

BY SHIP
There are daily coastal ships to KUCHING (29.-M$) and express boats (33.-M$), taking 18 hours or 6-7 hours respectively. Hourly up to 12:30 h express boats steam up the Rajang River to KAPIT, costs 13.-M$. Twin diesel engines get the boats really moving. The trip up river takes 4-5 hours. You can disembark along the way in KANOWIT, SONG, or another longhouse.

BY BUS
Since 1985 there's a daily bus to BINTULU. Leaves 7:00 h. Get your tickets one hour in advance.

Kapit

A crazy place with that middle of nowhere atmosphere! At the same time it's also the capital of Sarawak's 7th Division. Exotically tattooed Iban bring their latex, pepper, and vegetables down the river to market in dugout canoes. Later they provision themselves with civilized goods from the small shops around the central square. In one of the shops a dentist practices with ancient equipment. But not far away is a well-equipped hospital. About 30 cars and four taxis drive up and down the 15 odd miles of road - you'll see them again and again. They had to be brought up the Rajang from Sibu. Plans call for a connecting road to Kapit, but not in this decade! Occasionally a proud car owner will invite you to a quick tour of the area.
Around Kapit are several longhouses, but they aren't worth the high cost of a taxi.

HOTELS
Three hotels in town: The clean **HIAP CHIONG***, 33 New Bazaar (tel 96514), **REJANG****, 28 New Bazaar (tel 96359) and **KAPIT LONGHOUSE**** (tel 96415). The people in Rejang Hotel arrange trips to longhouses. Beware of strange guys offering you the same for tremendous prices! Behind the central square near the church, cheap accommodations in **METHODIST GUEST HOUSE***. Good meals in **ISLAMIC FOOD** right next to the hostel.

LEAVING KAPIT
If you're planning a river trip further up stream, check in Kapit at the State Government Complex whether you'll need a permit for your itinerary. Sometimes you can go without registering, but the regulations change frequently.

BY BOAT
River boats leave regularly for **ENTAWAU** (8 M$) on the Baleh River. If you want to go even further upstream, try to talk to one of the Iban going up in an outboarder. The overland trip north leads to Belaga. River boats depart at 05:00 h in the morning, cost 17.-M$ and take a whole day. During the dry season, particularly from July to September, there're usually no boats because there's too little water in the upper reaches of the Rajang.

Just beyond Kapit the scenery becomes fascinating with the Pelagus Rapids, jungle, longhouses, and other boats. You can get off along the way to visit a longhouse and take the boat the following day.

BY AIR
The airstrip is 2 km west of town. Twice a week a BN 2 does the route Sibu, Kapit and Belaga (just 10 kg baggage limit so put everything heavy in your carry-on bag!). The MAS office is near the big dock (Hua Chiong Co.). The flight to SIBU costs 48.- and to BELAGA 47.-M$. During the dry season when boats to Belaga are dried out, the flight is often booked up for weeks.

BELAGA
In Belaga there's a Resthouse** and two hotels** on the Main bazaar, where you'll also find a few places to eat. Electricity runs only from 6:00 to 22:00 h.

If jungle hiking isn't one of your strong points, you'll have to turn back here. Go either by boat back to Kapit, or take the twice weekly BN-flight for 47 M$ to Kapit or 76 M$ to Sibu. The MAS agent is Lau Chun Kiat on the Main Bazaar.

Overland from Belaga to Bintulu

Otherwise you'll have to organize your jungle trip. People will come to you with proposals, since hundreds of people do this tour each year. There's even a travel agency. The price for the whole trip now runs between 300 and 500 M$. Important! Be sure to bargain, and don't pay until the end of the trip or at a change of guides.

Some years ago the trip ran as follows: Your first objective after a half hour by longboat, a six hour hike, and another half hour by boat was **LONG BANGAN**. The next day you're off to **LONG UNAN** - two hours by longboat, followed by another six hours of hard hiking over mountains and across rivers. However, a large part of the jungle has been logged over. From Long Unan it took another day by longboat to reach **TUBAU**, from where you could get an express boat for 10 M$ which dropped you off about 5 hours later in **BINTULU**.

New logging tracks have shortened this route considerably. Try to get the latest info in Belaga. There are other, less travelled paths over the mountains, though they're generally very strenuous and expensive. For example, in Kapit you'll often be offered a trip via Sungei Metah and Sungei Mayeng to **TATAU**. It takes at least five days and costs around 600.-M$ including boat, gas and guide.

Bintulu

You're back in civilization here with real hotels, movie theaters, and even a bar in the HOOVER HOTEL****, Keppel Road. CAPITOL**** on the same road toward the bus station is a bit cheaper. Or try NEW CAPITOL HOTEL**** across from the Hoover.

The largest natural gas reserves in Malaysia were discovered off Bintulu at the end of the 1970s. A huge LNG (liquified natural gas) plant has been in business since 1982. The LNG is transported by special tankers to Japan. Total cost of the project is estimated at 3 billion M$. Shell holds a 17.5 % share of the LNG project, Mitsubishi has 17.5 % and the state owned company Petronas has 65 %. This has turned the once sleepy little town of Bintulu into the "boomtown" of Sarawak. Since there isn't a lot to see here, the town is just a pitstop for you.

SARAWAK 261

HOW TO GET THERE
There are daily MAS flights to SIBU for 53 M$ or to MIRI for 57 M$. Heading north (to Miri, 214 km or Niah) you can go by bus or taxi. Price: Bus to NIAH JUNCTION about 14 M$, taxi 24 M$ (sometimes they'll demand 100 M$!); bus to Miri 17 M$. Or try the newly finished road to SIBU.

Niah Caves

Spread over a total area of 100,000 m^2, the archaeological importance of the limestone caves wasn't discovered until the 1950s. prehistoric wall paintings were discovered along with a 35,000 year-old skull. Further graves have also been uncovered.

Millions of swallows and bats live in the caves. From the many bamboo trestles which are everywhere, reaching sometimes up to the ceiling, the swallow nests are collected and used to prepare real bird's nest soup. Way back during the Ming dynasty, Sarawak was the most important exporter of this Chinese delicacy.

A couple years ago the caves were placed under the administration of the Sarawak Museum in Kuching. The forest around the caves has become the **Niah National Park**. The swallow nest collectors are now licensed to prevent too many nests from being taken.

HOTELS
Batu Niah has several not too expensive hotels such as **NIAH CAVES HOTEL****, **CHAI LODGING*** or **KIM HOE HOTEL****. Another possibility is the **GOVERNMENT HOSTEL** in Pangkalan Lubang. In two large rooms, up to 15 people can sleep for 2.50 M$. Cooking facilities are provided, You're best off booking in advance in Miri or Kuching at the Forestry Department. On the other side of the river (boats across available) the path to the caves begins.

HOW TO GET HERE
Take the bus from MIRI to BATU NIAH, leaving every morning at 7:00 and 12:00 h for 8.-M$. Taxis over the same route run 15.-M$. Taxis from BINTULU should cost 24.-M$ but they'll demand much more. Alternative: get the bus to Niah Junction for 14.-M$. To BATU NIAH (13 km) either take a taxi or hitchhike. Charter a boat to PANGKALAN LUBANG for 25.-M$ or walk along the river (45 min.). Park boats cost just 5 M$ per person if available.

From Pangkalan Lubang, the famous 4 km-long wooden walkway, runs 1 m above ground to the caves. After a rain it's slippery and you can easily take a one-meter dive. Under normal conditions, you need 45 minutes to reach the Great Cave (western entrance). A guide costs 15 M$.

Miri

The uninteresting capital of the 4th Division. Oil was discovered here way back in the 1920s. Today drilling has intensified on offshore oil rigs. A couple kilometers north is a large refinery in Lutong connected by pipeline to SERIA in Brunei.

HOTELS
There are several hotels on China Street such as **TAI TONG***, no 26 - including a dormitory for 4.-M$; **THAI FOH***, no 18-19; **YEO LEE LODGING HOUSE***, no 12, **MALAYSIA LODGING HOUSE****, no 1 or try **MONICA LODGINGS***, 4 Kwang Tung Road. Good too is the **NEW MIRI HOTEL****, 47 Brooke Road.

LEAVING MIRI
BY AIR
MAS office, 239 Beautiful Jade Garden, tel 34544.
SAMPLE PRICES: BARIO 70.-, BINTULU 57.-, KOTA KINABALU 82.-, KUCHING 136.-, LABUAN 57.-, LAWAS 59.-, LIMBANG 45.-, LONG SERIDAN 57.-, MARUDI 29.-, SIBU 75.-M$.
Some of the flights are BN-Flights without regular schedules. To avoid the expensive Sultanate of Brunei with its cosmopolitan hotel prices, it's worth getting a flight to Labuan or Lawas.

BY BUS / TAXI
From Miri to BRUNEI (KUALA BELAIT) are four direct buses daily starting at 7:00 h for 9.50 M$. Takes about 3 hours. The ferry from Shell across the Baram runs regularly. Buses to NIAH for 8.- and to BINTULU for 17.-M$.

Gunung Mulu National Park

The national park covers a 530 km^2 area in the 4th and 5th Divisions. At 2376 m, **Gunung Mulu** is the second highest mountain in Sarawak. To the north lie the massive chunks of limestone - **Gunung Api** and **Gunung Benerat**. Be sure to visit the Melinau Gorge, where the river courses its way between the mountains - with steep 600 m high cliffs. Teams of sci-

SARAWAK

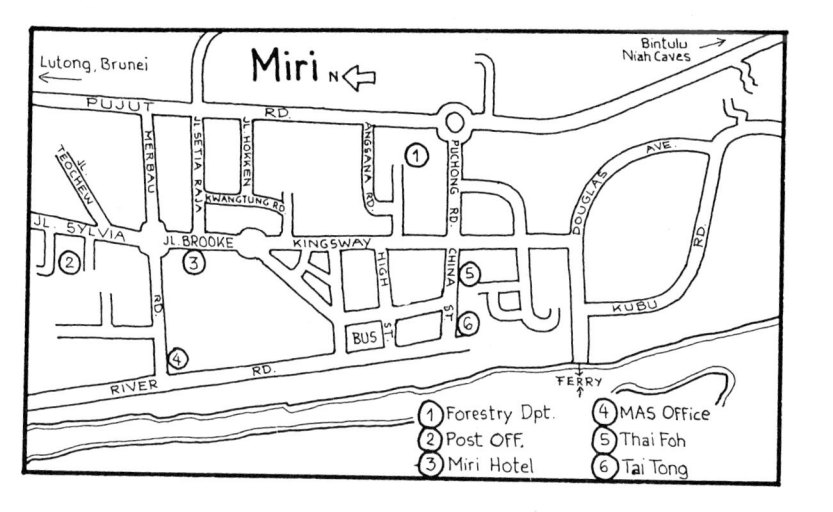

Miri N ←

Map legend:
1. Forestry Dpt.
2. Post Off.
3. Miri Hotel
4. MAS Office
5. Thai Foh
6. Tai Tong

entists spent two years in the park studying the geological structure and cataloguing the flora and fauna. Here you'll find macaques along with gibbons and other kinds of monkeys, anteaters, mouse deer, plus many different types of birds including the hornbill. There isn't any big game: there aren't any tigers on Borneo, and the only elephants are in Sabah. Many paths lead through the jungle; try the one to Melinau Gorge (19 km) or to Lubang Rusa (3 km). Gunung Mulu can be climbed from Melinau Gorge.

HOTELS
Since there are only a few beds in **LONG MELINAU PAKU**, you should book in advance at the Forest Department in Kuching or Miri (between Angsana and Puchong Road, tel 36637).

HOW TO GET THERE
Get a bus (2.20 M$) or taxi to KUALA BARAM at the mouth of the Baram. Express boats run from here at 9:00 and 13:00 h on the two hour trip to MARUDI (12 M$). In town is GRAND HOTEL** and MARYLAND HOTEL****, tel 55106. The 8 hour boat ride to LONG TERAWAN costs 12 M$ (no daily boats). Stay the night here. In the morning head to LONG MELINAU PAKU. Ask at the Forest Department about the latest connections since the park is constantly being improved.

Bareo

This tiny market town is situated in the comfortable climate of the highlands bordering Indonesia. The nights can be quite cold. The best pineapples in Malaysia grow here! Stay the night in LODGING HOUSE** right by the airstrip. The restaurants and shops are expensive, so stock up on food in Miri or Marudi.

Of interest is a trip to (or across) the Indonesian border at LONG MIDANG. Lots of Indonesians cross over here. From Bareo take the path to PA UKAT (one hour). Then it's another three hours to PA LONGAN, where you should stay the night. In LONG MIDANG is an Indonesian 'imigrasi' outpost. LONG BAWAN is just 10 km away and has a regular 'imigrasi' office. From Long Midang you can head back to Sarawak (BAKELALAN). In Bareo you'll meet lots of Indonesians who are heading back to Long Midang or Long Bawan. Taking the trip alone is not recommended!

HOW TO GET HERE
Flights from MIRI cost 70.-M$ or from MARUDI 55.-M$. The overland trip from Marudi takes one to two weeks and is expensive. MAS flies from BAKELALAN to LAWAS for 46.-M$.

SARAWAK'S NATIONALITIES

Dayak is the general term used for the proto-Malayan tribes of Kalimantan. Of the 1.307 million Sarawak population, about half are tribal members. Around 200 different tribes make their home on the island. The most important ethnic group in Sarawak are the **Iban** making up about one third of the population. Other nationalities according to the 1980 census: **Malay** (19.7 %), **Melanau** (5.7 %), **Bidayuh** (Land Dayak; 8.2 %), **Orang Ulu** (Kenyah, Kayan, Lun Bawang, Kelabit, Kedayan, Bisaya, Kajang, etc.; 5.3 %), **Chinese** (29.5 %), others (1.3 %).

Iban or Sea Dayak are mostly settled in the 2nd, 3rd, 4th and 7th divisions of Sarawak. Large numbers also live across the Indonesian border which was arbitrarily drawn by the colonial powers.

Characteristic of their culture (as with most Borneo tribes) is living in a longhouse. Up to 180 m long, 15-20 m wide and set on piles up to 5 m high, some 300 people can live in a longhouse. Each family has its own room **(bilek).** Most longhouses are on rivers with the kitchens **(dapor)** always looking inland. Some tribes also have an unroofed porch. Towards the river side is a long, roofed porch **(ruai)**. It serves as a big living room, and all the 'bilek' have doors opening onto it. Here people work, meet, grind rice, mend fishnets, and gather for festivities.

The chief of a longhouse is called **'Tuai Rumah'**. He settles disagreements, calls together the council of elders, declares divorces and is the community representative for outsiders. The 'bilek' of the 'Tuai Rumah' is in the center of the longhouse. Often his doorway is specially decorated and carved. Once in a while you'll see dusty old culverins in front. On arrival you'll have to present yourself to him for a talk and a cigarette.

The title of chief is not inherited; the most important men in the longhouse elect one of themselves to be 'Tuai Rumah'. The name of the longhouse changes with the new leader. There is only a superficial class system. Usually the bilek on the outer ends of the longhouses belong to less influential families.

Religious power among the Iban is in the hands of a medicine man **(manang)**. In other tribes he is called 'dayong' or 'dajung' or sometimes 'wadian'. The latter can also be a woman. He or she possesses magic powers, heals the sick, places people in trance and is the longhouse legend and storyteller.

If you've ever spent the night in the jungle among the sounds of cicadae, insects, frogs, birds, and monkeys - plus occasional thunder and lightning - you'll be able to understand why the religious perceptions of the Dayak are centered on the kaleidoscope of background noises. The inhabitants of the more isolated longhouses are still animists - although where missionaries have been busy, the spiritual beliefs have taken on a Christian variant.

DAYAK LONGHOUSE

1) DAPOR-kitchen
2) BILEK-livingroom & bedroom
3) SADAU-storeroom
4) TEMPUAN-corridor
5) RUAI-commons
6) PANTAR-sleeping area for guests
7) TANJU-outer veranda

The Iban, like other tribes, live from agriculture (rubber, mountain rice, corn, pepper) as well as hunting and fishing. Today many young Iban are leaving their traditional homes to seek work in the cities, in industry or on plantations.

A FEW WORDS OF IBAN

The Iban language belongs to the Malay language family, but is quite different from Bahasa Malaysia or Bahasa Indonesia. The numbers, however, are the same in all three languages. Here're a few expressions:

Hello!	Tabi!
I'm sorry	Minta ampun
Do you understand?	Nemu nuan?
How are you?	Kati nuan gerai?
What's your name?	Sapa nama nuan?
I want to pay for it.	Aku kamayaar nuan.
Where is the boat?	Dini perau?
We brought our own food.	Kami bisi mai bekal.
May I take your picture?	Oleh aku ngambar nuan?
My friend.	Pangan aku.
We like it fine.	Kami rindu.
Where is...	Dini endor...
Please bring me there.	Bai aku kien.

Land Dayak, about 107,000 strong, most live in Division 1 today. They are peaceful people who in the past have been pushed around by the more aggressive Iban.

Kayan and **Kenyah** are generally settled in Indonesian Kalimantan – in Sarawak you'll find them on the upper courses of the Baleh and Rajang Rivers. They are estimated to have about 20,000 members. There are some interesting differences between the Iban and Land Dayak on the one hand, and the Kayan and Kenyah on the other. The latter are aristocratic societies, meaning that some families have more privileges and authority than others. Slave holding was once widespread. The families lowest on the social scale today are the descendants of slaves.

Kayan and Kenyah are excellent metal workers and makers of parangs. Their tattoos are especially interesting. They are real works of art, created by an extremely painful procedure. Often the design is first cut into a kind of wooden stamp. This is then smeared with a mixture of lampblack, sugar cane juice and water and then stamped onto the intended part of the body. Two utensils are necessary for tattooing: a sharply pointed steel nail with a long handle attached **(ulang)**, and a metal rod. The nail is then repeatedly driven into the skin with light taps from the rod.

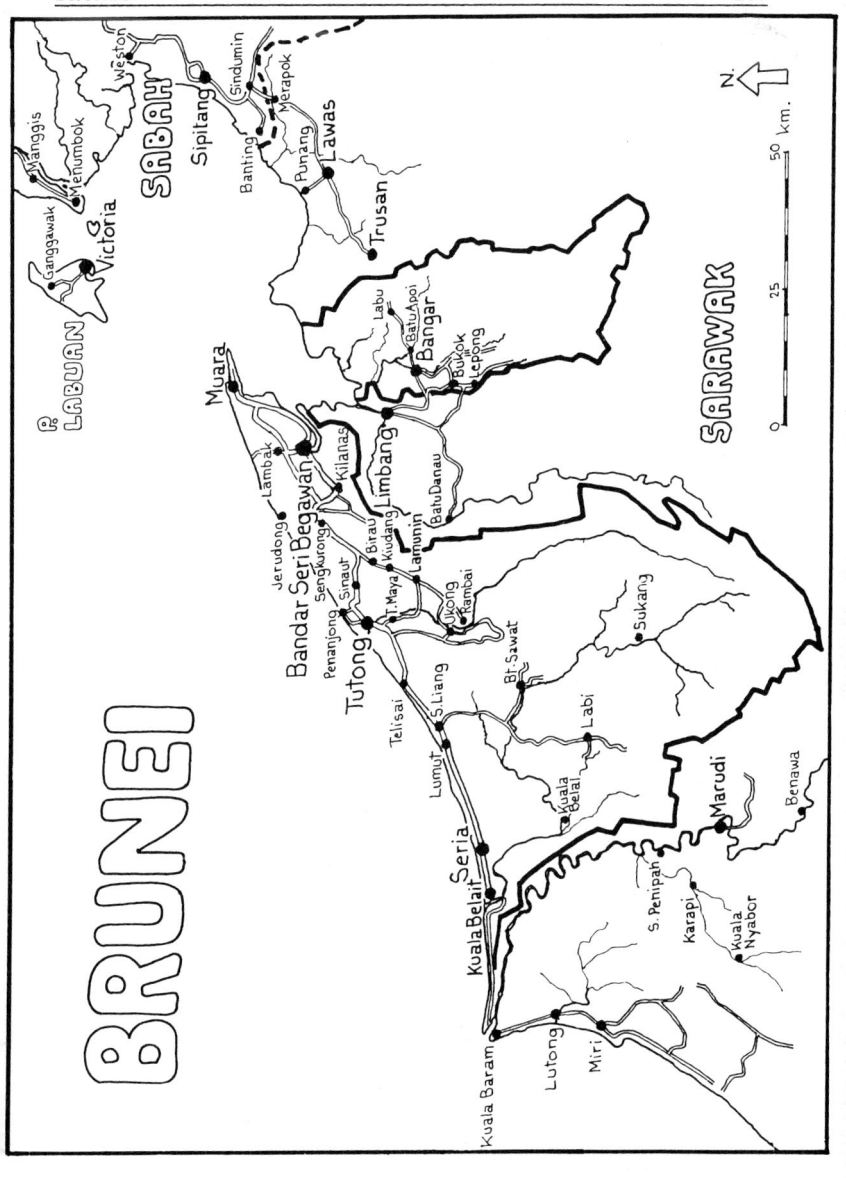

BRUNEI

BRUNEI

Brunei, the last Islamic sultanate that's still as British as in colonial days, is for most people a modern, car-choked capital city locked in by impassable jungle.

This relatively obscure country of 5765 km² on the north coast of Kalimantan (Borneo) was a British protectorate until 1971; since 1984 it is independent of Great Britain even in defence and foreign policy. Brunei's standard of living is high compared to the rest of South-East Asia due to oil exports. Prices reflect this affluence.

75 % of Brunei is covered by tropical rain forest. The country is divided into two parts by a sliver of Sarawak. A paved road runs parallel to the coast from the border of Sarawak to Bandar Seri Begawan. There is not much of interest to tourists in the sultanate; it is mainly a way station for people on the road from Sarawak to Sabah.

Bandar Seri Begawan

The capital of Brunei is a pleasantly quiet place to visit if you have the money or are able to get a bed in Pusat Belia. One of the most imposing mosques in South East Asia, **MESJID SULTAN OMAR ALI SAIFUDDIN**, was built in 1958. Take the lift to the top of the 44 m high minaret (closed at prayer time on Fridays). You have a nice view of the city and the **KAMPONG AYER**. Take a walk on the concrete footbridges connecting the pile houses in the 'water village' (Malay: kampong = village; ayer = water). Unlike less affluent counterparts elsewhere in South-East Asia, this water village has both running water and electricity. The big street in front of the village is packed with cars. Near Kampong Ayer is the **ARTS AND HANDICRAFT CENTRE** where traditional crafts are produced and sold. You'll find traditional work in silver, brass, bronze, along with beautiful sarong, plaited mats and baskets. A river tour can be fun too.

The **CHURCHILL MUSEUM** (Churchill Memorial Gallery) is Brunei's one of a kind reminder of English influence in South-East Asia (open daily except Tuesdays). Next door, the **SULTAN HASSANAL BOLKIAH AQUARIUM** is open daily except Mondays with a good collection of tropical fish; admission: 30 cents.

Official events in the capital are held at the Royal Ceremonial Hall **(LAPAU)** and in the Legislative Assembly **(DEWAN MAJLIS)**.

About 4 km from town (bus to KOTA BATU - 50 cents) is the **BRUNEI MUSEUM** and the nearby **MAUSOLEUM** of the famous Sultan Bolkiah, fifth sultan in the dynasty. As sights go, the new **SULTAN'S ISTANA** is reputed to have cost 350-600 million US$.

HOTELS

Try to get into **PUSAT BELIA** a youth center set up by the government. The complex includes: a dormitory, gym, swimming pool, library, and a restaurant. Normally you'll be asked to show an ISIC or an International Youth Hostel Card but they aren't absolutely necessary! The first three nights cost 10 B$, thereafter 5.-B$. Everything else is expensive: **CAPITAL HOSTEL*****, Jl. Berangan right behind

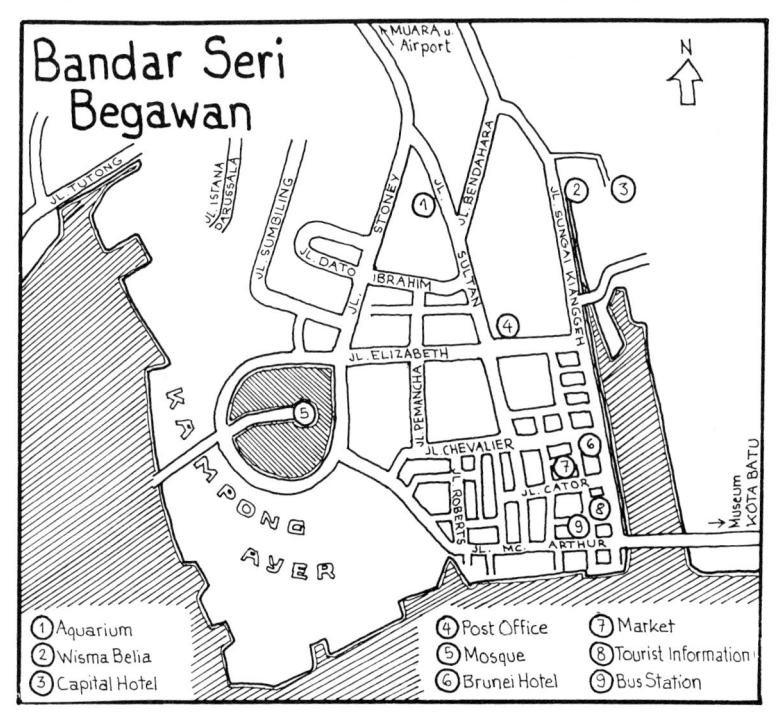

Pusat Belia. Or try **ANG'S HOTEL****, Jl.Tasek Lama (tel 23553) or **BRUNEI HOTEL****, 95 Jl.Chevalier (tel 22372). There are also international hotels such as **SHERATON UTAMA**** and the **ROYAL HOTEL****.

FOOD
In BSB, as elsewhere in the sultanate, are lots of Chinese, Malay, and Indian restaurants and food stalls. Try **MOHAMMED'S COFFEE SHOP** on Jl.Sultan for Malay-Indian fare. Good but expensive Chinese food can be found at **HOOVER**, Jl.Sungei Kianggeh. Alcohol is only available in Chinese restaurants.

DAY TRIPS AROUND BSB
Only to be considered if you fly into BSB. Otherwise make a stopover on the land route between Sabah and Sarawak.

TUTONG / KUALA BELAIT / SERIA
These are the centers of the Brunei oil industry. However, Tutong and Lumut do have nice beaches. Two hotels in Kuala Belait, SENTOSA*** and SEAVIEW*** are on Jl.Seria. Buses run regularly to TUTONG (1.80 B$), SERIA (4.50 B$) and from Seria to KUALA BELAIT (1.20 B$).

TEMBURONG
This is the smaller part of Brunei surrounded by Sarawak. A boat trip from BSB takes 45 minutes and costs 6.50 B$. There are several Iban longhouses, but not as interesting as in Sarawak.

LIMBANG
Over the border in Sarawak, the boat from BSB costs 6 B$. A good idea for people who want to save themselves the high cost of staying in a Brunei hotel. Several relatively cheap hotels include: SOUTH EAST ASIA**, 27 Market Street, tel 21013; AUSTRALIA**, 63 Bank Street, tel 21860 and NAK** on the same street.

From LIMBANG you can take the 7:00 h express boat to LAWAS. MAS flies to LAWAS for 25 M$ and MIRI for 45 M$.

LEAVING BANDAR SERI BEGAWAN
BY AIR
The following airlines serve BSB: MAS, British Airways, Cathay Pacific, Singapore Airlines, and Royal Brunei Airlines. A taxi to the airport (5 km) costs 15 B$. No airport tax. SAMPLE PRICES:

HONGKONG 596.-, KOTA KINABALU 65.-, MANILA 444.-, JAKARTA 531.-, KUCHING 172.-, SINGAPORE 320.-B$.

OVERLAND TO SARAWAK
The early morning bus to SERIA costs 4.50 B$. From Seria to KUALA BELAIT takes 30 Minutes for 1.20 B$. At 7:00, 9:00 and 14:00 h catch a thru bus to MIRI for 9.50 B$.

OVERLAND AND BY SEA TO SABAH
You have several possibilities. The simplest is the boat to LABUAN, leaves at 8:00 and 13:00 h, costs 13 B$. You'll find more info on the route Labuan - Kota Kinabalu in the Sabah chapter.

Another possibility is the boat to LAWAS for 15 B$. WARNING: The boat only goes as far as PUNANG where you switch to a bus or taxi (cost included in the 15 B$ fare). From Lawas get the bus to MERAPOK - costs 3.50 M$, departs at 14:00 h. Check the Sabah chapter for more information.

HISTORY
Old Chinese writings between 518 AD and 616 AD mention a place called Puni or Poli located between China and Java. Today it's assumed this refers to Brunei.

The 15th century marriage of a Johore/Riau princess with the Brunei king inspired his conversion to Islam. Under this first Sultan, Mohammed, Islam began to spread over the north coast of Borneo. The Sultanate of Brunei developed over the centuries, particularly under Sultan Bolkiah, into a power dominating large parts of Kalimantan, the Sulu Archipelago and Mindanao. Brunei-made

James Brooke

cannons were well known throughout the region. Trade relations were expanded, particularly with Portugal. During the rule of Sultan Bolkiah, Brunei was visited by the Italian historian, Pigafetta, who described the royal court as "of exceptional greatness". The city itself was built on piles over the water, with only the palaces and royal residences on land. Despite two attempts by the Spanish fleet to capture the sultanate, Spain was only able to occupy the capital city for a short time in 1578.

Brunei lost power over the next two hundred years. This was due to the waxing power of England and Holland, and to increased local piracy. The White Rajah of Sarawak captured ever more territory until by 1904 Brunei had shrunk to the mini-state size we find it today. Protectorate status established in 1888 gave Britain political control.

Brunei, under former Sultan Sir Omar Ali Saifuddin, decided not to join the Federation of Malaysia when it was founded by the British in 1963. The sultan didn't want to share Brunei's oil with Malaysia. In 1967 Sir Omar abdicated in favor of his son, Hassanal Bolkiah Muizuddin Waddaulah, the 29th ruler in the dynasty. After final independence on January 1, 1984, the country became the world's 169th independent country and the 6th member of ASEAN.

****
THE BLIND CAN'T SEE WITHOUT EYES!
Be our eyes and ears. Write to us. Tell us where you stayed, what it cost, where to go or what to avoid.
A special gift for the best letters.
****

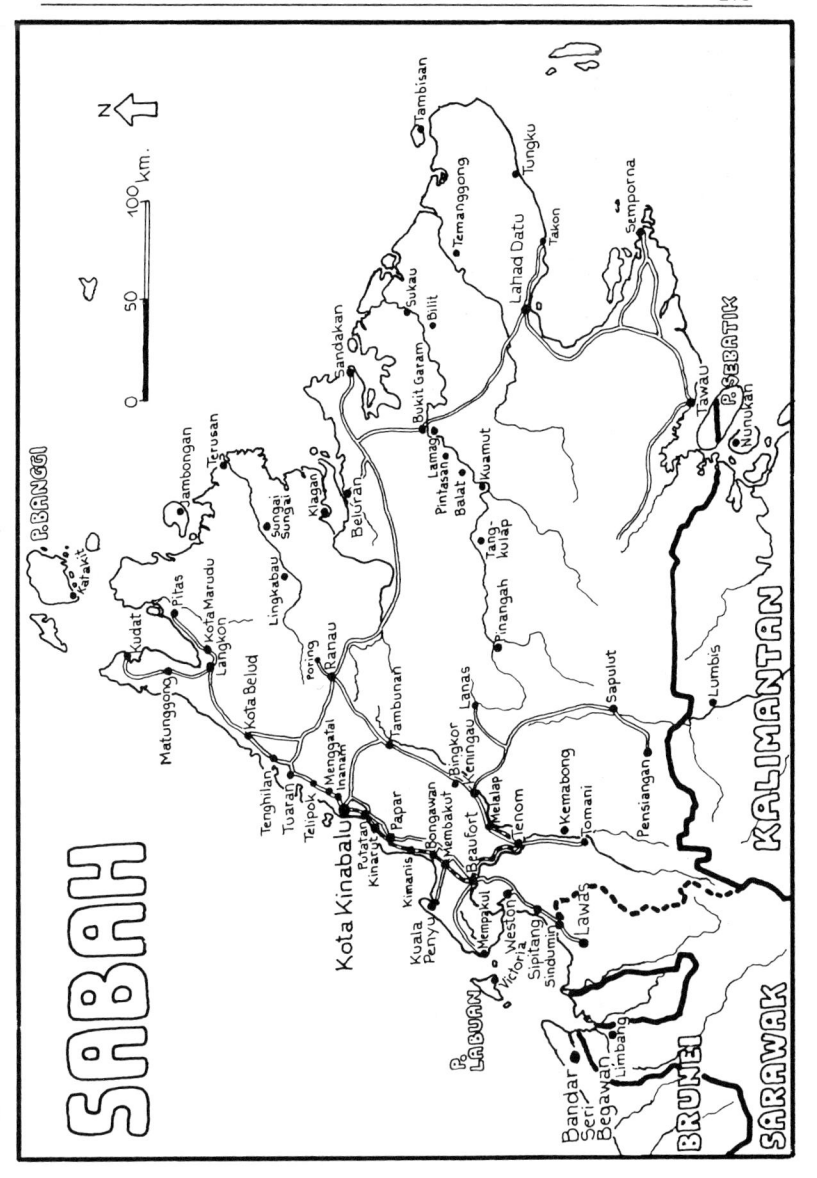

SABAH

SABAH

Malaysia's eastern most state is about twice as big as Switzerland but harbors only 1,002,000 people. The coastal areas were once infamous pirate sanctuaries. Even today sea robbers ply the Sulu Archipelago between Sabah and the Philippines. Typhoons don't come this far south, lending this state its name 'land below the wind'.

Until 1963 when Sabah, under UN auspices, voted to join the Federation of Malaysia, the crown colony was known as 'British North Borneo'. In the mean time there has been economic progress. Half the rare woods exported by Malaysia come from Sabah. The rape of the rain forests in recent years has led to irrevocable erosion damage. Reforesting programs and a reduction of exports are two methods being in an attempt to rectify the situation.

In Sabah, Malays make up only 8 % of the population. There are several tribes: Kadazan on the west coast, Murut in the interior who live off of slash and burn agriculture, and the largely Muslim Bajau, 'cowboys of Borneo', settled around Mount Kinabalu.
The port towns of Sandakan and Lahad Datu are trading centers for wood as well as smuggled goods. A large part of the military supplies destined for Moro rebels on Mindanao (the Philippines) goes via Sabah.

Sabah is an expensive place to visit. Like in Sarawak and Brunei, accommodations and transportation costs are the highest in Malaysia. Kota Kinabalu is the departure point for climbing Mount Kinabalu, the highest mountain in South-East Asia. Adventure trips can be made into the interior all the way to Indonesia. Or you can relax on the empty beaches of Kudat.

Kota Kinabalu

'**Api Api**' was the old Malay name for this town, meaning 'fire'. Pirates burned down the town so many times no other name fit. During the British colonial period, the town was renamed Jesselton after a director of the North Borneo Company. When the break with colonialism was made in 1968, they renamed the town after the nearby mountain Kinabalu – Kota (= town). Typically of Malaysia, it's been shortened to KK. After KK was completely destroyed during World War II,

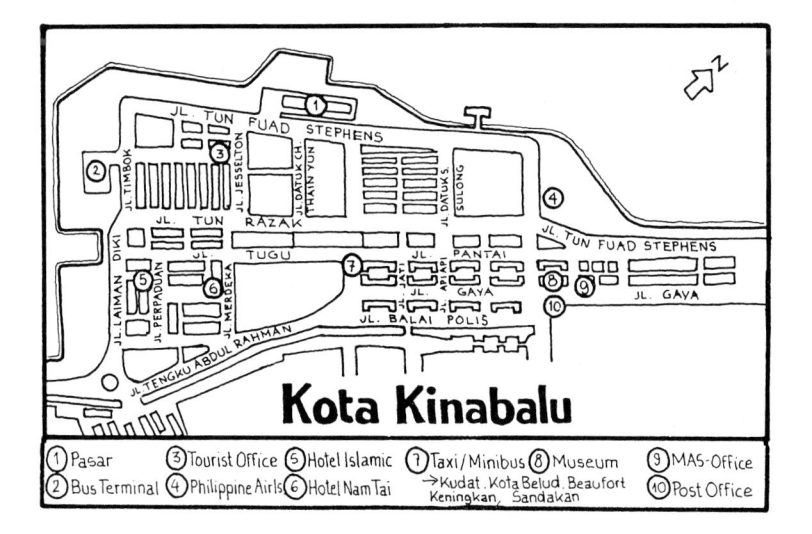

① Pasar   ③ Tourist Office ⑤ Hotel Islamic ⑦ Taxi/Minibus ⑧ Museum   ⑨ MAS-Office
② Bus Terminal ④ Philippine Airls ⑥ Hotel Nam Tai →Kudat, Kota Belud, Beaufort ⑩ Post Office
                                                  Keningkan, Sandakan

'modern' reconstruction spelled an end to any romantic 'Raja
Brooke' atmosphere still remaining in Kuching. Much of the
town (150,000 strong) is built on land reclaimed from the
ocean.

On the way to the airport south of town, you pass
MASJID SABAH, the second-largest mosque in Malaysia, built
in a modern style.

In town be sure to visit the little **MUSEUM**, which
boasts a collection of various objects from the Sabah tribes
as well as old photos. It's located on Jl.Gaya.

Take a walk up **SIGNAL HILL**. From here you have a
good view of the town and the sea.

For those who want more, 4 km northeast of town, a
hundred meter high concrete and glass structure dominates
the countryside. The **SABAH FOUNDATION COMPLEX** seems almost futuristic. From its rotating restaurant at the top you
can enjoy the view if you've enough traveller's checks.

HOTELS
'Cheapies' are in the area around Jl.Perpaduan, such as
ISLAMIC***, 8 Jl.Perpaduan (tel 54325), a bit rundown.
Partly furnished with ac rooms are **KIN FAH*****, 7 Jl.Haji
Yaakub (tel 53833) and **NAM TAI*****, 7 Jl.Merdeka (tel

54803). Several middle priced hotels can be found in the new Segama Quarter: **BILAL****, Block B, Lot 1 (tel 56709) or **ORIENTAL***, Block B, 6-8 (tel 56712). International class prices can be found in the hotels downtown such as the **Hyatt, Capitol** and **Shangrila.**

FOOD
Get good and cheap Indian food in **TAJ**, Jl.Tugu. It's not quite as good in the **ISLAMIC**. The foodstalls around the bus station and at the night market on Jl.Tugu are cheap. Try Chinese in **SUI SIEN**, 46 Jl.Pantai and in **JADE FOUNTAIN** behind the Cathay movie theatre.

GENERAL INFORMATION
TOURIST INFORMATION - good material at the **SABAH TOURIST ASSOCIATION** (tel 52424) on Lorong Jesselton. TDC Malaysia and Sabah Tourist Promotion also have their offices here.

Just round the corner, in Jl.Tun Fuad Stephens, is the office of **SABAH NATIONAL PARK HEADQUARTERS**, POB 626, tel 211585. Open Mon to Thurs 8:00-12:45 h, 14:00-16:15 h, Fri 8:00-11:30 h, 14:00-16:15, Sat 8:00-12:45 h.

IMMIGRATION - at the Federal Building, Jl.Mat Salleh (on the road to Tanjong Aru).

POST OFFICE - GPO with poste restante in Jl.Gaya (Colonial Building).

RENT-A-CAR - as yet, there are two rent-a-car companies in Sabah: AVIS, Lot 1, Block 1, SEDCO Complex (Jl.Laiman Diki), tel 58360; SINTAT, Block L, Lots 4-6, Sinsuran Complex, tel 57729 (Hornbill Tours next to Tourist Office). AVIS asks 570.-M$ per week for a Toyota Corolla. Try and bargain for a lower price! Only a few kilometers of road are paved (KK - Papar; KK - Ranau; KK - Kota Belud). You can't do any cross-country driving in a Corolla!

DAY TRIPS AROUND KK
PULAU GAYA - PULAU SAPI - PULAU MANUKAN
In the Bay of KK are a number of mostly unpopulated islands just a few kilometers offshore. They have been joined together to form the Tunku Abdul Rahman National Park due to their wonderful coral reefs and beautiful sandy beaches, The big negative: You may have to rent a fishing boat to get there, and they charge incredible prices. Alternative: check at Hornbill Tours next to the tourist office.

PENAMPANG
13 km southeast of KK, bus 80 c, taxi 10.-M$, is a nice Kadazan village with pretty houses and one of the oldest churches in Sabah.

TANJUNG ARU BEACH
Nothing special, but still a nice spot near the airport. Crowded on Sundays. Everyone picnics under the casuarina trees (foodstalls and a restaurant at your service). After your meal, join the promenade in Prince Philip Park. Those who can afford it keep a yacht here or play at the nearby golf course. Take the airport bus or come by taxi for 3 M$.

LEAVING KK
INTERNATIONAL FLIGHTS
The airport, 6.5 km from town, is regularly served by the airport buses 12 and 13, taxis cost 7.30 M$. Airport tax, like everywhere else in Malaysia, is 7 M$ for domestic flights, 10 M$ to Brunei and Singapore, and 15 M$ for international flights. MAS office is on 1 Jl.Sagunting, tel 53560. The following airlines also serve KK: Cathay Pacific (tel 54733), Singapore Airlines (tel 55444), Philippines Airlines (tel 57870) and Royal Brunei (tel 53211).

SAMPLE PRICES: BANDAR SERI BEGAWAN 65.-, HONGKONG 658.-, MANILA 414.-, SINGAPORE 346.-M$.

DOMESTIC FLIGHTS
There are daily flights to West Malaysia. Especially good deals are the night flights to KL and Johore Bharu. However, they're usually booked up well in advance. Be sure to book any flight well ahead of time. The Fokker-flights to Sarawak are much cheaper than the jets. SAMPLE PRICES:
BINTULU 110.-, JOHORE BHARU 301.- (night flight 256.-), KENNINGKAU 38.-, KL 380.- (night flight 266.-), KUCHING 198.-, KUDAT 50.-, LABUAN 43.-, LAHAD DATU 88.-, LAWAS 47.-, MIRI 82.-, RANAU 38.-, SANDAKAN 69.-, SIBU 156.-, TAWAU 80.-M$.

Those who don't shun the risks can go with the barter-traders: smugglers and small merchants sailing from Sabah to the Philippines. The best places to hook up are in Labuan or Sandakan.
The boats are frequently held up by pirates, and you might have to shoot it out with Philippine police. The officers at Sabah Immigration told us about two Dutchmen who'd been recently shot on the Sulu Sea. One man, badly injured with an upper arm wound, made it back to Sabah.
Sabah Immigration will give you an exit stamp for that kind of trip only upon special request. Upon arrival in the Philippines, expect difficulties. There're not likely to send you back, since entry and exit by boat are strictly forbidden. For that reason don't expect an entry or exit stamp in Davao or Zamboanga. In Sabah you will, however, get the important entry stamp.

BY RAIL
The Sabah State Railways is a relic of the colonial era that does not run any more between KK Tanjong Aru and Beaufort. The diesel and steam-powered trains only carry passengers between Beaufort and Tenom.

BY BUS/TAXI/LANDROVER
Sabah's road system experienced a real uplifting with the completion of the stretch from KK to Sandakan, Lahad Datu and Tawau. However, the Trans Sabah Highway is only partially paved.

Sample prices per person for Landrover (L), Bus (B) and Taxi (T): KOTA BELUD 12.-(L)+(B), 16.-(T), MT.KINABALU 17.-(B), RANAU 23.-(T), KENINGKAU 19.-(L), 24.-(T), SANDAKAN 50.-(B), KUDAT 19.-(B), 23.-(T), BEAUFORT 10.-(T) M$.

Taxis and minibuses depart for Kota Belud, Beaufort, Sandakan and Kudat from the corner of Jl.Polis/Jl.Tengku Abdul Rahman. Everything else leaves from the bus station.

Mount Kinabalu

Kinabalu National Park covers 767 km². Thousands of tourists visit the park yearly, but not everyone climbs the 4101 m Mount Kinabalu, the highest mountain between northern Burma and New Guinea. If you're reasonably fit, plan to make the climb. You'll need four days to make it up the noticeably cold heights.

Equally interesting are treks through the tropical rain forest at 912 m in altitude. The tropical mountain forest rises up to 1824 m in altitude, thereby covering most of the national park. The vegetation here is lower and thicker on the ground since more light gets through. This is home to tremendous numbers of epiphytic plants, so typical in tropical forests, particularly orchids. Botanists have detected about 1000 different varieties of orchid at Kinabalu. The park headquarters is right in this vegetation zone.

Most fascinating is the tropical 'foggy-mountain' forest. The short trees, frequently pines, are covered over and over with liches, moss, and orchids. Bamboo, rattan, rhododendron, and bushes make it impossible to leave the trails. In this vegetation zone you'll find the most monkey-cup plants (Nephenthes). More than half of all the plant types growing over 912 m are endemic to Kinabalu, i.e. are only found here.
Another typical South-East Asian plant (and the world's largest flower), the Rafflesia, blooms at certain times of year around Poring.
The national park's fauna is just as bountiful. Orangutan still live here, particularly in the northern areas which haven't been opened with tracks. And the Sumatra rhinoceros is said to be around. About 300 types of birds, two-thirds of all the Borneo species, make their home in the park.

HOW TO GET THERE
Like all Malaysian national parks, you have to book in advance; the address: Park Warden, Kinabalu National Park, POB 626, Kota Kinabalu. You can take care of this verbally at the office (BANDARAN SINSURAN), next to the Tourist Office.

In the morning at 7:30 and 12:30 h, the minibuses from the Tuaran United Transport Company will take you for 8.50 M$ to the park headquarters and further on down the road to Ranau. It takes about 2 1/2 hours to do the 100 km to the park.

ACCOMMODATIONS

Register in the old headquarters. They also have a canteen. In the new main camp, there's a Steak & Coffee House serving good food, as well as a small museum with exhibits on the flora and fauna. A possible place to stay is across the way in Twin Bed Cabins with bath****. Otherwise there's a youth hostel with a 46 and 52 bed dormitory*, offering student rates, and renting sleeping bags for 2 M$.

Other accommodations:
Duplex Two-bedroom chalets (6 person)	100.-M$
Single Storey Deluxe Cabin (5 person)	100.-M$
Double Storey Deluxe Cabin (7 person)	150.-M$
Twinbed Cabins (2 person)	60.-M$
Basement Rooms (2 person)	60.-M$
Annex Rooms (4 person)	120.-M$

THE CLIMB

Among your equipment you'll need a thick jacket, good shoes, and a sweater, kerosine to cook, food, a flashlight, and a sleeping bag (which you can rent after registering in KK).

Guides are only necessary for the last bit of the climb, cost 25 M$ per day for 1-3 people, or 30 M$ for 4-6 people. A jeep for 12 people to take you from the headquarters through the tropical rain forest to the **POWER STATION** costs 20 M$, on foot you'd need 1 1/4 hours. Here you are already 2000 meters up.

In another two hours, you're in **CARSON'S CAMP** (2960 m). Here there's drinking water, plus cooking and sleeping accommodations. It's another 2 1/2 hours to **PANAR LABAN HUT** (3660 m). Since the new cabin has been built, up to 65 people can spend the night. In Gunting Lagadan New Hut, there's a two-way radio connection to the headquarters, a small kitchen, sleeping bag rental (reserve in advance), toilet, showers, and double-deck beds. However, it isn't heated, so 'brrr' at night.

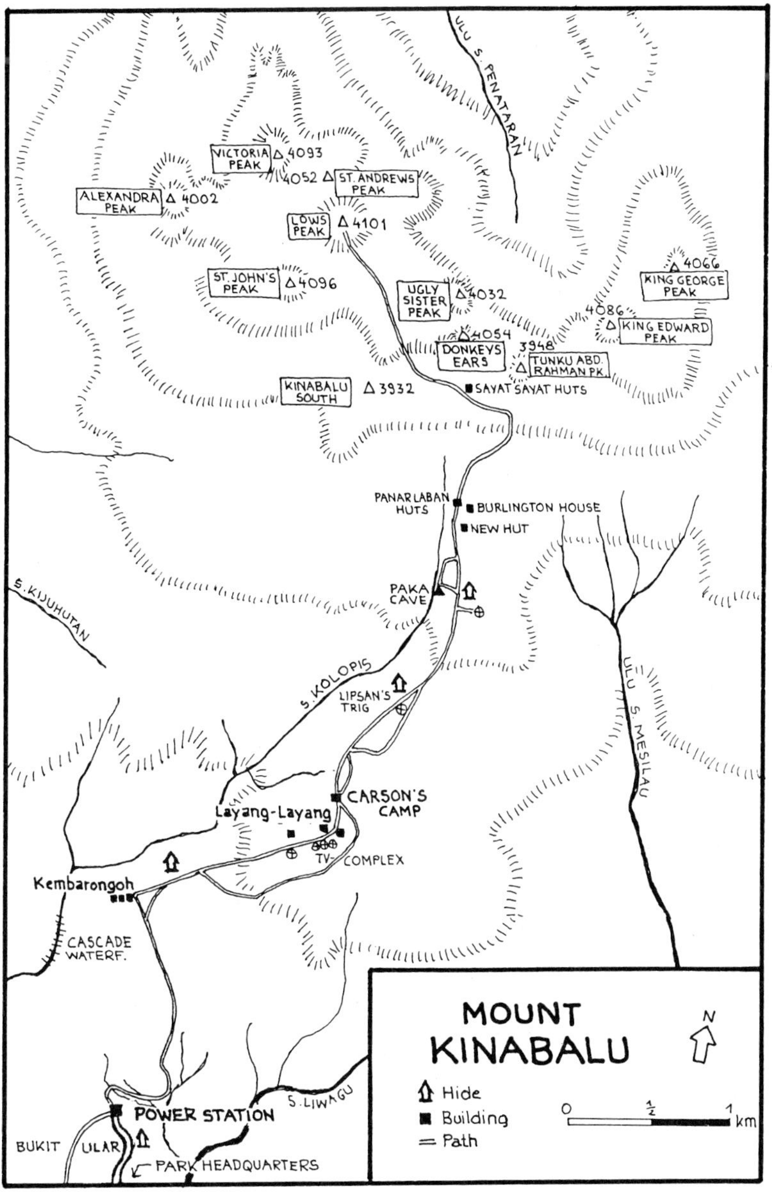

ULU S. PENATARAN
VICTORIA PEAK
4093
4052
ST. ANDREWS PEAK
ALEXANDRA PEAK
4002
LOWS PEAK
4101
ST. JOHN'S PEAK
4096
UGLY SISTER PEAK
4032
4066
KING GEORGE PEAK
4086
KING EDWARD PEAK
4054
DONKEYS EARS
3948
TUNKU ABD. RAHMAN PK.
SAYAT SAYAT HUTS
KINABALU SOUTH
3932
PANAR LABAN HUTS
BURLINGTON HOUSE
NEW HUT
PAKA CAVE
S. KIJUHUTAN
S. KOLOPIS
LIPSAN'S TRIG
ULU S. MESILAU
CARSON'S CAMP
Layang-Layang
TV-COMPLEX
Kembarongoh
CASCADE WATERF.
POWER STATION
S. LIWAGU
BUKIT ULAR
PARK HEADQUARTERS
MOUNT KINABALU
N
Hide
Building
Path
0
½
1
km

Those who still have the energy can go on up another hour to **SAYAT SAYAT HUT** (3800 m). On the smooth granite cliffs, hardly anything grows. The peak is clouded over, but on both sides you can see other lower peaks. A bit further along you come to the **SACRIFICE POOL** where they used to sacrifice seven roosters and seven eggs to the spirits of the mountains. At **LOW'S PEAK** you've reached the top of the highest mountain in South-East Asia. At sunrise the view can't be beat. The climb back down to the headquarters will take you a day.

DAYTRIPS IN KINABALU NATIONAL PARK
A number of people stay at headquarters to enjoy the many marked trails. **PORING** offers a good alternative. Get the first minibus for 3 M$ to **RANAU**, takes 50 minutes, HOTEL RANAU****, tel 75351, and the RESTHOUSE*, tel 75256. Here you'll have to organize your own wheels. The simplest is to take a share taxi in the morning or on weekends to the Poring Hot Springs (18 km) for about 4 M$. Otherwise you'll have to rent a car for 20 to 30 M$. In Poring you can find accommodations in the BUNGALOWS*** or the CLUBHOUSE*. But since the clubhouse doesn't have enclosed walls, be sure to bring a mosquito net. Next door are three small shops offering drinks and canned foods. Best of all is a bath in the hot springs. Several basins can be filled with hot or cold water. They were installed during the Japanese occupation. The hot sulphur baths were a very Japanese refreshment for the Tenno troops. Many paths lead through the jungle to waterfalls, caves, bamboo forests and to the rafflesia - the largest flower in the world.

From Kota Kinabalu to Brunei

An overland trip is the most interesting way to reach Sarawak and Brunei. After completion of the last missing bit of road between Trusan (Sarawak) and Labu (Brunei), you'll be able to do the whole trip by car. Until then you have two choices:
Beaufort - Menumbok - (boat) - Labuan - Brunei
Beaufort - -Sipitang - Merapok - Lawas - Brunei.

PAPAR
Your first stop should be this Kadazan village about 40 km south of KK. There's a RESTHOUSE*, tel 088/73518. Check out the old Chinese temple or make an excursion into some of the surrounding villages. A big Tamu is held every Sunday. Get to Papar from KK by bus in two hours for 2.50 M$ or overland taxi. Then go on by minibus or taxi to

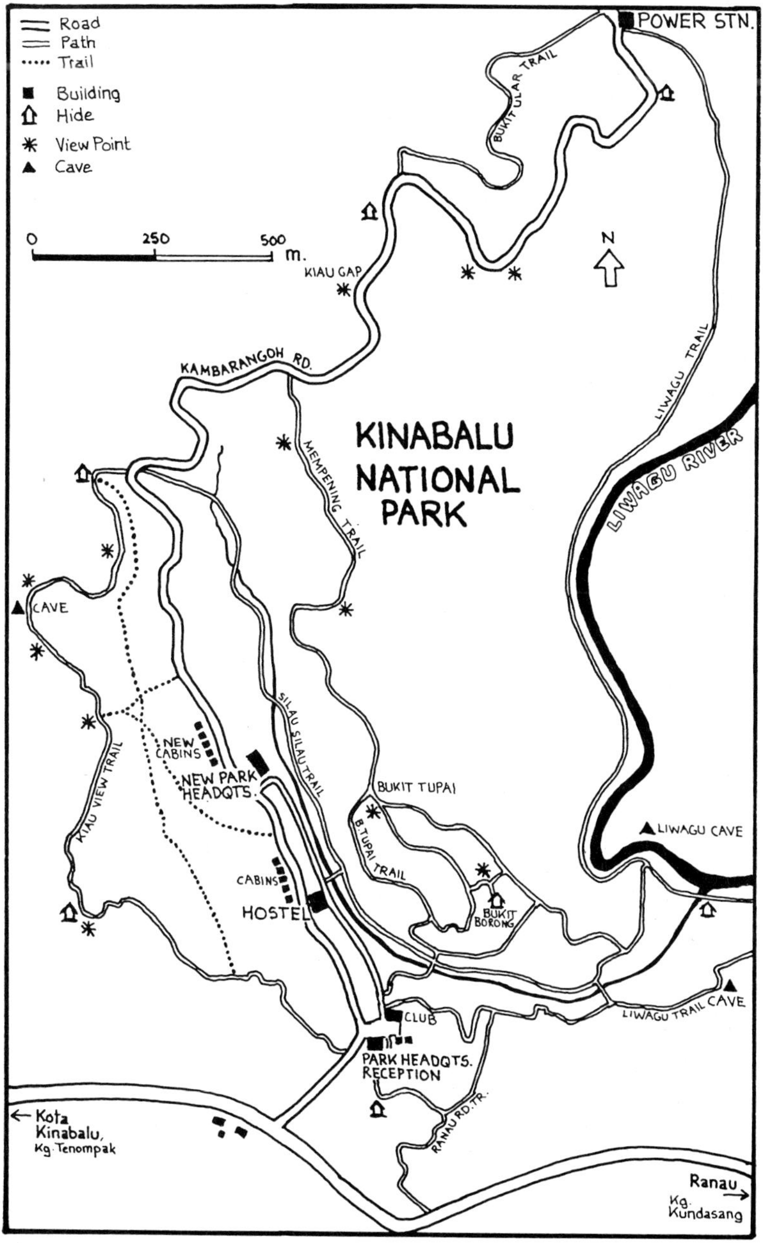

Road
Path
Trail
Building
Hide
View Point
Cave
0
250
500
m.
N
POWER STN.
BUKIT ULAR TRAIL
KIAU GAP
KAMBARANGOH RD.
MEMPENING TRAIL
KINABALU NATIONAL PARK
LIWAGU TRAIL
LIWAGU RIVER
CAVE
KIAU VIEW TRAIL
NEW CABINS
NEW PARK HEADQTS.
SILAU SILAU TRAIL
BUKIT TUPAI
B. TUPAI TRAIL
LIWAGU CAVE
CABINS
HOSTEL
BUKIT BORONG
LIWAGU TRAIL
CAVE
CLUB
PARK HEADQTS. RECEPTION
RANAU RD. TR.
← Kota Kinabalu, Kg. Tenompak
Ranau →
Kg. Kundasang

BEAUFORT
Named after a governor of the British North Borneo Company. In the village, the FOH LODGING HOUSE* is right across the station (usually full), PADAS HOTEL****, tel 211441, with a good restaurant or ECONOMY INN**** right in town. Go by minibus (2 hours) to

MENUMBOK
From there you can go right on by speedboat (carries 12 people) for the 45 minute ride to Labuan, costs 7 M$.

LABUAN
Still a duty free port, at one time it belonged, along with Penang, Singapore and Malacca, to the British Straits Settlement. An Australian military cemetery is a reminder of the heavy fighting here just before the end of WW II. A stone memorial reminds visitors of the handing over of the island by the Sultan of Brunei to the English.

There aren't any cheap places to stay. You can try on Jl.Okk in KIM SOON LEE*** (no 141) or in AURORA*** (no 112).

There's a speedboat connection from Labuan for 12 M$ to Bandar Seri Begawan and flights to BINTULU 96.-, KK 43.-, KUCHING 173.-, LAWAS 31.-, MIRI 57.-, SIBU 130.-M$.

In recent decades Sabah's cacao cultivation has been greatly increased. At the moment mostly just cacao beans are exported, but the processing industry is receiving federal support.

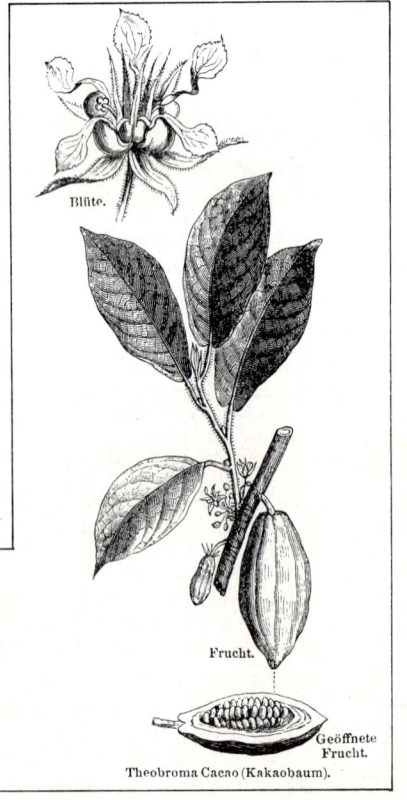

Theobroma Cacao (Kakaobaum).

The second alternative is to go on from Beaufort to **SIPITANG** and then to **MERAPOK**. Bytaxi you'll need 7.50 M$ for the first bit and 10 M$ for the second. In **SINDUMIN**, just before Merapok, you'll have to get a Sabah exit stamp in your passport.

The Sarawak entry stamp can be had in **LAWAS** (if you come from BSB), reachable by bus on the new road for 4.50 M$. Just in case, be sure to track down the immigration authorities, otherwise you'll have problems later on.

You can stay the night in RASA SAYANG LODGING HOUSE*. From Lawas you can go by bus/boat (12.-M$) to Bandar Seri Begawan. Another possibility is to go by plane inland to **LONG SEMADO** or **BAKELALAN**, near the Indonesian border for 36 M$ or 40 M$ with a small Twin Otter (see Bareo in the Sarawak chapter).

TENOM
People who like unusual trips should go from Beaufort to Tenom by rail. It follows the river and passes through a ravine where a huge hydro-electric plant has been built. The cost from Beaufort is 8.35 M$ (1st cl.) or 2.75 M$ (2nd cl.). Since the train goes very slow, you have lots of time to enjoy the countryside. Tenom is Murut country.

HOTELS
There're five hotels in town. The cheapest is **KIM SAN****, tel 611, dormitory for 10 M$, but not exactly clean. The owner is helpful, but very businesslike. Better in **TENOM******, tel 587. Or stay at **SABAH HOTEL*****, across from the police station. Try the food across from the Shell station in **KEDAI MAKAN YUN LEE**.

From Tenom there're taxis to **TOMANI** and Keningkau. In Tomani, there's no hotel, but a big open resthouse where you can spend the night for free. The nicest suspension bridge in Sabah is here! For 5 M$, you can get a taxi to **ULU TOMANI** (BEKUKU). Then go on by foot into the villages.

In the morning there're taxis from Tomani to Tenom (7 M$) as well as from there to **KENINGKAU** for 9 M$. Stay the night in HOTEL RIA***, ALISHAN*** or HIAP SOON***. The village was one of the best fortified Japanese bases during WW II.

If you want to go back to KK, get a Landrover for 19 M$ or a taxi for 24 M$ via **TAMBUNAN** (Resthouse*). Tambunan was the last hide-out of the national hero Mat Salleh.

In 1897 he reduced the first British settlement on Gaya island off KK to rubble. He then retreated to Tambunan where he built a fort. In 1900, the British using Dayak troops stormed the fort and murdered Mat Salleh.

There is also a second route back to KK right through the Crocker Range to **PAPAR**, but it isn't paved.

From Keningkau, take the new road down to **PENSIANGAN**. You can get to **LUMBIS** in Indonesia by way of the Sungei Sembakung. Up till now the exit stamp must be procured in Pensiangan (though this might change!). The people in Lumbis know well that the only way through is via the river. This makes the price high. The trip takes you from longhouse to longhouse until you reach the coast.

From Kota Kinabalu to Kudat

Tamu - the famous Sabah markets, can be found north of KK. They feature an interesting mixture of Sabah's various ethnic groups. Besides the Kadazan, there are Bajau, Chinese, Indians and Malays, all offering their wares. The markets don't take place daily, however. So check in advance with the tourist office in KK before you head out.

The 'tamu' in Kota Belud, Tuaran and Tamparuli are the most famous. **TUARAN** and **TAMPARULI** (market on Wed) are on the road heading north, taxis cost about 12.-M$.

KOTA BELUD
is located about 80 km from KK. Minibuses make the trip in about 2 hours and charge 12.-M$ per person, otherwise there are taxis. There're two hotels, TAI SENG**, tel 551 and KOTA BELUD***, tel 576. The largest and nicest tamu takes place here every Sunday morning behind the mosque.

KUDAT
The road then goes on to Kudat. Minibuses charging 10.-M$ for the 2 hour ride leave from the Shell station between 9:00 and 10:00 h. Kudat has four hotels: HASBA**, KING NAM TONG**, KUDAT*** and SUNRISE**** (great seafood). Otherwise there's a RESTHOUSE** with a large terrace.

Out here are beautiful white sandy beaches with offshore coral reefs and islands. From Kudat itself, you can visit the beaches north of town. When passing the airport runway, stay on the road running along the coast. Even under the casuarina trees on the main beach at Bak-Bak, it's peaceful during the week.

The whole Kudat peninsula is one big coconut grove. On the coast in **SIKUATI**, the Sabah Tourist Board built a longhouse just for tourists. No one seems to have discovered it yet. It's pretty quiet.

From Kudat you can get flights to SANDAKAN 54.-M$ and KK 50.-M$. Taxis to KK cost 23.-M$, a minibus will take you for 19.-M$.

From Kota Kinabalu to Tawau

The new Trans-Sabah Highway goes right through Sabah from KK to Sandakan. The road circles Mount Kinabalu and through Ranau and the timber region to the old capital of North Borneo. In early 1984 we had to take a boat across a river and board a new minibus on the other side.

SANDAKAN
Can be reached from KK by Landrover in 8-10 hours for 50.-M$. MAS will fly you there for 69.-M$. The city is Malaysia's most important port for wood exports. Like KK, it was almost completely destroyed during WW II. The new town consists of monotonous blocks of houses. Visit the **SANDAKAN ORCHID HOUSE** with its remarkable collection of different rare orchids. There are other botanical exhibits, along with hunting weapons and art objects in the Forestry Exhibition.

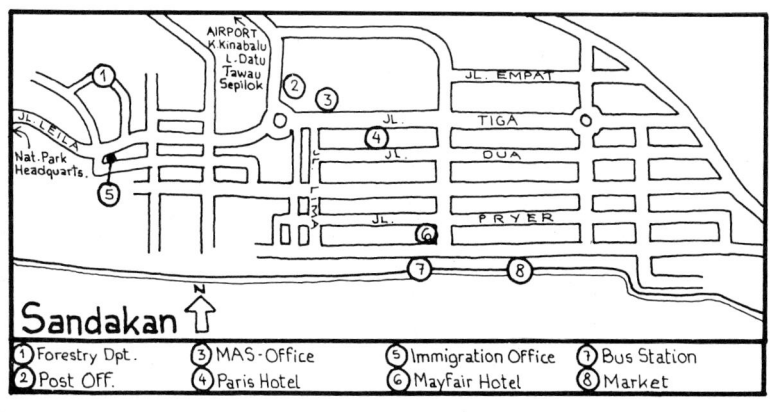

Sandakan

1) Forestry Dpt.
2) Post Off.
3) MAS-Office
4) Paris Hotel
5) Immigration Office
6) Mayfair Hotel
7) Bus Station
8) Market

HOTELS
This is the most expensive town in all of Sabah, all hotels****. Expect to pay about 50 M$ for a double in **MAYFAIR**, Jl.Prayer, **PARIS**, 45 Jl.Tiga, tel 21488 or in **KIN NAM SING**, 51 Jl.Empat.

DAYTRIPS AROUND SANDAKAN
PULAU SELINGAN
This island is also known as Green Turtle Island due to the many turtles, some 100 years old, populating the island. Get a permit to visit from the National Park Warden in Sandakan (Pejabat Taman Negara, Jl.Laila by Hotel Ramai). Unless you can get a ride on a park administration speedboat (leaves several times a week), the trip out could be very expensive, it takes about 2 hours. The island of Lihiman, just 2 km away, already belongs to the Philippines.

SEPILOK ORANG UTAN SANCTUARY
You can cover the 25 km in 45 min. with bus Batu 14 (1.- M$). Other buses with the signs 'Batu 16, 17, 30, or 32' go in the right direction, but you'll have to get off at the branch-off and walk 2 km to the park. Register in the park (free of charge) and perhaps list the trails you'd like to hike. There's a small exhibit about the species of flora and fauna, plus good maps. It's a 45 minute walk to where the orangutans are fed - feeding time is 11:00 h.

Lots of trails for hiking through the jungle. We enjoyed the path through the mangrove forest surrounding the Bay of Sandakan. Another path (about 35 minutes) leads you past several waterfalls and pools where the swimming's great.

GOMATONG CAVES
Located 32 km south of the Bay of Sandakan. As in Niah, swallow nests are collected from the shaky structures. Travel agencies charge high prices to take you here. Why not just ask some of the nest collectors to take you with them over the bay?

LAHAD DATU
The new road from Sandakan to Lahad Datu is now complete. Buses cost 14.-M$. Those who'd rather fly should check with the MAS office on Jl.Tiga in Sandakan, tel 42211. Flights cost 40 M$. The hotels in Lahad Datu are expensive, as you'd expect. In MIDO (home of the MAS office) rooms will set you back 100 M$. Try the KUNAK***, tel 85200, the PERDANA****, Jl.Bajau or VENUS****, Jl.Seroja, tel 81900. Buses from Lahad Datu - Tawau cost 25.-M$ and take five hours.

The 'forest people' (=orangutan in Malay) only live on Borneo and Sumatra. Some scientists estimates that only 5000 still live in the wild. People are constantly pushing back the territories of the individual animals. Their freedom of movement has been greatly reduced, and no single part of Sabah contains more than 100 of the animals. The main reason for the reduction of the orangutan population is deforesting by the timber industry of the great forest areas. Also not to be underestimated is the capture of wild orangutans for zoos and as pets around the world.
The mother thereby is killed so that the baby animals can be captured and sold. An attempt is being made in Sepilok to prepare tame orangutans for the wild so that they can be released. They are having success.

TAWAU
The town, a center for smugglers to the Philippines, is located in an intensively farmed region. Here you'll mostly find travellers on their way to or from Indonesia.

HOTELS
Accommodations are relatively cheap for Sabah, try the **NAM WAH LODGING HOUSE***, 893 Jl.Masjid, tel 72269. If it's full, check **FOO GUAN*****, 152 Jl.Chester, tel 71700 or **SOON YEE******, 1362 Jl. Stephen Tan, tel 72447.

It's possible to take a trip up to **SEMPORNA**, about 110 km north of Tawau. Landrovers or taxis cost about 15 M$. Two hotels: ISLAND VIEW*** and SEMPORNA****. Many islands and coral reefs. Since the town was frequently attacked by pirates in the past, the British North Borneo Company built a blockhouse, which is now made of stone.

LEAVING TAWAU
Taxis to LAHAD DATU charge 30.-M$ per person. You can fly it for 40 M$. If you want to go on to Indonesia, you'll have to fly since the boats to NUNUKAN are closed to foreigners these days. For the 35 minutes of airtime with BOURAQ to TARAKAN, expect to shell out 152 M$. You can book at the Merdeka Travel Service, 41 Dunlop Street, tel 2531. There is an Indonesian consulate (Jl.Kuharsa).

THE PEOPLE OF SABAH
A number of ethnic groups make up Sabah's population. Of the 1.1 million inhabitants, 56 % are younger than 20, 27 % are between 20 and 40, while just 17 % are over 40 years of age.

Almost one third of Sabah's people are **Kadazan**, about 20 % are **Chinese**. Other important ethnic groups are **Murut**, **Bajau**, and **Malay** (most of whom arrived after Sabah joined the Federation of Malaysia). Other smaller groups include **Brunei Malays**, **Kedayan**, **Bisayas**, and **Orang Sungei**.

Kadazan live mostly on the fertile plains of the west coast, but also around Ranau, Tambunan, and Keningau. Sub-tribes are the **Dusun** (around Tuaran) and the **Rungus** (around Kudat). With slight dialectic differences, all Kadazan speak the same language. Traditional longhouse life is only preserved among the Rungus near Kudat.

The sub-tribes differentiate only slightly in their traditional clothing, which they, like the other tribes on Borneo, only wear on special occasions. The basic color of their clothing is black. Kadazan women wear crown-like woven hats, from which one can determine their geographical origin.

Today they work mostly as peasants, owning their own land. The average farm size of 1-2 ha per farm is large by South-East Asian standards. Many Kadazan no longer work on the farm, but have gone into politics, administration, or trade. For this, the importance of Christian missionaries and their school system in providing a high level of education shouldn't be underestimated.

Bajau make up about 15 % of Sabah's inhabitants. They live on the west coast between Kudat and Papar. Another group can be found on the east coast, mostly around Lahad Datu. They migrated here in the 19th century. their forefathers were feared pirates between the Sulu Archipelago and Sulawesi. Today about half the Bajau live off fishing and the other half from agriculture. Especially in the Kota Belud area, cattle raising has become important, and the Bajau here have earned a name among tourists as the 'Cowboys' of Borneo.

Murut have a population of about 40,000 in the Tenom region of southern Sabah, in the uncharted regions along the border to Indonesia, and in the 5th division (Lawas - Trusan) of Sarawak. Many Murut practice slash and burn agriculture. Originally the Murut were semi-nomadic hunters who were pushed back into the less accessible jungle by the late-coming Kadazan. They have generally long since turned in their blowpipes for rifles. Nowadays many Murut farm rice paddies under projects supported by the Sabah government. In addition they plant sweet potatoes, manioc, and sugar cane. In Keningau and Tenom, the state has established Murut settlements.

Chinese make up a third of the Sarawak population, and about 20 % in Sabah. The Chinese made their big push into the northwest coast areas of Borneo during the last century and into the 1930s. As in other parts of South-East Asia, most came from southern China (Hokkien, Hakka, Teochew, Canton and Hainan). They control the retail trade, industry and transport, but in Sabah are also important in agriculture.

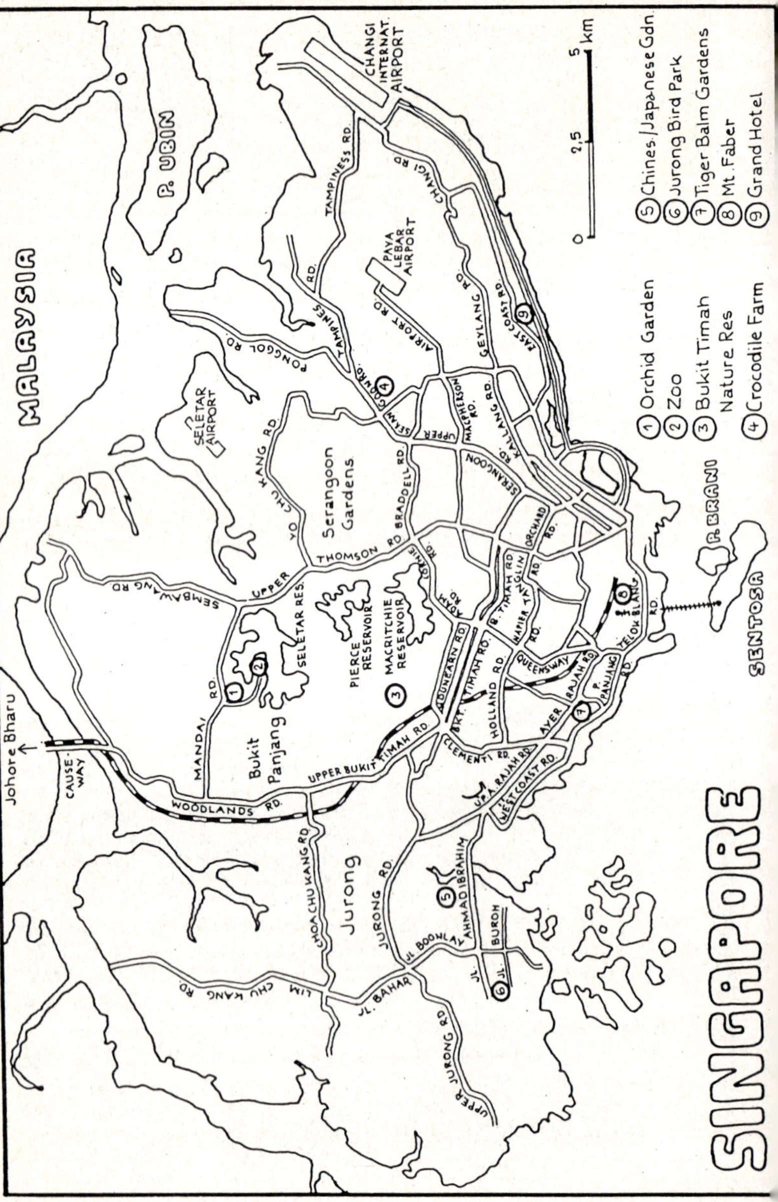
MALAYSIA
P. UBIN
CHANGI INTERNAT. AIRPORT
SELETAR AIRPORT
PAYA LEBAR AIRPORT
Johore Bharu
CAUSE-WAY
WOODLANDS RD.
MANDAI RD.
SEMBAWANG RD
UPPER THOMSON RD
YO CHU KANG RD.
PONGGOL RD
TAMPINES RD.
TAMPINESS RD.
CHANGI RD
AIRPORT RD.
GEYLANG RD.
EAST COAST RD.
SERANGOON RD.
UPPER SERANGOON RD.
MACPHERSON RD.
KALLANG RD.
BRADDELL RD.
LORNIE RD.
ADAM RD.
ORCHARD RD.
B. TIMAH RD
TANGLIN RD.
NAPIER RD.
QUEENSWAY
HOLLAND RD.
BKT. TIMAH RD.
ADUNEARN RD.
UPPER BUKIT TIMAH RD.
CLEMENTI RD.
AYER RAJAH RD
U.P.A. RAJAH RD
WEST COAST RD.
P. PANJANG
TELOK BLANG. RD.
SELETAR RES.
PIERCE RESERVOIR
MACRITCHIE RESERVOIR
Serangoon Gardens
Bukit Panjang
Jurong
CHOACHU KANG RD.
JURONG RD.
AHMAD IBRAHIM
BUROH
JL. BOON LAY
JL. BAHAR
JL.
LIM CHU KANG RD
UPPER JURONG RD.
P. BRANI
SENTOSA
0
2,5
5 km
① Orchid Garden
② Zoo
③ Bukit Timah Nature Res
④ Crocodile Farm
⑤ Chines./Japanese Gdn
⑥ Jurong Bird Park
⑦ Tiger Balm Gardens
⑧ Mt. Faber
⑨ Grand Hotel
SINGAPORE

SINGAPORE

Singapore is a Chinese city, whose population is spiced with 6 % Indians and 14 % Malay. These dynamic people have made Singapore into the most important trade and finance center between Hongkong and the Persian Gulf. Ancient tradition has been thrown to the wind in the name of progress. In the process, a lot of atmosphere has been lost, much to the detriment of nostalgia-seeking tourists. Bicycle rickshaws are out of place on the multi-lane highways. The old Chinatown has almost completely given way to high-rise office buildings. Multi-level shopping centers, offering an international selection of wares, have just about replaced the tiny Chinese shops. Only the splendid architecture of the British colonial past remains immune. Sir Stamford Raffles, founder of the former crown colony, still has his place in front of the parliament building.

About 2.5 million people inhabit this island nation of 619 km^2, about the size of West Berlin. The country had no natural resources when it seceded from Malaysia in 1965.

Since then an authoritarian regime has pushed 'Planned Capitalism' and the search for profits. The buy and sell mentality prevalent here has brought a high standard of living within a short time.

For some, the atmosphere is too sterile; others enjoy the comfort of a modern city - especially after a long trip through underdeveloped regions. Those who are pleased to see the clean streets should also keep in mind that even the thoughtless toss of a cigarette butt can lead to a heavy fine.

As a duty-free port, the strong Singapore dollar has laid waste to the one-time 'shopping paradise'. But the incredible selection is still there, enticing you to buy. But don't forget the basic rule of the east - bargaining and price cutting (outside of department stores) is part of the ritual.

The City

Strictly speaking, this is the part of Singapore along the river. A better description today would be what the city fathers have tenderly christened the CBD (Central Business District). Private cars can only enter this area from Mon thru Sat from 7:30 to 10:15 h if they pay a 5 S$ toll (taxis 2 S$) or have at least four passengers. This is supposed to reduce rush-hour madness. All traffic lights heading into the CBD are then permanently turned red.

Begin your tour on **RAFFLES PLACE**, the city's old business center. Highrise offices, banks, airlines and shopping centres have shot up like mushrooms. The old English colonial atmosphere has made way for 21st century architecture. A profit oriented, steam-hammer policy has led to the ripping down of just about everything of aesthetic value.

Go through **CHANGE ALLEY** (quite small) to **RAFFLES QUAY**. Most of the people here are tourists. Notice how the clever shop and stand proprietors have signs up in Russian; why not lure in the odd Soviet sailor in need of a Japanese watch or a custom-tailored suit.

Be wary of fast talkers: there are no 'one-time offers' - and careful what you buy.

CLIFFORD PIER is surrounded by shopping arcades. The pedestrian bridge is a magnet for business-minded hawkers.

The pier itself has little economic importance. This is the
departure point for harbor tours (see 'Islands'). Sampans
can be rented for 20 S$ per hour. Access to the open sea has
been reduced in recent years by land reclamation and the
new highway. The perfume smell of kretek cigarettes (made
of cloves!) is pungent because Clifford Pier is the hang-out
for young Indonesians working (unaccompanied) in Singapore.

Heading north you come to the **GENERAL POST OFFICE**, a
tremendous colonial-style building which hopefully will be
spared the modernization boom. Just a few meters further,
office buildings set new record heights each year.

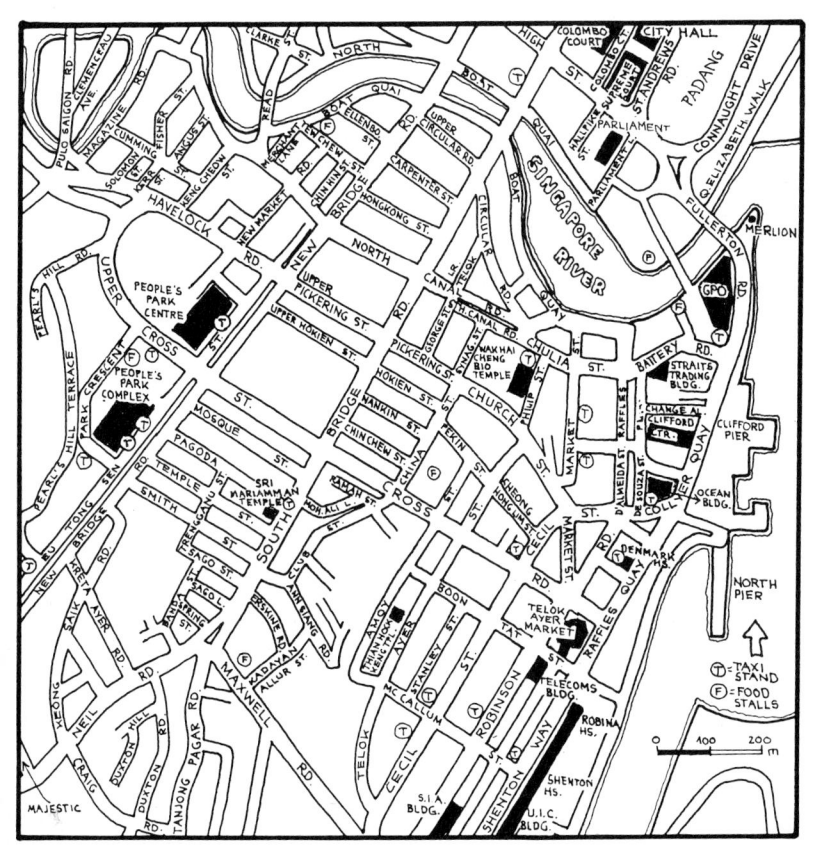

Before crossing the Singapore River, have a look on the headland at the statue of **MERLIN**, an eight-meter high, water spewing mixture of fish and lion, the city's emblem. Notice how the barges pass fully loaded under the highway bridge and skillfully steer their way up the Singapore River.

QUEEN ELIZABETH WALK begins on the other side of the river. It's a small green park right on the sea. A new city highway runs in a big curve over the ocean (or newly reclaimed soil) making the new world optically present even here.

On the Singapore River (North Boat Quay) is one of many **STAMFORD RAFFLES MONUMENTS**. Raffles is said to have landed here in 1819. A bit further upstream the 'tongkangs' (lighters or flat barges) are unloaded. Since most seagoing vessels lie at anchor, freight is transferred using lighters. It's busiest here early in the morning. But these old Chinese boats are certainly condemned by the advent of modern harbor facilities.

Lots of Victorian buildings can be found near Raffles' landing: **VICTORIA MEMORIAL HALL**, **SUPREME COURT** and **TOWN HALL**. The **CRICKET CLUB** is still one of the most exclusive clubs. **ST.ANDREW'S CATHEDRAL** is stylishly neogothic, dating from 1856, open daily 07:00-18:00 h. More than cricket is played on the huge lawn: the **PADANG** is site of pageants and parades held on state holidays.

Another leftover of British colonialism is **RAFFLES HOTEL** on Beach Road at Bras Basah Road. Everything else in Raffles' City just beside may be modern, but time has stood still here. The hotel was built in 1886 and soon developed into the social rendezvous for Europeans. Rudyard Kipling, Joseph Conrad, Somerset Maugham and Noel Coward mixed among the select clientele. So visit the Writer's Bar. Those with a few extra dollars might try breakfast or a Singapore Sling (6 S$). There's a nice story about the Billiard Room and two cool Englishmen: The gentlemen are playing billiards, when with that English imperturbability one mentions that a tiger is sitting under the billiard table. "Oh, the second one this week!" comes the not very surprised reply. Next to the hotel is futuristic **RAFFLES CITY**.

Chinatown

(or that which is left of it)
The old traditional style buildings are being chewed up by highrise offices and apartment buildings. Only a few sections

will be kept for the benefit of tourists. On the other hand, even hard-core nostalgia freaks have to admit that the houses are very old, lack sanitary facilities, and don't serve todays expectations.

For all practical purposes, Chinatown is northwest of Raffles Place. In the evening things still hop, proving it's Chinese. People play mahjong (a kind of dominoes). At the ever-changing night markets, it's buy and sell, snakes are skinned for the next meal, while durian are sniffed and selected. Old people practice a kind of shadow-boxing (tai chi chuan) to keep in shape while achieving peace and harmony.

Along the main streets, New Bridge Road, South Bridge Road, Cross Street, or Cecil Street, this atmosphere has been lost. If you want to experience old Chinatown, then wander through the back streets. STPB publishes monthly, a 130 odd page brochure, **The Official Guide to Singapore**, containing suggested tours of Chinatown. Many small shops offering a colorful mixture of traditional Chinese wares are noted. It's hard to believe what is sold as medicine at the druggists (on Sago Lane and China Street), or how many unknown foods can be discovered and sampled in the small speciality shops.

Start your tour at **PEOPLE'S PARK COMPLEX**, one of the large shopping centres. You can get here via bus 2, 11, 22, 32, 33, and others from North Bridge Road, or bus 143 from Clemenceau Ave. at Orchard Road. Cross the street and check the side streets (from west to east: Sago Lane, Sago Street, Smith Street, Temple Street, Pagoda Street). A **FRUIT AND VEGETABLE MARKET** is held in the early morning between Sago Street and Smith Street. Come evening, most shops are still open, and foodstalls on the street offer dishes which in many cases can only be compared to good restaurants.

In Chinatown at the corner of Pagoda Street and South Bridge Road, you can visit one of the city's most important Hindu temples. The **SRI MARIAMMAN TEMPLE** was built in 1850 and provides a vivid contrast to its Chinese surroundings. Above the main entrance is a colorful tower upon which Hindu figures are packed one next to the other. Before entering, everyone must respect the Indian tradition of removing their shoes. If you keep in the background, you're very welcome to stay and observe the faithful. For 1 S$ you can perform a sacrificial ceremony. Open from 06:00 - 12:00 H and from 16:30 - 20:30 h.

A bit further west is an Islamic place of worship, the **JAMAE MOSQUE**, built in 1825-1830 - but not as colorful.

Across South Bridge Road, at the corner of Maxwell Road is **MAXWELL MARKET**, featuring lots of foodstalls. We recommend a walk along Ali Lane, China Street, Club Street, and the narrow alleys south of Amoy Street which cars can't enter.

One of the oldest Chinese temples **(THIAN HOCK KENG TEMPLE)** can be found between Amoy Street and Telok Ayer Street. The 'Temple of Heavenly Happiness' (dedicated to Ma--Cho-Po, patron goddess of seamen) is mostly visited by Taoists from Hokkien. In 1840 Chinese workmen were imported along with all the granite columns, woodcuttings, and deity statues from China. The much-visited temple is open from 05:30-09:00 h.

Little India

It's India in Singapore on **SERANGOON ROAD**, and its side streets. This is where you get the best cloth for saris, or freshly mixed curry and other spices. The tiny shops, where you can bargain with the garrulous shopkeepers, are packed to the roof with wares. The smell of incense, jasmine, and curry fills the air. Men in white dhotis and women in saris crowd their way through the narrow arcades in front of the shops. Completing the scene are street hawkers selling cigarettes and newspapers. Refresh yourself along the way with strong Indian tea or a spicy vegetarian dish served on banana leaves (see FOOD).

Anybody whose travel itinerary doesn't include Thailand should take the opportunity to visit a buddhist temple. The **TEMPLE OF 1000 LIGHTS** is on Race Course Road, near Lavender Street, and open from 09:00-17:00 h. If you're staying near Bencoolen Street, you can walk to Serangoon Road, otherwise on Orchard Road get bus 64, 65, 92, 106, or 111 - or bus 146 from Cecil Street or Empress Place.

Arab Street

Unlike the very Hindu Serangoon Road, this section of town is home to Muslim Indians and Arabs. Between North Bridge Road and Beach Road are a number of interesting shops, though many cater to tourism.

SINGAPORE

The most important mosque for Singapore's large Muslim community is the **SULTAN MOSQUE** on North Bridge Road. The original structure was destroyed and replaced in 1924 by the present building featuring large, shiny-gold cupolas. Even here the 20th century has gained admittance in the form of a huge digital clock. To the mosque, get a bus from Victoria Street (2, 11, 12, 22, 32, 33, 41 etc. from Chinatown, bus 13 from Orchard Road and bus 100 from Robinson Road or Empress Place). Get off at Arab Street and walk to North Bridge Road (the one-way street heading into town).

Around Central Park

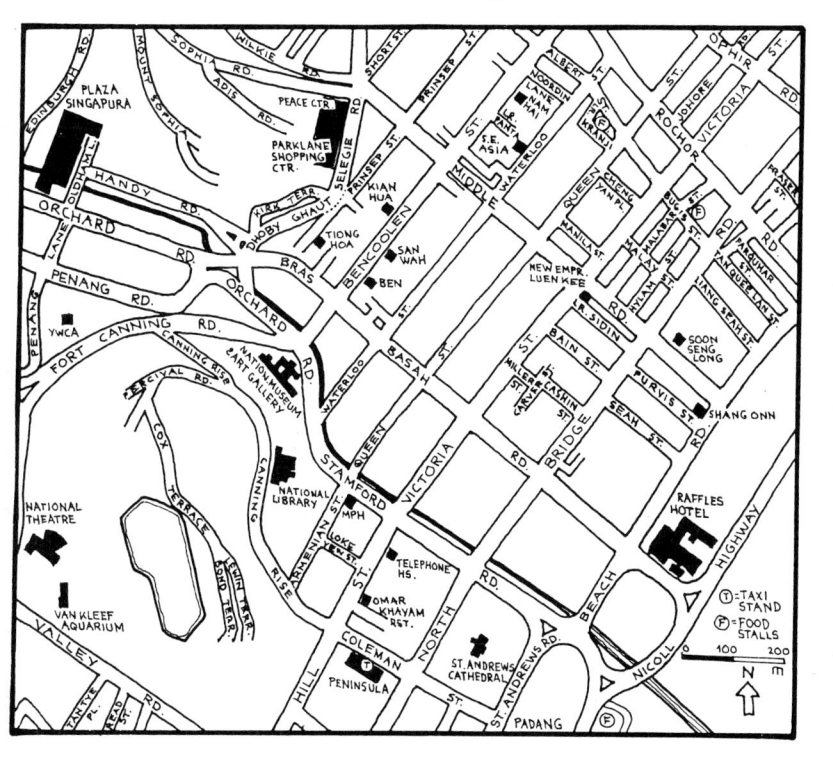

Worn out from shopping, take a break in the 40 hectares set in the heart of the city. Wander through the hilly grounds up to **FORT CANNING** (of which nothing remains). The oldest cemetery in Singapore is on the way to **VAN KLEEF AQUARIUM** (open daily 9:30 to 21:00 h, admission 60 c). The aquarium has a good collection of tropical fish - more than 4000 species. Right next door is the **NATIONAL THEATRE**, featuring a huge open-air stage.

On the other side of the park on Stamford Road is the **NATIONAL MUSEUM** (open daily 9:00 to 17:30 h, free admission). It's a well equipped museum with historical, archaeological and ethnological exhibits from Indonesia, Malaysia, and China. And, of course, you can learn about Singapore's history. The Art Gallery features regularly changing exhibits by local artists. Remarkable handwork in the **Haw Par Jade Collection**.

Parks & Gardens

BOTANICAL GARDEN
If you're on the upper end of Orchard Road, have a look in the Botanical Garden (Cluny Rd., open daily 5:00 to 23:00 h, free admission). There are beautiful strains of orchids and paved paths through a bit of virgin jungle! Young people like to take evening walks here under the floodlights. Early in the morning, you can see the Chinese practising Tai Chi Chuan.

TIGER BALM GARDEN
Chinese millionaire businessman, Aw Boon Haw, had a park built on Pasir Panjang Road. Tiger Balm, his creation, is by now well known everywhere; you can find the little red jars even in Europe or the States. By the way, it works wonders against headaches! In the park are many grotesque Buddha figures made of brightly painted cement. Scenes from Chinese mythology and history round off the Disneyland set up. The depictions of Hell are quite good! Get bus 10, 30, 143, 145, 146, or 192.

JURONG BIRD PARK
This is the oldest part of the modern industrial quarter. About 600 businesses have settled here since the 60s. Of interest is the huge bird sanctuary. About 2 ha of land on the slopes of Jurong Hill have been covered over by a net creating a free-fly zone for hundreds of birds. Admission: 3 S$. Open daily from 9:00 to 18:30 h, Sat/Sun/Hol until 19:00 h. First take a bus to Jurong Interchange: 10, 30, 154, 157, 165, 178, 183, 184, 196, 197, 198, 199. Then get bus 250 to Jl.Ahmad Ibrahim.

CHINESE GARDEN
In Jurong are two other parks: the Chinese Garden (Yu Hwa Yuan) contains 13 ha. Buildings and facilities are an imitation of the Peking Summer Palace. Open daily, 8:00 to 19:00 h, costs 2.-S$.

JAPANESE GARDEN (Seiwaen)
This is reportedly the largest Japanese garden outside of Nippon. Admission 1.-S$ or 2.50 S$ for both parks. Take the bus mentioned above to Jurong Interchange, then bus 242 or 240. None of the three parks are too far from the Interchange.

BUKIT TIMAH NATURE RESERVE
This is the last remaining piece of jungle area on the island. About 75 ha in size, it's located east of Upper Bukit Timah Road, 12 km from town. A hike here is especially worthwhile for people who otherwise won't get a chance to go on jungle treks. We even spotted a few flying lemurs and macaques. Good paths lead through the forest. Take buses 170-173, 177, 179-182, 193 up to Jurong Road. Another road leads from Jl.Anak Bukit to the forest. A map of the hiking trails is available at the information stand by the parking lot.

SELETAR RESERVOIR
The largest water reservoir on the island has been turned into a park. On weekends, the lake and park are popular recreation areas.

ZOO
Nearby is the zoo which, unlike other such facilities in South-East Asia, is well tended. Admission: 3.50 S$, open daily 8:30-18:00 h.

ORCHID GARDEN
Not far away is the largest orchid garden in the city. Open daily 8:30-18:00 h, admission 3.-S$, for which you can buy an orchid. Get bus 171 from Queen Street.

The Offshore Islands

MOUNT FABER
At 130 m, the name may be a joke, but still it offers a good view of the city and harbor. Take bus 143 to Mount Faber Road. On the hill is a Sentosa cable car station. One way from Mount Faber to Sentosa costs 3.50 S$. By the way, you can also get a good view of the city from the top of one of

the highrises, try the 38th floor of the Mandarin Hotel or the 17th floor of the Dresdner Bank.

PULAU SENTOSA
The island is a not very impressive tourist attraction - mainly for visitors from neighboring countries who might have never seen a real Swiss cable car except in the movies. The ride is interesting; from 60 m you do have a great view of the city and harbor. Note: a gondola fell and crashed in February 1983.

On the island you'll find an artificial swimming lagoon, Fort Silosa, and a 'surrender chamber' with wax figures representing the 1942 capitulation of the allies and the Japanese surrender in 1945. There is also a coralarium. Pretty touristy! Prices: Admission Ticket I costs 6.50 S$ including the round trip boat ride. Admission for the above mentioned is included. Admission Ticket II costs 4.50 S$ and excludes the coralarium. Admission Ticket III costs just 3.-S$ and is valid only after 17:00 h. Open: Mon to Sat, 10:00 to 19:00 h, Sun and holidays 9:00 to 19:00 h.

ISLANDS TO THE NORTH
Several islands lie off Singapore to the northeast. The smallest is **CONEY ISLAND** (Pulau Serangoon). The two larger ones are **PULAU TEKONG** and **PULAU UBIN**. They are still pretty wild. You can reach them all from Ponggol Jetty. Buses 82 or 83 will take you from the city to Ponggol. Speedboats cost 50.-S$ for 5 people.

ISLANDS TO THE SOUTH
There are a bunch of southern islands besides Sentosa Island. A must for every visitor is a harbor tour given by the Port of Singapore Authority. HARBOUR CRUISE (1 hour), 9:00 and 14:30 h, Mon-Sat. Price: 5 S$, leaves from the World Trade Center Ferry Terminal. The WORLD TRADE CENTER is on Telok Blangah Rd. (Sentosa cable car), buses 10, 20, 30, 61, 125, 143, 145, 176, 186.

At CLIFFORD PIER, 'JUNK CRUISES' are offered. First of all, they are too expensive (20 S$), and secondly they're packed with 10-day package tourists who, while doing South-East Asia, want to get some quick photos of the harbor. Not recommended!

If you want to visit the islands on your own, your departure point is the World Trade Center.

PULAU KUSU/ST.JOHN'S ISLAND
Boats depart at 9:00 and 14:30 h; last boat back at 16:00 h, costs 5 S$ round trip. Nine boats on Sundays and holidays.

The islands west of Sentosa are almost all plastered with industry. You can see the oil refinery on **Pulau Bukum** from Sentosa's swimming lagoon.

The islands further south belong to Indonesia's Riau Archipelago. As Indonesia's **PULAU BATAM** is a visa-free point of entry (it's stamped in your passport at the border), and there are regular ferries from Singapore, it's worthwhile to visit **BINTAN ISLAND.** To visit Tanjung Pinang, you'll have to apply for a visa in advance (see LEAVING SINGAPORE).

HOTELS
Singapore has a huge selection of hotel rooms in all categories. Cheapest are the dormitories on Bencoolen Street. Charging 7 S$ per bed are **GOH'S HOMESTAY** and **GREEN CURTAIN** at no 175. Other dorms at no 173 and 53/54.

Double rooms*** are also available. At the very bottom of the price scale is **SIM'S RESTHOUSE***, 114A Mackenzie Road (tel 3364957). Dito at **FRIENDLY RESTHOUSE***, 357A Serangoon Road (Perumal Road), tel 294084. Since these places are only half legal - they aren't zoned as hotels - the scene can change very quickly. Worth recommending is **SUNSEEKER'S RESTHOUSE*** on the second floor of the National Maritime Building, 20 South Quay (tel 2223483), next to the Neptune Building, featuring a bar, restaurant and TV room.

The cheap hotels can be found in the neighborhood Bras Basah Rd./Beach Rd./Rochore Rd./Bencoolen St. You'll have to look around. Not bad is **NAM HAI****, 166 Bencoolen St. (tel 3375395). Lawrence Nathan, the manager, can also arrange a cheap flight. Other hotels on the same street: **KIAN HUA****, no 81 (tel 3383492); **SAN WAH*****, no 36 (tel 3362428), **BEN HOTEL*****, no 12 (tel 3370034). At 7 Waterloo St. next to the Chinese temple you'll find the **SOUTH EAST ASIA***** (tel 3382394). At no 55 **WATERLOO HOSTEL*****, tel 3361685. At 26 Middle Rd. is **SOON SENG LONG****, tel 3376318 and at no 81-97 is the **NEW EMPRESS LUEN KEE*****, tel 3383477. Also good is **TIONG HOA*****, 4 Prinsep St. (tel 3384522). Recommendable and clean is **SHANG ONN****, corner of Beach Rd./Purvis St. (tel 3384153). Or try the **TAI HOE HOTEL****, 30 Verdun Road (tel 2584911) across from El Amigo nightclub. Two reasonable hotels are located on Jl.Besar (extension of Bencoolen St.): **CENTRAL HOTEL**** (Allenby Road) and at no 407 the **PALACE HOTEL***. Bus 92 goes to Jl.Besar.

MIDDLE CLASS HOTELS: Those who want to stay a bit out of town should check into the **GRAND******, 22/26 Still Road South (formerly Karikal Road), tel 3455261, in Katong. In the city try the **MAJESTIC*****, 31/37 Bukit Pasoh Rd., tel 2223377, or **STATION HOTEL*****, Keppel Rd. (tel 2221551). An alternative are the two YMCAs: **METROPOLITAN YMCA******, 60 Stevens Rd. (tel 737755), or the **YMCA***** at 70 Palmer Rd. (tel 2224666). Both are a bit out of town.

Should you really want to spend a night in **RAFFLES**, get ready to shell out 150 S$ for a double. Doubles in the big international hotels are over 120 S$.

FOOD

For people with a well stuffed wallet, Singapore can be the greatest food trip in the world. From morning till night you can gorge on all the culinary delights of exotic Asia (and more!). But even at the foodstalls you can eat well and save.

First, here is a list of the evening markets where foodstalls are set up. The 'street hawkers' are being grouped increasingly together. The old-time atmosphere turns a bit formal, perhaps more antiseptic, which shouldn't hurt the quality of the food. Some hawkers take in more than 500 S$ per day. One advantage of the new 'Food Centres' is improved hygiene. Health inspectors make regular rounds, and each foodstand proprietor is required to undergo a periodical medical check up. Eat without qualms.

We really like **NEWTON CIRCUS**. Start with a Hokkien Mee (noodles with pork and shrimps), then have an oyster omelette and for desert fresh pineapple or fried bananas (pisang goreng). That should all cost about 5 S$. In the city, **TELOK AYER MARKET** is set in a huge markethall that's been declared a historical monument (Shenton Way/Raffles Quay). It's especially nice for lunch. Similar quality are **EMPRESS PLACE** and **BOAT QUAY**. Less well known is **FOOD ALLEY** (Murray St., near Maxwell Rd.). Old-fashioned atmosphere can still be found on **CHINA SQUARE** (Cross St./Pekin St./China St./Amoy St.). Of interest, especially after midnight, are the restaurants on **ALBERT STREET** - though overpriced. You're better off in **ALBERT CENTRE**. Malay satay is best sampled in the **SATAY CLUB** (at the end of Queen Elizabeth Walk). Each skewer costs 25 c. In general the food centers offer mostly Chinese food. Indian and Malay specialities are largely restricted to murtabah and satay.

Go real southern Indian style, meaning eating with your right hand off banana leaves, in **KOMALA VILAS**, 76/78 Serangoon Road. Good, too, are the two Indian non-vegetarian places across from Sultan Mosque (North Bridge Road): **JUBILEE** (no 771/773) and **ISLAMIC** (no 791/797). Cheap is **UJAGAR SINGH JOHAL**, 7 St.Gregory's Place (across from the USA embassy on Hill Street). You can try north Indian cooking in **OMAR KHAYAM**, 55 Hill Street (tel 3361505) - reserve a table in advance! The menu is sheer poetry! Start with a Tandoori chicken (9 S$) - the chicken is seasoned in 13 different spices for six hours. Then move on to prawn curry à la Kashmiri (11 S$). The art of mixing spices reaches the ultimate here. Also worth recommending is the fresh okra (Nentara, 6 S$). To top it all off, have a harem coffee - prepared at your table. It's worth letting a few dollars fly. Less expensive, but no worse, is **MOTI MAHAL**, 18 Murray St. (Food Alley), tel 2214338. The Far Eastern Economic Review praised it as "One of the best Indian restaurants anywhere!". Here, too, the specialities are from Kashmir and Punjab.

Those who lived off nasi padang on Sumatra and learned to prize hot food needn't miss it here. Try **RENDEZ-VOUS**, 4/5 Bras Basah Rd. (good but not cheap) or another nasi padang place on the corner of Beach St./Seah St. For the real thing, of course, you'll need plane tickets.

It's hard to write about the various Chinese restaurants - there're just so many of them. And of these many, too many are just too excellent. Before trying Chinese cuisine, read the Food & Drink chapter. What is sold in the west as Chinese cooking has little in common with the high state of the culinary arts found in the Middle Kingdom (or Singapore). Here are a few suggestions: You can get an excellent 'steamboat' with 'chicken rice' in **YET CON**, 25 Purvis Street. We paid about 40 S$ including beer for 6 people. Still, check the price in advance! The same goes for 'dim sum' during the afternoon in **EASTERN PALACE**, 448 Lucky Plaza Shopping Centre, Orchard Road. Dim sum and other Cantonese dishes are also served in **EVERGREEN**, 37 Tanjong Pagar Road. You'll find lots of Cantonese restaurants in **PEOPLE'S PARK**. Try Hakka food in **GOLDEN JADE**, 5 Seah Street. You might also order 'Golden Salted Chicken' or 'yong tau foo'. Hainanese chicken rice can be found in **SWEE KEE**, 53 Middle Road or in **VICTORIA**, 87 Victoria Street. Get Teochew shark's fin in **TEO HIANG**, 43 Middle Rd. or in **TAI SENG**, Maxwell House, 6 Murray St. another speciality: steamed crab. Szechuan cooking is available in the expensive **OMEI**, Hotel Grand Central, 22 Cavenagh Rd.

McDonalds and Kentucky Fried Chicken have hit Singapore (Liat Towers, Orchard Rd.; Shenton Way; People's Park and at the Airport). Westward-looking Singaporeans seem to like such things! There's English pub atmosphere in **FOSTER'S**, Specialist's Shopping Center or in **JACK'S PLACE**, 117A Killiney Road.

SHOPPING

Many travellers only go to Singapore to shop, get film developed, send mail, or pick up a visa. Just to make it plain: Singapore isn't the cheap shopping center of days past. Due to the strong Singapore dollar, it's hardly worth picking up a camera or roll of film here any more.

Advertisers hail Singapore as a shopping paradise. When the smart shoppers are gone, advertise! If you don't watch out, your financial resources can take a big dive. Whether this really is the time and place to buy a new stereo is something you'll have to decide for yourself. Just remember, the customs authorities back home are sure to take a big interest in your Sony or Toshiba boxes raising the price even more. Never believe a salesperson concerning custom duties back home - how should they know. And they don't see their customers swearing at the cashier's window in London, LA or Darwin.

DUTY-FREE GOODS - Since Singapore is a duty-free port, most imported goods are tax free, meaning no import duty. Here is a list of the most important duty free goods:

CAMERAS	ELECTRIC RAZORS	LIGHTERS
WATCHES	IRONS	CALCULATORS
RADIOS	ELECTRIC POTS	TYPEWRITERS
TAPEDECKS	VACUUM CLEANERS	SPORTS EQUIPMENT
RECORD PLAYERS	REFRIGERATORS	GAMES/TOYS
AMPLIFIERS	WASHING MACHINES	EYE GLASSES
TV SETS	SEWING MACHINES	MUSICAL INSTRUMENTS
RECORDS	RUGS	LEATHER GOODS
CASSETTES	SILK	PERFUME
TAPES	PEARLS	COSMETICS
JEWELERY	PRECIOUS STONES	OPTICAL INSTRUMENTS

DEPARTMENT STORES - If you have something in mind to buy, think about what the thing would cost back home (on sale!). And check the price in a big department store where they have fixed prices. Then, in most cases, you can get it cheaper after long bargaining from one of the small dealers. Addresses of the big department stores:

METRO GOLDEN MILE, Beach Road, open till 21:30 h.
C.K.TANG, Dynasty Hotel, open till 21:30 h.
CORTINA, Colombo Court, North Bridge Rd. (Coleman/High St.)
ISETAN, Liat Towers, Orchard Rd., open till 21:00 h.
JOHN LITTLE, Plaza Singapura, Orchard Rd.
YAOHAN STORES, Plaza Singapura, Orchard Rd.

CHINESE EMPORIUMS - visit the Chinese Emporiums featuring goods from the People's Republic of China. They offer a good selection of jewelery, silk, arts and crafts, as well as exotic odds and ends:

CHINESE, International Building, (upper) Orchard Road.
ORIENTAL, People's Park Centre, New Bridge Rd./Upper Cross St.
OVERSEAS + TASHING, People's Park Complex, New Bridge Rd.
YUYI, Orchard Building, Grange Road.

SHOPPING COMPLEXES – The shopping complexes, such as People's Park, Plaza Singapura or Lucky Plaza at first glance seem to be huge department stores. But actually they consist of hundreds of small private shops. Since similar wares are offered by a large number of dealers, they are a good place to bargain. In general the shopping complexes surrounding Orchard Road have a higher price level than those in the less well known streets, but the selection of wares is larger. Besides the following major shopping complexes, there are a number of smaller ones, often in the international hotels.

PLAZA SINGAPORA, LUCKY PLAZA, FAR EAST SHOPPING CENTRE and numerous others all on Orchard Road.
TANGLIN SHOPPING CENTRE, Tanglin Road.
PENINSULA PLAZA AND SHOPPING CENTRE, and **CAPITOL SHOPPING CENTRE,** behind St.Andrew's Cathedral.
PEOPLE'S PARK CENTRE and **COMPLEX,** New Bridge Rd. at the corner of Upper Cross Street.
CLIFFORD CENTRE, CHANGE ALLEY AERIAL PLAZA, OVERSEAS UNION SHOPPING CENTRE on Collyer Quay.

ADDITIONAL SHOPPING TIPS
FILM – is more expensive in Indonesia and Malaysia than in Singapore, so stock up. You can have Ektachrome film developed by KODAK within 24 hours at 305 Alexandra Rd. The shops offer good prices for color prints.

CAMERAS / STEREOS – when purchasing cameras and other expensive items, be sure that an international guarantee card is included and that the date and serial number are noted on the receipt.

BOOKS – you'll find the largest selection of English language literature in South-East Asia, including books about Malaysia and Indonesia. Check the large shop on the second floor of Plaza Singapura (Shizuoka Yajimaya). MPH has three branches: at 71 Stamford Road (corner of Armenian St.), Centrepoint and in the Afro-Asia Bldg. on Robinson Rd. Times Bookshop is rapidly expanding (Centrepoint and Airport).
 Find books about South-East Asia at Selecta Books, Tanglin Shopping Centre. It is the only bookshop in South-East Asia specialized for books on the region.

WESTERN FOOD – after weeks of eating Asian, a simple bottle of wine with cheese and 'real' bread can be worth a few dollars. These delicacies are available in any big supermarket, such as Cold Storage Supermarket (Centrepoint) or Fitzpatrick's on Orchard Road (Promenade near Bideford

Road). Cold Storage has a branch behind the Albert Centre that is open 24 hours a day.

HANDICRAFT CENTRE - South-East Asian arts and crafts can be found on Tanglin Road behind the Tourist Office. The prices, however, might convince you to do the travelling. For 'old-stay-at-homes', there are more reasonably priced handicraft shops all around town.

CHINATOWN - in the area between New Bridge Rd., South Bridge Rd. and on to the south, there are just a few remaining streets reminiscent of old-fashion Chinatown. A walk through the side streets is still rewarding. Many interesting tiny shops offer temple accessories, jewelery, porcelain, traditional medicines and specialities.

Early in the morning on Smith Street there's a nice market specializing in food. In the evening the same area transforms into a night market where textiles and foodstalls predominate.

Before flying home you might stock up with orchids at the Morning Market (30 c a piece), or try a garden center. Another tip: there are Chinese medicines based on natural ingredients for just about every ailment - some are said to be better than what's offered by modern chemistry. But many countries forbid such imports.

EQUIPMENT - for treks through tropical forests, jungle boots have proved their worth: you can find a pair on Weld Road (the extension of Arab Street). Look for mosquito nets here too! Diving masks and snorkels at Aquila Aurea, Specialist's

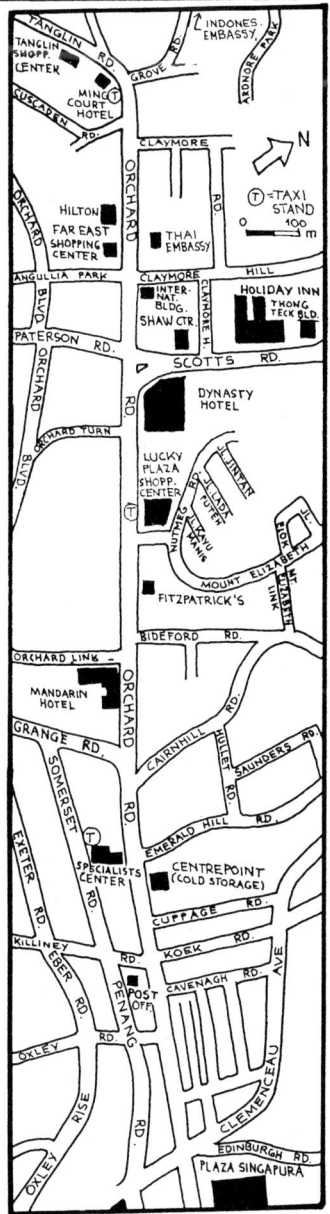

Shopping Center, or at Chop Hock Heng, 247 Beach Road. But the whole are is due to be torn down soon. In that case try at Ong Say Kuan & Sons, Lucky Plaza.

GENERAL INFORMATION
TOURIST INFORMATION – the STPB (Singapore Tourist Promotion Board) has its main office at 131 Tudor Court (off Tanglin Road), tel 2356611. Open daily except Sun and Fri from 8:00-17:00 h. Several magazines and brochures are available free of charge offering tips as to what's going on and where to buy. Look for: **The Singapore Visitor**, **Singapore Tourist Guide Book**, **Lion City**, or **Weekly Guide**. They are also available in all the big hotels.

POST OFFICE – the General Post Office is on Fullerton Road, open Mon-Fri 8:30-18:00, Sat 8:30-14:00 h, Sun closed. Singapore has the cheapest and most reliable postal system in the region, so send your letters and parcels home from here. However, parcels shouldn't weigh more than 10 kg. If you have heavier stuff to send, check Stevensons International, 420 Katong Shopping Center, 865 Mountbatten Road. Since the mails here are X-rayed, **don't send film by mail** except in special development bags.

TELEPHONE – local calls are free. From the phone booths you pay 10 c for three minutes. Many international calls can be dialled direct: a three minute call to Western Europe costs 22.50 S$. Collect or reverse charge calls aren't permitted. Open round the clock are the GPO, Fullerton Building, the Telecom Building at 35 Robinson Road, and the Telephone House at 15 Hill Street.

BANKS – almost every major international back has an office in this financial center. This makes Singapore an ideal place to receive money wired from home. You're best off using one of the major backs from your home country.

BANK OF AMERICA, 24 Raffles Place, Clifford Centre.
THE CHARTERED BANK, 21 Raffles Place.
CHASE MANHATTAN BANK, 50 Raffles Place, Shell Tower.
FIRST NATIONAL BANK OF CHICAGO, 150 Cecil Street, Wing On Life Building.
 Because a lot of bad checks have floated through the city, many banks are very careful about cashing checks, even Eurochecks. If you aren't a regular bank customer, you might have to pay a 20 S$ fee per check. So you're best off with traveller's checks. When changing money, take note of both the exchange rate and the fees, which can be very expensive.

Stamford Road, Singapore.

MONEY CHANGERS – to change cash money, can be found particularly around Raffles Place, Collyer Quay, in Change Alley, and in the major shopping centres. Every currency in the world is for sale. Especially cheap are weak Asian currencies such as the Indonesian Rupiah, Indian Rupee, Burmese Kyat, or Philippine Peso. Check import restrictions for the countries in question! Before bargaining for a good rate, check the most recent edition of **Far Eastern Economic Review** or **Asiaweek** for the latest exchange rate.

AMERICAN EXPRESS – 9/10 Ngee Ann Building, Orchard Road, tel 7349095.

CITY MAPS – The various brochures available at the tourist office contain city maps which are adequate if you keep mostly in town. Clyde Surveys, England, offers a useful folding map. Unfortunately, there aren't any more maps showing the bus lines.

NEWSPAPERS – besides the papers in Chinese, Tamil and Malay, there are two English-language dailies, **THE STRAITS TIMES** and the **SINGAPORE MONITOR**. In the international hotels you can also find a wide selection of international newspapers and magazines.

RADIO / TELEVISION – Singapore's airwaves are as multilingual as the printed media. Two TV stations transmit news and films in English – interrupted by countless advertising spots.

BUSINESS HOURS – the major shops are open Monday to Saturday from 09:00-18:00 h, some until 22:00 h, and Sunday mornings. Banking hours are Monday to Friday 10:00-15:00 h and Saturday 09:30-11:30 h. Other offices open between 07:30 and 09:30 h, and close between 16:00 and 18:00 h. Most take a lunch break from 12:00 to 14:30 h. Offices are usually open Saturday mornings.

FIRST AID – the two most important hospitals are the Alexandra Hospital, Alexandra Rd., tel 635222 and the Singapore General Hospital, Outram Rd., tel 2223322. You can call an ambulance at 999. Private medical practitioners and dental surgeons are usually outfitted with modern equipment, especially those located around Orchard Rd. Addresses are listed in the yellow pages. Expect to pay about 30.-S$ per doctor's visit. Vaccination clinic in the PSA Building (Port of Singapore Authority), 7 Keppel Road.

FOREIGN CLUBS – for those who want to meet some of their countrymen, or read a newspaper from home:
AMERICAN CLUB – 21 Scotts Road, tel 3448319.
BRITISH ASSOCIATION OF SINGAPORE, F9, 4th Floor, Maritime Bldg., tel 984390.

SINGAPORE CULTURAL THEATRE – on Grange Road behind the Handicraft Centre, the INSTANT ASIA CULTURE SHOW is held for tourists at 9:45 each day. For information about this 'instant' look at various cultures call 2352102. Hourly from 12:00 to 18:00 h the SINGAPORE EXPERIENCE is presented – an audiovisual slide show offering an interesting view of the city's present and past, call 7343456. Each show costs 5.-S$.

KEEP SINGAPORE CLEAN – is a campaign to make Singapore the cleanliest city in South-East Asia. But this isn't an appeal to reason. Severe laws see to that. This can also affect you, should you discard cigarette butts or other trash thoughtlessly (500.-S$), smoke in subways or other public transport (500.-S$), or not use the crosswalk (50.-S$).

NIGHTLIFE AND ENTERTAINMENT – begins on Orchard Rd. It's happening on the first and second floors of the Tropicana Bar in the Holiday Inn, and at Lost Horizon disco in the Shangri-la. What the Chinese consider a night club can be seen in El Amigo Blueroom & Niteclub, on Kitchner Road. The

SINGAPORE 313

city also offers a number of movie theatres (more expensive than in Malaysia). The films are usually subtitled in several languages including English, Malay and Chinese. Enjoy traditional song and dance in the three international hotels:
In Raffles the show costs 8.-S$ (starting at 20:00 h), with dinner 30.-S$ (starts at 19:00 h). The Hyatt offers an evening of culture around the pool on Tuesdays and Fridays, costs 35.-S$. In the Mandarin the show costs 32.-S$ including barbecue or 20.-S$ without (daily except Mondays). All prices include 13 % tax and tip.

HORSE RACING - held at the Singapore Turf Club, Bukit Timah Road. Most races are held on Saturdays. Get info from the newspapers or call 4683366.

FESTIVALS AND HOLIDAYS
OFFICIAL HOLIDAYS: January 1st, Good Friday, Easter Sunday, and December 25th (Christmas Day). The 9th August is NATIONAL DAY: Especially impressive are the huge parades, (participated in by all ethnic groups), military parades and dances (featuring traditional Chinese lion and dragon dances).

CHINESE HOLIDAYS: The stores start hopping several weeks before the CHINESE NEW YEAR. One, two, or even three months extra wages are paid out by employers. Huge family gatherings have to be prepared and holiday clothes sought. The whole town is on its feet until, with everyone on the point of exhaustion, they retire to relax and celebrate with their families.

The BIRTHDAY OF THE MONKEY GOD is celebrated twice a year, especially in the two temples on Cumming Street and Choon Ong Street. They include both processions and Chinese opera. Men stick needles through their tongues and cheeks while in a trance. Parents pray to the powerful Monkey God to stand as godfather to their children so that they will have his strength.

Other splendid birthday festivals can be found in the White Cloud Temple on Ganges Ave. where the BIRTHDAY OF THE SAINT OF THE POOR (Kong Teck Choon Ong) is celebrated, and in the Taoist Temple on the corner of Clarke St./North Boat Quay, where the BIRTHDAY OF THE THIRD PRINCE is celebrated.

For four weeks in October and November, the Taoist faithful pilgrimage to Kusu Island in homage of the GOD OF PROSPERITY. Ferries depart from Clifford Pier by the World Trade Center.

GETTING AROUND SINGAPORE
Most tours are easy to do by foot. But distances within the city are great enough that you'll need public transport occasionally. Try to avoid travel during rush hour, you'll only move at a snail's pace anyway.

BY BUS
The cheapest way to get around is by SBS (Singapore Bus Service Ltd.). Routes for all the buses are listed in the somewhat confusing SBS guide, available for 70 c at newspaper stands and stationery shops in the city and at the airport. One ride costs between 40 c and 80 c depending on

SINGAPORE

how many fare stages you pass through. Besides buses with a conductor, there are also OMO lines (One Man Operation), where you just pay a standard rate. These include the CBD Ring Buses running within the Central Business District. All bus stops are clearly marked. But some bus drivers only stop if you flag them down.

BY TAXI
From Airport $3 Surcharge, $1 for boot luggage.

There are more than 10,000 taxis on the island, which are still relatively cheap. In the city center, they are only found at certain taxi stops. Most are air conditioned. Rates: The first 1500 m 1.20 S$ (non-ac 1 S$), every further 375 m 10 c, nights between 1:00 and 6:00 h add 50 %, every additional person (above two) and piece of baggage costs 10 c. From 07:00 to 10:15 h, a ride in the CBD costs a 2.-S$ surcharge if there're less than four passengers. You can order a radio-equipped taxi by calling 4525555. Any complaints should be made to the Registry of Vehicles, Middle Road, tel 3379115 or at the Tourist Office.

BY TRISHAW
Every once in a while, you'll see a trishaw in Chinatown or in front of the tourist hotels. Normal prices are paid by elderly Chinese women who ride them to the market in the morning. Tourists, however, pay for an expensive, nostalgic sightseeing tour.

BY RENT-A-CAR
Private and rented cars are expensive. The rates aren't much higher than in Malaysia, but the heavy toll to enter the CBD during rush hour and the high cost of parking downtown make a car uneconomical.

LEAVING SINGAPORE
BY AIR
Singapore's role as the trading center of South-East Asia is well served by one of the biggest harbors and most modern airports in the world. Changi Airport, in service since 1981, gives a first impression of the city's dynamism. Its huge duty free shop ensures that even on the briefest stopover you still have a chance to spend money. The modern Changi Airport is 20 km east of town. You reach the city via a multi-lane expressway by taxi (normal rate plus 3 S$ airport tariff, count on 15 S$), by the airport bus (SABS) for 4 S$, or cheapest of all with the regular city bus (SBS) for 80 c - get bus 390 to Queen Street.

The airport tax is 12 S$ for international flights, and 5 S$ for flights to Malaysia or Brunei.

ADDRESSES OF THE IMPORTANT AIRLINES
AEROFLOT, Sinsov Building, 55 Market St., tel 5326711.
AIR INDIA, 17th Floor, UIC Bldg., Shenton Way, tel 2205277.
AIR NIUGINI, 220 Orchard Road, Orchard C & E, tel 2354958.
CATHAY PACIFIC, Ocean Bldg., Collyer Quay, tel 911811.
CHINA AIRLINES, Lucky Plaza, Orchard Rd., tel 7372144.
CSA, Holiday Inn Bldg., Scotts Rd., tel 7379844.
GARUDA, 101 Thompson Road, Goldhill Square, tel 250288.
LUFTHANSA, Tanglin Shopping Centre, Tanglin Rd, tel 7379222
MAS, Singapore Shopping Centre, Clemenceau Ave, tel 3366777.
PAKISTAN INTERNATIONAL, Hilton, Orchard Road, tel 7373233.
PHILIPPINE AIRLINES, P.S.M, 35 Selegie Road, tel 3361611.
QUANTAS AIRWAYS, Mandarin Hotel, Orchard Road, tel 7373744.
SINGAPORE AIRLINES, SIA Bldg., Robinson Road, tel 5456666.
TAROM ROMANIAN AIRLINES, 3 Coleman Street, tel 3381467.
THAI AIRWAYS INTER, Denmark Hse., Raffles Quay, tel 2242011
UTA AIRLINES, Ming Court Hotel, Tanglin Rd., tel 7377166.
YUGOSLAV AIRLINES, F.E.S.C., 545 Orchard Road, tel 2353017.

Here are sample prices for flights to neighboring countries, one-way, in S$, ISIC prices in parenthesis:
BANDAR SERI BEGAWAN 320.-, BANGKOK 494.-(257.-), COLOMBO 847.-, DENPASAR 475.-, HONGKONG 842.-(421.-), JAKARTA 345.-(181.-), KOTA KINABALU 346.-, KUALA LUMPUR 103.-, KUCHING 170.-, MADRAS 847.-, MANILA 699.-(489.-), MEDAN 251.-(177.-), PAKANBARU 172.-, PALEMBANG 225.-, PENANG 150.-(107.-), TAIPEI 955.-(563.-), TOKYO 1371.-(727.-)S$.

In most cases you won't have to pay the official IATA tariffs. Besides student rates, there are the excursion tariffs. Otherwise, cheap travel agencies offer tickets at way under the official rates. Check ads in the newspapers.

Book your ISIC flights from Holiday Tour & Travels, Ming Court Hotel, 4th Floor, tel 7345681.

If you're flying to Europe, Australia or the US, first check the student rates. The cheapest are PERTH for 303 US$, MELBOURNE 424 US$, SYDNEY 424 US$. Flights to Western Europe with an ISIC cost 440 US$ no matter where you fly into. SEATTLE costs with Thai 582.-US$.

MAC (Malaysian Air Charter Co. Sdn. Bhd.) flies a small plane for 95.-S$ to MALACCA and TIOMAN (95.-S$). Departs from Seletar Airport.

Agent: German Asian Travels Pte. Ltd., 9 Battery Road, 1503 Straits Trading Building, tel 5335466.

SINGAPORE

BY BUS
Cheapest is bus 170 from Queen Street for 80 c to JOHORE BHARU. For 1 S$ there's the Johore-Singapore Express non-stop. At the border, everyone has to get out and walk through Malaysian immigration before getting on another bus to the JB bus station. Bus 170 leaves every 10 minutes from 5:20 to 00.10 h. In JB you can get local buses in all directions.

Right from Singapore, Pan Malaysia Express and other companies' buses leave from New Bridge Rd. (parking lot near the General Hospital) to all major Malaysian cities. For info call 2216601. The Malacca-Singapore Express office is across the street at 579 New Bridge Rd. (tel 2238868).

SAMPLE PRICES: SEREMBAN 17.-, KUALA LUMPUR 17.-, IPOH 25.-, BUTTERWORTH 30.-, ROMPIN 8.50 (ac 12.-), KUANTAN 13.50 (ac 17.-), KUALA TRENGGANU 17.- (ac 23.-), KOTA BHARU 26.- (ac 31.-), MERSING 7.-, MALACCA 9.-S$.

BY TRAIN
The train station is on Keppel Rd., bus 20 from Beach Rd. or bus 10, 30, 125, 145, 146, 176, 186. Information tel 2221791. Six trains leave daily to KL (6:30, 7:30, 8:30, 15:00, 20:00, 22:00 h). The Ekspres Rakyat/Sinaran (7:30 and 15:00 h) arrives in KL at 14:20 (21:35 h) and in Butterworth at 21:30 (7:10 h). The Ekspres Rakyat booking office is open from 8:30 to 12:30 h and from 14:00 to 19:30 h.

SAMPLE PRICES: SEGAMAT 6.10(9.70, 20.60), GEMAS 7.20(11.50, 24.30), WAKAF BHARU 23.10(36.80, 78.20), BANGKOK 77.40(only 2nd cl., 163.- 1st cl.), KL 12.50(19.90, 42.30), IPOH 19.-(30.40, 64.50), BUTTERWORTH 24.60 (39.30, 83.50). **Ekspres Rakyat/Sinaran:** KL 15.50(ac 26.-), IPOH 22.- (ac 37.-), BUTTERWORTH 27.60 (ac 46.-) S$.

BY SHIP
There are fewer regular ship connections every day, and Singapore is no exception to this trend. The Straits Steamship Company has discontinued its routes to Sarawak and Sabah. Passenger steamers to Hongkong and Australia are also a thing of the past.

INDIA: The Shipping Company of India's CHIDAMBARAM leaves Singapore once every three weeks on the route Singapore - Port Kelang -Penang - Nagapattinam - Madras. The trip takes about 12 days. Agent: Jumabhoy & Sons, 10th Floor, Straits Trading Bldg., tel 912511.

INDONESIA: Daily jetfoils and smaller ships leave Singapore for BATUAMBAR (Pulau Batam). The trip costs around 40 S$. Departure point is Prince Edward Pier. Take bus 80 from Beach Rd./Bras Basah Rd. Otherwise the following buses: 17, 40, 70, 82, 100, 140, 141, 161, 163, 172, 175, 196. You can get tickets right on the pier or in advance from German Asian Travels. Pulau Batam is a visafree point of entry into Indonesia. Kantor Imigrasi is at Batam Island Country Club where the jet foil docks. Take a bus from here to the harbor. Several boats leave daily to Tanjung Pinang (5000 Rp). From **TANJUNG PINANG** you have daily boat connections to **PAKANBARU**. This combination is the cheapest route to Sumatra.

Stamford Raffles joined the East India Company as an office clerk at the tender age of 14. He quickly made a name for himself at the main office in London. In 1805 he was sent as assistant secretary to Penang. A trip by ship to the Far East in those days took several months, and Raffles made wise use of the time to bone up on Malay language and culture. Soon he was an accepted expert. By 1808 he was already working for the High Court in Penang. In 1810, Stamford Raffles was in Calcutta where the British Governor General Lord Minto appointed him Governor of Java. Since Holland had been annexed by France, British troops occupied the Dutch colonies to keep them out of French hands. Raffles tried to institute liberal reforms on Java, but the colonies were returned to Dutch control in 1816. Raffles, a confirmed nationalist, warned the British government and the East India Company of the consequences for British trade. His attempt to get other bases in Sumatra besides Bencoolen received only half hearted support. Sometimes he operated on his own initiative. On the 29th of January 1819, Stamford Raffles landed on the island of Singapore and signed a treaty with the rightful Sultan of Johore, Hussein. Hussein's brother had usurped the throne and was known for his friendship with the Dutch. The Union Jack was raised over the island on the 6th of February 1819. In 1824, the seizure of the island was confirmed in a treaty between England and Holland.

In 1823, Raffles left Singapore for England where he died three years later. His two volume work, **A HISTORY OF JAVA**, was a great scientific achievement, offering the most wide ranging study to date of the history, culture, ethnology, zoology and botany of Java.

SUGGESTED READING

GENERAL REFERENCE
INFORMATION MALAYSIA - 1984 Yearbook (Ed. Cheong Mei Sui & Faridah Ibrahim; Kuala Lumpur 1984)
A wide-ranging reference book offering the official point of view.

INTRODUCTION TO THE PEOPLES AND CULTURES OF INDONESIA AND MALAYSIA (Koentjaraningrat, R.M.; Menlo Park, Cal. 1975)

SOUTH EAST ASIA - Race, Culture, and Nation (Hunter, G.; Kuala Lumpur, London, New York 1966)

HISTORY
A HISTORY OF SOUTH-EAST ASIA (Hall, D.E.G.; London 1964)
A standard work on South-East Asian History.

A PORTRAIT OF MALAYSIA AND SINGAPORE (Tan Ding Eing; Kuala Lumpur 1980 - Oxford Progressive History)
An informative and easy to read history book ranging from the Malacca Empire until today. Economic and social problems are well handled.

MALAYSIA, SINGAPORE AND BRUNEI 1400-1965 (Jessy, Joginder Singh; Kuala Lumpur 1974)
A highschool textbook for Malaysian students, wide-ranging, easy to read.

THE FIRST 150 YEARS OF SINGAPORE (Moore, Donald & Moore, Joanna; Singapore 1969)
A recommendable history of the city.

SARAWAK 1839-1968 (Rawlins, Joan; London 1972)
An easy to read historical work; however, the Brookes are praised uncritically.

THE WHITE RAJAS - A HISTORY OF SARAWAK FROM 1841 TO 1946 (Runciman, Steven; Cambridge 1960)
Wide-ranging book about the people and their history.

THE KINGDOM OF JOHOR 1641-1728 (Andaya, Leonard Y.; Kuala Lumpur 1975)
A specialized, study of the golden age of the Johore Kingdom up to the intervention of the Bugis and the Minangkabau.

MAHATHIR - A PROFILE IN COURAGE (Morais, J. Victor, Selangor, 1982)
The story of Mahathir's journey from political nowhere to Prime Minister of Malaysia.

JUNGLE WAR IN MALAYA - The Campaign against Communism 1948-60 (Miller, Harry; London 1972)
An extensive discription of the EMERGENCY, by a British journalist.

THE UNDECLARED WAR - The Story of the Indonesian Confrontation 1962-1966 (James, Harold & Sheil-Small, Denis; London 1971)
A military history of the conflict in East Malaysia.

ETHNOLOGY

ORANG ASLI - The Aboriginal Tribes of Peninsular Malaysia (Carey, Iskandar; Kuala Lumpur 1976)
An important work about the aboriginies of West Malaysia by a former commissioner for Orang Asli Affairs.

NINE DAYAK NIGHTS (Geddes, W.; Oxford 1973)
An anthropological research paper, but still easy to read, looks at the mythology of the Bidayuh (Land Dayaks).

THE PAGAN TRIBES OF BORNEO (Hose & McDougall, Reprint 1966)
A standard work about the tribes of Borneo, particularly the Iban and Kayan in Sarawak. First published as two thick volumes in 1912.

LIFE IN A LONGHOUSE (Morrison, H., Kuching 1962)
A four-language photobook featuring photos from the 1950s, put together by an energetic woman, whose husband, an anthropologist, administrated the Sarawak Museum for many years.

VANISHING WORLD - The Ibans of Borneo (Morrison, H., New York, Tokyo 1978)
The best photographic look at the Iban, available in Singapore, Malaysia, and in Europe.

NATURAL SCIENCES

THE MALAY ARCHIPELAGO - The Land of the Orang Utan and the Bird of Paradise (Wallace, Alfred Russel; 1st published 1869, Reprint 1962, New York)
A classic by the great English natural scientist, who spent years on the mainland and islands of Malaysia. Emphasis on flora and fauna.

MALAYSIA'S GREEN AND TIMELESS WORLD - An Account of the Flora, Fauna and Indigenous Peoples of the Forests of Malaysia (Shuttleworth, Charles; Kuala Lumpur 1981)
The wide-ranging report of a nature lover featuring lots of black and white and color photos.

THE SINKING ARK - Environmental Problems in Malaysia & Southeast Asia (Lee, David; Kuala Lumpur 1980)
A recommendable look at Malaysia's various ecological problems and their effects.

TROPICAL RAINFORESTS OF THE FAR EAST (Whitmore, T. C.; London 1975)
A starndard work on the tropical rain forests of South-East Asia, unfortunately, too expensive.

ORANG-UTAN (Harrison, Barbara, London 1962)
An easy to read paperback.

THE LAND AND WILDLIFE OF TROPICAL ASIA (Ripley, Sidney Dillon, Time-Life 1975)
A look at tropical Asia, featuring lots of photos and sketches.

MALAYAN ANIMAL LIFE (Tweedie, M.W.F. & Harrison, J. L.; Kuala Lumpur 1977)
A complete look at the fauna of West Malaysia, lots of pictures, first published in 1954.

TRAVELOGUES

THE GOLDEN CHERSONESE - Travels in Malaya in 1879 (Bird, Isabella L.; Reprint Kuala Lumpur 1980)
The adventure packed trip of Mrs.Bird through Selangor, Negri Sembilan, Sungei Ujong and Malacca, recommended.

THE EASTERN SEAS - Or Voyages and Adventures in the Indian Archipelago in 1832-34 (Earl, George Windsor; Reprint Kuala Lumpur 1971).

LIFE IN THE FORESTS OF THE FAR EAST (St. John, Spenser; Reprint Kuala Lumpur 1974, first published in 1862)
Great discription of Sarawak and Sabah with lots of maps and graphics, two volumes.

IN MALAY FORESTS (Maxwell, George; London 1907)
A classic by a great Malaya lover, fifteen stories.

IN BRITISH MALAYA TODAY (Sidney, Richard J.H.; London 1924).

AMONG THE BELIEVERS, AN ISLAMIC JOURNEY (Naipaul, V.S., London, 1981)
A critical look at Islamic fundamentalism in Malaysia.

CULTURE - LITERATURE

CULTURE SHOCK! What not to do in Malaysia and Singapore, How and Why not to do it (Craig, JoAnn; Singapore 1980)
A well recommended paperback, originally written for expatriats, but which fits nicely in the hands of every tourist.

THE MALAYS - A CULTURAL HISTORY (Winstedt, Richard; Singapore 1981, 1st published 1947)
A classic by a great Malaya expert. The new edition features an excellent appendix by Tham Seong Chee on new developments.

PLACE-NAMES IN PENINSULAR MALAYSIA (Singam, S.Durai Raja; Kuala Lumpur 1980)
An amusing explanation of almost all geographical names in Malaysia.

MALAY WEDDING CUSTOMS (Haji Mohtar Bin M. Dom; KL 1979ff)
TRADITIONS AND TABOOS
MALAY SUPERSTITIONS AND BELIEFS
THE BOMOH AND THE HANTU
MALAYSIAN CUSTOMARY LAWS

MALAY MYTHS AND LEGENDS (Knappert, Jan; KL 1980)
An easy to read introduction to the ancient Malay myths.

SEJARAH MELAYU (Malay Annals) (Ed. and translated by Brown, C.C.; Kuala Lumpur 1970)
The best translation to date of the classic of Malay literature.

NOVELS

COLLECTED SHORT STORIES (Maugham, Somerset; volume IV, London 1951)
A paperback look at colonial Malaya of the 1920s and '30s, an absolute must for Malaysia travellers.

PASSAGE OF ARMS (Ambler, Eric; 1959 London)
The exciting story of weapons smuggle during the uprising on Sumatra in 1958-59.

KING RAT (Clavell, James; 1979)
The personal experiences of a successful author as a POW in the Japanese camp, Changi.

THE SINGAPORE GRIP (Farrell, J.G., Glasgow, 1978)
A look at Singapore, on the eve of the Japanese invasion.

MALAYAN TRILOGY (Burgess, Anthony; Harmondsworth 1981)
Three autobiographical novels situated in post-war Malaya.

ALMAYER'S FOLLY (Conrad, Joseph; London 1859)
A Conrad novel about the life of a European during the colonial era. Other Conrad novels for readers on the road:
TALES OF UNREST, VICTORY, AN OUTCAST OF THE ISLANDS, and **LORD JIM.**

SAINT JACK (Theroux, Paul; London, 1973)
Story by an American who lived as a pimp in Singapore.

THE CONSUL'S FILE (Theroux, Paul; Harmdonsworth 1977)
A look at life in Ayer Hitam (Johore) as seen through the eyes of an American consuls.

TANAMERA (Barber, Noel; London 1981)
The spellbinding story of two lovers and two great dynasties; one British, the other Chinese. The novel sweeps from British ruled Malaya of the 30s thru the Japanese occupation to the birth of the new nation.

TRAVEL GUIDES

MALAYSIA, SINGAPORE & BRUNEI - a travel survival kit (Crowther, Jeff & Wheeler, Tony; South Yarra 1982)
A wide ranging guide, but offering little background information.

MALAYSIA & SINGAPORE (Insight Guides, Singapore)
Both guides follow the familiar Insight format, extensive route descriptions and color photos, little concrete info.

SUBJECT INDEX

A
adat	182
agriculture	33
airplane tickets	63
Albuquerque, Alfonso d'	25
American Club	312
ancestor worship (Chinese)	40
animism	39
atlas moth	15

B
Baba Chinese	20
Bahasa Indonesia	44
Bahasa Malaysia	44
Bajau	290
batik	54
berok	13
bird's nest soup	98
bird singing contests	103
Bisayas	290
blowpipes	133
bomoh	40
British Association	312
Brooke, Charles Vyner	28
Brooke, James	27
Bugis	25
Bumiputra	34
butterflies	15

C
cacao	284
Cameron, William	131
caoutchouc	33
caste system	42
Chinese	19
cholera	66
climate	59
climate chart	61
cloves	163
cobra	14
Confucius	42
cost of living	79
culture	52
currencies	78
customs regulations	58, 84

D
dance	53
Dayak	22
Deepavali	105
deutero-Malayan	23
Dragon Boat Festival	104
drinks	100
Dusun	290

E
ecology	16
ecosystems	16
elephants, Indian	13
embassies	57
Emergency	29
England	26
entry formalities	56
estuarine crocodile	14
exchange rates	78

F
fauna	12
Festa de San Pedro	190
festivals	102, 125, 158
flora	12
flying lemur	14
flying squirrels	14
food	96
Chinese	97
Indian	99
Malay	97
foreign trade Malaysia	34
Fraser, James	130
fruit	100

G
gado gado	97
Gawai Dayak	103
geography Malaysia	9
Gunung Jerai	168

INDEX

H
haj 38
Hari Raya Puasa 104
head hunting 256
health 66
Hikyat Abdullah 45
Hikyat Hang Tuah 45
Hinduism 42
history
  Brunei 271
  Malaysia 23
  Sabah 27
  Sarawak 27
  Singapore 27
holidays 102
Holland 25,140,187
hornbill 13
hotels 93

I
Iban 22
ikat 55
immigration
  Chinese 19
  Indian 21
income 79
Indians 21
industry
  Malaysia 34
  Singapore 36
inflation rates 79
inoculations 66
insects 15
ipoh trees 143
Islam 24,37

J
Japan, WWII 28
jawi 44
Johore Empire 26,197
jungle treks 251

K
Kadazan 290
kain songket 55
kancil 13
Kayan 266
Kedayan 290
Kenyah 266
kite flying 54
kongsi 152
Koran 37

L
laksa 97,155
Land Dayak 266
Langkasuka 23
language, Malay 44
Laotse 42
Larut War 148
leatherback
  turtle 225
leeches 240
Lee Kuan Yew 30,32
Leith, George 150
Light, Francis 150
literature 45

M
macaque 13
Mahathir,
  Mohamad 30
mail 82
main gasing 54
Majapahit 23
Malacca Empire 24
malaria 67
Malaya 19
Malayan
  Communist Party 29
Malays 19
Malaysia,
  Federation of 29
Malaysian Chinese
  Association 29
Malaysia Indian
  Congress 29
mangroves 15
Marco Polo 24
Maugham,
  Somerset 26
measures 81
media 51
medical
  treatment 66
Minangkabau 25
monsoons 60
Munshi Abdullah 44

murtabah (k)	99	proto-Malay	21, 23
Murut	290		

N

National Holidays
- Malaysia — 104
- Singapore — 104

national parks
- Bako — 250
- Endau-Rompin — 206
- Green Turtle Island — 288
- Gunung Mulu — 262
- Kinabalu — 279
- Taman Negara — 234

newspapers — 51

New Years
- Chinese — 103
- Islamic — 105

Negritos — 21
North Borneo Company — 28
nutmeg — 163

O

oil — 36
opera, Chinese — 54
Orang Asli — 21, 132
Orangutan — 14
overland taxis — 86

P

palm oil — 34
Parawesmara — 24
pawang — 40
People's Action Party — 30, 32
Petronas — 33
photography — 106
plantations — 33

population
- Brunei — 22
- Malaysia — 19
- Singapore — 22

Portuguese — 25, 190
precipitation — 60
press — 51
primary jungle — 12
proboscis monkey — 14

R

rafflesia — 12
Raffles Hotel — 304
Raffles, Stamford — 26, 318
Rahman, Tunku Abdul — 29
railroads — 86
Ramadan — 38, 104
rent-a-cars — 90
resthouses — 94
reticulated python — 14

rhinoceros
- Sumatra — 13
- Javanese — 13

Rungus — 290

S

Sabah
- history — 27

Salleh, Mat — 28

Sarawak
- history — 27

satay — 97
secondary jungle — 13
Sejarah Melayu — 45
seladang — 13
Senoi — 21
shark's fin soup — 98
silat — 34
Sri Vijaya — 23
States, Federated Malayan — 26
Straits Settlement — 26
swamps — 15

T

taboo — 40
Thaipusam — 102
Taoism — 42
tattoo — 266
tamu — 104
tea — 136
telephone — 84
television — 51
Templer, Gerald — 125

theater	53
thermometer	81
time differences	85
tin	144
top-spinning contests	54
tourist offices	107
transport, public	36
travel expenses	80
Trengganu Stone	24
typhoid	67
tropical mountain forests	15
tropical rain forests	12

U
UMNO	29, 31

W
wages	79
wagler's pit viper	14
Wallace, Alfred Russel	196
wayang kulit	53
weights	81
wood carving	55
World War II	28

X
Xavier, Francis	188

Y
Yang Di Pertuan Agong	31
Yap Ah Loy	114

INDEX OF TOWNS

Alor Setar	171
Arau	174
Aur, Pul.	202
Ayer Hitam	197
Babi Besar, Pul.	202
Bakelalan	264
Bako, Kg.	250
Balikpulau	163
Bandar Seri Begawan	268
Bandar Sri Aman	254
Bareo	264
Batu Ferringhi	164
Batu Maung	162
Batu Niah	261
Batu Pahat	196
Batu Rakit	220
Bau	247
Beaufort	284
Bekuku	285
Belaga	259
Belimbing	230
Beras Basah, Pul.	179
Besar, Pul.	194
Beserah	229
Bidong, Pul.	220
Bintulu	260
Brinchang	134
Bukit Larut	148
Butterworth	167
Cameron Highlands	131
Chenering, Kg.	222
Cherating, Kg.	228
Chukai	228
Dayang Bunting Pul.	179
Desaru	200
Duyung, Pul.	221
Emplanjau	255
Endau	205
Entawau	258
Fort Skanda	232
Fraser's Hill	130
Gaya, Pul.	276
Gerik	170
Gertak Sanggol	162
Gua	254
Gunung Jerai	168
Gunung Mulu	262
Gurun	168
Ipoh	142
Jambu, Kg.	217
Jasin, Kg.	206
Jerangau	227
Jerantut	234
Jerteh	219
Johore Bharu	197
Juara, Kg.	204
Kangar	174
Kapas, Pul.	224
Kapit	258
Kayu Papan	202
Keluang	197
Keroh	169
Kemaman	228
Kemasik	228
Keningau	285
Kijal	228
Kota Belud	286
Kota Bharu	212
Kota Johore Lama	200
Kota Kinabalu	274
Kota Tinggi	199
Kuah	175
Kuala Baram	263
Kuala Belait	270
Kuala Berang	222
Kuala Besut	219
Kuala Dungun	226
Kuala Kangsar	145

INDEX

Kuala Kedah	172	Mersing	202
Kuala Krai	218	Miri	262
Kuala Kubu Bharu	131	Mount Kinabalu	279
Kuala Lipis	233	Mount Ophir	196
Kuala Lumpur	113	Muar	195
Kuala Pilah	184		
Kuala Rompin	206	Niah Caves	261
Kuala Tahan	236	Nilam Puri	216
Kuala Tembeling	241		
Kuala Teriang	178	Padang Besar	179
Kuala Trengganu	220	Paka	228
		Pa Longan	264
Kuantan	208	Pancing	209
Kuching	244	Pangkalan Lubang	262
Kudat	286	Pangkor, Kg.	140
Kukup	196	Pantai Cinta Berahi	216
Labuan	284	Pantai Dasar Sabak	216
Lahad Datu	288	Pantai Merdeka	168
Langkawi	174		
Lawas	285	Pantu	255
Limbang	270	Papar	286
Long Bangan	260	Pasir Mas	216
Long Bawan	264	Patah, Kg.	206
Long Melinau Paku	263	Pekan	207
Long Midang	264	Pemanggil, P.	202
Long Semado	285	Penambang, Kg.	215
Long Unan	260	Penampang	277
Lubok Antu	255	Penang	149
Lubok Paku	231	Penarek, Kg.	220
Lumbis	286	Penggerang	201
Lumut	141	Pensiangan	286
Lundu	247	Perhentian, Pul.	219
		Petaling Jaya	125
Macap, Kg.	197	Pontian Kechil	196
Makam, Kg.	200	Poring	282
Malacca	187	Port Dickson	186
Manukan, Pul.	276	Port Kelang	126
Marang	223	Pulau Aur	202
Marudi	263	Pulau Babi Besar	202
Maxwell Hill	148		
Menumbok	284	Pulau Beras Basah	179
Merang, Kg.	220		
Merapok	285	Pulau Besar	194
Merobok	168		
Merlimau, Kg.	195		

Pulau Betong	162	Sarikei	255
Pulau Bidong	219	Segamat	196
Pulau Dayang Bunting	179	Segu Benuk	247
		Sekayu	222
Pulau Duyung	221	Selepong	254
Pulau Gaya	276	Selingan, Pul.	288
Pulau Kapas	224		
Pulau Keladi, Kg.	207	Sematan	247
		Semporna	289
Pulau Langkawi	174	Sepilok	288
		Seremban	180
Pulau Pangkor	139	Seri Menanti	184
Pulau Pangkor Laut	140	Seria	270
		Setindan, Pul.	202
Pulau Pemanggil	202	Shah Alam	126
		Sibu	256
Pulau Perhentian	219	Sindumin	285
Pulau Rawa	203	Singa Besar, Pulau	179
Pulau Redang	219		
Pulau Rusa, Kg.	223	Singapore	292
		Sipitang	285
Pulau Sapi	276	Sitiawan	142
Pulau Selingan	288	Sungei Lembing	209
Pulau Setindan	202	Sungei Patani	167
		Sungei Ular, Kg.	229
Pulau Singa Besar	179		
Pulau Tenggol	227	Taiping	146
Pulau Tioman	204	Taman Negara	234
Punan, Kg.	206	Tanah Rata	134
		Tapah	139
Raja, Kg.	219	Tambunan	285
Ranau	282	Tamparuli	286
Rantau Abang	224	Tanjong Aru	276
Rantau Panjang	218	Tanjong Bungah	164
Raub	233	Tanjung Keling	192
Rawa, Pul.	202		
Redang, Pul.	219	Tanjung Rhu	178
Ringlet	134	Tasek Bera	232
Rusila, Kg.	223	Tasek Chini	230
		Tasek Chenderoh	170
Sabak	216		
Salang	204	Tatau	260
Sandakan	287	Tawau	289
Santubong	247	Tekek, Kg.	204
Sapi, Pul.	268	Telok Assam	250

Telok Bahang	163
Telok Chempe-dak	208
Telok Kumbar	162
Telok Limau	250
Telok Mahkota	202
Temburong	270
Temerloh	231
Templer Park	125
Tenggol, Pul.	227
Tenom	285
Tioman, Pul.	204
Tomani	285
Tuaran	286
Tubau	260
Tumpat	216
Tutong	270
Wakaf Bharu	218

NOTES: MALAYSIA

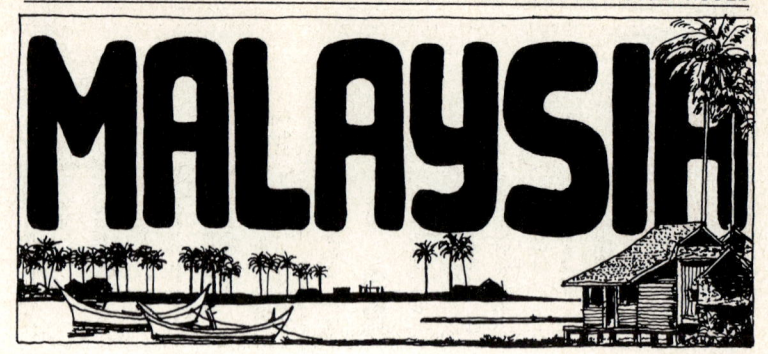